To

Dee

Enjoy

With Love from

Jan X

Janet S Rogers

13TH May 2017

Surviving Strangers...

...Now Who's the Div?

By

Mumma Grimmer
Aka; **Janet S. Rogers**

grimmers
Ink
Publishers

Surviving Strangers

Written by Janet S. Rogers
Aka Mumma Grimmer
Edited by Lee Cleary

© Janet S. Rogers. All rights reserved.

For more information contact:
janierogers44@yahoo.co.uk

Surviving Strangers...
...Now Who's the Div?

Introduction

So... if you begin to write the story of your life, where would you start? Stories have a beginning, middle and an end.

So the question... Is the beginning the first day; meaning the day of your birth, or your first memory?

The middle... Well, again easier but for all I know I may be well past the middle, I'm forty-eight, is that the middle or nearing the end?

And then... If you were to include the end, the final chapter, you'd have to know when that would be and be able to write the last word as you drew your last breath.

I guess you'd have to say that the beginning is your first sketchy recollection, then you add the story so far; the bits good and bad in between and then you'd have to end it there.

But if there's a chance of a future and I hope there is, then I've got my sights set on a somewhat happier phase ahead.

But who knows?

Chapter 1

In the beginning...

I'm a middle child; my sister, Verity is three years and eleven months younger and my brother, Aaron is eighteen months older. I was the odd one, that's what I've always considered - the unwanted one and I still think like that now, you'll probably agree by the time you've read this but then again you may not!

My sister would say she was the unwanted one and I admit I certainly didn't want that intrusion into my life; this baby sister who took my Mum away but worst still my Pop-pop, My Grandad, the only person who gave me time and attention. He died the day she, my sister was born. I believed that had she not been born, he wouldn't have died.

I still remember him: A little man about 5'6", balding and grey but always smiling. He'd put a swing in his garden, especially for me; two lengths of old rope and a tatty bit of wood, tied onto the bow of the cooking apple tree. I used to eat those apples; preferring them to the eating apples that were on several other trees in the garden, or the pears from the tree that hung over the fence from the next-door neighbours, even the plum at the very bottom of the garden. The fallers were always best, bruised and maggoty but the best in the world and to this day cooking apples are my favourites, flavoured with the best memories of my life.

My Pop-pop would push me on the swing or sit me on his big grey old 'Ford' car with running boards, he would sit me on the bonnet and I'd slide off but he always caught me. Mum sat on my swing and broke it. My sister was born and he died. I remember the day my sister was born, sitting on the stairs on my own, waiting for the nurse to come out of Mum's room, I heard the baby cry and she - the nurse, came out and walked past me, she told Dad, who was now at the bottom of the stairs, that he had a baby daughter, a girl. They both walked past me without a word and went in to see this baby girl. Ages later she left and my Dad came out, I suppose I must have been able to see her aswell but I don't remember. I do remember my Nan coming to see the baby, it was about four days after she had been born, but to me, as a memory, it seems like the same day, Nan wanted to talk to Mum about something and so Aaron and I had to leave the room. We went and played buses on the stairs, I pretended to be a passenger and Aaron was always the

1

bus conductor; I'd give him pretend money and he'd give me a scrap of paper as a ticket. Eventually we went back into the room, a solemn room, where my Nan and my Auntie were sat very straight faced and my Mum who, judging by her red and swollen eyes, had obviously been crying and of course the baby, who it seemed, did nothing but cry! It was then that my Mum had been told that her Dad, my Pop-pop had died; I assume we were told as well but I don't remember. I did learn later that Mum had had an argument with her Dad, the week before his death and never had the chance to make it up with him, something I know she always regretted.

We had lived with Mum's parents until I was eighteen months old, when Mum and Dad were given a three bed-roomed Council house. My Dad was a carpet fitter and he loved his garden, he also bred rabbits - New Zealand whites, he would kill them and sell them to the neighbours for food, I had thought of them as pets and didn't know what happened to them until I was much older. He loved fishing too and would go every Sunday, taking my brother Aaron along... Me, I didn't know where I fitted in.

I did have two friends, who lived either side of us, Laura; six months younger at number three and Molly; six months older at number seven. I played with them in our front garden making rose petal perfume or daisy chains and building camps in the overgrown allotments out at the back of our houses, where the grass was so high that when you walked into it you couldn't see or be seen. We spent many hours there, with a bottle of water and dry bread; that was my picnic, its funny I've always liked dry bread … Cooking apples and dry bread, maybe I can put my diet down to memories. We would sit on my front porch on a Sunday morning, making our watery perfume whilst Mum cooked the dinner. I can still smell the roast lamb, caught in the summer breeze, coming through the open kitchen window, accompanied by family favourites on the radio. Always lamb on Sunday and always the same routine: Dad and my brother would get back from the river at about 12:30pm in their black welly boots, carrying their boxes of tackle on their backs, their rods in hand, encased in green canvass. They were like two peas in a pod, they looked alike, walked alike and even smelled alike; that fresh water, fishy, earthy smell of the river, they'd kick off their boots in the back porch and put their tackle in the shed. My brother would then feed and check on his toads, newts, frogs and lizards that he always kept in various tanks or buckets in the garden and Dads greeting was always the same;

"All right then, what you up to?"

Then he would go into the lounge and read his 'News of the World' whilst Mum dished out the dinner and at about 1pm, we'd all sit around the old, yellow, Formica top table for dinner. Mum never really spoke to Dad at anytime; Dad would chat away to Aaron and if he did try and speak to Mum her answers were always very short and straight to the point. We knew no different then but as the years went by we learnt how very unhappy Mum was. Verity was always with her and they always seemed happy together, although in the latter couple of years of Mum's life, with her illnesses, Verity was less happy; the strain of looking after Mum and her own family did take its toll.

Those early days of my life were reasonably happy. Truth be told, we were pretty poorly off too, this assumption is due to the fact that Mum would always mend and make do, her clothes had been passed down from somewhere and I could never remember her buying herself new clothes, with the exception of an occasional cardigan. Our clothes too were hand me downs, although she made us a few dresses, summer ones, from some old piece of material stitched on her old singer sewing machine. My sister and I couldn't wait for the warmer weather and at the end of May, we'd get really excited about wearing last years summer dresses, every day we would ask;

"Is it warm enough yet, can we wear our dresses?"

Verity was luckier because she got my old dresses too. She didn't get my penguin dress though, that was mine; a light blue dress with full skirt and covered in little black penguins. I wore that dress for four summers and it went from my calf to well above the knee in four summers. It was suggested, then demanded that I let my sister have it, but I hid it behind the panel at the end of our bath; there was no way she was going to have it and she didn't. When it was finally discovered, it was stained and dusty and although I wanted to keep it, Mum threw it in the bin. I was luckier with my winter coats, 'anoraks' and school shoes; strong tough lace up shoes with a leather toggle on the end of the laces. My Nan (Mums Mum) always bought them for me, just before the end of the summer holiday's to return to school in. I usually got a brown

3

anorak and shoes and I hated brown, although when I was about ten I did get the blue one that I had always wanted.

My gifts from my Nan were always hidden from the rest of the family and with them came the same line;

"Don't tell Catherine I've bought this for you!"
Catherine was my cousin, my Mum's brother's daughter and they came across as rich snobs. I don't think they ever liked me and I always felt it, every mistake I ever made was pointed out to any member of the family who'd listen and then everyone would agree (or that's how I saw it) that I'd never amount to anything. I really did live up to their expectations in the following years, still I suppose if you are told enough times how useless you are, you begin to believe it. Mum was the black sheep too; she was the youngest of four, with two sisters and a brother, all owned their own homes; they didn't have to live in local authority houses, they all had just one child each; Mum had three that she couldn't afford and they all stayed with their partners until death; Mum and Dad eventually divorced.

Mind you, I think even our neighbours were better off than us; they got orange squash as part of the weekly shop. Mum managed though, I mean we didn't go without, not really, we just didn't have as much as everyone else. Christmas wasn't bad, I remember one year I got a second-hand bike; Dad had walked four miles, on Christmas Eve to pick it up for me. My sister never got that either because, try as she may, she could never ride a bike; Mum tried to teach her, so did my brother but she never managed it and to this day she still can't. My eleventh Christmas was memorable; I got a second-hand, eighteen jewelled Swiss watch, "tick, a, tick, a, Timex, tra, la, la," and my first two records - 45 rpm singles; 'Eloise' by Paul & Barry Ryan and 'Those were the days' by Mary Hopkins.

I always wanted to be a pop singer; I was in the school choir for three years and once sang at the 'Winter Gardens,' it was my first ever-public appearance, well, I say first but I did perform once before; it was one Christmas, I was about five and I stood on a chair singing to my Aunties and Uncles, "Always something there to remind me" by Sandy Shaw, I sang that song for years, bare foot and with a hairbrush or some such thing, pretending it was a microphone. Then I was Sandy Shaw, later I was Mary Hopkins but never was I really myself. Mum always told me that I

4

would never make it as a singer, actually when I wanted to be a model, I had, as she said, 'the wrong shape legs' and for a ballet dancer 'I was too fat', today I'm just me. I'd sing every night in those days, until my Mum shouted at me;

"Will you shut up in there and get to sleep!"

Chapter 2

I was eleven years old when things really went pear shaped for me, I was still at primary school but being an over developed child and fat, I was the one who was bullied. Boys and girls had separate playgrounds, divided by a painted white line and we were never allowed to cross the line. The boys would stand on that line shouting abuse at me, things like 'fatso' and 'fatty,' I suppose they did it to most of the girls at one time or another but it seemed, at that time anyway, that I was the only one. I remember a particular day, with puberty looming, I just flipped; a gang of about eight or nine boys were shouting the usual abuse, it was just at the end of lunchtime play, calmly I walked towards them, not saying a word, they were still taunting and hurling abuse at me, then I suddenly ran straight into their playground and caught one of them next to a concrete fence post; grabbing his head I banged it against the post, cutting it open at the back. The satisfaction was great, he was taken to hospital and I had to stand outside the Headmaster's office until home time. We didn't have a phone in those days, so Mum couldn't be contacted to collect me but I was given a letter to take home, asking her to attend a meeting on the following morning with the Head master. Mum took me to school the next day, usually I'd have had to go on my own, dragging my little sister behind me, Mummies little girl.

I don't remember the punishment exactly; I think I had to do one hundred lines saying, 'I must not beat a boy's head against a post', or some such thing. Mum kept telling me how much I'd let her down, the Headmaster kept saying how much I had let the school down and they never took into consideration the months and months of taunting. It was then that I decided I didn't want to go to school, I went most of the time but quite often, if I didn't feel like it, I would take my sister in and when she was out of sight I'd walk out, but once in a while I kept her off with me and we'd walk for miles. Monday was always the best day not to go to school because first thing in the morning Mum did the family wash in the old Hotpoint twin tub and at about lunchtime she would go and have a cup of tea with one of the neighbours. In those days the doors could be left unlocked, so we would creep in through the old allotments and in through the back door, go up into our bedroom, hide under the beds and stay there. Somehow we always managed to get down the stairs and out again, round the block and walk in

6

as if we'd just walked home as usual. I think Mum knew, or rather suspected that I was truanting but she had already started to give up.

My brother had started to rebel too, he'd had two brief scrapes with the law; once, just before Bonfire night he put a banger through an old mans letterbox, he was with other boys but the Policeman said that he was the ringleader and that the victim, had almost had a heart attack. Aaron wasn't bothered and Mum was worried more about what the neighbours would think, concerned that the Policeman had been seen knocking our door. The second brush came early the following year when Aaron had broken into a bungalow; the occupant had died and the place was standing empty, although the furniture and belongings were still in there, that was, until Aaron got his hands on them. He brought boxes of old postcards, letters, old coins, medals and bits if silver home and hid them in the loft. Eventually, when the Police called, he did give some of the items back but said he didn't feel he'd done anything wrong, after all nobody seemed to be interested; it was all still as the owner had left it and even though there were family members, they were too busy arguing about the property. There was an inventory of missing items and it occurred to me then that they would do well to settle the property dispute quickly or there would be nothing left. We didn't have this extensive list of missing items hidden in our loft but my brother always seemed to have money.

It was then that Aaron developed an interest in antiques and his life of crime. He had a distinctive lack of conscience and empathy for anyone, that coupled with his ability to have no need for other peoples company or approval made him quite a formidable adversary. I'm sure this need on my part for other people's approval and acceptance has been the difference between myself and him; he was always able to be himself, I on the other hand always strived to be what people wanted me to be: To my Dad; he was his son, to my Aunties and Uncles; he was the favourite nephew - the likeable rogue. My sister was Mum's little girl and was the baby to everyone and then there was me. I just remember feeling so unwanted and unloved, with no real place, in short I craved attention. My brother and I fought continually, not just verbally but physically too. He also had the knack of compounding what was already well established in my mind - that I was fat, ugly and that nobody wanted or cared for me.

I was in the last few months of primary school, at almost twelve, when a new family moved in at the top of our road. The Mother was just nineteen, the Father twenty-one. They had three little girls, the older two, aged three and two and a baby that was three months old. They were beautiful children and as I looked far older than my years, I befriended the Mum and spent many hours with them, playing and helping with the children. I'm sure she was grateful; being so young, three babies was a lot for her to manage. I was allowed to baby-sit for them in the evenings. The first few times I asked my Mum first if it was all right and Mum in turn spoke to my new friend Ruby, who told her how good I was with the children and she confirmed to Mum that I was babysitting. I was sure it didn't make any difference to Mum anyway; she was by now working from five until eight in the evenings, cleaning at a bank in the town and often took my sister with her. If she wasn't working, she was going to a conservative club to play bingo and on Saturdays she'd take Verity with her to the club, to meet up with her newfound friends. Aaron was out doing whatever he wanted and Dad usually got home after Mum had left for work. By now, I never knew where anyone was, so I stayed out later and later in the evenings and if Mum wasn't at home I'd stay with one of the neighbours that Mum had tea with, or more often than not with my new friend and her family.

I learnt to smoke and drink cider at Ruby's; I'd pop to the shop for her and be given a cigarette for my trouble. Her husband was also a drinker and most nights he would disappear up the pub and she and I would sit, drinking and keeping each other company. He would come home and they'd start to argue but I'd leave before the violence started and the following day she would have a black eye or a swollen face, handfuls of hair were pulled out in lumps from her head too. I never understood why she stayed with him, not then anyway but years later I found out why, from my own experience. Stay with him she did until he died from lung cancer, just a few short months ago at the tender age of fifty-eight.

Chapter 3

I started secondary school at an all girls' school that summer and I hated it. I was by that time a well-established truant and felt I'd learnt enough anyway, besides I now had somewhere to go, where I could stay all day. I would take a change of clothes in my school bag, at one time truanting for three weeks and I'd become very good at forging Mums signature too.

I had a good time over those first few months but inevitably it caught up with me: One morning my Mum turned up on Ruby's doorstep with the Truant Officer, she demanded I get my things together and said that I was going to school. The Truant Officer advised Ruby that she was liable and may be prosecuted for encouraging me but I insisted it wasn't her fault and, as Ruby said;

"She's just been turning up; she'll do it anyway, better to be in doors safe than wandering the streets."

Even so, she had to agree that she wouldn't allow me to do it anymore, well, not at her home anyway! I was escorted back to school by Mum and the Truant Officer. Sat facing the Headmistress I have to admit I was nervous; she was very strict and very into discipline. The verdict... I was to be expelled. She sat stern faced with a stance that was meant to be intimidating and it was! Mum asked her if she would change her mind about the expulsion. Finally, she turned to me saying;

"I am prepared to give you one last chance Janet but you must guarantee you will come to school everyday."

With an attitude I had become identified with in the recent months, I replied with;

"I don't want another chance in your bloody school and I won't guarantee anything, you can stick it!"

With that, she simply turned to Mum;

"I'm terribly sorry, but under the circumstances I feel I cannot be expected to allow Janet to remain in my school, she is a very disruptive influence."

Mum was told that she would be better to find me an alternative school placement. We left the school there and then and Mum cried all the way home. As we walked, she asked me why I'd done this to her, saying how embarrassed she was and defiantly I answered;

"You don't care about me, you've never cared, you are never home, maybe if you had been there a little more often, then I wouldn't have done it."

And I truly believed that would have been the case at the time but she blamed Ruby's influence, I tried to tell her that it had started long before they'd moved in but she banned me from going there anyway. I suppose some people would interpret my behaviour as 'a cry for help', that's the normal diagnosis for problem children isn't it? Well that's what I was fast becoming.

I had by this time, become a smoker and needed to get my cigarettes somewhere, especially as Mum had taken to counting hers. My Dad too was a smoker, although never heavy, probably ten a day at most. He would smoke just half a cigarette, put it out and save the other half until later. He would put them in his jacket pocket and at desperate times I'd smoke those butts too. He would often leave odd pennies about as did Mum; I'd collect them up and buy cigarettes... At the time of writing this I'm still a smoker but I wish I'd never started.

So by the age of 12 years, I had been expelled from my first secondary school and I'd only been there three months. I didn't return to school until Easter of that year, to a new mixed school. For those few months Mum had kept an eye on me and seemed for the most part, to take an interest. This also meant that when she went to the club on a Saturday, she would, on occasions take me along with her; I saw this as my chance to see live musicians and to see what she was up to. I got fizzy drinks and crisps, just like my sister, I also sang a few songs on the stage with the bands; 'Those were the days' by Mary Hopkins was the favourite... A title true to my life!

I knew that that was what I wanted to be, people seemed to like my voice and I enjoyed the attention but it was to be short-lived and Mum stopped taking me soon after. I felt uncomfortable around her friends anyway, especially the men, Verity was already well established with them and had been accepted. She and Mum had learnt to ballroom dance together aswell, I had never learnt anything like that but then I'd never been taught. So they danced together and I sat with their friends, who were strangers to me and they talked amongst themselves as if I wasn't there. I really wanted to be a singer but I wanted to be accepted as part of Mum's world more; for her just to have said that she thought I had even an ounce of talent, or for her to admit that she had possibly made a mistake about me, would have changed my whole outlook and my behaviour, but it wasn't to be and I went back to my previous pattern of behaviour, even more convinced that she would never like me, no matter what I did, so why try?

By the time I was twelve and a half, I'd started wearing make up and short skirts, being twelve - looking eighteen. I was smoking, drinking and fighting my way through life, hating and rebelling against anyone who represented any kind of authority.

By now another family had moved in just three doors away from Ruby and her girls; Jo and her husband had six children, the youngest just one year old and the eldest was eight. Her husband was a long distance lorry driver and was away most of the week. She was alone a lot of the time with her children and so I befriended her too. I also babysat for her on occasions and now I had another place to be, staying late every evening either with her or with Ruby, anything rather than be at home with Dad, who'd sit, sulking and questioning me about what I thought Mum was up to.

I still went to see my Nan with Verity on a Saturday; we would walk the three and a half miles there and the same back but I had by now got to the point where I didn't want to go there anymore either, it was always the same;

"Your skirts are too short... Your blouses are too short... You'll get a cold if you don't wear a vest to keep your back warm... You want to put a comb through that hair... You shouldn't wear make up at your age!"
Of course she was right but I didn't think so at the time. I had stayed with her for one week every year, during the summer holidays, for as long as I could remember but this year was to be the last; at twelve and a half years old, I had decided I was too grown up, besides even though Nan had said that it was a holiday for just the two of us, I was now convinced that it was Mums way of getting rid of me.

It was on one Saturday afternoon, after Verity and I had visited Nan and had our usual lunch of fish and chips. Whilst walking home across a common between two main roads, I first discovered what men's genitals do when aroused. Although I thought I knew a bit about sex, I didn't have any real idea. The only penis I'd seen was my brother's, when we were about four or five and still bathing together on a Sunday evening to save hot water and all

11

I knew was that he used it to pee out of. Verity and I were walking along a path at the top of a hill, Verity was in front of me and standing at the bottom of the hill, just about fifty yards to the side of Verity, we saw a man. I still remember him to this day; he was aged around his mid twenties with short ginger hair, he was smiling, wearing a full-length grey coat that was open and he was rubbing his penis, which was now stood erect. I was puzzled by this strange apparition but instinctively knew it wasn't right.

"What's he doing?" Verity questioned.

I told her to look straight ahead and keep walking, which is what we did, he didn't follow us.

Neither of us mentioned it to Mum, instead I went and spoke to Ruby; she laughed at me and said that she couldn't believe I didn't know about these things at my age. She called him a pervert, a flasher and then she filled in the gaps. I'd never known anything about sex after all and the idea of actually having something like that between my legs didn't appeal to me in the slightest, in fact the idea was quite repulsive. It did however, seem the ideal opportunity to find love, well maybe not love but certainly the attention I wanted, I mean, what a weapon and at the end of the day I may even be able to have a baby, someone who would show me real love, a person to love me that I could care for, always.

I suddenly became very aware of the way men, all sorts of men looked at me. In the weeks and months that followed the 'flasher' experience, several men, usually when I was walking home at night, followed me, they'd probably been around all the time but only now was I aware of them and then I realised that's why Mum's always say; "Don't talk to strangers!" I remember one particular night, I'd left home after an argument with Mum and was walking around the streets thinking I'd teach her a lesson; 'If she didn't know where I am by eleven, she'll have to come and look for me, she'll check and find I'm not at Jo's or Ruby's and she's sure to worry, and serves her right!' I thought. I was walking down the road, alone, it was dark except for a few dull streetlights and I was picking the odd flowers from the gardens along the way when I became aware of a car following me, at first I ignored it and carried on but the car eventually pulled up just in front of me and stopped; there was a middle-aged man driving, he called out to me for directions, I explained that he had just passed his turning, he asked if I would get in and show him, I said I didn't think that was a good idea, he then asked me about the flowers and said how nice they were, I told him that they were for a friend and that I had to go. I started to walk on, but he continued to drive along side me, talking about how he had a daughter about my age and that his wife was disabled and couldn't satisfy him. 'Satisfy him?' I kept walking, praying that he would go away, or that one of the houses I passed would have a light on, thinking that if I found one I could pretend that that was where I lived. He suggested he give me a lift home but, still walking and looking straight ahead I explained that I didn't have far to go, he then asked me to give him a 'bit of satisfaction' by ways of a 'hand job.'

"You don't have to go all the way," he said, "you could even suck it like a lolly if you wanted to."

By now I was very frightened, I even considered doing it just to get rid of him but then I saw a call box on the same side of the road and decided I would head for that. I did but he followed, so I went inside the phone box, shouting to him to go away or I would phone the police and he pulled the car right up against the door but when I lifted the receiver and dialled 999, he drove away and was gone. Shaking, I put the receiver down and waited for what seemed like an hour, just to make sure he was gone, then I ran as fast as I could to Ruby's. When I got there she asked me what was wrong, I told her that it was nothing and that I'd had an argument with Mum. I didn't tell anyone at home either, after all Mum wasn't talking to me anyway and if I had explained to her what had happened, I was sure she'd say; 'serves you right!' Telling her would have shown her that I was vulnerable too.

She was so angry with me when I got in and her face showed every expression. Her eyes used to bulge in anger but then, more often than not she would burst into tears and walk away. Dad, well he never said anything, ever.

Chapter 4

Mum and I had several fights after that night. In the main we'd fought because I wouldn't get up for school; she'd shout from the bottom of the stairs for me to get up, again and again and when I didn't, she'd strip the bed off with me still in it; screaming, eyes bulging and telling me to get up as she hit me around the head. One morning she came in and the usual routine followed, only this time I stood up and challenged her, so she slapped me, I slapped her back and she walked away into her bedroom, shutting the door behind her. I went into the bathroom thinking that I'd won but it wasn't over; she suddenly burst in behind me, screaming that she was going to kill me;

"You little bitch!" She screamed as she pulled my hair from behind.

I lost my balance, hit my head on the floor and she sat over me, slapping me violently. I eventually fought her off and then I was on top of her doing the same when Dad came in;

"What's going on here then?" He asked in his usual flat, unflustered tone, "Janie get off of her and pack it in. I'm going to work now."

We were stopped in our tracks, I shut myself in my room and Mum went on out. I didn't go to school that day, Mum cooked the tea as usual and went to work; she didn't come home that evening but went to the bingo as usual, as if nothing had happened.

The following day she didn't get me up for school, instead she asked if I was going;

"Not today," I answered,

"Ok!"

And it was as simple as that. From that day forward I went to school when I wanted, we had occasional arguments but none were as serious as that first one, although one argument did frighten me; Mum was wallpapering her bedroom, I can't remember what I'd said or what it was about, only that I'd called her a;

"… Fuckin' old cow!"

She turned, those eyes bulging as usual and hit me with the roll of wallpaper across the head. I remember covering my head with my hands as she continued to hit me with it until she ran out of steam. She then collapsed onto her bed holding her chest, feigning a heart attack and I walked away, thinking that I had won but then, after a few minutes, when she didn't follow and no sounds were coming from her bedroom, the thought and the fear suddenly hit me; 'what if she wasn't faking?' When I went back to see if she was ok she'd told me that she was sure she was having a heart attack; I didn't want her to die, I wanted her to notice me! And instead of walking away again, I sat down and explained to her exactly how I felt and for the first time in years, she cuddled me and told me that it was going to be all right. We cried together and she told me then that things had gotten so bad between my Dad and her, that she didn't know how long she could carry on like this, meaning staying with him, or at least that's what I'd thought. I didn't realise until later that that conversation was a goodbye. I didn't realise that she meant she wasn't taking us children with her, well, not me or Aaron anyway.

I spent more and more time away from home, at Ruby's helping her look after the girls and running errands but I'd also found a new interest there: Ruby had a younger brother, Ryan, he was sixteen nearly seventeen and rode a Lambretta scooter with big mirrors and tassels. He had a friend also called Ryan, who rode a similar scooter and they had taken to visiting Ruby most evenings, I decided then, that I was in love and without doubt, I was certain this was the man for me; I was smitten and went there at every spare moment, talking to them. One night we went for a walk, it was early evening and I thought I was quite safe, I was with both the Ryan's, four other friends of theirs and a girl called Zara. We were all laughing and joking as we walked through a wooded area called 'Pucks Dell,' all the kids used it and there were old tyres hanging on the boughs of the Oak trees, tied on with bits of rope and we'd swing on them for hours.

This particular evening was no different to start with but I hadn't noticed that everyone had started to move to another area, about a hundred yards away. I was sat in one of the tyres, smoking and drinking from a bottle of cider, as had become my regular routine, deep in thought, as was often the case, when Ryan came up behind me. He grabbed the rope above the tyre and swung me around towards him, he bent over and kissed me, it was so sudden and at first a bit of a shock. He took me by the hand and led me into the long grass. We sat against the trunk of a tree and he started talking about his sexual experience; although I acted as though I knew everything and had experienced everything, he knew that I hadn't. He always carried a comb and whilst talking to me, with one arm around my shoulder he was combing his hair with the oth-

15

er, suddenly just as before, he kissed me and just as swiftly his hand was inside my bra. I was very nervous and although it wasn't unpleasant, I felt my insides churn again; I didn't know how to get out of this and my mind was rushing. The next thing I knew his hand was between my legs, he was fumbling about and I was on my back, he was then undoing his zip, I asked him to stop but he didn't seem to hear me. By now my knickers were down but try as he may he couldn't enter me. I was struggling and demanding that he let me go and he gave up but he warned me that if I was to say anything to the others, I would be sorry; he said they'd all planned that he and I would be having sex that evening. They'd even had a bet between them; that he wouldn't be able to 'screw me' but he'd told them that he would win the bet and warned me that if I denied it, I would regret it. I was sat on the ground with my knickers still down as he stood up, zipped up his jeans and walked away. I just sat there in shock and disbelief; I couldn't believe that someone, who I'd thought had similar feelings to my own, could treat me this way. I let the tears roll down my face but I made no sound, it was as if I had no control, all the anger, frustration and hurt was falling from my eyes, as if I'd finally overflowed. I had made a mistake in thinking that Ryan could have been interested in me, my brother was right; I was worth no more than a bet.

I sat alone, everyone gone; I later learned that I'd been sat there alone like that, for about an hour. The other Ryan returned to see if I was all right but by then the anger in me began to grow and as he asked if I was ok, I shouted;

"What have you come for? S'pose you want a ride too? Should I get dressed or wait until you've finished?"

He was hurt and I could see it in his face but he said nothing, he just took my hand and helped me to my feet, then he helped me re-dress, picked the grass out of my hair and we walked back to Ruby's together. I couldn't stay there that evening, not with everyone laughing and joking, as if nothing had happened, so I went home.

No one was at home and it was dark, but I didn't bother with the lights, I walked into our bathroom, took my Dad's razor blade from its casing and held it against my arm, I hated everyone at that moment but worse still, I hated me; I was fat, unlovable and ugly, nobody cared and I would be better off dead. I was slashing my wrists and arms but I couldn't slash deep enough, it didn't hurt, neither did it help; the pain was too much everywhere else. I couldn't see the wounds, nor did I want to, I went into my bedroom, got into my bed and pulled my knees up to my chest, holding them tight with my arms, like a foetus in a ball and eventually I fell asleep in that position.

I awoke the following day when Mum came in and said it was time to get up but then she noticed my arms;

"What the hell did you do that for you stupid little bitch?" She said, "you'd better wash it or you'll get an infection!" I didn't tell her why I had done it besides, she didn't stay long enough for an explanation and she just left the room yelling;

"Get up and get your uniform on or you'll be late! I assume you are going to school?"
As I was dressing I heard Dad shout;

"Have we got any razor blades? Someone's been using this one."

"They are where they always are!" Mum replied, followed by; "She used it, (meaning me I suppose,) to cut herself!"

"What did she do that for, what's the matter with her?" he asked.
But there was no answer from Mum. I didn't have any breakfast that day, just went off to school. I went to see Ruby after school, but she didn't want to speak to me; she had obviously been told that Ryan and I had had sex and I didn't deny it, after all I had been warned not to. She said she thought I was trying to get her brother into trouble, that I had encouraged him and that he would be in trouble for having sex with an underage girl. I left there and went to Jo's, I didn't tell her what had happened but she was concerned and she knew that something was wrong but she didn't push it, she just checked my wrists and said;

"You know I'm always here if you need to chat, about any-thing and you are always welcome to stay here, whenever you want."
I left there at about 10pm that night, Ryan and his friends were leaving Ruby's at the same time and Ryan shouted;

"Fancy another fuck?"

They all laughed, all except the Ryan that had come back for me. I did my best to ignore them and went home.

Chapter 5

It wasn't until the following year that I went back to see Ruby, instead I spent my time with Jo and her children; I would visit them before and after school, and quite often during the school day too. I used to come home from school at lunchtime everyday. Tuesdays was the day Nan that came to lunch, or as we called it; 'dinner' and on Thursdays we would go to her home for lunch. I came home from school one lunch time and as I walked into the kitchen Mum said;

"Thank goodness you're home!"

Both Nan and Mum were sat, with their feet up on the chairs. Mum screamed at me,

"Hurry up and move that ruddy thing!"

I followed the direction in which she was pointing and there, under the table, rolled up like a Catherine wheel was a grass snake, one of my brothers. I had no fear of reptiles and insects then, I mean my brother had always kept such things, Dad had also collected moths and butterflies and he'd pinned them to boards, he called it a collection but I called it cruelty, I felt the same way about his breeding rabbits, or killing fish and eels for food. It was nice to see that my Mum and my Nan were so pleased to see me, even if it was the snake that had caused this grateful display of my presence. It was short lived though and I didn't get a dinner that day, Mum had been sat in that position since 10:30am and hadn't had time to cook anything, I had a sandwich and laughed all the way back to school.

I had many problems at school, I didn't make friends easily and all my friendships were brief. I was, as I thought far more grown up than the other girls my age and I rebelled against the system. At school my only interests were in English, Art and Music and they were the only subjects I would take part in. Geography wasn't too bad, for other reasons; I had a crush on the teacher, Mr Thomas. I struggled with maths, disliked French and absolutely hated any kind of physical education; I'd refuse to take part and would always, absolutely refuse to take a shower. On one occasion I was confronted by the PE teacher, she insisted that I remove all my clothes and take a shower; she humiliated me in front of the rest of the girls. I wasn't a small girl and was very developed. She stood in front of me whilst I removed my clothes;

"No wonder you didn't want to show yourself!" She said, sniggering.

I was ordered into the shower, much to the amused jeering of the other girls but they were eventually led out and I was left alone. I was late for my next lesson and given a detention, but then this was nothing new; I was always getting detention for something, usually lateness, not doing my homework, not wearing the correct uniform or just for being me.

The cane was less likely but it did happen once, I was with a 'sort of friend' named Monica and another girl named Joan. Joan was always scruffy with bitten nails and a very bad haircut, cut by her mother, she was also a nervous girl and I always felt sorry for her, but I bullied her anyway, although no one else was allowed to. On this particular day we were in a maths lesson playing up and passing notes to each other. The teacher, Mr Pearson, spotted us and with a flick of the wrist he sent the wooden blackboard rubber whizzing past my ear. I stood up, shouting abuse at him and he demanded that the three of us leave his room and go to the Headmistress' office. We stood waiting for her to come to her door. She was a big woman and regularly taught PE or maths; not a good combination for my way of thinking. She told us all to stand in front of her desk, then she turned and made her choice from the selection of bamboo canes clustered against the wall; I remember her saying she didn't like doing this but felt she had no choice, apparently we would, however, all learn something positive from this experience. 'Stupid woman, what's positive about this?' I thought as we stood in a line, each with a hand out. She caned Joan who immediately burst into tears, then Monica, who held up very well, except for screwing her nose up a bit, then it was my turn, the cane came down on my fingers, she looked me in the eyes and asked;

"Did that hurt?"

"No, not at all!" I answered.

I was made to hold out the other hand and I got a second one, I never knew why; maybe if I had cried the first time, it would have been pleasure enough for her.

If I hadn't liked the woman before, I certainly didn't after that and it became my aim from that day forward to disrupt her life and anyone else in authority that crossed my path. My very last disagreement with her was when I turned up in school, wearing a leather jacket, covered in studs and chains and a very short skirt, that I couldn't even bend slightly in without showing my knickers, which I might add, were not the regulation blue ones. She called me into her office; she had selected a spare uniform from lost property and had demanded I changed immediately into it. I refused saying something along the lines of;

"Stuff it lady, you like it, you wear it!"

I then proceeded to walk away and she came after me, so I ran into the playground and she followed, demanding that I return immediately as she was puffing and panting. I reached the school gate and turning, I laughed and put my two fingers up. By the time she'd got to the gate I was at the end of the road, I waved to her and then I was gone.

I didn't go back to school for five weeks and when I did return, I went only when I wanted to. Mum still attempted to get me up in the morning and we would argue, but more often than not she'd walk away and leave me to it. I'd get up about lunchtime, after Mum had gone out to the neighbours. I would usually go to Jo's and help her with the kids. We had talked a great deal and the relationship between Jo and her husband had really started to break down. On one Friday evening he came home demanding his dinner and accusing Jo of having an affair. I stayed in the lounge with all the children while he argued with her about the state of the house. I must admit I would never eat a meal there, the kids; especially the two babies were always covered in dirt with snotty noses. They also had various animals, in particular dogs, but despite it all, Jo had a good heart. The two of them ended up pushing each other around, I could hear them banging about and shouting, then her husband threw her out of the front door and locked it. He came into the lounge where I was sat and said;

"I don't know how you're going to get out, because you are not going to open the door."

I tried to reason with him, telling him that he couldn't keep me locked up, I even tried to reassure him that Jo wasn't having an affair with anyone; I had been there most of the time so I would know. He said that I was bound to go to her defence; I was as he put it;

"Covering for her!"

She did occasionally leave me to baby-sit the children, and it was at odd times during the day, sometimes in the evenings too. She had told me that occasionally she just needed a little break from the children and I could totally understand that; they were hard work. Jo did rely on the older children though, especially her eight year old daughter, sending her to the laundrette with the babies, aged now two and three years, in an old pushchair piled high with washing and dirty nappies, I did feel sorry for that little girl, I felt sorry for them all, but in particular her. Contrary to what was expected, they all turned out well; the baby is now working for the ambulance service, next youngest is a trapeze artist in a family circus in Portugal, with her own two daughters, the next is a Heavy goods vehicle driver. There is one in the army, with over twenty two years of service under his belt and the little laundrette girl is happily married and has six children of her own. Only the eldest is still at home with his Mum. So there I was, still in the house with the children and Jo's husband asked me if I'd make him a cup of tea, I did as I was asked and he sat with us in the lounge. I had been a little nervous to start with, but I soon realised that I shouldn't be, he wasn't angry with me and did not intend to hurt me. Although I was still locked in with the children and Jo was still locked out, but he was far calmer now. I talked to him more and he was soon telling me all his troubles and fears, I was just thirteen but he spoke to me as if I were thirty, confiding in me and I felt so sorry for him, especially when he started to cry. I listened to him and he finally said;

"I'm going to bed, you'd better let her back in."
I did as he asked and we never mentioned that night again.

A few weeks later Jo's husband was gone and a divorce was filed. It was as if he'd never existed, the kids didn't mention him and Jo just said that she was relieved it was over. He popped in on Thursday evenings with a maintenance payment for the kids, I think Jo decided then and there that she wanted to live her life as if she were a teenager again and in the months that followed, she certainly did that. We started going out to pubs and nightclubs together. She met several men and would take them home, hippy types mainly; I would go on home at around 12am and leave her to it. Mum always thought I was babysitting or out with Jo visiting her Mother, besides my Mum was hardly ever home now.

On a Friday and Saturday evening Mum got a lift home from the club with a man, a little, short, fat man with a pencil moustache, he reminded me of Oliver Hardy. His name was Larry, Uncle Larry to us kids. He would come in with Mum, armed with

three large bottles of coke, some crisps and a bottle of beer for Dad.
We quite liked it, but Dad didn't; as it turned out, he had good reason not to. One evening when I was about thirteen and a half, I'd just left Jo's and as I went towards our house, I could hear the argument. I opened the door and there stood my little sister, with her coat on, her giant teddy under her arm and Mum was holding a suitcase; it was obvious what was happening, she was leaving. Mum ushered Verity out of the door as I tried to get in, she pushed past me without so much as a word or even a glance in my direction, Dad turned on me and said;

"Don't you let her go, go on?" Pushing me out behind them as he followed.
I walked beside my Dad, following Mum the short distance to the top of our road where she flagged down a taxi. Verity climbed in and Dad pushed me in too, but as Mum started to get in, she shouted at me to get out.

"You stay there!" Dad screamed.
This went on for what seemed like forever until eventually the driver turned to Mum;

"Are you going or not?" He asked, "I have got a job to do!"
Mum got out and the driver handed Dad her case, which she promptly snatched back. I helped Verity out of the taxi and the driver pulled away. Verity and I walked behind Mum and Dad, back down the road towards home with Mum screaming;

"You can't make me stay!"
Then she swung her suitcase at him, he dodged it and we laughed, although not out loud, Mum was already angry enough. Verity and I went straight to bed;

"I didn't want to leave you but Mum is unhappy." She said.
She was confused too and I didn't want her to go either; she was a pain and a real Mummy's girl, but she was still my sister and I loved her. 'Who knows when, or even if I'd ever see her again?' I thought, I knew things were bad, Mum and Dad had been arguing for as long as I could remember, but even with her threat of leaving on that morning, now over a year before, I still didn't believe that Mum would really go… I mean; Mums don't leave their children, do they? It's usually the other way round, isn't it? I had decided that I'd better not go anywhere the following day and my Dad came to see me while Mum was downstairs. Dad told me that Mum was still intending to go, but that we should act as if nothing

had happened. He then said that he would make sure she didn't leave over the weekend but he would have to go to work on Monday, it would then be my responsibility to make sure she didn't leave during the week. I didn't know how I could stop her.

On the Monday morning my sister got up as usual and went downstairs, I was listening all the time. Mum came up and told me to get up like normal but I knew I couldn't, if I did she'd go whilst I was at school. She pulled the blankets off of me but still I refused to get up, so she left the room. I then heard Verity leave for school and I could hear Mum still moving around downstairs; she had started the washing, so I convinced myself that she'd changed her mind and eventually drifted back to sleep. I woke up again at about 11:20am and the house was eerily quiet. I jumped out of bed and ran downstairs, it was clean and tidy but Mum wasn't there. I started to panic and ran to our neighbours, thinking she may have gone there for her morning cup of tea, but our neighbour hadn't seen her, she asked why I was so worried and I shouted back, as I ran towards home;

"I think she's left us!"

I ran indoors and up the stairs, into Mum's room and there, on the bed was a brief note which read:

"I've gone and I'm not coming back. I've taken Verity with me, I can't save the other two, but I may be able to save her. Janie wouldn't get up for school, this was the final straw."

I sat and looked at it for hours. 'What was I supposed to do to stop her?' I wondered, 'Dad had asked me to, but how else could I do it? I shouldn't have stayed home, I shouldn't have gone back to sleep!' I cried all day and Dad came in at about 4pm; I was still in Mum and Dad's bedroom, sat on the bed clutching the note. I handed it to him;

"So you let her go?" He said, "I told you to stop her, why didn't you just go to school? This is your fault, you never wanted her to stay, you've always been the same, now what am I going to do? I've got no life left and it's all because of you!"

I didn't know what to say to him, he was right; I got up, left the room and went for a walk. I didn't want to talk to anyone, not Jo, not Ruby, I would have talked to Mum if I could have found her, but where would I look? I wanted to die, just go to sleep somewhere and not wake up. I just kept walking; nowhere in particular and eventually I walked my way home again. It was getting dark, the house was quiet and the words were still ringing in my head; what she'd said in her note, what he'd said. I walked up the stairs and into my parent's room and there I found my Dad, sat on the edge of the bed with his head in his hands, surrounded by tablets and empty medicine bottles.

"Have you taken anything?" I asked.

"I don't think so," he replied.

"Have you?" I demanded.

"No, not yet, but I'd just as well, I have nothing to live for." I begged him not to and I tried to console him, trying in vain to convince him that, given time Mum would return and that I would be there to look after him and my brother until she did. I had already accepted the fact that she was gone and I told Dad for the first time ever that I loved him. I still tell him in various ways now and I always did love him.

I have never ever got over the guilt of Mum leaving. Even today I don't know whether or not it was entirely my fault that she left, she said it was partly my fault, but mostly it was down to my Dad and Aaron. I'm still not convinced, I suppose I could have been the excuse she'd needed to go, or just another line to fill the notepaper with as she left... A few words that have left scars with me for life and words that would change my life – forever.

Chapter 6

So there we were; Dad moping around, planning way's to persuade Mum to come back and Aaron out breaking the law by poaching deer, burgling, or coursing with his new love – his two greyhound/saluki cross dogs. And then there was me, I just spent a lot of time at Jo's.

Ruby also asked me to baby-sit for her occasionally; she had apologised for what she'd said, admitting that it wasn't my fault but she had been angry with Ryan and had taken it out on me. She had started going out on a Saturday night with her husband, or at least he'd go out early and she would meet him in the pub later, her babysitter had let her down. I had no reason not to step in; I had nothing else to do, so I started babysitting again. Ryan came in one day, as Ruby was getting ready to go out and he too apologised for the way he had treated me, but by then it didn't matter anymore; I felt so low, almost submissive and nothing anyone ever did or said surprised me and even though he had still told everyone that we'd had sex that day, I decided that it wasn't worth the denial, and neither was I.

A few weeks later and everyone had started coming round again. We would all drink cider and smoke, just as before and I found a new way to deal with and hide my emotions, I would act the fool and acquired the nickname 'Divvy.' I'd go round to Jo's when I wasn't drinking with the boys, or babysitting and we'd go on down the town to the Cave bars, or the Badger bars. One evening I was running a little late; I was expected to cook the dinner each evening for my brother and Dad and I didn't see a lot of point in protesting, it was the least I could do after driving Mum out and so this had become the routine. The gas had gone and I'd had to wait for Dad to come in before I could start cooking, so when I finally got to Jo's she had already gone out, but she'd left a message with her eldest boy, to tell me that she would wait for me in the Cave bar. I leapt on a bus and went to look for her, I wasn't afraid to go into bars alone because I had got to know so many people, obviously I looked eighteen because no one ever questioned or doubted it. I looked everywhere at the Cave bar but Jo wasn't there, so I walked on down towards the centre of town, to the Badger bars but she wasn't there either. I was then told by a couple of Jo's friends that she had gone down to a bar on the beach, I knew where it was and headed down there through the towns gardens.

25

It was now nearing 9:30pm and dark, it was also cold because it was early February. I was walking along a path between two rows of trees and bushes when I heard footsteps behind me. By now I was a little nervous and was relieved when the people following, tapped me on the shoulder and turned out to be the two men from the Badger bar. Another man had now joined them and they told me that they had decided to go to the beach bar as well, insisting that they walk with me. We were laughing and joking when suddenly, and without warning I was grabbed by two of them, one on either arm, the third man then grabbed me from behind and jammed his hand hard against my mouth. I was dragged into some bushes, frozen in fear and ordered not to scream; they told me that they didn't intend to hurt me, just to use me for a bit of fun, they promised it wouldn't take long and when they were finished, we could all go on to the pub together. I was being undressed, my legs were held open and then one of them was in me, another sat across my chest, he slapped my head and said;

"Open your mouth!"

The first finished and the second moved down my body and was in me, the third followed and then it was over. I had a pain in my stomach but I didn't move, they got dressed and I stayed there. One of them asked;

"Aren't you going to get dressed? Jo will be gone!"

I just stayed where I was and whispered to them to let Jo know that I had gone home. And just like that; they were gone.

Covered in blood, I tried to clean myself up a bit with a piece of tissue that I'd found in my bag and some leaves, I put the tissue paper between my legs and put my clothes back on. I couldn't see how much blood I had on myself, on my legs or my clothes but I thought it best not to go on a bus looking, as I imagined I must look, so I walked the five or more miles home. No one was in when I got back and I got into a cold bath, washed myself and went to bed, freezing cold. I stayed there for four days, getting up only to cook the meals for my Dad and brother. I was afraid that I would be pregnant but thought that; although on the one hand it would be awful, on the other; I would have that someone who would love me, so maybe that wouldn't be so bad. But I also knew that if I was pregnant, I'd have to tell Dad and he'd phone the police, I'd then lose all my friends because they'd close down the clubs; who would lose their licences for serving me under age, my friends would have nowhere to go, I'd be put into care and worse; they'd all know how old I really was. I decided it was best to say nothing and told Dad that I was ill with woman's things; an excuse I knew he would not question me about.

Four days later I went to school and decided that if I didn't fight this thing men had about sex, I may even manage to get something out of it for myself; they may buy my drinks or fags for a few days. I was determined to turn this terrible experience into something that I could use to my advantage. I suppose this was my way of dealing with it, my light at the end of the tunnel...

I was right I had lots of boyfriends after that night. Jo asked what had happened to me and I just told her that I didn't have much money and had come home. No more was ever said but from then on, if Jo went into town, as happened on occasions, I didn't bother, instead I seemed to spend my time equally between Ruby's and Jo's homes, drinking and babysitting; hanging around with all of Ryan's friends at Ruby's and the older men at Jo's. They were two very different types of people; there were the lambretta lads at Ruby's and the hippies at Jo's and whilst I mixed with them all, I always felt that I didn't really belong with any group. At home I was still the housekeeper, doing all the washing, cooking the meals and going to school, (only on Monday mornings, Wednesday afternoons and Fridays, no one said anything anymore, so to me it didn't matter,) but every evening I was out, either being the joker at Ruby's; the leather clad mini skirted girl, always up for it, or at Jo's... Beads, peace and love reigned.

The first time I tried drugs was at Jo's, first a bit of blow, she was well into it but she'd also been taking L.S.D.; the 'micro dot.' I had tried smoking cannabis twice but it had had no effect; I didn't want to, but to keep up appearances I thought I should. The first and only time I tried L.S.D. was awful, I'd made a date a few days before, with the nicer of the two Ryan's and I was to meet him at 7pm on this particular night. At about 2.30pm, on the day of the 'date,' I took half a tab of this stuff that the others were taking. When asked if I was ok, I'd told Jo that I was fine when actually; I was far from it and I left telling her that I was going to meet Ryan. I didn't get there until about 7:15pm and being the nice guy that he was, he was sat waiting for me on his scooter. I couldn't walk properly and was swaying all over, I could feel my pulse pounding and I thought I was going to die. He asked if I was ok and suggested I

27

get on his bike and we go for a ride. I said that I couldn't, that I was ill, and then told him that I didn't want to see him anymore. I couldn't focus properly but he looked hurt and puzzled and then he rode away. I had really liked him and because of my stupidity I had lost the only man, (all be it only seventeen but still a man to me,) that had treated me with an ounce of respect. I went straight home, got into my bed and listened to my pulse, so fast and loud in my head and I was sure my heart would burst; I just wanted to sleep, to take the hallucinations away and I swore that if I survived the experience, I would never do it again.

After that, I didn't go to Jo's place as often, but instead went to Ruby's; I'd decided that alcohol was better than drugs. Ruby also had an older male friend, Terry, who had a wife and two children. I'd met him a few times, when he'd pop in on odd days or evenings for a cup of tea. At that time he only knew me as; 'Divvy' but then he'd never heard me called anything else. Terry turned up one evening when I was babysitting, Ryan and all the boys were there and we'd all been drinking, I was a bit worse for wear and the boys were messing about and having a laugh. I remember going up to check if the girls were asleep and then went to the bathroom; as I turned to shut the door one of the lads put his foot in the way and grabbed me, but as he did, so Terry appeared behind him. He grabbed his shoulder and pulled him away, told him to leave me alone and get out. Terry then whispered to me;

"I'll wait out here for you," he said, "you're not staying here with them."

"What about the girls?" I asked.
He said that Ryan could look after them until Ruby got back, but that I was to leave with him there and then.

Downstairs, Terry popped his head around the door and shouted to Ryan;

"You can look after the girls and you can also explain to your Sister why we've left, Divvy is coming with me!"
We didn't go to my home or his; instead he drove us miles out, into the New Forest, where he parked in a picnic area. We had talked throughout the whole journey and continued the conversation there, I remember him saying how he thought that I was about to be raped and how I was in a dangerous situation. He asked me my real name, how old I was, and said he was afraid for me. He talked about his wife and children, I talked about Mum leaving, he said

that he understood why I had been acting the way I had and that he was amazed how much older than my years I seemed, he suggested the reason for this was because I hadn't had a proper childhood and he promised that he wouldn't allow me to be in that position anymore; he would be there to look after me from then on. He kissed me and told me how attractive I was and then I had my first experience of 'normal' sex. Terry told me that his wife wasn't interested in him anymore and in my naivety I believed him. He did look after me for many years, until I was well into my twenties; if I needed to go anywhere he'd take me, if I needed anything at all, he'd be there, all it would cost was the use of my body when he felt the need.

He, his wife and their children played a major part in my life after that, of course what he did was wrong, and in a way, to most people it was very morally wrong. But during those years, he gave me some positive answers and although, to the average person it must seem that I was used for his gratification, I also used him quite a lot too, to regain some self esteem and I believe that he did love me, in a way that was so lacking in my life, it made me feel safe, I could talk to him honestly about everything, and it didn't always end in sex, just more often than not.

Chapter 7

I had just turned fourteen. Dad was out at the pub most of the time; he'd come in from work, have his dinner, get ready and go out again. Anytime that he wasn't at work, or at the pub was usually spent either at the police station bailing Aaron out; my brother was still getting into various scrapes with the law, or, on the rare occasions when he was at home, he'd be sat, scheming in his head ways of getting Mum back, he kept calling her at her place of work too. I still hadn't seen Mum; it was by this point more than ten months since she'd left.

It wasn't long before I'd started going to the Cave again with Jo and I'd seen this guy there several times; he was gorgeous, tall, dark, leather jacket with cut off sleeves and hells angel colours, he also wore dark glasses, a cap with a chain around the peak and rode a triumph 650cc motorbike. Jo had spoken to him a couple of times and I'd told her that I really fancied him but also said that I didn't think he'd be interested.

"There's one way to find out!" She said then went over and asked him.

He never said a great deal, his answer was;

"Yeah why not, I'll give it a try."

He came over, took his glasses off to the end of his nose and looked me in the eye;

"So you're interested?" He asked and I just nodded.

I went home with him that night on the back of his motorbike, although I had no intention of sleeping with him. He came and picked me up from school on it for the rest of that week and I loved it. He'd take me out on his bike just for a ride and we saw each other everyday, eventually I even took him home to meet Dad. He'd called himself Cliff but his real name was Paul, although I wasn't allowed to call him that. Looking back, I remember him as being very moody and demanding, telling me what to wear and what to do, but I was besotted with him and I didn't see anything wrong with doing as he asked. The first month we were together, I saw him everyday but after that, it became less, I'd still managed to see him twice during the week and then at the weekends too.

It wasn't until April 1972 that I next saw Mum, the first time since she had left. I was ill with bronchitis and had been off school. I was lying on the settee and Cliff was there, although I couldn't have been that ill, because I was smoking away and laughing with him. Dad was at home and was loitering in the kitchen. I heard a voice; the door opened and in walked Mum. She looked at Cliff, then at my hand, loosely holding the cigarette, so casually.

"So you're ill are you?" She asked and walked out again. My immediate thought was that the school must have contacted her. She and Dad argued briefly and then, just as abruptly as she had arrived, she left. Cliff made his excuses and also made a hasty exit. It seemed to have all happened so suddenly and I was left alone – again. A few minutes later, Dad came in;

"You could at least have looked like you were ill!" He barked at me. "Maybe she would have stayed, maybe she would have come back home, but because of you she certainly won't now!" I found out later that Dad had told Mum I was dying and that I probably wouldn't last the night, he'd also said that I'd been asking for her. Apparently he had phoned her at work; she had believed him and had come straight over, after she had finished her cleaning of course. I didn't see her again until March the 7th 1973, the following year.

Cliff and I continued to see each other as regularly as he would allow. One Friday at the end of May, his parents went away and I went to stay with him for the weekend at his house. He'd had to go to work on the Saturday, but had wanted me there, to make sure his dinner was ready when he came in; I could cook whatever I wanted but was also warned that I would have difficulty cooking a meal to his satisfaction because his mother was a very good cook and if he didn't like the meal, it would go in the bin. He went off to work on the Saturday morning and I was left to cook. I needed ingredients but the nearest shops were some four miles away. There were only two buses a day and, had I taken the bus, I would have been back too late to prepare his dinner, so I walked the eight miles, there and back, and cooked the dinner, which he didn't like at all and true to his word, it went in the bin. He wouldn't speak to me for the rest of the evening, at the end of which I was ordered to bed, where he then punished me with violent sex; I say that as if it was normal, unperturbed, but I had come to expect nothing less. By the time he'd finished I was bleeding quite heavily and I'd had to get up and wash the sheets. He went out to the pub, leaving me alone and I had no way to leave, so I just waited for him to come back.

Sunday arrived and we went to watch the banger racing; his brother was taking part. I stood on the sidelines, alone, whilst Cliff helped his brother, it seemed like he was still angry with me and at the end of the racing he said;

"I'm dropping you home."

He'd brought all my belongings back during that week, and did so whilst I was at school. I phoned him most days but he was never in and he came to see me maybe three or four times after that week-end, but finally told me that he didn't want to know anymore.

It was a few weeks later that I started being sick, I'd had a very light period, although not a missed one and I was aware that something was wrong; I suspected the worst, but just hoped that I was wrong. My clothes were getting tighter and Dad had made a few comments about my weight gain. I must have been, by now, around four months pregnant and just about to have my fifteenth birthday, I was sure that it was too late to have an abortion, but even if it wasn't, I was determined that no one would be able to make me kill my baby. I still hadn't missed a period but I knew my body had changed and that I couldn't hide it anymore.

Dad was in the garden, talking to our next-door neighbour over the fence, I felt sure he would lose his temper, even though he never had before, but I was sure that this was the one thing that would make him lose it with me, even so I had to tell him. I walked out to the back garden; he looked at me and said to our neighbour;

"Don't you think she's getting fat?"

"Can I speak to you Dad?" I asked,

"I'll be there in a minute." He said and as I walked away he hollered; "Make me a cup of tea if you like?"

"Ok!" I answered.

When he came in I handed him his tea;

"I've got something to tell you," I whispered, his response was just as always, as if I'd been talking about the weather;

"Don't tell me, I know you're pregnant! I'll finish my tea and then I'll have to phone social services."

He did just that and a social worker came out to see me the follow-ing day. I was told that I would have to go into care, I was already under a supervision order, placed a few weeks before and I was pretty sure that I was pregnant when the order was placed, but it didn't show then and I was certain that they would have insisted on an abortion. At the time I'd begged of the court, by letter, to let me stay at home with my Dad; I'd written a very heartrending letter to them and they'd eventually said that I could stay at home, so long as I went to school. I agreed and since the order had been placed, had done as they asked and by doing so, it had bought me a few more weeks for my baby to grow. This time though, try as I might there was no way they'd let me stay. Dad said that he was sorry but it was for the best, although I was given a couple of day's grace, not for me but because there weren't any spaces available in the local home.

Two days later, I was examined by a doctor at the local venereal disease clinic; they couldn't get me an appointment at the local maternity hospital, at short notice. The clinic confirmed that I was pregnant and gave a rough indication of dates; I was then escorted home by the social worker and ordered to collect my clothes before I was whisked away to a local girl's hostel. Most of the sixteen girls, all older than me, were at work and the hostel itself was for girls who had left school, it wasn't for schoolgirls or pregnant girls – I was both and I was to stay there for a week. I was given a few hours to familiarise myself with the building. The matron was a bit like my Mum, but more 'Mumsy.' Okay, she was an authority figure, but she didn't make anyone feel like she was 'all powerful' and all the girls loved her. I soon learnt to love her too and still keep in touch with her to this day. That first week went by so fast but Matron was there with me, all the way: When I was interviewed by the police; they wanted to know who the Father was and said that I had to tell them because he (the Father) had committed a criminal offence, I refused and they came back three times during that first week, twice with the social worker, but still I wouldn't tell them anything. They were getting angry and I admit I felt threatened, but each time I'd felt like that, I only had to look at matron and she'd give me her reassuring look that made me feel instantly more at ease and able to handle the interrogation. Each time they left she'd say lets have a cup of tea and a chat;

"They were doing their job that's all, I know you are finding it hard to deal with but if you don't want to tell them, then that is your choice." She said.
She instinctively understood me and for the first time, in a long time, I trusted someone. Matron was wonderful and I wanted to stay, she said she'd have liked me to too and although my first

night there had been strange, sleeping in a room with two other girls but I felt I belonged.

I had to leave the following week and I cried, matron cried too and said that when it was all over, I would be able to go back, unfortunately not with the baby as they didn't have the facilities, and if, as I was determined to do, I kept the baby I would always be welcome to come back and visit her. I promised to do that and the social worker and I left. I was taken to a mother and baby home in Surrey and I learnt a lot about my social worker on the way there; something she would later regret. I never liked her and I always felt the feeling was mutual.

Chapter 8

The mother and baby home was a Victorian style house that was supposed to become my home for the next few months, but the moment I saw it I knew I wasn't going to stay. The social worker and I went in through a big oak door and I put my suitcase down in the entrance hall, where the Matron was waiting to meet us. She had a stern face, with not a trace of a smile and shook my hand as the social worker introduced me;

"Pleased to meet you." She said, but it was obvious to me that she wasn't.

"Goodbye," said the Social Worker, "I'll see you in a month!"

And without as much as a backward glance she was gone. I was shown to my room by Matron who told me that I would have to earn my 'time-out' (timeout being a privilege) and that I wouldn't be allowed outside for one week in order to obtain some 'credit.' I was told to unpack and to return back downstairs, to the main entrance hall in thirty minutes. My room was at the top of the house; a drab, cold, grey room with two metal beds, two wardrobes and a bedside locker, that I was to share with a girl called Lucy. I unpacked and went back to the entrance hall as instructed and there I was told the timetable for meals and given the instructions for my life for the foreseeable future: I would be given a multi vitamin and an iron tablet first thing in the morning with breakfast and they would be checking that I was taking them, I would have to attend a school room for lessons and then, after lunch; an hour and a half compulsory bed rest, then two hours of lessons again in the afternoon and tea at 5pm, we had to be in bed by 9pm, and that was that: My life in a timetable.

I had to see the resident Midwife, who was a lot younger than the 'sour faced' Matron and during our introduction and conversation had even smiled a few times. She'd noted dates of my last period, or in my case the first one that was less than ordinary, then she took blood and urine tests and did an examination to confirm my dates. She told me that I was roughly four and a half months pregnant, and that my due date was estimated as the 28th of February 1973. With that done it was dinnertime and I was shown to the dining room, told to take a plate and join the queue. I stood behind a queue of girls and nobody was talking to anyone else; the atmos-

35

phere was very sombre. As I looked around the room I noticed that some of the girls were almost full term, others had had their babies. I was shown the nursery, where the babies were to be kept and from that moment, I started planning my escape; I wasn't sure how, but I knew that I couldn't live there and neither would my baby, I was going to take care of it and not some woman in a nursery.

I was told from the start that adoption would be best for my child, the sensible thing to do; after all I wouldn't be able to take care of it because, according to law, I had to finish school. I would be able to live there, with my baby for 6 weeks but we would then be separated. The child, (my son or daughter,) would have to go into foster care and because I was already in care, 'it' would automatically be in care, Social Services acting as guardians, I didn't have a say in it. They seemed to have it all planned, but it wasn't going to happen. 'No way!' It was my child, my decision, and no one was taking it from me. The problem was; I didn't know which direction I would have to go to get home and so, for the first two weeks, I did exactly as I was told. During lessons I wrote directions on a piece of paper, taken from a road Atlas of Britain that was hung on the class room wall, and hid it. My escape route out of the building would be the fire escape outside my room; that would be the easy part. Dad had written me a letter, enclosing a cheque for five pounds, but I couldn't cash it; I would have had to open a bank account, and then waited a further ten days for it to clear. So I asked for permission to go to the post office and open an account; for all intents and purposes it looked as if I was settled and resigned to my new surroundings. I followed the same routine everyday; going out for a walk every afternoon after dinner, familiarising myself with the country lanes and taking note of road signs. I soon found a quick route to the dual carriageway that was on the right track towards London, Croydon and I decided that that would be my route; I was certain that I'd be able to hitch a ride going that way.

The chosen day of escape arrived and after first telling Matron where I was going, I went to the post office. I tried to draw the money from my account, but they'd only let me have four pounds; I would have to leave the rest to keep the account open and I figured that closing it down may have drawn attention and suspicion. So, taking my four pounds I went back to the home and started packing. I was throwing things into a bag when Lucy walked in;

Lucy, although not shocked that I was leaving said that she would have to say something, until I eventually persuaded her that it was a dangerous thing to do; if I got into trouble and had to stay then she would pay, she decided not to squeal on me. I didn't have a coat that fitted either; mine was now far too tight, so I told Lucy I was taking hers and told her to tell them that I'd stolen it; having every intention of sending it back when I got back home. I packed a small bag and put it at the bottom of the fire escape, out of sight, behind a bush and the following morning, before anyone was up, whilst it was still dark and raining, I left. I walked to the dual carriageway and put my thumb out, but ended up walking for about two hours before getting my first lift. By then I was soaked to the skin, even considering returning to the home, but just as the thought went through my mind, my luck changed and I was picked up by a woman with a baby in the back of her car; she took me all the way to Andover. I told her that my mum was ill and that I had no money but I needed to get home and she was very nice. As was the lorry driver who picked me up almost immediately after she had dropped me off; I told him the same story. He had a delivery to make in Winchester but said that he had nothing else to do after that. We stopped at a café on the way, where he bought me a much needed sandwich and a coffee, he then asked me if I was interested in having sex with him, but I explained that I was pregnant, he shrugged and said;

"Ok, never mind."

He took me all the way home, dropping me off almost outside Jo's front door, I thanked him and he was gone. I couldn't believe my luck; I knew just how dangerous hitching could be, but at the time I didn't believe I had any other choice, it hadn't cost a penny, I still had my four pounds and best of all; I didn't have to sleep with anyone either. I didn't go straight into Jo's, first deciding it would be best to call her from a call box up the road, just in case anyone had been looking for me.

"No, no ones been here, where are you?" She asked,

"I'm just up the road!"

"Oh god," she said, "Get round here now!"

I did just as she said, checking for strangers in cars that may have been watching the house, but there was no one.

By now, Jo was seeing a man that she'd had a relationship with years before. He was a strange guy and I have to admit that I wasn't completely comfortable with him; he claimed he knew everything, that he had experienced everything and had been everywhere in the world. She later married him and they are still together. I stayed there that night but the following day the police arrived, I was sat on the stairs out of sight. They asked Jo if she'd seen me, she said no. The police then asked if they could come in and look around, but before she had chance to answer Malc, Jo's new man, asked to see a warrant, they didn't have one;

"Well," he said, "I suggest you go and get one then, Jo's told you she's not here and that should be good enough."
They left and didn't come back again for a further three weeks and by then, I was sleeping at home, my home, with Dad. He'd said, in his usual way, that he ought to tell social services that I was there, but he understood why I didn't want to be in a place like that and my need to be at home. He warned that eventually they would catch up with me but said we would face it when it came; anyway, he was glad I was home for the moment.

Jo's boyfriend, Malc had a friend called Dan, he had been told my story and when I had met him for the first time, (two weeks earlier,) we'd hit it off straight away and by the time the police, finally caught up with me, we were quite attached; he said that he would stand by me through the pregnancy and even be happy to take the baby on as his own.

One evening the police turned up unexpectedly: I had left dad's and gone to Jo's but didn't realise that I was being watched; given the length of time that had elapsed, I suppose I thought that they weren't going to bother. I had just walked in through the front door and into the lounge when the knock came on the door, Jo opened it and the police, (two police men and a W.P.C.) pushed past her, straight into the lounge and grabbed me by my arm. I struggled and hit out at the W.P.C. and in the struggle the buttons flew off her tunic. Malc, who was being held back by a police officer, shouted at her to leave me alone, saying that there was no need for it. The Police claimed that they had seen me go in and didn't believe it when told that I hadn't been staying there. Jo was threatened with prosecution, I insisted that I hadn't stayed there and that they should leave her alone, they didn't prosecute; I don't know if the fact that I had said I would put in a counter claim for assault against the W.P.C. was reason for not pursuing the prosecution, but they didn't. I was taken to the police station and kept in the cells overnight; the walls covered in the names of previous detainees, including my brother, I had to laugh and during the night added my name under his. A midwife had to be called, because of my 'condition,' she checked me over and said that I was ok to be kept there; if I needed anything I could ring the bell. I didn't need anything, least of all her and even if I had needed medical help, I'd never have rung that bell. I was so angry, I was upset too; that I hadn't seen Dan before I left, I was told that I could see him if he was the baby's father. He wasn't the father, but he would be in trouble for having sex with a minor and I didn't want him to get into trouble, so I didn't ask to see him again. He was questioned, as I found out later, and he confirmed that he wasn't the father but told them he intended to be there for my child, if I wanted him to be. They didn't understand that, I mean, why some young man would take responsibility for the baby and me, unless he was responsible, was beyond them but they couldn't prove anything, or act on it unless I gave the fathers name.

I'd been free a month when I was taken back to the girl's hostel, where my lovely matron welcomed me with open arms. But the situation was as it had been before, and even though I begged to stay; promising that I wouldn't run away again, I would have no need to, this was my home town, but if they sent me back I swore to run away at the earliest opportunity. It fell on deaf ears and I wasn't allowed to stay; two weeks later I was back in the mother and baby home as before. The Social Worker told me that she'd had to beg them to take me back; they didn't normally but they were willing to give me one more chance, I told her that she shouldn't have bothered, repeating my intentions to 'run' again and she had already unwittingly confirmed that if I did, they wouldn't take me back. That was all I needed to hear; I was determined that in the end they would run out of places to send me. True to my word and one week to the day, I was hitching home again, I decided on a different route, just in case they knew which way I'd gone last time. It had been easy to get out and away this time, too easy, as if they'd wanted me to, but had had to go through the motions of looking as though they had given me a chance to settle there. I didn't leave until after four in the afternoon and being October it was quite cold. It occurred that I may even be out, on my own all night. I went via Brighton and almost immediately got a lift from an elderly man, probably ten minutes with my thumb up. I was quite comfortable with him, with the exception of a conversation about 'Devils Dyke' and the murders that were committed there but, although it made me nervous, I believe he was just making conversation. He dropped me on Brighton sea front and it was by now dark. Another car pulled up and the middle aged driver asked where I was going, I told him and he said he lived in Chichester and would take me that far, so I got in. It was obvious by now that I was pregnant. I told my story, again; that my Mum was ill and that I didn't have any money, the difference being was that this time, she wasn't expected to live. He was a lovely man and I felt a little guilty about my lies, especially when he took me to the railway station and paid for my ticket to Bournemouth. He gave me instructions to change in Southampton and I promised that if he gave me his address I'd pay him back; I'd send him the money;

"Don't worry about that," he said, "you just get home and see your mum."

He kissed me on the cheek and waited until the train pulled away, waving and smiling, that's how I remember him… I had been so lucky, considering that this was in the days that Fred West was murdering so many young girls, of around my age, who had been taken from the areas that I had travelled to on my previous journey home.

I arrived back in Bournemouth. at about 9pm and phoned Jo, as I had before. I told her I was in town and asked if it was ok to come round, she told me to get the bus;

"I'm waiting for you and so is Dan." (He was now staying with them.)

By 10pm I was inside with a cup of tea, a sandwich and my friends. I went to see my dad at about 12am and again he was pleased to see me;

"I knew you'd be back," he said, but he gave me the same warning; "They'll catch you!"

I had a good week, nobody called and I slept two nights at Jo's with Dan, the other five at home on the settee, so that I would be able to hear anyone approaching and if necessary, disappear out through the back. I was wrong: It was a Friday morning and I was awoken by my social worker, stood in the room shouting;

"Wake up and get up!"

I refused, calling her all sorts of names. Eventually I calmed down, as did she and I promised her I would get up, but, as I was not dressed I wouldn't get up with her in the room; I promised that I wouldn't go anywhere if she left and she could come back and get me in half an hour.

"I trust you to be here." She said.

"Of course I will, where am I going to go?"

She left and I was up, dressed and gone in less than ten minutes. I didn't go to Jo's this time, instead I went to Ruby's; I could keep a watch on Jo's house from there. I told Ruby I was home for the weekend and thought I'd pop in and see her. I watched my Social Worker come and go from the window, laughing to myself at her naivety. I stayed at Ruby's for a while, Terry was there and he was really pleased to see me, he asked if I wanted to go for a drive, I declined and told him that I was going to see Jo. He told me to write and said;

"Don't forget, if you ever need anything just give me a ring, or drop me a line."

I left and went to Jo's. Jo, Dan and I had a long chat and we decided that it was a good idea to phone the Matron, at the girl's hostel and give myself up; maybe they would change their minds and let me stay now, after all, where else could they send me? My dear Matron, Mrs Mills was trying desperately to be cross, she told me to go straight there and when I arrived we would call the relevant departments. She said that she would see if I could stay but didn't hold out much hope; it wasn't her decision. I arrived there about an hour later and she was waiting at the door; it was like coming home again. She welcomed me with open arms and I just felt that she cared; to this day I remember that feeling, it's the only place I have ever felt the warmth of belonging. I know it was her job, but to her it was more, she had a real gift and she respected us, she listened and was fair, and in return we respected her. The next day my social worker arrived and as she got out of her car the disapproval was obvious on her face. I was watching her through the window and left it to someone else to let her in; I couldn't be bothered. I sat and listened to her enraged threats; how I'd let her down, how I couldn't go back to the mother and baby home because they wouldn't have me back, I couldn't stay where I was and she was at a loss as to what to do with me, I'd caused her so much trouble, more trouble than I was worth. (God, if only I had a pound for every time I'd been told how worthless I was.) She finished by telling me that she could arrange for me to be sent to a lock up in Scotland.

"Go ahead," I said, defiantly, "I'll come back."

"You wont you know!" She replied and my response;

"Watch me!"

Mrs Mills gave me a disapproving look and she and the social worker, Mrs Morris, went out to have a chat. Mrs Morris came back about ten minutes later;

"We've agreed you can stay here," she said, "just until I can find another mother and baby unit to take you."

'Yes!' I thought and I hoped she wouldn't find anywhere, but two weeks later Mum, (Mrs Mills,) called me into the office and Mrs Morris was there;

"They've managed to find you a placement in Bristol," she said, "but it won't be available for another week."

She left and I was alone with Mum, she put her arm around me and I burst into tears, years of tears. She said she had tried to persuade the department to let me stay but they wouldn't allow it. She told me she was worried about me, but it was only for three months and it would all be over and maybe, once the baby had been fostered, I would be able to come back permanently, or at least until I was able to be discharged from care, I couldn't speak, just sob. I managed to calm down after a while and mum made a cup of tea; funny how, no matter what the situation, tragedy or triumph, a cup of tea is the great British answer and funnier still is the fact that it really does seem to make things better.

CHILD OF A CHILD

No more can I hide this feeling inside,
The movement defines the fear of release,
To a world full of judgement where all will believe,
That the plan all along was to conceive,
The feelings of love from a child to a child,
In the mind of the confusion seemed restless and wild,
But the truth will be told the opposites true,
In this physical world where they must see you.

I longed for acceptance and love,
Not of my making but chosen above,
In reality all that I wanted was you,
No substitute love would ever do,
But now that I feel this movement inside,
With no one to turn to and no place to hide,
This life that exists is now part of me,
Whatever the right or the wrong it maybe,
This fate is now cast your shadow in view.

A child born of child but this also is true,
This mother's love will never leave you.

Chapter 9

The following week, the Social Worker (Mrs Morris) and my Dad arrived at the home in a taxi, hired to take me to Bristol. I didn't acknowledge Mrs Morris but I was really pleased to see my Dad and we sat together in the back, chatting about how things were for him. He talked about my brother, who was by now in a detention centre near Southampton. I hated the idea of Dad being alone, although he said he was doing ok. The drive was good, the countryside as beautiful as ever, and I made mental notes of land marks and the places that we passed through; I'd need them to find my way back. I never hid my intentions to do a 'runner' again, happily telling both Dad and the Social Worker.

So there we were in Bristol. I remember thinking; 'What a drab, dull place,' driving through street after street of grey buildings, covered in soot from car exhausts and road dirt. I spotted the coach station; we travelled just two minutes past it and stopped, 'that's handy,' I thought. The taxi driver took my case out of the back and wished me good luck; Dad looked at him and said;

"I wouldn't bother mate, she'll be back before we are!"

"You're not wrong!" I added.

Mind, it did take a little longer than that, one week to be exact. The social worker said goodbye, I kissed my Dad and he told me to behave myself and off they went. The home was three storey's high, a filthy grey building and there were only eleven girls here, although room for sixteen. Only four of the girls were white, the rest were coloured; I had never had any dealings with coloured girls before, I once made a friend of a man, working on a fairground, he was thirty-three and half cast, but he was only around for about a week. I'm by no means a racist, but for a young girl, on her own in a strange city, with absolutely nothing even remotely familiar around her, it was very bewildering; these girls were alien to me. I decided I wasn't going to make friends with any of them, what was the point; I had no intention of staying anyway, so I figured I needn't bother. The feeling was blatantly mutual; white with white, black with black, they didn't mix and the only thing I really learnt was that the coloured girls would coat their hair in a special wax, wrap it in brown paper and then press it with an iron to straighten it; 'very strange' I thought, but it worked.

Two days after I arrived, I received a card from Dad, with just a few lines written inside and a five-pound note, so off I went again. I had an hour to get my bearings and find the bus station. I asked at the home for directions to the nearest post office, saying that I had a letter to post. I found the bus station and the bus times for Bournemouth, the last one left at 7pm. I went back to the home but had taken a little longer than I was meant to and I was questioned by the matron as to why; I said that I had got lost and hadn't realised how long I was out. She told me that an hour a day was all we were allowed and for the next few days, if I wanted to go out, I would have to be supervised and earn their trust again. So I stayed in, I knew how and at what times I'd be able to go now anyway. A couple of days went by and I went out alone again; after all I'd convinced them that I liked it there, and that I felt it was in mine and my unborn child's best interests to stay. I was allowed out but reminded of the 'one hour' rule and off I went, running most of the way. I bought a ticket for the 7pm bus to Bournemouth and returned to the home in record time; just forty-five minutes, the next problem was getting out later to catch the bus. I decided that if I missed it, I was still leaving; I'd walk if I had to but I was definitely going! I followed procedure for the rest of the afternoon; had lunch and then school work until about four, compulsory bed rest until five, then dinner. I ate my dinner but was watching the clock and time was going fast. I said I didn't feel too well and didn't want desert and went up to my room, by now it was six o'clock. I looked at my belongings; I had no chance of getting out with them, so I stuffed clean underwear in my coat pocket. I even had to leave my toy monkey, Jacko behind; he'd been with me everywhere, I had thought that they'd send him on later, with my belongings, but I never saw him again. The fire escape that was out of a door on the landing was to be my exit but the bottom of the steps ran past the dining room; if I were going to get caught, that's where it would be. Fortunately, once again, luck was on my side; I managed to slip by unnoticed and was down the road faster than my legs could carry me. The bus was waiting and five minutes later we were on our way; I'd done it again. I asked the driver to tell me when we were nearly there and somehow I had fallen asleep, the next thing I knew, a passenger was waking me, on the instruction of the driver;

"Wake up, we're here."

I thanked him and got off the bus in central Bournemouth, it was 10:20pm and once again I went to the call box and phoned Jo;

"Has anyone been there looking for me yet?" I asked,

"No, why, where is ya?" She replied.

"Bournemouth!"

"Oh God, not again!" With a sigh she said; "Ok, get the bus, I'll be waiting for you, Dan's still here, he can meet you at the bus stop, just in case anybody is about."

So half an hour later I was back and Dan was waiting as arranged; he was pleased to see me but annoyed that I'd done it again. I wanted to phone Mrs Mills and tell her I was all right but decided it wasn't a good idea, not yet anyway; they'd send me back again, or maybe even further a field this time and Christmas was only a few weeks away and I wanted to be home for that; to spend it with my friends and family. Dan went to see my Dad and told him where I was and that I was safe, telling him that I'd try and pop in later, when I was sure no one was watching. We had several visits from the police over the next three days and each time they were told I wasn't there. I thought perhaps they'd given up because, it was a further six days before they turned up again. I went with them willingly this time and they rang Mrs Mills; no cells this time, I was to be taken straight to the hostel instead and they took me in a panda police car. I was fed up with hiding away; I hadn't had any medical checkups, I was feeling pretty unwell and hadn't eaten properly for what seemed like forever. I discussed it with Jo and my dad and told them how I was feeling; Jo said she thought I was doing the right thing, especially as I would need medical help sooner or later.

"You must do what you think is best." Said Dad, in his usual manner.

Once again the warm welcome and the feeling of being home; a warm bed, decent food and a cuddle from my surrogate mum. It had been discussed in my absence, between the Social Services department and Mrs Mills (Mum) that if, or when I was found this time, would Mum be able to cope and accommodate me, ensure immediate registration with a G.P and accompany me to my ante natal appointments? She hadn't hesitated, even though it wasn't part of her job description; finally I would be able to remain in the hostel and Mum would be willing to look after my needs, at least until the baby was born. After the birth, they would have to reassess the situation and decide the next course of action. Mum, or rather the hostel could not accommodate me once the baby was born if I was, as I had maintained throughout, still intent on keeping him or her. I knew this but I was just happy and relieved that I had a couple of months before the birth, to rest and get myself back on my feet. The following day I was at the doctors and then straight to the hospital for a check up: In those days there were no scans but I had a general examination; blood pressure check, baby's heartbeat, blood test and quick inspection of my abdomen to check position and size of the baby. Everything seemed to be fine but as a precaution, vitamins and folic acid were prescribed. Mum was with me the whole time, a warm friendly smile, that was genuine, there was never anything false about her, not then and not now; I knew she was getting paid to do this job but she really did love and care for all the girls who passed through her hands in the home. I built up relationships with many of the girls there too, they were from all walks of life and were in the hostel for various reasons, under a mixture of care orders, or place of safety orders, some for their own protection and some for the protection of others. One in particular, was Penny, she was there because of an order by the court; she had committed G.B.H. She was eight months older than me, at almost sixteen, came from Blandford and she was so funny, with a real Dorset accent, like a female version of the comedian Jethro. She liked everyone to think that she was a real hard nut, very much like me in many ways and always dressed in her leather jacket and one leather glove on, with rings on over the top; Penny was a fan of Alvin Stardust, hence the glove! She played acoustic guitar quite well, but 'The House of the Rising Sun' was her favourite, played over and over again, eventually with me singing along. Penny couldn't sing but she was and still is a real character; we still speak on the phone most days. On Monday evenings everyone had to stay in, do their washing and change their beds. On Friday's or Saturday's we were allowed out until 11pm, but for the rest of the week the curfew was 10:30pm and if we were late, we were in for a week. Needless to say; Penny was late quite a lot and was in quite a lot but she always accepted it and made Mum laugh, sulking and protesting her innocence; blaming her watch for being wrong, or the bus broke down, even that she wasn't walking as fast as she thought. She gave me some really happy memories, both then and now but she is also very hard work at times and she likes a drink, although she drank cider in those days, now she has to stick to beer; everything else has an adverse effect on her health, or her temperament. We shared a room, three of us; my bed just inside the door, Penny next, and at the far end of the room another bed, which seemed to be occupied by many girls and nobody ever seemed to stay in that one for long; probably because Penny and I were always talking, laughing and singing until late at night, until that is Mum went to her flat on the same floor, she'd put her head around the door of our room and say;

"Shut up and get to sleep!" Always with a little smile.

Not like my own Mum used too, she never smiled. Mum's accommodation was right next door to our room and she lived there with her husband, Uncle Don (who was in the navy) and her two children; a boy and a girl, both aged roughly the same as the girls in the home. John, the son had quite a lot to do with us but the daughter kept herself to herself and lived her own life. Dan was allowed to come and see me most days and I went visiting Jo, Ruby or Terry and his wife Iris; by now they had three children and the fourth baby was due the week after mine, 7th of March 1973.

I was happy for the first time in my life, although I was slipping out at night, whilst everyone was asleep; going to Jo's to be with Dan and breaking back in before breakfast. I had been doing this a few weeks and I really thought that I had blown it again, when Mum called me into the office;

"I know you are slipping out at night," she said, "but could I ask you to stop? Not because you will get into trouble, it's a little late for that, especially given your condition, but simply because everyone else is doing the same and following you. I get up to do breakfast and there's no one here." She laughed and I laughed;

"Ok I'll stop!" I said and I did.

Chapter 10

Christmas 1972 was great and all of the girls received a sack full of presents from Mum (Mrs Mills.); she was given an allowance for each of us by Social Services but always added to it from her own pocket. Everybody had a big gift of choice and then some small ones of perfumes, underwear, chocolates and individual personal things, all were different and all had been chosen with such care and individuality; she had read each personality exactly, even me. My sack contained personal bits and pieces and a set of baby clothes. The outfit was white lace,

"I hope you're not disappointed, getting baby clothes?" Enquired Mum.

I wasn't in the least, in fact the feeling was totally the opposite and I was quite overwhelmed. She told me that it had been difficult to get out and find the things she wanted to get for me, limited as she was in her time off, I had only been there a short while too… Her care would have been enough.

I went and saw Dad later in the afternoon; he'd bought me two orange bedside lamps - funny the things you remember! Dad had bought them with his new girl friend Sash, or 'Go fast eyelashes' as I liked to call her. She was a strange woman; she lived at home with her elderly parents but worked as a barmaid at Dad's local and fluttered her eyelids when she spoke; I'm not sure, to this day, whether she did this to impress, or whether it was a nervous twitch. Dad and I were invited round to Sash's parent's home for tea on Boxing Day; I remember that Sash's father wouldn't allow her to do something or other and she actually had a tantrum, a full blown tantrum: Sash had been trying to impress, dancing around the room like a demented ballet dancer, singing some strange ditty in a high pitched squeaky voice, that she was making up as she went along, when her dad said;

"That's enough!"

And without warning she started stamping her feet, saying;

"Please Daddy, please let me?"

I looked at Dad and him at me; we were both quite bemused, although Dad was also obviously embarrassed and this annoyed me somewhat, so I made my excuses and left. I didn't see her again and their relationship didn't last long either; some three months later and Dad was alone again. I can't say that I was too upset about that, I couldn't have imagined her as a stepmother.

I was still seeing Dan regularly and on most days I went to Jo's. On one of these days I met Mandy, a new friend of Jo's; Jo had met her in town, at a café where she'd been spending a lot of time with her hippie friends. Mandy was eighteen years old and homeless, so Jo had offered her a temporary place to stay. I liked a number of Jo's friends but took an instant dislike to Mandy, I tended to be like that now; analysing people, learning very quickly what they were about and first impressions had counted for a lot. Unfortunately Mandy's reputation had preceded her; she was known as the town bike, sleeping with anyone and everyone and she never denied it. She had treatment several times for various venereal diseases and she also took an infection called 'scabies' into Jo's home; everyone who was also living at Jo's around that time had to have treatment, even Dan. I really didn't like him living in the same house as Mandy, especially given her reputation, but Dan assured me that he wouldn't touch her with a barge pole;

"Not with someone else's, let alone my own!" he had said. But I still felt uneasy and asked him if he would like to stay at Dads for a while, he agreed and so I asked Dad. He was happy for Dan to stay; my brother was away and Dad said that he could do with the company. Dan still visited Jo and Malc most days. At around that time, Terry introduced me to a man called Eric; they had known one another for many years and Eric came from Bournemouth but had lived most of his adult life in Yorkshire. He got to know Dan and Jo too and we were all pretty friendly, he even came to the hostel to visit me with Dan. Eric also had a wife and two children but I hadn't met them at that time and he was a typical Yorkshire man; the wife (his wife) is supposed to be at home, making the gallons of tea that he drank a day. The woman's place as he said was;

"Barefoot, pregnant and chained to the kitchen sink!" I don't think he really believed this was the way it should be, just felt that he had to give that impression.

It was the 21st February 1973 and Dan and I went to the pictures to see a film called 'Soldier Blue'. I'd had a mild stomach ache all day but nothing much. It wasn't until just about the end of the film, around ten o'clock, that the pains, although irregular, were getting more painful. I hoped it wasn't the start of labour; the longer I could hold on with this baby inside me, the longer I'd be able to stay at the hostel. I tried to ignore it and Dan asked several times if I was ok; I tried to shrug it off, saying that it was just a few twinges. He was a little concerned, but I covered it well;

"Maybe you should mention it to mum?" He suggested.

"No, its ok, it'll go off in a minute." I replied, while in my head I was saying; 'Please, please, don't let it be time!'

We said our goodbyes and off he went. When I got in I didn't mention the pains; I just whispered that I was feeling tired and was going off to bed. Mum put her head around the door;

"Goodnight," She said, then asked; "are you sure you are all right?"

"Yes." I replied,

"Well don't forget, you call me at the first signs, we don't want to get caught short do we?"

I told her not to worry and laughed it off.

"Night, night!" She said with a nod and left.

All night the pains got worse, they were every ten minutes, then every seven. At 7am mum came in to wake us as usual and I was sat up in bed; she only had to look at me;

"Ok, how long has this been going on?"

"All night," I replied, wincing but still trying to play it down. She wasn't too impressed. "Well I didn't want to disturb you," I said.

She helped me to sit on the side of the bed, asked if my case was ready and then she called the ambulance. As I stood up to get my case there was a pop; my waters had broken. Penny grabbed towels on impulse and threw them at me, then ran out to tell mum, who came rushing back into the room;

"Oh God," she said, "Well never mind, the ambulance is on its way. I'll make you a cup of tea, just keep your nightie on and I'll bring your clothes to the hospital later."

I had so wanted her to go with me to the hospital but she had to get the other girls off to work. She assured me that she would keep in touch with the hospital and that she would contact Dan and my Social Worker, Mrs Morris. Off I went in the ambulance, with Mum, Penny and most of the girls waving me off and wishing me luck. The ambulance staff made me sit in a wheelchair and when we arrived at the labour room, a nurse helped me into bed. She checked me over and said;

"You've a long time yet; someone will be round to shave you in a while!"

Thank goodness they don't do that anymore. I was left alone for what seemed like forever and I remember thinking; 'I really don't want to do this, I've changed my mind!' But then I knew that I would soon be holding that little person that I could love. A lifetime later and I heard footsteps; I was laying flat and could hear a rustling of papers, packaging on a trolley and then a scraping of metal instruments on metal. The bed was up high and I couldn't see anyone, then, the footstool was pulled out from under the bed and this little lady appeared; she could only have been about 4'6"and she had a German accent. She was telling me that she was there to shave me but she could tell that I was really unnerved; for which she apologised and after a long chat about the procedure and what I was to expect, I began to relax and she assured me that she'd performed this hundreds of times. She stayed with me most of the morning and I liked her, she was very sweet, as was the doctor. The doctor was blonde, Australian I think, probably about 6' tall, with nothing out of the ordinary apart from a huge scar he had around his throat; it went back as far as I could see, extended to his Adams apple at the front and was about a quarter inch thick - my God, it was like a freak show!

At about 11:45am, they gave me an epidural for the pain; I had been inhaling the gas and air but it wasn't doing much. Dan was in the waiting room and Mum had been told how I was doing. I was told to push and then they had to do an episiotomy. Another couple of pushes and it was out – a beautiful boy. It was 12:15pm when I heard him cry;

"Good girl, well done!.." They congratulated me and then;

"...Oh look!"

Everyone took a look at my baby, everyone except me. I asked to see him;

"What's wrong?" I stammered,

But he was whisked away with the nurse saying;

"You can see him soon; we've got to clear his airways!"

"We'll clean you up and stitch you first." Said my little nurse; "You'll be able to see him soon."

I was stitched up and cleaned; had a cup of tea and was moved to another room, on a ward; which I later learnt was the ante-natal ward. Dan came in and congratulated me;

"So it's a boy! He weighs 6 lb 4 oz! Somebody will be in, in a minute." He said.

We had decided some weeks before on a boy's name, together; it was to be Carl John. At 1:30pm the doctor came in and said that they were concerned about something they'd found, but wouldn't confirm any diagnosis until a specialist, who was on his way from Southampton children's hospital had seen him. I asked when I could see him, the doctor left saying;

"As soon as the specialist has confirmed it."
At just before 2pm the specialist walked in; he introduced himself, but I can't remember his name because the conversation that followed left me totally disorientated and numb:

"Miss Smith?" He asked, shaking my hand;

"Yes, I am," I replied.

"Do you know what spina bifida is?"

"Vaguely,"

"Well I'm sorry to tell you this, but your baby has got it."
Dan held my hand as the specialist continued; "We are taking him to Southampton general now in an escorted ambulance, the sooner the better but you should prepare yourself for the worst, first impressions suggests a severe abnormality."
All I could say was;

"Please, can I see him before he goes?"

"Yes, but it will have to be brief."
A few minutes later the nurse wheeled Carl in; he was dressed in a little blue bonnet, wrapped tight in a shawl, with just one hand and his little face showing and his blue eyes flickering open and shut, as if trying to look at me. He looked so perfect with his dark brown hair showing from under his bonnet, but I couldn't hold him, just stroke his hand. I had to say hello and goodbye, almost in the same breath, I then gave them his name and he was whisked away; A few minutes later I watched at the window as the ambulance drove away and then; he was gone. I didn't speak to Dan and he didn't speak to me; it sounds silly but something changed between us at that moment. He stayed an hour or so and then made an excuse to leave; saying he'd be back later. I was numb, it was like a bad dream and I thought; 'I'll wake up in a minute,' but then I was awake, wasn't I? This was real. Nurses and Doctors came and went, checking my stitches and my blood pressure, but I didn't really notice. Dan didn't come back that day. Over the next few days I had time to think; I thought I was responsible, I mean I had made Carl that way, I didn't get the medical help I should have and I had been running around the country, not eating properly, getting soaking

wet. I also remembered that his kicks were felt very late; the first flutter wasn't until about six months and even then they weren't strong movements, but then what did I know; I was only fifteen. I figured that I was being punished; punished for letting my Mum leave, for my Dad's loneliness, for not going to school. I had to be punished and God had decided that this was it, but why punish me by making this baby suffer, making him deformed? Why use this child? I couldn't cry, even when Mum came to see me, not my own Mum, I needed her then but she didn't come, neither did Dad but I was told they had been informed.

Three-women came in the following day; they were also patients on the ward and it was then that I learnt I was on the ante-natal ward. All three were still pregnant;

"Just thought we'd say Hi, when's your baby due?" One of them asked,

"I've had it." I said,

"Oh, what did you have?" She said, sounding surprised,

"A boy,"

"So, where is it?" She asked,

"*HE'S* got spina bifida and *HE'S* been taken away to South-ampton," I said.

At which point, the nurse called them away;

"Come ladies, Miss Smith needs some rest."

The shock on their faces was so obvious that I even felt sorry for them and I thought; 'What sort of hospital was this? Letting them face me, who's to say they won't give birth to rejects aswell?' The nurse came back to me and apologised;

"That should never have happened!" She said, "You won't be disturbed again."

I asked to use the phone and it was brought to me, I needed to speak to someone; 'Why should I suffer this alone? Who else should suffer?' And then it hit me; 'Well Cliff of course, or should I say Paul? He should be informed shouldn't he? After all he is the father.' I dialled his number and he answered;

"Hi, it's Jan," I said.

"So, what do you want?"

"I just wanted to let you know that I've had your baby, it's a boy, but he's in Southampton hospital. He's got spina bifida and they don't expect him to live!"

He started to say something but I put the phone down. I was in hospital for five days in total, the Doctors wanted me to stay longer but finally agreed to let me go; Mum would be there at the hostel, she would look after me. They said that the midwife would remove my stitches at home, on one of her daily visits and that it was a bit unfair to expect me to stay, surrounded by expectant Mums… 'Unfair on who, them or me?' I decided it was best for them, and anyway I needed to get to Southampton to see Carl; if Social Services wouldn't take me, then I'd walk, but either way I was going.

On Monday 27th February I was discharged from hospital, Dan came straight up to the home to see me as did Mrs Morris; she said how sorry she was and that she couldn't imagine what I must be going through, having not been able to have children of her own. She told me that they had found a placement for him in a local nursery, if he survived; it was residential and I could work there part time as a nursery nurse, I'd also be able to stay at the hostel, even though I was still supposed to be at school but they had to sort that out too. 'Well thanks then; it takes giving birth to a disabled child to get any support from them!' That's what I had read into those words, but then in those few days my world had turned upside down and my outlook had changed completely. There was no point in crying or protesting, this was my lot in life; nobody loved or cared, and that wasn't surprising; being the sort of terrible, evil person that I was.

I was to find out later the next day, just how disabled my son was: He was a little stronger and had increased his intake of food, from 5ml to 10ml of milk, per feed and was considered strong enough to withstand the operation that had been scheduled for 12pm. My Social Worker had said that she'd take me to the hospital and that Dan could come too, so at 10am the next morning she was back. Dan sat in the back and I in the front of the car. The Social Worker chatted to me but when I didn't respond she chatted away to Dan, chatting and laughing. Given that my baby was going under the knife in just a couple of hours, I felt that they shouldn't be laughing and I felt my anger welling but said nothing. We arrived in the hospital and waited to see the Doctor, as for Carl, I knew that we probably wouldn't be able to see him that day; the doctor said he'd expected the operation to take about two hours and from what he'd seen so far, Carl was paralysed from waist down, it was also usual for hydrocephalous (water on the brain) to be present; this was the case with Carl, although his head was not enlarged yet. I was told that they would be able to put a shunt in (a

tube behind the ear)at some later date, where by they could periodi-
cally drain the fluid from his brain to relieve the pressure. He had
clubbed feet too but this was also common and I was told that an
operation to straighten them would be possible, also at a later date,
did I have any questions?

"No!"

"Please be prepared because this is a severe case and as
much as I'd like to say he will be all right, I feel there is no more
than a twenty per cent chance that he will pull through, although
we will keep you informed. Meanwhile, there is a café in the
grounds, or you can walk in the gardens, feel free to wait."

We left the room and found the café, which was around the back of
the main building and outside the windows of the operating thea-
tres; frosted windows to prevent the public from seeing in. There
were a lot of people in the café; most were children with various
tubes and bandages. I found a seat with Dan and Mrs Morris went
to buy us coffee, she asked if I'd like something to eat but food was
the last thing on my mind and I felt so sick, I was sure that I'd be
sick if I tried to swallow anything. I didn't tell her that, I just gave
her a look and said;

"I don't think so do you?" Dan ordered a sandwich.

There were two little girls sat at the next table; they looked maybe
five or six years old and were identical twins. Such pretty little
things, with long blonde hair pulled up in ponytails, they wore identical, little pink dresses and white cardigans and they smiled, giggled and looked like normal, healthy little girls; with the exception
of a tube protruding from under each dress, the tube carried what
appeared to be urine and was connected to a transparent bag with
white, plastic carrying handles, which were hung on the back of
their chairs. They stood up together and each turned and picked up
their bags; one with the left hand, the other with the right, which
appeared to be the only difference between them. Each took the
others free hand and as they walked past me, one turned towards
me and smiling she said;

"Hello!"

"Hello!" I replied, smiling back.

That little girl's image stays with me; they seemed happy and
friendly, regardless of their illness... Maybe there was hope for
Carl, perhaps he wouldn't be unhappy or blame me for his disability, he may even have a chance of a life!

Chapter 11

A nurse came and found me, to tell me that the operation was going to take a lot longer than anticipated, but if I felt I couldn't stay, they would understand. There was no way I was leaving until they were finished; no matter what the out come, I was going to be there and I told her as much. Mrs Morris though said that she would have to get back to work and that she would arrange for a taxi to bring us back to Bournemouth later. She left and I was glad to see the back of her, convinced as I was that she was just doing a job and had no feelings what-so-ever. Dan and I sat and waited, and it was 4:30pm before the nurse came back;

"Carl is back on the ward," she said, "the doctor will see you now for a little chat,"

We walked through the corridors of the children's wards in silence; the walls were covered in cartoon characters and teddy bear pictures. We followed the nurse, still not saying a word; the only sounds were our hollow footsteps. I had difficulty keeping up because my stitches were pulling and had become infected, I winced with the pain.

"You should really have stayed at home," Dan had said, but nothing short of death would have stopped me being there. We walked into the doctor's office and were greeted with a solemn handshake. Before I had chance to sit, his words spilled out and I remember thinking; 'What nice teeth he has!'

"Well, baby Carl has come through the operation well, but he is still in a very critical condition and is a very poorly baby. We have opened his spine from the nape of his neck to the base of his spine and as far as we can see, his spine had not formed properly, as a result of this procedure his spinal cord is exposed all the way down and the spine is open. He is presently paralysed in the legs and given the extent of the damage, he will gradually lose feeling from the waist up and eventually he will almost certainly lose the use of his arms. I'm afraid he will also be extensively brain damaged and the chances of him surviving, or even living for more than a few days are very slim. But he certainly is a fighter Miss Smith!"

It was at that point that I stopped listening, he carried on but I wasn't hearing any more. Although I did hear, as we got up to leave;

"You mustn't blame yourself, it's nobody's fault. This happens in the first few weeks in the womb and nobody could have known. Normally nature aborts such abnormal foetuses but probably given your age... Blah, blah, blah!"

"Can I see him?"

"Yes, but you'll not be able to pick him up and he is laying on his tummy because of the stitches. There are tubes taking the waste from his body and he also has a drip to stop dehydration and to dispense medication into his blood stream."

"Thank you." I said.

He shook my hand again and the nurse took us back down the corridor. We were told to scrub our hands and given gowns and masks before entering the room. It was open visiting;

"This is because the babies in this room are so very poorly," the nurse informed us. "You will probably be shocked by the tubes and the wounds but it looks worse than it actually is." The nurse was trying to reassure me.

We gowned up and entered the room: There were eight little plastic cribs, all with tiny little deformed bodies in them, Carl was the third from the right; he had a little nametag with a teddy on it and it was the first time that I'd noticed his name written, I hadn't even written it down anywhere myself. A white cotton sheet was placed over his legs, but he was naked from his hips upward and that vision will haunt me forever: There were two tubes placed into bottles at each end of his crib and they disappeared under the sheet, his tiny back was exposed and a line of black stitches ran down the centre of his back, from top to bottom and just above his waist there was another, larger patch of stitches, like a darn in the top of an old sock and there was a mass of stitches, about an inch or so across his spine; he looked as though he had been sown up, like an old toy that had had the stuffing knocked out of it. Aside from all of this he looked so faultless; his perfect little face and his shock of dark hair. I stood and watched him sleeping peacefully and there was no sign of pain and, for the first time since his birth; the tears started to roll out of my eyes, no sound, just tears, dripping. I stood there for over two hours. A nurse came in and spoke to Dan, she said that the social worker was on the phone and wanted to know what time would we like the taxi. I didn't want to leave, who would know if Carl would live through the night, or if I'd ever see him again;

"Eight thirty." Dan told her.

The nurse checked Carl's condition and STATS but I couldn't watch, so I looked into the other cribs: In the first crib on the left there was a little girl; she was smaller than Carl with an abnormally large head, she also too had two darn patches and a mass of stitches down her back. Yet another with such a pretty face, but I knew that she would not be alive much longer.

"Poor little soul, we can only do what we can." Said the nurse, leaning over my shoulder and nodding in the direction of the baby girl. She then turned to Carl;

"There you are then, he's doing well and I'll be back shortly. In the meantime, if I don't see you before you leave, please feel free to phone anytime or visit, all right my love?"
She left the room and I stood there for another twenty minutes, watching him sleep. A flicker of his eyelids and a little sigh were the only signs of life I'd seen in the three and a half hours of that visit. I touched his little hand and whispered into the crib;

"Goodbye little man, I'll be back really soon." And then I left; the taxi was waiting. Dan put his arm around me as we climbed in and he kept saying how lovely Carl was, how much of a fighter he must be and what he'd do for him if he made it, but I could feel the anger inside me building up;

"Why don't you shut up?" I yelled. "Any idiot can see he's going to die, and even if he did live; he'd be a bloody cabbage!"
He looked at me as though I'd kicked him in the teeth. I wasn't angry at Dan, I was just angry full stop, unfortunately for him; he was there. He didn't speak again, except to say goodbye at the door of the hostel;

"I'll be back to see you first thing in the morning." He said pulling the door towards him. I walked inside and Mum was waiting; she looked at me and the tears started again, hers and mine.

"Cup of tea?" She asked and put her arm around me. The place was silent, sixteen girls in and still silence; no music, only sad faces looking at me, waiting for news. "She's had enough for today; we can talk about it tomorrow." Mum said to the girls and led me towards my room. I went to bed and still there was silence.

The next day the midwife took my stitches out, I had a bath and went down to breakfast and much to my relief; everyone had gone to work. It was 9:30am and Mum had already phoned the hospital; she said that Carl was doing well, that he had taken his feed and was quite bright, so that was good news. During the next few days I told Mum the conversation I'd had with the doctor's, I explained Carl's condition and description and Mum relayed it to the girls. I saw Dan everyday and Jo and Eric came round as well. Terry's wife was pregnant too and due any day, and although I didn't get to see him, he asked after me. Penny went home for the weekend; we'd become quite close and she made me laugh, she also cried with me too. On Sunday the 5th March the hospital phoned and asked Mum to ask me if I would like Carl christened; he'd taken a turn for the worse. I said that I would but I wanted to be there; the christening would be arranged for the Monday. 'What if he doesn't make it?' I thought and every time the phone rang, I thought; 'This is it!' But it wasn't. Mum kept saying;

"No, its ok, he'll be ok! It's just a precaution."

Monday the 6th, at 10am and the Social worker was there to pick us up; off we went to the hospital again, she asked how I was; 'Like she cares!' I thought, although she did actually sound genuine and I did learn her first name on that journey too; June. We arrived at the hospital, scrubbed and gowned and went straight in, June aswell. I noticed that the little girls crib was empty; the nurse said that she had gone, died. June Morris looked at Carl;

"Oh he's beautiful," she said.

By now he was very yellow – jaundiced; this was apparently to be expected according to the nurse. I was asked if I would like to hold him and I was afraid of hurting him, or pulling out a tube, but the nurse said that he wasn't in pain and if I sat down on a chair, she would pass him to me. I took him and he folded into my arms almost double, like a floppy rag doll and I knew then that he wasn't going to live. I sat for an hour; June Morris and Dan watched me. With her eyes full of tears, June said;

"I've got to go. I'll give you the train fare to get home."
I couldn't take anymore and at that point, the poison words spilled out from my mouth;

"Go on then, off you go, you can't face it can you? You are responsible for this; making me trek all over the country. You made this happen, just because you can't have children of your own and just as well, I'm glad you can't!"
She ran from the room in tears.

"What was that for? A bit nasty don't you think?" Asked Dan.

"No, she deserves it!" I replied.

Calming, I shifted my attention back to Carl; I knew I'd gone too far and that I had hurt her so badly and I was ashamed, although I would never admit to it, after all, I couldn't change it now.

I sat with my baby boy for several hours and he opened his eyes, he'd also had wind and so, occasionally, it was as if he'd smiled. I'm sure he knew who I was and it was as if he'd been waiting for me to hold him. I kissed him several times that day, told him that I loved him and said goodbye and at 4:30pm we caught the train home; I knew that that was the last time I would see him.

Chapter 12

The call I'd been expecting came at 2:30pm, on the 7th of March 1973: Mum called me into the office;

"Come and sit down," she said.

"You don't have to tell me, he's gone isn't he?"

She nodded, her eyes drowning in tears; he had died at quarter past two. I didn't cry; I knew it was inevitable and walking out of the office, I said;

"I'll go and pack the baby stuff away and get rid of it."

Mum was concerned but I couldn't talk about it anymore; it was over and that was that. I went into the recreation lounge and looked out of the window; I needed to tell Dan but he hadn't come round yet. At 3pm Eric turned up without him, he said that he'd been around to Dad's to pick Dan up but he wasn't there; he'd thought that Dan had already come up to see me, he hadn't. 'He's probably at Jo's,' I thought, I needed to tell him that Carl had died and I needed to take the baby clothes to Dads;

"Would you give me a lift?" I asked Eric.

He said he would, so I told Mum where I was going. We went to Dad's first but the door was locked;

"We'll have to go to Jo's," I said.

I wrote a note telling Dad what had happened, left the case of baby things on the doorstep and went into Jo's; whilst Eric waited in the car. I called out to her;

"Up here!" She hollered. "I'm painting the landing!"

"Have you seen Dan? Only, I need to tell him that the baby has died."

I said it so matter of factly that she looked at me almost dumb struck, and then gestured towards one of the bedrooms at the end of the landing. I opened the door to see Mandy pulling on one of her boots and Dan zipping up his trousers, Mandy grabbed her other boot, pushed past me and ran down the stairs. Dan looked at me;

"I'm sorry!" He said.

"So this is what you do on the day my baby dies?"

I then turned on Jo, who was now standing behind me;

"This happens under your roof and you don't think to tell me? Some friend you are!"

She was protesting as I went down the stairs, closely followed by Dan saying;

"Wait Jan, talk to me?"

I told him to fuck off, but he kept following. As I walked towards the car, I spotted Mandy heading up the road and proceeded to run after her; she took flight and Eric and Dan followed me in the car. They spun up onto the pavement in front of me and the next thing I knew; I was being thrown onto the back seat. Eric then took off back down the road, which was probably just aswell; I would have killed her and I wanted to kill Dan too. We went back to the hostel and Eric waited outside whilst Dan came in with me; he went in to tell Mum what he'd been caught doing and I went into the recreation room; nobody was there, they were all still at work. A few minutes later mum came in;

"Dan wants to talk to you, but it's up to you?"

"If I must," I said.

He came in and sat next to me, full of apologies and waffle: He told me how she'd offered it to him on a plate, that he'd been lonely and upset and that he wanted me to forgive him; he said that he couldn't believe how stupid he'd been, that he loved me and that it would never happen again. He suggested he go to Dads and not go to Jo's again and left saying that he'd be back at 7:30pm; then we could go for a drink and I could tell him my decision.

7:30pm came and went, and I was still numb from the days events but somehow angry and yet accepting of the whole thing. At about 8:30pm, Eric came in;

"I need to talk to my Dad." I said and he agreed to take me. We went to Dads but the house was in darkness;

"He's probably down the pub, I'll take you there." Said Eric, motioning me back towards the car;

"No chance, I'm going to Jo's," I said,

"No, get in, I'll take you!"

I started running and I got to Jo's as Eric pulled up; I didn't knock, I just flung open the front door and stormed in. Jo was stood in the hallway with Malc and Dan was stood to my right, in the kitchen, talking to Mandy, who was stood with her back against the back door. I passed Jo in a flash and headed for Mandy; there was large bread knife on the side and I grabbed it, as I did, so Dan lunged for me and somehow threw me over his shoulder onto my back; Mandy ran out of the door and was gone again. Dan said he'd been there five minutes and was just explaining to Mandy that what had happened was a mistake and that nothing was going to come of it; Jo and Malc confirmed what he said and told me I should calm down. We sat, the four of us, for an hour, all apologising for what

63

had happened; Malc even told Jo that that slut was not to stay there ever again, to which Jo agreed, for me she said.

Eric had taken me back to the hostel that night and I didn't see Dan for another two days. The vicar came to see me on the Friday to make arrangements for the funeral service and Social Services said that they would pay but; I was to understand that it would be a 'Paupers grave,' meaning no headstone. I wanted him to have a burial and I wanted it to be at St Mark's church, as near to my Pop-pop as possible; if anyone would be waiting for my Carl, he would and he'd take care of him in the afterlife too, if there were such a thing. 'The lord is my Shepherd' was the hymn I chose and the service was scheduled for the following Wednesday. I decided to write to my own Mum; a brief outline of what had happened and to let her know when the funeral was. On Monday I got a reply; this was the first time I'd had contact with her since the short visit, when she thought that I was dying:

> Dear Jan,
> I'm sorry to hear about the trouble you've been involved in and the death of your baby, but it's probably just as well, it's for the best. Maybe now you can try and sort yourself out. I don't know if I will come to the funeral, Auntie Pat (her eldest sister) will be there and so will Nanny, but I'll have to see if I can get time off work. Look after yourself.
> Love mum x

I phoned Cliff again and asked to speak to him, he wasn't there but I left a message with his mother: I explained who I was and she remembered me vaguely and then I told her that her Grandson had died after thirteen short days;

"Perhaps you could let Cliff, or rather Paul know?.." I asked.

"...Thank you!"

She didn't say much, although it was pretty obvious that she knew nothing about any of this, I said goodbye and put the phone down before she had chance to ask any questions and I never spoke to them again.

I went to Jo's on the Monday before the funeral; she asked me if I would come and see her. When I walked in, Mandy was there, but before I had chance to say or do anything she said;

"Hit me if you want, I am sorry and I don't blame you for hating me."

64

'Hate her!' I thought I had no feelings for her; feelings, or emotions would've meant that she had importance to me and she meant less than nothing.

"But if you can forgive me," she carried on, "then I'd like to see Carl at the chapel of rest?"

I didn't know quite what to say; besides if I said anything at that point I was sure I would choke on my words. Jo and I had discussed going to see Carl one last time; she said it would help me come to terms with the loss. Mum (Mrs Mills) had offered but I said I didn't want her to see my reaction, should it be too much but I found out later that she had been with a couple of the girls and two of the care workers from the hostel. In the end, with a nodded agreement, I allowed Mandy to go; I couldn't have cared less at that point, my only concerns then were that of my dead son; besides, Dan was obviously willing enough to bed her. I wouldn't allow her to go to the funeral though and she understood that. We went to the chapel of rest that evening and there he was, in a little white coffin, with blue silk lining and his perfect little face, lying in the silk, facing out, his dark hair with pale complexion; he looked so peaceful, as if fast asleep. I was told that if you kiss a loved one goodbye, it eases the pain of that loss. Mandy kissed him, I looked at Jo and she gave me a reassuring look and asked if she could do the same, I nodded. I asked Mandy to leave, so I could spend my last few moments with Jo and Carl alone, she left the room.

"What about you, are you going to kiss him?" Jo whispered. I was reluctant, I touched his face with my hand; it was firm and cold like porcelain, or marble, not frozen just cool. 'My little china doll,' I thought. I looked at him for a while longer and then kissed his tiny head;

"Sleep tight little angel," I said as I turned and left.

Dad came to see me and it was arranged that the undertaker's car would pick Dad, Dan and I up from Dad's home. The boys at the 'Horse and Jockey' (my Dads local) had had a collection and ordered a wreath; I'd been there with him a couple of times and they were a good bunch. There were also flowers sent from a local Gypsy family, who were great friends of my Dads and later me; they were flower sellers in Bournemouth Square. There were wreaths from Social Services, Mrs Mills, the other staff and all the girls at the hostel. Jo made a wreath of daffodils weaved into chicken wire and there were bunches of flowers from Mum, Nan and my Auntie. Dad and I had a wreath made together.

The car picked us up on Wednesday, at 10am. Dad, in his usual tone greeted me when I arrived.

"All right then?" he said.

'Always the same,' I thought, 'just as he had always been,' remembering when he would return home from his fishing on a Sunday morning; it seemed so far back in the past now but I longed to be able to turn back the clock and take it all back. The funeral was at 10:30am and we arrived before Carl. As we got out of the car, I noticed my family; including my Mum. I didn't speak to her; everyone seemed to be consoling her over the loss. What did she know about anything? She was glad it happened. It was her justification for leaving me behind, then confirmation that I had turned out to be exactly as she had predicted. A lot of people attended, some thirty or more and none of them had known my little angel. A grey saloon pulled up in the driveway of the church and the tiny white coffin with little, golden handles was taken from the back, carried into the church by the undertaker and placed on a small table. The service passed quickly, although I didn't take much notice of what was said; I felt like I was going to burst watching my Mother cry. 'What was she crying for? What right did she have? She wanted him dead!' I was screaming inside and the feeling was so intense and so concentrated but nothing came out. I didn't cry that day or in the weeks and months that followed, I had changed and I was so very angry; angry at the world, at God and at myself, especially myself... I didn't see my Mother again for over a year.

Chapter 13

Dan and I continued to see each other throughout March, I didn't trust him anymore, but he carried on visiting me and living at Dads. Mum hadn't discussed me being moved to another hostel, although I'd thought it would be inevitable. Eric had started seeing a girl called Sarah, who I shared a room with at the hostel and she had decided to run away with him. Dan and I had talked about taking off together and looking for work up country somewhere, so we agreed to run away too; I had nothing to stay for now. It was the first week of April when we took off: I hid my case around the back of the hostel with Sarah's; she'd had to go to work but it was arranged that Eric and Dan would pick me up around the back at 3pm, we'd pick Sarah up from work at 4:30pm and then go.

We headed north and it was starting to get dark before we hit the motorway. We weren't sure where we were going before we left but Blackpool seemed to be the agreed destination; we arrived about 3am. Sarah and I didn't have much money, nor did Dan, but Eric had a lot of cash; he said that he'd taken out a loan at the bank;

"After all, one of us had to do something!" He said and we didn't question it.

I'd thought that Blackpool was all lights and holidays, but it looked dead when we arrived; dark and dreary. Eric parked up outside a derelict hotel, or at least it looked derelict; he said that it belonged to some friends of his, that he knew where the key was and that they had given him permission to use it anytime he was there. We went in and tried the light switch, there was no power and the building was old and shabby; It had been converted into holiday bed sits or was in the process of conversion, either way there was no furniture and no curtains at the windows, just a few old cups and some cutlery. Eric checked the fuse box;

"I'll have this on in a minute!" He announced and I watched him as he by passed the meter with a piece of wire. Sarah and I found some old curtains and we decided to get our heads down for a few hours; we used the curtains and our coats as blankets... Blackpool in April is extremely cold. The next morning we went to a café for breakfast. Eric said that he had to meet someone to pay the rent on the flat. The plan was that I would stay at the flat whilst they all went out to look for work: It was decided that, because of my age, firstly; I wouldn't be able to get a job and secondly; because people may have been looking for us, the fact that I couldn't give a National Insurance Number, might have aroused suspicion. We bought some peroxide to dye my hair from mousy brown to blonde. Dan said that he could do it but it went totally wrong; it took hold at the roots, but only about the first two inches or so and I looked like a natural blonde who had dyed my hair brown. We decided that that wouldn't do and so Sarah went out and bought a jet-black dye; luckily it wasn't a permanent colour. The result; from tip to roots the shades went from black to dark brown, then to orange and finally green... In the days of glam rock I was probably the first punk and if I was trying to remain incognito; I had failed miserably. I remained in that flat for the duration of our stay, which was almost two weeks. The others had no success finding work and Eric and Dan took the car to a garage to sell it; Eric wanted to buy something cheaper. We had all thought that he owned that car, but we found out later that it was in fact on Hire Purchase. The garage let them exchange it anyway and Eric bargained a two-seater sports car, (he was given a cheque for the difference - about five hundred pounds,) but there was obviously not enough room in that for all of us, so they bought a motorbike too, that was advertised privately. They persuaded the owner to sell it to them, excepting the cheque from the garage as payment and then parting with some £250 cash as well; which was the difference between the cost of the motor bike and the face value of the cheque. Eric had told the seller that we had to go home to London in a hurry and that we didn't have time for the garage cheque to clear. When they finally got back to the flat they told Sarah and I to gather our things Together;

"We are heading further north!" They declared cheerily. We put everything in the boot of the car. Dan and I set off on the motorbike, Sarah and Eric in the car; Eric had told us that we were going to Scotland. The sun was shining but it was so cold on that bike and we had to stop several times just to warm up; the sports car kept disappearing from view, and then would stop so that we could catch up. After Dan and I had warmed up for what felt like the hundredth time, we set off again but as we came around the bend, we saw Eric parked on a gravel area in the centre of the road, a sort of central reservation and Sarah was leaning over the boot of the car. As we approached nearer, I noticed that she was crying and that her leg, from calf to thigh was grazed; apparently, as Eric had attempted to swing the car around, the passenger door had swung open and she had fallen out, her coat had gotten caught and she had been dragged;

"She needs medical help!" I said, but Eric was adamant;

"If we do that, then we'll all be in trouble!" He said.

It was then that we realised what he'd done with the car and that if we got caught; he would be arrested for fraud and deception. He had, as he told us at that moment, also left Bournemouth with the wages of several men, who worked on a painting job; he was the foreman and had to collect their wages from the bank, to pay them. He hadn't taken out a loan as he had claimed, he'd stolen the money. As we carried on towards Scotland, Dan and I discussed the situation; Dan said that we were really in the shit now and that it was probably a good idea to get as far away from Eric as possible, but we had no money. About 10 miles further we stopped at a roadside café and I went with Sarah to help clean her leg up; she told me that Eric had shouted at her for leaning on the door and that he had threatened to drop her off in the road if she kept grizzling, she said that she was afraid of him. I hadn't seen that side of him before but I wasn't surprised, after all; he was a man.

We arrived in Glasgow at around 4:30pm. As we headed through the city, over to our right, there was a park and in there were kids throwing things. They launched a plank of wood at the car, so Eric pulled the car over, got out and ordered Sarah to stay put, he then told me to get off the bike and got on behind Dan, it was then that I noticed he had a shotgun in his hand, I hadn't seen it before. I stood with Sarah as they disappeared into the park, chasing the kids; none of them could have been more than about 12 years old. I asked Sarah about the gun and she said that he'd had it all along; I really had misread this man. Dan and Eric returned about 10 minutes later and thank goodness; the kids had got away and I was back on the bike. We passed the old tenement buildings and the 'Gorbals;' it was an awful place and I could understand those kids from the park; what future did they have living in such slums? Bournemouth was where I wanted to be. We decided that Glasgow wasn't for us, but we had travelled a long way so we stayed in town for the night. The room in the hotel was three floors up and there were bars on the windows; this was totally alien to me, as were the armoured type land rovers that were patrolling the streets as police cars… This was one place that I could never imagine living in.

The following morning we were all up early, we had breakfast and left. We headed back towards England, to Yorkshire and Leeds; Eric wanted to show us Yorkshire before we decided what to do next and the money was almost gone. The countryside was beautiful but Leeds was not; Eric suddenly picked up speed along one road and we only just kept up. When we did finally stop, a few minutes later, he told us why he had bombed so fast;

"That's one road whites don't stop in," he said, "its called 'love lane' and is full of Asians, they'd kill you before you get to the other end."

I couldn't help but ask why he'd even bothered to take us down there;

"Well, just so you can see how the other half lives, besides if we live around here you need to know where you can and where you can't go, don't you."

I had no intention of living there either. Bournemouth at that time had very few ethnic minorities; there were only ever students during the summer months and my only real contact with other cultures was during my stay in Bristol, in the mother and baby home. We stayed that night, in the 'Black Bull,' a public house on the outskirts of Leeds. It was quite nice, but had a view from the window of a demolition site; I wasn't too bothered about the view but it was better than Glasgow. I was starting to feel really homesick, and Dan and I discussed going home to face the music;

"Anything would be better than this!" We said in unison. We talked to Eric and Sarah; they had obviously had another disagreement but seemed to have come to the same conclusion. They also agreed that we should split up; the only problem was that Dan and I had no money. Eric disappeared early the following morning and came back at about 10am, minus the motorbike; he sold it and gave us half the money. He told us that he had decided to stay in Yorkshire; his wife was there, staying at her mothers and he'd decided that he was going to try and patch things up with her. I asked him if he thought she would take him back;

"Well yes, she always has before!"

"So where does that leave me?" Asked Sarah,

"Sorry, but it isn't working anyway." He said and shrugged his shoulders.

He gave us a lift to the motorway, dropped us off and left. It was now just the three of us, until Sarah said that she thought she would have more chance of thumbing a lift if she was on her own. It was agreed that we'd meet her at the end of the motorway, at a motel on the outskirts of London; I was concerned that something could happen to her alone, but she said she'd be fine and walked on down the motorway. We kept back but still had her in sight and almost immediately a lorry picked her up and she was gone. It took about an hour before we got our first lift and we passed Sarah some miles on, thumbing her next lift. That was the last time that I saw her; she never met us at the motel. One more lift and we arrived in London but it was getting dark and I was concerned about Sarah, to the point that I was annoying Dan; he said that if I didn't shut up, he'd leave me too. We waited for her and then asked around to see if anyone had seen her but no one had. We booked a room and asked that we be notified when she arrived. At about 9pm, we had a message from reception to say that Sarah had phoned and said that she wouldn't be coming after all; she'd met someone and was going back to Blackpool. The last I heard, a couple of months later, was that she had married the man that she'd met and was still living in Blackpool... I hoped that she was happy.

The following morning, after breakfast Dan and I headed off again, hitching home. I think we'd decided then that that would be the end for us too and I was quite upset; we had been through a lot together and I was quite attached to him, even after all he'd done. We got back to Bournemouth and went to the youth club, that I believe is still there today, called the '8.9.6., Numbers Club.' I'd been there several times with Dan. We wanted to test the water and the people in there knew us; they would know how much trouble we were in and we would find out if anyone had been looking for us. I phoned Mum from there;

"You are in real trouble!" she said. "You need to come back here now and I'll see what I can do!"

I agreed, but told her that it would take a while as I had no money, so she asked to speak to a youth worker and they gave me taxi fare; Mrs Mills promised the department would repay it. Dan waited with me for the taxi, I kissed him goodbye and thanked him for getting me back safely; at least I could be grateful for that. It was over between us, although I still saw him a few times at Jo's. A gap of many years passed and then I saw him, recently, about five years ago; he was completely bald and had a long beard. Jo had brought him round to see me;

"I see you have your head on upside down." I said.
It was really one of those moments when you say what's in your head without thinking. I'm sure that it was taken as it was meant in jest, although I do think he was a little hurt; he'd had a full head of shoulder length hair all those years before.

Chapter 14

Mum was angry but also relieved to see me. She said that she'd worried so much;

"Where is Sarah?" Was her first question.

I told her the whole story from start to finish, over a cup of tea and a welcomed sandwich; I was starving and had lost a lot of weight, which she commented on. Actually she'd said that I looked ill, but then I hadn't really recovered from Carl's birth and I had been missing for a month; which to me had seemed like a year. I told her that Dan and I were finished, to which she said;

"Well something good came out of it then? That is definitely good news."

I hadn't realised how much she'd disliked him until then. Eventually she got around to asking me why I had left in the first place, after all I had made such efforts to live at the hostel, she thought that that was where I had chosen to be after all; wasn't that the reason for returning every time that I'd been sent away? I told her my fears; that I was afraid I'd be moved anyway, Carl was gone and as I still wasn't of working age, I was technically still a school child, so I wasn't eligible to stay. As it turned out, Mrs Mills had been talking to the department and had asked them to make an exception to the rule, she was going to tell me when they'd made their final decision. She'd wished she had told me sooner, I knew I wouldn't have run away if I had known; now it would have to be talked about again and it was policy to discuss things with the other girls too. I knew, as did they, that if any of them had done what I had done, they would almost definitely not have been given a second chance, they would have been sent to Redhatch: A lock up home with complete supervision at all times.

A meeting was called the following evening and I had to give reasons as to why I should be allowed to stay, the girls then told me their opinions and I was sent out whilst they voted. I was voted out by two votes; I called my Dad at the pub and he arrived by taxi about half an hour later. We went into the office to discuss it further, that was the first time in my life I'd seen my Dad that angry.

"What a ridiculous state of affairs!" He said. "You mean to say that you allow young girls to make a decision on my daughter's future? There is no way she is going anywhere, I'll go to prison first!"

Mum assured him that I wouldn't be going anywhere immediately and that he could appeal to the Social Services. She then asked me to leave the room so that she could settle things with Dad but I protested; if she had anything to say, she could say it to me too.

"Just give us a minute, please!" Dad interrupted.
Reluctantly I left the room and I stood outside. A couple of minute's later Dad came out with Mum, saying;

"I will be in touch in a day or two." He put his arm around my shoulder and as we walked to the door he said; "It's not going to happen, Mrs Mills has said you can stay, it has been arranged, and it's just that they have to follow procedure."
I didn't know whether to believe him or not, I wanted to hear it from Mum, but Dad said he wasn't supposed to tell me. I was so tired and upset that I couldn't sleep and I sat up talking to Penny; she had missed me, she said that she didn't vote because she didn't feel it was right. She was the only person who was really still talking to me, I even felt Mum as if hated me too and she became Mrs Mills again.

I saw the doctor the following day for my check-up; I hadn't had my postnatal examination but he considered that I was very well considering. June Morris came to see me too, and gave me a lecture about what Social Services could and couldn't do to me, what she was going to do, etc, etc. It went in one ear and out the other; I was by now convinced that what I'd said to her at the hospital was justified. She spoke to Mrs Mills and left, saying that she would be back next week; that meant I had another week there at least. Mrs Mills called me into the office again just before bedtime; she couldn't keep me hanging anymore and even though the girls had voted on a decision, the overall decision was that of the department: They felt that I'd learnt my lesson and had decided to allow me to stay, there was only one condition; I would have to go to school and earn their trust again. As punishment for running away I had to stay in for a month and was also told not to be too surprised if certain girls gave me a hard time for a while; some did, but only the ones that I had never originally liked anyway.

During the month I was grounded, I learnt a lot about the life histories and characters of the other girls. Penny and I spent a lot of time together, doing normal stuff that girls our age should be doing, like listening to records; 45's and LP's and Penny's Alvin Stardust impressions were hysterical. We played 33 1/3's on an old record player in the 'Rec Room' and Penny would strum away on her acoustic guitar, with me singing along; 'Streets of London,' 'The Seekers' stuff, or 'House of the rising sun,' over and over. We had another girl who played guitar and sang; her name was Cathleen and she was a tiny speck of a girl, with short blonde hair and a truly lovely voice. She was always so sad and was accommodated there under 'a place of safety' order, she had a younger brother, also in care, but he had been fostered and they'd been separated for a few years; she didn't or couldn't talk about it, which always concerned me. Such a sad vulnerable girl and it often showed in the songs she sang: The two I remember so well were 'Ben' by Michael Jackson - a song about a rat, although I think it held a different meaning for Cathleen and the other was 'Love story.' I can still hear her singing as I write this. Sadly Cathleen died in early 1974, I had been at home with Dad for the weekend and when I got back she had been taken into hospital. She had become very ill with what they thought was a kidney infection and that was what she was treated for. On the Thursday Cathleen had phoned Mum to say that she was feeling well and would be home the following day; we were all relieved. The call came again at about 10pm: Cathleen had collapsed and she'd had Meningitis; she died early on Saturday morning, she was just sixteen years old.

God had done it again, Cathleen had been to hell and back in her life and just as things seemed to settle and she was on track for a better future, she was dead, gone. All the girls went to the funeral, paid for by Social Services. There was to be no head stone as had been the case with Carl. She was buried at a different cemetery, just a little way from where I live now; I memorized the place because I knew we'd never be able to find it once the flowers died. The sadness and disbelief in that home lingered for months; Mum, all the staff and the girls, without exception were equally distraught... I now had two faces to remember.

Chapter 15

A place was found for me in a school; it was a 'special' school, for kids with learning difficulties or behavioural problems, not that I was one of those but no main stream school would take me and according to the law; I had to be in school until the age of sixteen. I had visited this school briefly prior to Carl's birth to meet people, it was quite close to the nursery where Carl would have been placed and it would have been ideal; I would be able to go and see him at the end of each school day and take care of him, at least that had been the plan anyway. I started there in the June of 1973 and Mr Lewis, the head, welcomed me on the first day; he was a big man with a Welsh accent and a wicked sense of humour. After shaking my hand and introducing himself he said;

"Well Janet, where are we going to place you? You are not going to be disruptive?!"

'Was he telling me or asking me?' I thought, he continued;

"You are intelligent and so I'm not sure what we can teach you, if anything. I think I'll call you a teacher's assistant and put you with Miss Callum. She teaches music to our eight to ten year olds and she could do with your help. We will call you Miss Janet. I know you smoke and you can if you like, but not in front of the children. You can take your breaks in the staff room, we will even let you have coffee, so long as you make mine occasionally and don't forget my biscuit. But remember; to all the children you are a teacher, and I don't want any of them to know otherwise or we will have problems, especially with the older boys." He went on without taking a breath and his voice and his accent were just like music, deep and lyrical and I could have listened to him talk forever;

"Right, let's go and show you where you will be. Remember, any problems, not just about this place; my door is always open for you, whatever it is and I expect Miss Callum will tell you the same." We went out of the main school building and into a house next door, it was attached to the school by a front wall and it had been converted into a classroom downstairs, with the staff room and the bathroom upstairs. We walked into the classroom together and I was introduced to Dorris Callum, and then the children; there were just ten in that class.

"Please excuse me Miss Callum?" He said, addressing the class. "Children, this is Miss Janet, she is here to help Miss Callum to help you with your work. You can ask her anything and if you need help, she will be happy to help, wont you Miss Janet?" He winked at me. "Right, I will leave you in Miss Callum's capable hands!" He said to me as he left the room.

Doris Callum became a good friend in the two years that I was there. I was comfortable and happy helping these children with varied disabilities; I imagined Carl being in a school like this, had he have lived. But then there were no children here with such severe disabilities as he'd had. I taught art - making collages out of old wallpaper books, papier mache` heads of clowns, pasted around inflated balloons and painted, even puppets made of clay, with jointed limbs, tied through holes with string. Some were hung on display in the school for years, long after I left; in particular a papier mache` witch on a broomstick, it was made for Halloween but remained hung in the main corridor all year round.

I helped teach music with Doris, whilst she played her guitar, eventually I sang with her and helped with evening events; including two Christmas concerts in the school. At break times I'd have my coffee, after making Mr Lewis his; he'd always say thank you and ask if everything was all right. The only real conventional schoolwork I had to do were spelling checks and basic maths tests once a month or so, I was tested by Mrs Garrett; she too was welsh, in her fifties and another wonderful woman. She'd said that, had I been in the main stream school I would, without any doubt, have got a G.C.E in English and maths and Doris considered o'level art and probably music aswell, but they had no facilities for me to do it there. It was a shame and I regret not having those; it has affected my whole working life since, but then all I really wanted was to get married, have children and be a singer.

By October 1973 I was allowed home every other weekend to stay with Dad; although he was hardly there. I'd leave the hostel on a Friday afternoon, after tea and return by 10:30pm on the Sunday. Penny had started to go home too, to Blandford: She had a boyfriend there but sadly, he was killed, in the September, on his motorbike, on his way to visit her; his name was Rainbow. I had never met him and I never realised how much he'd meant to her at the time; she didn't show emotion easily, to the point where I almost didn't believe that he'd even existed. Apparently he had hit a farm gate after the back wheel of his Suzuki had seized, just as he rounded a bend and he was killed instantly; Penny had told me so matter of factly that I'd sort of dismissed it. So she would go off home and I'd go off home too. My weekends were spent with Jo, Ruby or more often than not, with Dad in the pub; I played darts with him or watched him play and I became quite good. Dad had many friends there but there was one in particular I remember; Old Tarpot, a short, dumpy man and a real character. Every pub has one: He was always drunk but he was happy; he'd sing at the top of his voice and I'd sing along with him. He lived in a caravan park with his brother, about four hundred yards away from the pub doorway and it would take him about half an hour to get home; two steps forward, one step back, invariably in the middle of the road. Dad and I were convinced that one of these nights he would, without doubt, be run over and he had some near misses but was never hurt; the cars would blow their horns, he'd put his two fingers up and carry on singing and stumbling on his way.

Another of my Dads friends, that he played darts with was a man they called 'Ginger' and he was only nineteen. After some weeks of minor conversations he offered to give me a lift home, with Dad of course. Dad got out of the car and Ginger and I sat together, he asked if I would consider going out with him; he wasn't exactly good looking, with ginger, shoulder length hair, freckles, even on his hands, about five foot nine inches tall and not at all my 'usual' type. I found out that his name was Dan but it took me months to stop calling him Ginger, it had become a habit and besides; I wasn't keen on the name 'Dan' after the last one.

We arranged to meet at lunchtime the following day and he picked me up in his old A40 car; the car as tatty as it was, was a bonus. We went to the pub and then for a walk along the sea front and we seemed to get on quite well. He gave me a lift back to the hostel at about 10pm that evening and I introduced him to Mum; she was obviously suspicious but said that he'd seemed nice. He said he'd like to see me again and was so polite; which again was something I wasn't used to. We arranged that he would pick me up on Tuesday and we could go out; I explained that it was compulsory to stay in on Monday.

Dan was an apprentice welder for the Ministry of Defence, in Christchurch; not only a job but ambition aswell. He was from a good family who owned their own home, not like my usual friends which were, for the most part, council tenants. I didn't tell him the reason why I lived at the hostel, although he did ask, I just told him that Mum had left and Dad couldn't cope with having to go to work and looking after me and my brother as well, so it was best for me; I would tell him eventually, but not until much later in our relationship. We went out again on the Tuesday to the pub and had a good night. I wasn't going to see him again until after Christmas, he would be at home with his family all over Christmas and it was too late to re-arrange things, also far too early to introduce me to his family. I didn't think I'd see him again, I thought that I wasn't good enough. I went home myself for the few days over Christmas; I told them at the home that I was spending Christmas with Dad and my brother, although that couldn't have been further from the truth because by now, my Dad was seeing another woman and had been invited to spend Christmas with her and her family, (she had six children,) and my brother was off poaching, with his friends. Dad had thought that it was a bit early in his relationship with this woman to introduce me to her; it would raise too many questions that he didn't feel he could answer and once again I had those old feelings of rejection; I was no good, no one wanted to be around me.

I opened my presents at the hostel; make-up, hairbrush, hairdryer and underwear. I said thank you, kissed everyone and wished them all a great Christmas.

"I hope you have a lovely Christmas too." Mum said, "Enjoy it, you deserve it after the year you've had."

I smiled and left. I went straight home to find that the house was cold and empty, the electricity had been cut off; Dad had not paid the bill, he was never there anymore. I didn't take my present's home to show Dad, but I already knew that he wouldn't be there for me to show him and there wasn't much point taking my hairdryer, there was no power. The only sign that anyone had been there was a piece of venison in the gas oven; I did have that to eat at least. I wandered around the house and garden, looking for anything that I could make Christmas decorations out of; I found a small branch in the garden, well it was more of a twig, I broke some cotton wool into small pieces to put on the branch ends like snow balls, found some glitter in a kitchen drawer, sprinkled it over and then placed it on the side board. I was going to light the fire in the lounge, but all I could scrape together was the coal dust in the back of the shed, some paper, old clothes and a few twigs that I found in the garden. So there I sat in Dads chair, alone, and proceeded to burn the things I'd found... Coal dust and Memories burning in the fire place to keep me warm.

My brother came in, removed the venison from the oven and put it on a plate saying;

"You can have a bit if you want, but not much, I'm taking it round my mates." He murmured something under his breath about not knowing what I was doing there anyway, and then laughed at my pathetic attempt at making a Christmas tree, he told me I was sad and that I should piss off back to where ever it was I was living.

"I won't be back for a few days and I doubt Dad will be back at all." He said as he left, carrying the venison under his arm. It got dark, the fire went out and I sat alone and hungry. I slept in Dad's chair and covered myself with blankets and my coat. Christmas dinner was dry bread and a tin of garden peas. I did have a bit of chocolate, I'd found it in Dads drawer; I had no idea how long it had been there, it was plain chocolate but it tasted ok. There was a dribble of milk and a bit of sugar, but no tea bags. So milk, hot water and sugar it was then... Warm, sugared water! There was no way I was going back to the hostel to tell them what had happened though, besides they'd stop me going home for weekends in the future. I went to Jo's and Ruby's briefly to wish them Happy Christmas and had a cup of tea in both places, but they had family round and were busy enjoying themselves; Christmas is for family isn't it? So I made my apologies and left, saying that I was having dinner with Dad and his new girlfriend; had to go or I'd be late.

I went back to the lonely house and wandered around from room to room, seeing what memories were tucked away, the Christmases I'd spent with my family. I remembered my Aunties, Nan eating Satsuma's, Mum's home made Christmas cake, when she was making it she'd get us all to give a stir and make a wish. I don't remember any of the wishes that I'd made before but if there was one wish I could have made for that Christmas, it would have been to be able turn the clock back, even just to see and spend one minute with my whole family, my Mum. I went into Dads bedroom, opened the wardrobe and still hung there was Mums wedding dress; she had said that one day I would wear it on my wedding day. It had started out as a pearl white colour but now it was nicotine stained yellow. How could things have gone so wrong? They must have been happy then or they wouldn't have

80

married? Probably went wrong when I was born, it was more than likely my fault, Mum had said as much during one of our arguments, I still hear those words;

"Yes, you were a damned mistake, I wanted your brother and your sister but you, you've never been anything but trouble!"
She apologised later saying that she didn't mean it, but it sticks. What she had meant to say, or so she said, was that there was not a big enough age gap between me and Aaron.   I found some old high-heeled shoes and tried one on; it was too tight now but years before I had dressed up in them. Still rummaging I came across Mums old wooden box, with her private papers and little mementos of the past, photos and clippings of our birth announcements in the local paper, mine too, it said;

'Mr and Mrs Smith are proud to announce the birth of a daughter; Janet Susan Born on the 8th of September 1957, sister for Aaron.'

I don't know how long I sat there but it was getting dark and felt so cold; I had to find something to make a fire with, I wouldn't be able to see soon. There were the remains of two candles in Dad's room; they'd give me about an hour or so of light if I was careful. I burnt Mums wedding dress that night; I was angry, angry with them, with myself and the world, and as I sat in Dads chair, watching the last glow of the fire go out; I fell asleep.

Boxing Day morning I awoke to find a frost covering the inside of the windows, and the sun shining through it made leaf patterns in the frost. It shone onto my so called Christmas tree, lighting up the glitter on my snow ball cotton wool. I felt happier today.   I decided that I'd probably get away with going back to the hostel that night, a day early; I could say that I didn't want to go to the pub with Dad or something and I'd probably get approval for making such a responsible decision. One more day; I got up and had a quick wash in cold water, just my face. I'd tried to heat the kettle but the gas was finally gone. There was no way I was taking all my clothes off; if I stripped off I'd freeze to death. A change of clothes, some make-up and I thought; 'that'll do!' I collected all my things and packed them back into my weekend bag. I would go and see Jo first; I could get a cup of tea there. Jo was still in bed, she shouted down and asked me to make the tea and said that she'd be down in a minute. It was warm, the tea was hot and I made toast for us all, even me; that stopped me feeling sick. Jo asked how my Dad's had been;

"Yes it was ok." I answered.

For a moment she believed me but something in my face must have told a different story because she asked;

"Ok, so where did you spend Christmas day?"

I told her and she called me a stupid cow, not in a nasty way and said that I could have stayed there, but it wasn't right; I didn't want to ruin their Christmas. Anyway I got through it and I was going to the pub at lunchtime; Dad would probably be there, so alls well that ends well. I did go to the pub at lunchtime and Dad was there with Ginger (Dan). They and a few others were having a friendly game of darts. Dad was pleased to see me, if a little nervous; the reason was that his new girlfriend and her daughter, her youngest child and her boyfriend were with him, sitting at a table;

"Please don't make any trouble, I like her." He whispered. What did he think I was? "I'll introduce you; just let me finish this game."

Dan was much happier to see me and bought me half a light ale. (I have drunk that for a long time, up until about ten years ago.) I sat at the bar waiting for Dads introduction and I couldn't help but study this woman; she was very smart, slim and clean looking, as was her daughter, although I instinctively knew that I wouldn't get on with her.

"This is my daughter Jan," Dad said startling me from my thoughts, "Jan, this is Diane, her daughter Cindy and Brian."

"Pleased to meet you, your Dads said a little bit about you." She didn't elaborate and I didn't ask, Cindy, the daughter, just nodded in acknowledgement. I stood for a moment, whilst they continued their conversation as if I weren't there.

"Well I'll possibly see you again?" I said smiling graciously and retreated back to the bar where Dan was sat, he broke off his conversation with his friend to talk to me; a very small thing to anyone else, but it meant so much to me. He said he'd have to go in a minute, that his dinner would be ready and that his Mum had told him to make sure he was back. He asked what I was doing for the rest of the day;

"Well, going back to Dads and then home tonight I guess, that's the only plans I have right now," I replied.

"Ok," he said, "I'll pick you up this afternoon from your Dad's. Is about 3pm Ok?"

He did just that and we went for a drive, we talked a lot in those couple of hours, mostly about him and his family: He was one of three boys and was the eldest, his youngest brother was ten years younger and he had a step father, ten years younger than his mother, he also had a step brother. Dan's own father had been killed in a car crash in another country, or so he'd been told, although he had no proof. He didn't really care, his Dad had been a violent man, had been forever beating his Mum up and had gambled away their home; they'd been homeless when his little brother was just a few months old. They'd lived with his Auntie, Uncle and her three boys for a while. He did have another stepbrother, who was eleven years younger, but he had tragically drowned in Spain while they were on holiday; he was just five years old. I began to think what a dreadful life he'd had and yet, he was doing ok; the biggest difference between us seemed to be that his Mother loved him and would do anything for him and her family. I got him to drop me at Jo's with the excuse that I needed to say my goodbyes; the real reason was that he might have asked to come into Dads house, I would then have had to explain the lack of electricity, I thought that would definitely put him off and I didn't want to do that, even with his ginger hair and freckles, he was quite nice and who knows if it were to work out, I might just be able to better myself. Mum would without a doubt like him, if I ever got the chance to introduce him. He asked me if I'd see him later, he had to go home - his Auntie, her family and his Nan would be round. I asked him to pick me up outside Jo's and off he went. I told Jo about him and she was pleased for me, but with the joy also came the warning;

"Just take it slowly."

Dan came back for me at 8:30pm as arranged and as I got into the car I asked;

"Where are we off to?"

He smiled and glanced my way, he was taking me home to meet his family. I was an absolute wreck;

"What if they don't like me? I'm not ready for this!" I stammered.

He re-assured me saying that his Mum had insisted on it; she wanted to know what or who had got into her sons head recently.

We pulled up outside a house, in a tree-lined avenue, with two cars parked in the drive and a neatly presented garden, with its well-kept lawn. A Christmas tree lit up in the window, between the draped net curtains that matched all the others in the front of the house. The holly wreath on the white front door was illuminated by an outdoor lantern. 'These people will hate me,' I thought, 'they'll say I'm not good enough.' I was a nervous wreck and felt sick.

"Please drive on," I pleaded.

"Don't be daft, they're expecting you." He insisted.
We walked into the entrance hall at which point his Mother came to meet us; she was just about five foot tall with short, auburn hair, obviously dyed, she was well dressed and smiling;

"I'm really pleased to meet you, come on in, Dan wouldn't tell us a lot, but we knew it was a girl he has been spending all his time with recently. All we have is your name; Jan isn't it?"
I nodded and smiled. As we entered the lounge I was confronted with all these people, all smiling and all shook my hand as I was introduced to them, one by one: Sam – Dan's Stepfather, little Gran – as they called her, as she was a tiny lady, Dan's Mum Lou, Auntie Susan, Uncle Frank and their boys Simon, George and Phil, Dan's brothers Mark and Neil, and their step brother Alan.

"Dan, take her and get something to eat." Lou said motioning us towards a door. We walked together into the dining room where the table was laid out with every sort of Christmas food you could think of, including an enormous turkey with half covered breast. We never had turkey; I'd had it at school years before but it never tasted like that. I still felt sick and where I hadn't eaten, I found it difficult to eat much, besides I was nervous about eating with strangers but it was good food though. A good family and a proper family Christmas, I felt welcome there from then on. Yes they were obviously comfortably off, but in particular, Lou was down to earth. She became my best friend as the years passed; I thank God for her and miss her every day. At about 10pm I said I should go soon as I had to be in, Dan explained that I lived in a hostel and that I needed to be in by 11pm. We left with Lou kissing me on the cheek saying;

"It was really nice to meet you and I hope we'll see you again."
Hand shakes all round.

"Wasn't so bad was it?" Dan said as we got into the car.

"No I'm ok; it was just a bit sudden. I was surprised by the kiss and the lipstick mark that it left."

"That's the usual," Dan laughed, "Nobody gets out without a lipstick stamp."

I had many of those over the year's aswell; it's a pity I couldn't have preserved each one. We arrived back at the hostel and sat in the car park; we made plans to call each other the following day. Dan pulled me towards him and kissed me and it was the action more than the kiss that was memorable, but that was enough for me. Mum (Mrs Mills) was surprised I was back early, I lied;

"I got bored at home; I prefer to be here with you, besides I've missed you!"   "Well I missed you too!" She said smiling.

"I bet you say that to all the girls?" I said and we laughed. I was glad to be back, in my bed, with food, light and people, or at least one person who really did care.

Chapter 16

1974 - I went to school, I even enjoyed it and my life at the hostel was settled and quite good too. Dan (Ginger) and I were together. I had finally told him about the situation at home; I told him about my brother and the electricity being off, which I found out wasn't because dad hadn't paid the bill, it was actually that my brother had robbed the meter and it had been turned off because of that; Dad didn't want it back on because he knew that Aaron would only do it again.

My weekend home visits were spent with Dan, I only had to sleep at the house and for most part, Dan stayed overnight with me. Dad was living with Diane at her home, although he was still paying the rent on our house and Dan and I went to the pub in the evenings. We bought food and locked it in my wardrobe; my brother was rarely in but when he was, he would steal the food. I did introduce him to Dan early in the year, but he'd shown no interest except to say;

"He looks a complete prat!"

On several occasions Aaron did threaten to beat Dan up if I didn't give him some of our food. He was by now some 6'2" in height and broad, not fat and Dan was small in comparison, if he Aaron had hit him, he probably would have killed him. It was easier to give him the food, besides I didn't want Dan hurt and I didn't want my brother in any more trouble than he already was; when all was said and done, he was and is my brother and for all his faults, I do care about him and what's happened to him. One evening, after the pub, we arrived back at Dads to see an ambulance was outside a neighbour's house; Mum had always had her morning cuppa with this neighbour. The woman was in the back of the ambulance, sat up in a chair; she looked at me with a lost, vacant look and waved. I had had quite a lot of time for her before Mum left, that was until her son – Jack, started taking too much interest in me. I had several encounters with him during the year after Mum had left and it was attention that I didn't want; he was 24 and so I stayed away. I didn't know his Mum was ill though and felt guilty for that, more so when she died a few days later, aged 52; I didn't get to say goodbye. Then little Cathleen died and I was beginning to think that being around me was dangerous; it seemed to me that anyone I became close to died. I found out where my Mum was living and went unannounced to see her, with Dan. The idea was that I could use her friend's death as my excuse to see her and introduce Dan at the same time; I knew she would approve of him and in some way it might prove that I wasn't all bad, I could find a decent boyfriend, from a good family without her.

It was a Sunday morning; Dan picked me up and we went to the flat where Mum was living with a man that she'd met at the conservative club: He was 20 years older than Mum, with a daughter, just a year or two younger than Mum, who lived with them along with my sister. I knocked the door; she hadn't seen me since Carl's funeral.

"What are you doing here?" She asked when she answered the door; "Just a minute!" She said and shut the door again.
Dan looked at me puzzled and put his arm on my shoulder. She came back;

"Ok you can come in for a minute, but it's not my flat, it's Jim's."
She led us into the kitchen.

"Just thought I'd let you know that Mrs Thomson has died!" I said.
She was a little shocked but not surprised;

"It was probably caused by a broken heart when her husband had left her for another woman." Mum said.
The first Mrs Thomson had known about her husbands affair was through the local newspaper: He was the captain of a ship that had caught fire at sea and there was a photograph of the captain and his wife on board ship; the wife was in fact the other woman, his mistress. Mum said she'd only seen her couple of times since she'd left Dad, because she had hidden herself away. I introduced Dan, who was given the third degree about what he did for a living, where he lived and how old he was. My sister Verity came in and had time to say;

"Hello!" Before Mum said;

"I thought I told you to stay in there."
She turned and was gone; I caught a glimpse of Jim before Verity shut the door. He had grey hair and a moustache; he looked older than I'd expected, although I knew of the age gap.

"Anyway I've got to get on," Mum said, "Phone before you visit next time." And then she wrote down the phone number;

"Thanks for letting me know."

She then ushered us out and shut the door. I knew that she was impressed by Dan and I also knew that all the time I was with him; I'd have a chance of seeing her.

It wasn't long after my visit with Mum that a young girl moved into the hostel, she was just 12 years old and had been diagnosed with schizophrenia. She had been placed with foster parents, but they couldn't cope with her anymore; she had become violent, had broken a girls arm during a fight at school and was very disturbed but her medication had, in the most part, controlled her condition. Her name was Vicky and she was very pretty with thick dark hair and big dark brown eyes. She unnerved me a little, especially when she was about to have an 'episode' or an outburst; her pupils became enlarged until her eyes looked black, she'd scream, run at people, even hit out and then run out of the building; heading off towards an estate just around the corner where her Father, also with a similar condition lived. Mum was instructed not to stop her, just notify the police immediately, which she did many times during Vicky's stay. Nobody wanted that little girl and nobody knew how to handle her. Penny was very frightened of her and Vicky knew it. She was put into our room to sleep and I changed beds with Penny so that I was in the middle. One day I walked in to find Penny pinned to the bed, with Vicky sat across her chest trying to shave her eyebrows. I ordered Vicky off, which she did immediately;

"I only wanted to shave her eyebrows, what's the fuss?" She laughed.

I laughed so much that tears were rolling down my face; Penny was petrified, and told me that I was never to leave her alone with Vicky again and as far as was possible, I didn't. I developed a rapport with Vicky, I'd just say;

"Don't start!" and she'd calm down.

Besides I liked her, there was only ever one exception; Vicky was having a row with Mrs Mills in our room and as I walked in I saw Vicky kick Mum in the stomach, sending her flying backwards into our wardrobes, where she sat on the floor winded and shaken. I was so angry and I didn't think of the consequences; I laid into Vicky, punching her in the face and body, calling her all the ungrateful bitches in the world. Vicky was crying and I was summoned to the office. Vicky looked at me in shock, with the tears streaming down her pale face, from those big brown eyes;

"I'm sorry Vicky, but you shouldn't have done that!" I hugged her.

"I'm sorry!" She sobbed and we went down to the office together.

She apologised to Mum, who was still very cross with her, but she forgave her, this time. Vicky was then told to leave the room while Mum had a chat with me; she was cross with me too and said that she should report it, she'd never seen that side of me. But on the other hand she was grateful; she'd never been frightened of a girl before but even so, I shouldn't have done it. I wasn't about to let that go; nobody would do that to her and I told her so. From that day on Vicky and I got on better than ever, if she had her outbursts it was almost always when I had gone home for the weekend. She even went to school everyday with me, but only as a pupil; she was accepted and for the most part was as good as gold, that was until the week after I left school. She returned and just three days into the week, she had beaten Mrs Garrett so badly that she needed hospital treatment. Vicky was arrested and put into a local mental hospital; she was admitted to several after that.

I left school in April 1974 and I was sad to go; the whole school and staff had signed a card. I stayed in touch with Doris Callum and her husband as, on odd occasions, I'd been looking after their 10-year-old daughter, Pamela. We became good friends and remained so for a long time after I left school. I went back occasionally to see the other staff until they moved on and the school closed.

I started going home for longer periods - a week at a time in preparation for me leaving. I was full of dread, Dad didn't live there anymore, but Aaron did, when he wasn't in prison. I had security at the hostel with Mum and I had Dan's family too; I'd had dinner there many times, usually on Sundays and I had Dan too. We'd had a few rows and he'd go off for a few days, but I'd phone him and apologise, even if it wasn't my fault and he'd come back. I really didn't want to lose him; I loved him in a way, or as close as I could and I loved his family. Everybody liked and approved of him and that was so important to me; without him I'd be back to square one, alone, even my own Mum liked him, she had told me so on one of my brief visits.

"You've got a good one there," she said, "don't mess it up!"

At the end of January 1975, after several weeks' trial at home, I left the hostel. Dan came to pick me up; I said my good-byes to the girls and promised to come back and see them all. I had a lump the size of a marble in my throat saying goodbye to Mum; I thanked her for caring and she handed me a card, telling me not to open it until I got outside, I hugged her so hard and we cried together;

"Be happy Jan." She said.

The words in the card read;

Good Luck, I consider you to be a success.
Love from mum (Mrs Mills).

Short but it had meaning to me. Shortly after that, Dan moved into our home ; the hovel and I couldn't understand why he'd chosen to live with me there rather than his beautiful, comfortable home with his family, but live with me he did. With a little fiddling, Dan managed to bypass the meter and so we had light again, I couldn't stand to live there without light. One night we watched a film called the Exorcist and I had nightmares that were so vivid, there was one in particular that I still remember as clear as day: I walked into a room with thirteen chairs and there were monks sat on twelve of them, all with their heads down, wearing brown robes with the hoods up. I sat on the thirteenth chair and they all looked up but they had no faces; it was just emptiness, black. Then a door opened, on the opposite side of the room; I got up and walked through. There was a tunnel with a bright light in the distance and although I couldn't see them, I was aware of caves either side of me and voices crying, almost wailing and moaning, and the feeling was so sad and oppressing. I walked on towards this light and that was all I could remember. I awoke in floods of tears and I woke Dan; I had to get out of there. He got dressed and drove me to Terry's and Iris's, where I explained what had happened. We sat there for a couple of hours; Terry had tried to keep contact with me since Carls death and as he lived just round the corner from the hostel, I had been round to his home a few times, but I stayed away as much as possible, one reason was that he would expect me to sleep with him, the second and more important was that his wife had had their daughter, just 5 days after my sons death on 12.03.73; I couldn't face looking at her, watching her grow, I mean,

90

my baby was in the ground. Dan also knew about Carl by now, but said that I should forget it and never mention it to his family, so I never did. When I had calmed down Terry took me out to the back of the house to show me something he'd made; it was a headstone, an open book, carved with carls name, birth and death dates and inscribed at the bottom, it said; 'Safe in the arms of Jesus.' It was hard but I had to tell him that we could never put it on Carl's grave; a pauper's burial and he'd made so much effort. I realised then how much effect the death had had on him and how much he did actually care about me, for me, and that it wasn't just about the sex.

He told Dan to take care of me and we went home. I had a lot more nightmares after that; various topics but nothing like the first one, and the drives became an almost nightly occurrence; I would sleep with the light on. My Dad also gave me some advice, it was one evening after one of our drives, we got back and Dad was there; I didn't ask why but I think he'd fallen out with Diane. Dan explained what I'd been experiencing and dad told me that I was safe at our home;

"You will not die and nothing will happen!" He said, "Go through it and you will come out on the other side. Trust me, you will see."

.Anyone who has ever suffered anxiety attacks will recognise this advice.

After a while the midnight jaunts were becoming a bit of a strain and I decided to write to a local vicar, I don't remember the content of his reply, but the very day I received the letter the night-mares stopped. I still have a fear of lofts and my beliefs changed... They recently re-released the Exorcist on D.V.D. but I will never watch it, even though my kids tell me that it is quite tame in comparison to films that are released today.

Chapter 17

Dan and I got engaged in February 1975; we didn't have a big party, just a few drinks in the pub. We told everyone and most were pleased, although a few said that it wouldn't last. Mum was happy for me but I learnt, much later, that she'd told Dan he would eventually regret it. We also found out that Dad had missed a few rent payments, so the house would ultimately be repossessed by the council and we would have to find somewhere else to live.

I missed a period the same month that we got engaged, I didn't want to tell Dan until I was sure but I couldn't wait the week it would take to get the pregnancy results from the doctor either, so I contacted L.I.F.E. - a voluntary organisation, who did pregnancy tests and gave the results whilst you waited. I wasn't going to make the same mistake as I had made with Carl and I phoned and made an appointment for the following day. With my first urine sample safe in an old screw top medicine bottle, well washed out first as I'd been instructed, I got on the bus and headed to the address I'd been given. I was scared, scared if I was pregnant and scared if I wasn't: 'What if it was like Carl? What if Dan didn't want it? He had said he didn't want to share me with anyone, but not even his own children, surely he couldn't mean that? But then what if he did? What if he left me?' Well there was no way that I'd abort it on the say so of a man, even if it were like Carl. I walked up to the door of the private house, a lovely Georgian style house and I thought; 'I'd love to have a home like this one day, but then people like me just aren't lucky like that.' A lady, dark haired, I would say roughly aged about mid fifty, opened the door;

"Come in love and we'll have an answer in a few minutes." She was friendly, accepting and not in the least bit judgemental. She listened to my story of Carl and my fears and her whole demeanour was that of understanding. She dropped her chemicals onto a lid and then added a droplet of urine into the same dish. She continued to explain the procedure and she had a leaflet showing a picture of a negative result and one of a positive.

"Well," she said, "that's a positive result. We will leave it another minute, while you finish your coffee but it won't change." She was right and she wrote me a certificate, for proof of the result, I thanked her and left. I was apprehensive about telling Dan but secretly elated. I knew we had a long way to go and the situation was far from ideal, but from the moment that lovely lady confirmed I was pregnant, my mind was made up; whatever people thought, whatever Dan wanted and whatever the condition of this child, it would be born, and I for one would love it, I already did. That evening I made Dan his dinner, as was expected and as he sat down to eat, I handed him the certificate. He looked at it;

"What the hell is this?"

Ok, he'd said he didn't want to share me, but this was totally unexpected. He left his dinner and the certificate on the table and walked out of the kitchen. I looked out of the window; he didn't leave the house, so I waited, I thought he'd calm down but he didn't. I went to see where he was and found him in our bedroom; I sat down next to him;

"Well, you'll have to get rid of it, we're going to be homeless and we can't afford it. I told you I didn't want kids!"

I argued and said (wrongly); "Well I'm not killing it for you or anyone!"

With that he stood up, picked up a chair and threw it at me, then he went to leave but I got to the door first and stood in his way; I pleaded for an explanation, but he pushed me back onto the bed and left. I had a bruise on my cheek where the chair leg had hit me and it ached for days, although I felt far more numb from his reaction. He didn't come back that night; he eventually came home at teatime the following day, asking where his dinner was;

"I didn't make any; I didn't think you were coming back!" I said.

"Why wouldn't I? I didn't mean to do that," he pointed to the bruise "you just made me angry. I still don't want kids but it looks like I've got no choice, no say in it, unless of course you lose it!"

That was the first of many assaults and bruises; more than I care to remember.

Dad's house was repossessed a little while later and we had to stay with Ruby and Tim for four weeks before we could get our own place, meanwhile the bailiffs moved in and stripped our house bare. We waited until the day before the eviction was due before moving out and I watched them through Ruby's kitchen window as they threw all my childhood memories, onto a council lorry to take to the tip; those workers couldn't have known the importance of those bits and pieces, or that I was watching them. Mum's bedroom suite, the Formica kitchen table; each piece conjured up a memory. The lounge curtains; I'd helped Mum hang them when she'd bought them off a catalogue, she loved them and they'd been hanging there for so many years, I must have been about 7 years old when she'd bought them and they'd seen it all. I wondered where my brother would live and I was worried about him but I needn't have: He had found a room in an old man's home, rent free; the old chap had felt sorry for him, but then I suppose Aaron had spun him a line... Mind you, he had the luck of the devil. The day after the repossession, Dan left for work in the car we had then; an old 'Triumph Herald' Convertible, nice to look at but it had a problem starting, you had one chance to start it and if it didn't go on the first turn of the key, it would have to be pushed. On this particular day it did start at the first turn, I waved Dan off and he headed off down the hill, but as I turned to walk away I heard the engine stop and turned back to see that there were uniformed police everywhere; they had pulled Dan over, believing him to be Aaron and it seemed that every road leading off was blocked with police waiting for him. I found it very amusing; I had no idea what Aaron had done to warrant this, but Dan's face was a picture, bright red with his orange hair and funnier still was that once the police had established his identity, Dan had tried to start the car again and it didn't want to know... Half a dozen police had to push it to start it again. Although I didn't condone my brother's criminal behaviour, it did have its funny moments. It also had its frightening moments, I was used to the police knocking on the door looking for him with warrants for his arrest, but on one particular occasion though, when the knock came, I opened the door and there were two plain clothed police officers stood there, one asked;

"Is Aaron here?"

"No!"

He wasn't and I hadn't seen him. Our little dog, Rocky, didn't like uniforms, he was after all Aaron's dog and although the men weren't wearing uniforms, he knew they were policemen and started barking. He slipped past me, out of the door and up the road, a'' the while the policeman kept saying;

"Are you sure he's not in?"

I was annoyed, firstly; because the dog had gone and secondly; that they didn't believe me. I said;

"I tell you what, go in and help yourselves. I'm going to find the dog, the doors open, it's all yours!"

I ran after the dog but he was gone; I knew he'd come back, he always did. I went back home to find the police still there and asked;

"Well do you believe me now?"

"Have you seen him today?"

"No, I've told you, I haven't seen him, why?" I hadn't seen him, although I was a little concerned by their persistence.

"Well we believe he was involved in a car accident!" I was now very concerned, he could be dead somewhere; "We believe he must have been badly hurt."

"If I knew where he was, I'd tell you!"

"Well if you have any idea, or anyway to contact him, please do so, thank you." With that they left.

'Now what could I do? Seriously injured they'd said so where was he?' All this was going through my mind as Aaron walked in through the back door, with the dog, bold as brass; he'd seen the police arrive and had stayed out the back until they'd gone. He proceeded to call me all the stupids under the sun; the dog might have given him away, but lucky for me he hadn't.

"Where the hell have you been? They weren't here to arrest you; they said you were badly hurt in a car accident! Were you?" "Do I look hurt?" I had to admit he looked ok, then he continued; "Yes, I was in an accident, with a tree but I've just grazed my back!" He lifted his shirt to show me the so-called 'graze;' it was about six inches wide and the full width of his back, it started from just above his waist and it made the hair on my back of my neck stand on end, it was seeping. A graze on your knee hurts enough; it stings, so that must have been really sore, but all Aaron said was;

"Stings a bit, but it's ok!"

"It needs cleaning!" I told him.

"So clean it!" He replied.

I found a bowl, filled it with warm water, got a piece of towel and started to clean it,

"Well clean it then, what're you frightened of?" He shouted as I dabbed gently; I couldn't believe his pain threshold. He told me that he and his mate had been speeding through a local Park, messing about; his mate was driving and had lost control, hitting a tree. My brother had been thrown out onto the road and had skidded along on his back. I asked about his friend and he said;

"He's an idiot, banged his head a bit, but he's ok."

I was angry and I shouted;

"You could have been killed, you could have told me!"

"Blimey, I didn't know you cared," He said with his usual grin.

"Of course I care, you're my brother!"

"Would I care if it were you?" He then laughed at me. I don't know if he would care, but I'd like to think that he would; I certainly wouldn't like to be his enemy, it seemed that nothing touched him. I still smile when thinking of the things he did, and still does but on a larger scale in comparison. He is a likeable rogue and I missed his antics for a while; Dan was a nice, law abiding, hard working man and not at all what I was used to. Even though that was the life I was used to and that was where I had grown up; I was still glad to move from Ruby's, I didn't like the idea of seeing new people in Dad's home, my home and Terry had taken to coming round on most days to see Ruby, so he said but the offer was there anytime, if I needed him.

We had to find two hundred and fifty pounds deposit for the flat and the first months rent, which was a further hundred pounds. Dan's wages were just eighty pounds a week, not that bad at the time, but his Mum came to the rescue, giving us the deposit. She helped us out many times over the years and we were lucky to have her; I couldn't call on my family, they never had much anyway, well apart from my brother, he did well on his ill gotten gains, the expression; 'crime doesn't pay' obviously didn't apply in his case, although he has done a lot of time for it. We had to go all the way to London to pay the landlord the deposit, collect the keys and complete the tenancy agreement. It was worth it; our first real home together: A fully furnished, one bedroom, self-contained flat and it was great not to have to live with other people, to be able to close my own front door. In just a couple of weeks I would be married, someone's wife, then another few months a mother, this was all I'd wanted. Dan and I had a few arguments, but that's what all young couples do, don't they? So the odd slap didn't matter either, did it?

The wedding preparations were well under way, Lou and Sam paid for everything, they bought my dress and the flowers, and the reception was held at their home. My dress was dusky pink, loose from under the bust to cover my now obvious bump; my posy of flowers would also help to cover it. I wore a black, wide rimmed hat with a pink flower; white would have been nice, but didn't seem quite right given the circumstances, pink wasn't really my colour either but the thought was lovely all the same. They bought Dan's suit too, a flared, three-piece, brown pinstripe one; it was difficult to find a colour that matched him with his orange hair. I was told that I wasn't allowed a hen night; Dan had said that he didn't think it was appropriate, considering I was pregnant, although I could go to the pub with him if I wanted.

The day of the wedding arrived; the 7th of June 1975. Dan and I drove to the registry office together; I hadn't wanted to be at the flat alone overnight and Dan wasn't prepared to allow that either, so we broke with tradition; it didn't matter, we had done the same with everything else. We arrived at 10:30am and everybody was waiting, even my Mum and sister; even though they were invited, I didn't really think they'd turn up. I'd invited Jim too but he had declined; Dad would be there and he didn't think it was appropriate. Diane didn't come either and I was quite relieved about that. My family weren't all stood together but they were there, the only one missing was Aaron; Dad said that he was otherwise detained, on remand, although he wasn't sure what for. It was so hot that day and yet, just a couple of weeks earlier it had seemed like mid winter with night frosts. We filed into the registry office and Dad and Lou were witnesses; the idea was to keep Mum and Dad apart, except Mum wanted to take photos of us as we signed the register. It was a tense moment, the first time that they had had any kind of contact in a while. As mum attempted to take a picture, her flash cube blew up, fell to the floor in pieces and left a small scorch mark on the carpet; I had trouble trying to contain the laughter at Mums obvious embarrassment; everyone else giggled and the registrar said not to worry and it lightened the atmosphere. I felt it was like a little pay back time; there were always plenty of photos taken of Verity and Aaron, not so many of me and now that she'd wanted one, she couldn't have one. Lou said she'd got a couple of good one's and that she would send them to Mum later. The day went well; all things considered. A little later Mum asked to speak to me outside, everyone was in the back garden, stripped off, playing cards and chatting. I told Dan where I was going and met Mum out the front; without warning she turned and hugged me and said how pleased she was for me, especially given our history and she wished she could have done more. By now Mum was crying and she seemed genuine. She had bought me a second hand, cylinder

Hoover and I was grateful for that as I did need one, but try as I might I couldn't feel sorry for her, I didn't show my reluctance, instead I said that it didn't matter, the important thing was that she was there and that she'd done what she could. I told her not to worry and that I would like to see her and Verity a bit more often. And perhaps one day she could introduce me properly to Jim; it was a pity that he hadn't felt he could come but it was understandable. I broke off the conversation and motioned to her to come back inside, before people started to miss us.

"You go, I'll be there in a minute," she said and turned away.

Finally, I'd seen a little regret for what she'd done and I was, in some sick way, happy that her leaving had had some effect on her, until then I'd never seen anything but resentment for me; as a result, I'd become like that towards her. I wasn't like her though, one thing was for sure, my baby would never be alone and I'd never leave it. Another thing was also to remain true: I knew then, at that moment that I could never really forgive her for robbing me of my childhood. Jim picked Mum up from outside the house about an hour later; I said goodbye to Mum and Verity at the gate and waved as they pulled away. Jim also waved back, with a smile; maybe he was all right after all, I had thought that perhaps he didn't like me, but I was wrong, as only time would tell.

Dan and I left for our honeymoon; a weekend away. We didn't know where we were going but Lou and Sam had given us one hundred pounds to spend; that on top of everything else they had done for us. The car was covered in tin cans and 'Just Married' squiggles and Dan wanted to remove all that before we drove too far. When we got to the top of the road, there was a terrible smell coming from the engine and it was the worst thing I'd ever smelt. Dan pulled over, opened the bonnet and there, tied to the engine, was a fish, rotten and smelling. Dan wasn't amused but I saw the funny side; it had been his brothers and stepfathers idea of a joke. He removed it carefully and threw it into the gutter, he was annoyed at the smell on his hands; he hated dirty hands. We had to go back to the flat and collect our luggage and we left later than we'd wanted to; it was past four in the afternoon, because Dan had had to wash the engine compartment out, then half an hour washing his hands, and he was pretty annoyed by the time we left. We headed towards the West Country, thinking that maybe we would go to Cornwall. We didn't speak much but I was enjoying the drive and beautiful countryside and when we reached the borders of Devon and Cornwall, it was getting dark. Dan said we should try and find a bed and breakfast and perhaps have a meal, so we tried a couple and passed half a dozen more with 'No Vacancy' signs. Finally, the third one that we stopped at had one room; a twin bedded room but we had no choice. Just our luck, single beds on our wedding night; we pushed the beds together and to be honest it wasn't so bad, it wasn't as if it mattered; I was pregnant with swollen feet and backache, and Dan was tired from driving. Our first night as a married couple; we slept well.

The next day we drove down to Cornwall and visited a few little villages with old smuggler cottages and cobbled little streets, gift shops of trinkets, tat, postcards and rock candy, and everywhere we went we were offered 'Cornish Pasties' and scones with clotted cream. I loved that area of Britain; if I didn't live in Bournemouth and love it so much, then that would be the place for me. Dan wasn't too keen, he always saw himself migrating to Australia; I just couldn't do that, ever. We started the journey back a different way, we decided to go across the Severn bridge, into Chepstow just to say that we'd been to Wales. We did go into Chepstow, turned around and came back; we were probably in Wales some ten minutes: Next stop; Weston- Super- Mare. We parked in a side street and it was so hot that once again my feet were swollen. I was complaining about walking, but Dan told me to keep up or he would leave without me; he was hungry and we'd seen a café as we drove through, so we headed there and we had a sandwich and a cup of tea over looking the sea front. Another half hour and we were on our way home; we decided it would be better to have a meal on the way back, somewhere nearer home. It was still early when we reached Wareham; about 6pm and too early for dinner, so we had a wander around there. We lay in the dunes for an hour and then headed into to a pub called 'The Black Bear' where Dan fancied a cold beer. We set off for home again at about 7:30pm and decided on a restaurant on the outskirts of Christchurch for our final honeymoon meal; we just about had enough money left. We had been there before so we knew the steaks were good. The steak didn't disappoint, but I really wasn't keen on the small caterpillars in the watercress; I glanced down at my plate, as one was half upright, looking back at me. Dan had already taken his first mouthful of steak when I said;

"Stop, Check your meal! Have you got caterpillars?"
He checked, found that he had them too and called the waitress over; we pointed them out to her, with honest disbelief and she just removed the watercress from the plates, saying;

"Oh gosh!"
She put it on the tray in her hand and walked away. We waited for a few minutes, thinking she may come back for the plates but she didn't, so we ate it. I wasn't keen but Dan said;

"Well, she's taken the caterpillars away and I'm hungry!"
We never went there again.

Chapter 18

Dan's family were thrilled about my pregnancy from the start and his Mum, Lou, was over the moon at the prospect of a grandchild, although she was concerned and curious about the kind of tests I had to have: I would have to have an 'Amniocentesis,' as well as a scan; it was a new procedure back then and the test involved taking amniotic fluid from around the baby, by way of a syringe, through the abdomen and it would establish whether or not the baby had 'Spina Bifida' or 'Downs Syndrome.' There was a risk of miscarriage but, because of my history, it was advised. Lou had asked why it was so important for me to have this test, especially with the risks and I hated lying to her, but I had been warned not to say anything by Dan, I was not to say anything, ever; I eventually told her that my Mum's sister had had a disabled child, with a condition called 'Spina Bifida' and he had died. I'm not sure if she believed me but she didn't ask again. I had the test done when I was 18 weeks gone but the results would take a further 3 weeks. Dan wouldn't come with me for the test but told me to ring him when it was done and then he'd pick me up from the hospital entrance. I went in and was prepared for the procedure; I was told that my baby was fine, growing well and seemed normal, they checked that I understood the risks and I signed the forms. The nurse held my hand; I couldn't believe the size of the needle, it was like a size ten knitting needle. I was told to expect pressure as they inserted the needle, but I didn't expect the popping noise as it went in, neither did the nurse and whilst holding my hand, she jumped twice but it in went well and I had to lay still for a while. They checked the baby again before I left and said that everything was, or seemed ok and that I should try and rest for 24 hours. I phoned Dan and then told them he would be collecting me at the entrance, obviously concerned, the nurse said;

"You can't walk down; I'll get a wheel chair and take you. Does your husband realise what you have had to go through?"

"He's a man and hates hospitals." I replied. "He would probably have fainted anyway!"

I didn't want them to know that he didn't welcome the prospect of this child but when Dan arrived he was really nice and very pleasant to the nurse; he thanked her for taking good care of me and said that he was no good at these things. She smiled and told him to make sure I got some rest as it had been quite an ordeal: That was an understatement; I now felt that I knew what it was like to be stabbed. Dan didn't speak to me at all on the way home.

It was July 1975, three weeks after the test and I had to phone the hospital for the results between; 9:00 and 10:30am. My pulse was racing and I was so afraid of the answer, even though this pregnancy had been very different from the one I'd had with Carl; this time I had felt movement, which was something that I hadn't experienced with Carl. The other obvious difference was that I hadn't had any bleeding, at all, so that had to be a good sign too. The nurse came to the phone;

"Yes, everything is absolutely fine. Did you want to know the sex?"
'Did I?' Yes I did; I'd secretly hoped for a girl, but as long as this baby was healthy; that was all that really mattered.

"It's a boy!" She said.

"And you are sure everything is ok?" I questioned.

"Yes, everything is absolutely fine and we'll see you for your Ante-Natal."

"Thank you, so very much!"
I walked back to the flat smiling; 'A boy and healthy too, thank God!' And my son's due date was the 14th November 1975. I wandered around the flat; I had to tell someone and Dan was at work, so I walked back to the call box and phoned Lou who was ecstatic;
"Boys are easier," she'd said, although she had never had a girl herself.
Dan came in late, he didn't ask about the results but I told him anyway;

"Its good news," I said, "everything's ok and we're having a boy."

"That's good then." He responded. "Better make the most of our time out now, because we won't be able to go gallivanting once it arrives, or at least you won't."
I'd thought that he would have come round to the idea of having this baby by now, but I was wrong.

I started to see a bit more of Mum, about once a week; I was after all a respectable, married woman now. She even came to my flat to see me and I was invited to hers for dinner on my birthday, and she cooked my favourite: Stewed steak with Yorkshire pudding (always home made), sautéed potatoes and garden peas. It was a bit strange being with her but I was glad to be spending time with my sister and if Mum was part of the package; then so be it.

They were at my flat when the pains had started on the 10th of November 1975. I'd been cooking dinner whilst getting the first slight pains; they were about ten minutes apart and irregular, but by 10pm they had become stronger and I'd had difficulty not showing it.

"You're getting pains aren't you?" Mum asked. "How long have you been sat there like that?"

She sounded concerned and I told her but she was about to leave to go home. I didn't want her there; she did offer to stay but I graciously declined, I said that I'd be fine with Dan. She went home but left instructions for Dan to let her know, he told her he would. By 12:30am the pains were almost too much but I told Dan to leave the phone call a bit longer; I wanted to have a bath but he insisted on phoning, I think he was a little scared or rather – terrified.

"Well tell them I'm having a bath first!" I shouted after him as he rushed from the flat to call the hospital. The contractions were now four minutes apart; it sounds daft but I felt that the longer I left it before going to the hospital, the more chance I'd have that they wouldn't have time to shave me again. I knew that everything was all right but Dan was starting to panic and lose his temper so I relented;

"Ok, let's go!" I declared.

We arrived at the hospital at 1:30am; a porter brought a wheelchair and said that I had to sit in it. Dan put my bag on my lap and I was wheeled into the lift and up to the labour ward. Memories filled my mind as we passed by the delivery room that I was in the last time; for which I was grateful and I think I would have insisted that I wasn't in that one, I'd rather have given birth in the corridor.

"Ok, get yourself into bed." Said my Midwife, as she helped me up. "We'll give you an examination and see where we are at."

Dan was looking very uncomfortable and the Midwife asked if he'd like to wait outside whilst they got me ready; he looked at me and his expression was almost like a startled rabbit, caught in the head lights of a car and it would have been wrong to laugh, so instead I smiled and nodded;

"I'm ok, go on." He'd shown me a vulnerable side that I hadn't seen before.

"I'll go and have a cigarette."

"We'll come and get you in a few minutes." The midwife assured him.

He was out of that door in a flash, and it was too late for a shave, thank goodness but I was asked if I'd like an epidural; I declined, I wanted to be fully aware of all that was happening this time. Dan came back in but he didn't have much to say, he just sat on a chair, in the corner until the Midwife left the room;

"How long is this going to take?" He asked and continued with; "I'm not going to get much sleep tonight!"

"Well stay home tomorrow." I replied, "You can take the day off you know? I wont be having a baby everyday; I'm sure they'll understand."

He was concerned about his dinner as well, so I suggested that he go to his Mums. The last hour of labour flew by, with the help of the gas and air. I needed no stitches and at 3:30am he arrived, weighing eight pounds and two ounces: Our son - Lee David (we had chosen the name, or at least I had with an 'ok' approval from his Daddy months before,) and he was beautiful; perfect, with a mass of black hair and the most amazing colour eyes. He was handed to me straight away and the relief was immeasurable, I'd kept thinking; 'Please don't take him from this room!' I was totally in love with my son from that very moment. Dan had left the room half an hour or so prior to the birth; there was no way that he wanted to be in the delivery room but he came back in about ten minutes or so later and he was smiling as he entered the room. The midwife handed him our son saying;

"Congratulations Daddy, would you like to hold your son whilst we give your wife a quick clean up? I think you could do with a cup of tea too, couldn't you?"

I could see Dan was nervous holding Lee for the first time but his face said that he was happy;

"He looks all right to me," he said, smiling from ear to ear.
'Maybe it would be all right after all?' I thought.

At about 5am I was taken up to the postnatal ward and Dan kissed me and Lee goodbye; he was going to phone everyone and then get some well-deserved sleep. He was tired and had been more supportive than I'd ever expected. He assured me he would be back in the afternoon for visiting. I couldn't sleep; I could only watch my perfect baby. I gave him his first feed at about 6am, a full 2 ounces straight off - poor little Carl had only ever taken 10mls at a time, hard to imagine watching Lee swallow this so easily. At 3pm

Dan was back with flowers, a card, a teddy and a big smile. He gave me a kiss and went straight to the baby,

"Shall I pick him up?"

"Yes, if you want to."

He was asleep and other than stirring slightly when he'd filled his nappy or when I changed him, he didn't wake throughout the whole visit. I did ask if Dan would like to change him but he declined saying;

"I draw the line at that one."

He never did change a nappy.

Lou came in a little while later, also armed with flowers, chocolates and a beautiful shawl she'd croqueted herself. She was so overwhelmed by how much hair Lee had and she approved of his name. She said how beautiful he was, nurses had commented on his looks as well, so it wasn't just me then? I thought perhaps I was biased, every mother believes their baby is the most beautiful don't they?

Mum didn't come and see me then, but phoned telling the nurses she would be in the next day. She kept to her word and arrived with my sister. Lou was there too, she said she wanted to be known as granny, my Mum wanted to be Nanny so that was easy, no grumbles and it would avoid confusion later.

Lee was good as gold in the hospital, I was nervous about being alone with him at home, I had never found it easy, given my past, to ask for help, I'd never have asked my Mother, besides everybody has their own ideas on how to raise their children. I had looked after Jo's and Ruby's children and I had learnt from them how to make up bottles, about sterilising, nappy changing, but having one of your own was very different: Lee was mine, I was solely responsible for his welfare. I also started to find I had difficulty in the hospital with Lou, with the 'when Dan was born' and the 'do it like this', 'I wouldn't' or 'I didn't do it like that.' I was very torn because the last person in this world I wanted to fall out with, or more than likely hurt, would be Lou. I had asked Dan if he would arrange it so that no one was waiting at home when he collected me from the hospital. I just wanted a few hours whilst I settled Lee in and made up his bottles - just the 3 of us, my own little family.

Dan arrived at the hospital at 11am. He'd told Lou that I'd be home at 2pm, but if she wanted to come over it would be better if she left it until about 4pm, before doing so, she said she would. Unfortunately she didn't, Dan had left her a key and she had said she wanted to get things ready for me and the baby. She cooked dinner, made up the baby feeds, the cot in the way she'd chosen, our bed was even made up the way she had chosen. As we opened the door of our flat she was stood waiting, she took Lee from me before I'd got over the threshold. I turned into our lounge where little Gran and Auntie Susan were also waiting,

"We'll look after him, you go and unpack," they said.
I said nothing, Lee was due his feed but Lou fed him, he was passed around the room back and forth. I wanted him to get accustomed to his carrycot - start as we meant to go on but I was told that it wouldn't hurt for a while and he'd know no different.

Finally after his next feed and we'd all had dinner and I'd washed up, they went home saying,

"You look tired, maybe you should rest. I'll see you in the morning."
I'd wanted to say, NO, give me some space but I didn't, instead I turned on Dan;

"She's your Mum, why didn't you tell her?"
He claimed that I was being stupid, possessive,

"She is only trying to help!" He barked.
I knew she was. Dan and I ended up not speaking for most of the evening. Whether it was the disagreement, the change of surroundings or that the milk formula was made up wrongly, but Lee cried and screamed from 10pm until 5am. Dan went and slept in the lounge, he went to work at 7am with no kiss goodbye. I finally dozed off, after feeding Lee and he eventually settled just as Dan was leaving. Lou woke me at just after 9am; she was taking Lee out of his carrycot. She said he needed to be bathed and fed before the midwife came, I protested and told her about our night, but she did it anyway. The midwife told me how lucky I was to have such support, I didn't feel lucky, I was very tired and pretty weepy, I had an interfering Mother-in-law, a husband that wouldn't speak to me and a baby that wouldn't sleep, he obviously didn't like me either.

He was settled all the next day, but come 8pm on the second night he started again, by 3am Dan said if I didn't shut him up he was going to smother him, or throw him out in the rain. Of course he didn't, but sadly, I did believe that he was capable of it and from that moment on I knew I would never get support from him. By the third night, when Lee was only five days old he settled, he had his feed every four hours, he hardly cried, with the exception of his colic that usually occurred between 6pm and 7pm. After one week I increased his feed to 5oz. He missed his 2am feed and by the time he was 2 weeks old, he slept all night. The first time he did it I slept until 9am, I awoke with a start. I thought Lee was sure to be dead in his carrycot, he must be. My heart in my throat, I peered in, he was fine and sleeping peacefully. From then on I checked him every few minutes during the day and woke several times at night to check he was breathing.

Terry and Iris came in to see me the week after I came home. They and their children wanted to see Lee. There youngest was about 18 months old now, I found it easier to face her, she sat on her Mummy's knee cradling Lee in her chubby little hands, her blonde curls dangling in his face, as she gave him sloppy kisses. Looking at her I imagined my Carl at the same age.

I went to make tea for us and Terry followed me into the kitchen saying he'd help. He came up behind me and kissed me on the back of my head,

"You may have just had a baby, but I still fancy you, I'm here when you feel the need, anything for you."

I couldn't look at him, I was disgusted, but there were things he could do, I was alone with this baby, with the exception of Lou's help. If I went to their home, perhaps once or twice a week, I'd at least get a bit of a break from her, besides Terry wouldn't try anything now I was married, I had convinced myself of that much and Terry liked Dan, Dan liked him, so as long as the dinner was ready when Dan got home, it shouldn't be a problem. So on Tuesdays and Thursdays I went to Terry's home and Thursdays he'd take us to do the food shopping, his children in tow. He would always get me home for 4oclock to make sure Dan's dinner was on time. He mended plugs and decorated the flat for me.

Dan and I had started to struggle financially, we got behind with the rent and our relationship was becoming strained. We couldn't keep borrowing off people. It was even more reason for Dan to support his opinion that this baby was a mistake. He started losing his temper regularly, more so after he'd been drinking, which he'd taken to doing 3 nights a week. At other times he would force an argument to justify walking out. I obviously didn't want him to go out at all and so, more often than not, I stood in his way. At the beginning, he would push me aside with an occasional slap, and I gave as good as I got, at least I did in the early days, but the frequency of the assaults and severity of violence, left me with lumps, bumps and bruises, usually on my head or body where they would not be seen. I believed in some way that I had caused these outbursts, I had been late with his dinner a couple of times, or his washing wasn't in his drawer when he wanted a specific item to wear, he did try to provide for us as best he could. There was also the point that his father had been violent towards his Mother, these violent outbursts weren't anything like the injuries inflicted upon her, besides I didn't want to be alone.

Terry found out by accident that this was happening, he tapped me on the shoulder after saying something he thought was funny, my arm was badly bruised and I flinched away, I said it was a one off, that Dan had pushed me and I'd fallen on it. He didn't believe me, but he didn't say so. On the days I didn't go to his home, he took to calling in with his wife, but more often he was alone. Dan then lost his job, he had been late several times and work was slow, so he was laid off. By the time Lee was just 4 months old, we were homeless... again. We could find nowhere to live, unbeknown to me Terry had spoken to Dan and arranged for us to stay with him and his family in their council home. I had no choice, with nowhere else to go. Dan didn't want to impose on his family and was ashamed that he couldn't provide for us. We had a young baby and no money. If I had spoken out and confessed my real reasons for not wanting to stay with Terry, Dan would surely have killed him. To be honest Terry had become the only person I could really talk to.

It was cold and early march 1976, when we moved in with them. Terry's wife, Iris, had said it would be fun and quite nice having the company of another woman. I did feel sorry for her, Terry treated her very differently to the way he treated me, for as long as I knew her, she had washed his feet, shaved him and combed his hair, at the same time as having to care for four young children, all under school age. As a result the house was less than perfect; it was not to my standard of cleanliness, certainly not for my son. I was very particular with Lee, he was a hungry, windy baby and he would swallow a full bottle, bringing a lot of it back and with such force, it would reach across the room. He was on solid food by 2 months, but he'd had a couple of chest infections aswell, so cleanliness was my priority and I found it difficult living there. We lived there though for 4 months, in the latter 2 months Dan found another job and I was at home with the family alone. Terry took to sitting with his arm around me in front of his wife and on occasions molesting me, touching my breasts in front of her, she seemed to think it was funny. I knew differently and on two occasions whilst she was in the house, Terry had forced me to go all the way. The first time was in the bathroom: I had just had a bath and I thought he had gone out, there was no lock on the bathroom door; Iris had broken it off, when the eldest boy had locked himself in. Terry didn't mend it because he said it might happen again. He was worried for the children. He came in and approached me, saying it was only right that I let him, as we had been living there rent-free for all those weeks and I knew what his wife was like. He said Iris was grateful for the rest; I couldn't tell Dan, he would leave me and I couldn't stop Terry or he would tell Dan and kick Lee and I out. I was damned if I did and damned if I didn't. I never really knew until years later, whether Iris did know and turned a blind eye, or whether she really was naïve. One thing was for sure; she idolised him, he never worked, he was just there, he said he got more on the dole than he could earn working with 4 children, if he needed extra money he could do the odd decorating job.

It took its toll on me and I became depressed. I felt trapped, I decided that it would be better if I spent my days out of the house, or as much as I possibly could. I'd put Lee in the pram with his bottles and food and walk for miles. I visited Jo or Ruby or just walked around the shops. I went to visit Mrs Mills a couple of times. They were about to close the girls hostel and she was retiring, she'd had enough, things weren't the same anymore since we'd all left. We lost touch with each other for many years, especially as she moved to Brighton and when she left, I'd had no address for her to contact me, and she had gone. I lost touch with everyone, including Penny. I took Lee to visit my old school just before they closed their doors too, Jo was remarried and I felt she and Ruby had moved on without me, I was very lonely, I'd seen Lou just a few times and hadn't seen Mum at all since moving into Iris's.

I was out one day going to the shops, as I crossed at a zebra crossing I noticed a couple coming the other way, also pushing a pram. The man said hello as I passed and I turned to see who it was, it was Jack, Mrs Thompson's son – my Mum's old neighbour. We shouted back and forth, asking how each other were, nice to see you, the usual pleasantries. I couldn't help noticing the angered expression on the woman's face, I didn't know her and I had never seen her before. I was annoyed by her look and decided if I saw her again I'd ask her what her problem was. I walked on and then turned again, I could see the woman was obviously arguing with Jack, I thought poor guy, he had only said hello.

As luck would have it, just the next morning I was walking with my pram, past a house at the other end of the same road as where I was staying, when I saw that very same woman sat on the wall. As I got closer, Jack walked out of the driveway pushing a pram;

"Hello again," I said and went to walk past, then thought better of it and decided to stop. Jack was obviously uncomfortable; I turned to the woman;

"Hi, I'm Jan, I've known Jack for years," I said extending my hand,

"I know," she said, "I'm Gemma," responding to my gesture,

"I did tell her how we knew each other, but she didn't believe me," said Jack,

"Yes I did," she said smiling, but only ever so slightly. I ended up having a cup of tea with them and talking about our baby's and my temporary situation at Terry's, I didn't give details. Their baby was also named Lee and was 3 months younger than my Lee. The weather was quite warm, and it turned out to be a very hot summer. I explained to them how strained and cramped things were at Terry's.

"Well if you're ever fed up, you come on down here." Said Gemma.

Iris was a little peeved because I'd taken to going out and she thought it was because of something she'd done; Terry said I should stay with her more often, besides he wanted to see me too. By the end of that week, I had been to Gemma's everyday. In the end Terry said;

"Well you'd best see if you can live there instead, you obviously prefer it there."

A conversation that I'd relayed to Gemma and Jack. They looked at each other and Jack said,

"Well we could do with the extra money; we've got the room, why not?"

I spoke to Dan and we went back to see them that evening, it was agreed that we would move in at the weekend, in just 2 days. Dan was also really fed up living at Iris's, he couldn't cope with his own son, let alone their four, he confessed that he had even considered going back to live with his Mum for a while, but was deterred because then he wouldn't be able to keep an eye on me, particularly at night, so had thought better of it.

Since leaving the flat we had seemed to get on a little better, he still went out with his friends, still drank, but there was no violence, I knew he didn't want people to know about it, he wanted people to think highly of him and I would have to say that the majority did.

Those last 2 days at Iris's were very strained and difficult. I told Iris that it wasn't anything she had done and that I hoped we would remain friends, I would still go and see her regularly and that I was only down the road. We told them that Dan and I felt that we were taking up space that they needed for the children and themselves. We thanked them for letting us stay and Dan handed Terry some money, I never knew how much, but one things for sure Iris would never benefit from it, and even though I'd spoken to Iris, I still felt an atmosphere and felt we left under a cloud. We knew that it was temporary anyway, that's how we'd seen it but, I'm not sure about Terry.

So we moved in with Gemma and Jack. Dan and I had been registered with the local council on the housing list since losing our flat and we had visited the housing offices regularly, we were always fobbed off. We couldn't get an appointment to see the director of housing for Bournemouth, I was sure that if he knew our situation he might move us further up the waiting list. I was grateful to Gemma and Jack, but we needed to find our own place, our own home and a place for Lee.

I decided to write to the Prime Minister, James Callahan, not for a place to live, just an appointment to see the director of housing for Bournemouth, Mr Bradley, even his wife, who was responsible for allocations and accommodation. It was some weeks before I got a reply and in the meantime, Dan found another job working nights, Jack also worked nights and so Gemma and I spent our time together with our two Lee's. We got on very well, more importantly; I was able to stay in without fear of being molested, or under pressure to put out to keep a roof over our heads.

It was a very hot summer; we'd do our washing and housework, whilst the baby's slept in their prams in the back garden. Every Friday we'd go on the bus into Bournemouth to the housing office, then walk up to the law courts to pay fines for Jack, I didn't know what they were for. Dan would receive fines for motoring offences, such as: When we'd been in dire straits financially, we hadn't been able to afford tax on the car, we got caught out. We hadn't been able to afford insurance on the car, we got caught out. Another time we had defective brakes, we got caught out. Each time we were caught out, resulted in a fine. Dan was very upset about it all; he'd never been in trouble for anything, whereas I'd had plenty of experience with the law. I did feel sorry for him though, especially when he finally told his Mother, his stepfather, Sam, gave him a very hard time, also inferring that Dan hadn't any problems until he'd got involved with me, Lou defended me saying, it was an unfortunate set of circumstances rather than any fault of mine. After paying the fines, Gemma and I would walk down into Bournemouth gardens or onto the sea front, there we would feed the baby's with a tin of cold Heinz baby food and a bottle, then catch a bus home again in time to get the men up for work. I enjoyed my time there and a friendship formed then with Gemma which still remains today, almost thirty years on.

A reply came from 10, Downing Street, telling me that a further response would come from the ombudsman. A few days later it did and an appointment was arranged for three weeks later.

Dan had met and made friends with someone at work called Joe. I knew Dan was restless, he wanted more money, some security and this chap filled his head with wild ideas about being a mercenary in Angola, had been telling him how he could make a fortune. He had some 'contact' in Ipswich and said Dan had to meet him. I didn't want him to go, what about us? What if he were killed? If he was going to Ipswich then I was going with him.

We packed the car up, Joe's girlfriend Loraine sat in the back with me, Lee on my lap all the way. We didn't leave until gone 4:30pm. I thanked Gemma and said I hoped to be back in a day or so. The idea was ridiculous, although if I hadn't gone, Dan would have gone without me and God only knows what he'd have got dragged into. Lee was restless, he kept crying, especially as we had to sleep in the car over night. We were to meet these people the following morning at 11am. Dan and I had a very big argument during the night, he gave me a back hander in the face, his friend seemed to find this amusing, he said I would be better off if I went home, I shouldn't have come in the first place. With Lee crying and no sleep, combined with my bruised face, I had to agree. As it happened though, when we found the address where we were to meet these people, to find that the house had been demolished. I was relieved, although it was suggested that there was another address in Guildford that we could try on our way back. I couldn't help thinking, why didn't we try that first? It was after all a lot nearer home; this was definitely a wild goose chase. I was right, we didn't find the address or anyone who knew anybody, we arrived back at Gemma's at about 8pm. Dan dropped me off, baby, belongings and all, he had something to do and went off out. Gemma was relieved to see me and I her, whatever happened, whatever hair brained scheme he came up with, I wouldn't be going with Dan again, I should never have put Lee through that. Dan came in the following morning, he'd been to work, and got his job back and had done a night shift. He apologised for putting us through that, I suppose that included the bruise? I told Gemma I'd caught my face on the car door.

Chapter 19

We walked into the carpeted office, it had a large oblong table of oak and a big leather armchair, and there sat Mr Bradley, the director of housing, who greeted us saying;

"You see, I do exist."

We explained our situation and had been there about ten minutes when he said;

"I understand you are homeless and living in your car, as it happens we have just had a temporary flat become available, my wife will show you around in a while. In the meantime, if I find out you aren't really homeless, I will be very annoyed."

He handed us a set of keys and a tenancy agreement to sign. I thanked him, shook his hand, as did Dan and then we left following his wife who gave us directions to the flat, she would meet us there in an hour.

We pulled up outside an old hotel, right by the sea front; it's not there today, it was demolished to build the Bournemouth International Centre. It was the beginning of September 1976 and raining. Mrs Bradley took us into the entrance hall, there were four families housed on the ground floor, where we were to live temporarily for three to six months in flat 4; we occupied three rooms - a lounge that looked out over Bournemouth beach and the pier, a bedroom with a bed, which was supplied by the previous occupant and a kitchen, all had a key and we were advised that each door should be locked if we weren't in the room, as each door opened onto the entrance hall. We had to share a bathroom with everyone on the ground and first floors. The previous occupants had also left an old fridge; 'Circa 1950', a hob with two rings and an oven in the kitchen, and two old armchairs in the lounge. Mrs Bradley assured us several times that it was only temporary and it was surely better than the conditions we had been living in, it was the first step on the ladder.

I fumigated it and scrubbed it, there was a damp smell that I couldn't get rid of, the sash windows leaked each time it rained and in the 3 months that we were there, it rained almost everyday, Lee had several chest infections while we were there. The view of the sea was lovely though and I couldn't help thinking; 'if only it had been the summer.' Dan wasn't keen on it, but he at least agreed that it was a step in the right direction. Once we had our own things in it, it wasn't so bad and Dan found another job working days.

Our neighbours were in the same position as us; a young girl, 16 years old and married with a baby just 6 months old. The other side there was another married couple, he was half cast, with a baby daughter who was only a year old, she was a beautiful child with dark curly hair and the biggest brown eyes I've ever seen. I soon became friends with them all and we were supportive of each other. I didn't have to lock my doors all the time either and the baby's all played happily together.

Lou visited regularly, as did Gemma, Terry and Iris, and... My sister! My little sister had grown up when I was distracted with my life and I hadn't noticed. She was now fifteen, with a boyfriend. She brought him with her to meet me when she came to baby-sit. It turned out though that I already knew him, from my days at the special school, he would be on the bus with his Mother and she had known Jo and recognised me from there; they'd get on the bus out-side the bingo hall most afternoons. I didn't know then the part she and all her 8 children would play in my life; it certainly is a small world. It just so happened that Mary, my 16 year old neighbour, had been at school with my sister and they had been friends... Very small world.

Mrs Bradley called back again at the end of October and delivered letters to all of us on the ground floor, the fourth family had already moved out, I never knew them. The three of us that were left were given letters, offering tenancies to brand new flats, on a new housing estate under development. We were all to be housed in the same block; two bedroom self contained and all on the ground floor. They were beautiful places compared to what we'd been used to and we all moved in on the 6th December 1976.

Dan and I ordered furniture from a shop in Boscombe on Hire Purchase; a three piece suite, a bed and a dining set. We took the fridge from the old place, it was old but it worked. Lou gave us curtains and bought us lots of useful things, it seemed that every-day that she visited, she was laden with goodies for the flat, be it, food or money. She was also less pushy than she had been before or maybe I had miss read her intentions after the birth, maybe it was me and my hormones, either way I was grateful for her, then and so many times over the following years. Mum and I just didn't see each other, so Dan's family were my family now. I ordered a Christmas tree complete with all the decorations from a catalogue and it arrived a week later, I had been concerned that I wouldn't get it in time, the Christmas post being what it is. I was excited about Christmas, finally we had our own permanent home and my son could have a proper family Christmas, we could begin our lives as a little family. Dan and I seemed more settled together, we didn't argue as much and he hadn't hit me for sometime, maybe, just maybe, we would make it. It was only a registry office marriage, I know, but my vows that we would be together forever, whatever, had meant so much to me.

We had a wonderful Christmas; Lee was walking, just, and was interested in all the presents. We helped him unwrap them and his little face lit up with every one. Granny and Grandad bought him his first tricycle, although he didn't ride it properly until well into the summer. He wasn't tall enough and his feet didn't reach the pedals properly until then. He had everything you could think of and more, I was determined that my little man would never go without, never know Christmases like mine had been, that his life would never resemble any aspects of mine.

In 1977 the winter was bad and cold, for a while we'd had quite deep snow. We had to walk to the shops on the main road to get our milk because the milkman couldn't get to us to deliver. Dan collected milk for everyone in the block, he played with Lee building a snow man, throwing snow balls, I watched them laughing together from the window remembering my Christmas alone, how cold it had been in Dad's house, not here though with my central heating.

It was that year that Lee developed a nasty chest infection again, it was so bad that I thought he had pneumonia. The doctor was called 3 times over 4 hours, he said, after his second visit that if he was no better on his return in an hour or so, he would consider hospitalisation, we had a vaporiser burning with antibiotics and gave him paracetamol, to bring his temperature down. I held him on my lap all night watching his breathing, his little chest rising and falling so fast, like waves on the water, I was so frightened, I couldn't lose him too. On the third visit the doctor said he thought he would be all right, he suspected that Lee was asthmatic. It turned out that he was and from then on he was given Ventolin syrup, later on inhalers and he still uses them today.

Terry and Iris would come down once a week to take me shopping, I'd stay with them for the day and be home, as before, to make sure Dan's dinner was done and the flat was clean and tidy. He still got angry if things weren't just so. Lee was well into a routine, Daddy came in at 6pm, his dinner ready, he'd kiss Lee good-night and I'd put him straight to bed. Dan liked his peace and quiet, his home tidy, and no toys in the lounge when he got home. Terry did all the D.I.Y for us, with strings attached, not all the time but it happened. What could I do, he still threatened to tell Dan; he even said that, first and foremost I belonged to him, Dan only married me, because he liked him and allowed it, he told me that he didn't mind me being with Dan because he was able to look after me but I wouldn't like Dan to know what had gone on before between us, would I? No, I wouldn't, so I put up with it.

It was April 1977 and my Nan fell ill, I'd been there just a few times since I'd had Lee, just so that she could get to know her great grand child. They had discovered, the year before, that she had a heart murmur; she'd probably had it all of her life caused, as they thought, by rheumatic fever when she was 5 years old. She gave up smoking and lost weight, she went from fifteen stone to just ten. My sister still went to see her every Saturday and kept me informed of her health, I would have liked to have gone more often, but with everything that had happened I felt slightly uncomfortable with her, I didn't have the closeness with her that I'd had when I was little and I sort of missed that. I invited her to the flat, I thought it might make a difference if she could see how well I was doing and to my surprise, she agreed to come, Mum and Jim would bring her, with my Auntie too. Maybe we could build bridges after all. I made sandwiches and cakes, which they enjoyed. My flat, my son and my husband impressed Nan, she stayed most of the after-noon, but said she was feeling a little tired and they left. Jim had been friendly too and I quite liked him after all; he wasn't my Dad, there was no one like my Dad but he wasn't all that bad, besides, it annoyed Mum that Jim and I got on so well. He was a bit of a joker and we laughed together, Mum didn't.

I got a call 4 days later; Nan was in hospital. I went to see her while Lou looked after Lee for me, I met my sister there. Nan was propped up in bed with an oxygen mask on, she looked so small and frail, and not like the strong woman I'd known. She smiled and held my hand, she asked me to help with her pillows – they weren't quite right - we plumped them. She pulled the mask off the line; if we reconnected it once, during that visit, we did it a dozen times; it was so out of character for her, she seemed to find it amusing. She kept looking at me with such sadness in her eyes, the next moment she'd laugh. Finally she said;

"I don't think I'm going to get better, I'm not coming out of here."

I kissed her head and said;

"No, I know Nan, but you will be all right, I promise!"

She seemed calm and happy when we left, we waved goodbye, I knew I'd never see her again and I'm sure she knew too. The following day my uncle went to see her, he returned home saying, I think we should go to Mum, it's just about over. Awful but amusing - Nan had feigned death; she had lay there pretending, with her eyes closed, through the whole of his visit. Mum phoned the hospital only to be told that she was fine and had just got up to go to the toilet. My uncle was annoyed, I thought it was funny, even more so when the on following day ,on the 12th may 1977, they all went to visit her; Mum, her two sisters and their partners, my uncle and his partner. During the whole visit Nan said over and over;

"It's no good them waiting at the bar, it's too late, it's after time, they wont get a drink now!"

Nan had never been in a public house in her life, she hated the smell of beer, to the point that it made her vomit, she couldn't even wash a glass that had had beer in it, but she kept on and on about not being able to get a damn drink. She told them all, one after the other what she'd thought of them, Mum never said exactly what she had said but it wasn't very nice. She also said she wanted no crying at her funeral, she had said that before, along with things like;

"I've had my 3 score years and 10," "I'm living on borrowed time now" and   "I've eaten my pound of dirt."

They were all upset by her comments. My uncle and his snobby wife had always looked down on me; they were really upset, especially with her last comments about me. She said;

"I will be all right; do you know how I know? Because Janie said so!"

As I'd said those words, I really did feel that she would be all right.

She died peacefully, during the night, on the 13th of May 1977, aged 75years. Those final words meant more to me than anything she'd ever said or done, she did still love me. I knew she had died before I was told because early, on that same morning, as it was getting light, I opened my eyes to see her standing at the end of my bed, smiling, it frightened me and I closed my eyes again, when I opened them she was gone.

On the morning of the funeral we all met at Nan's, Dan came with me. I overheard my Auntie's criticizing me for wearing trousers; they were black and part of my suit, but they felt I should have worn a skirt. Dan and I went into the church ahead of them; I really didn't want to be in their company any longer than I had to. It was very difficult for me to enter the church; I hadn't been there since Carl's funeral. Nan was also being buried with my Pop pop, her husband. The grave had to be opened, coupled with Carl, just at the head of the grave in the next row. It was very hard to hold back those tears, but in accordance with Nan's wishes, I did just that. I did ask my Auntie to refrain from standing on Carl's grave, she said she didn't know it was there because there was no stone, I just said thanks for the reminder and Mum gave me a dirty look. I was quietly annoyed that none of the mourners had remembered my Nan's 'no tears' wish.

We all went back to Nan's again after the funeral for sandwiches and tea. Dan and I stayed for about half an hour whilst they argued about who should have what, like a bunch of grave robbers, my snob of an Auntie was the worst, saying;

"Caroline would like this," "Caroline wants that."
I couldn't stand it anymore, I said my goodbyes and we left, Dan was disgusted with their behaviour. I was happy to have my memories, especially those last words she'd said;

"I will be all right because Janie said so!"
That memory was and is mine. A few weeks later, Mum gave me some sheets, towels and a few plates, one plate, although cracked I still have. I was told it was what was left, nobody else wanted it; 'a bit like me really,' I thought. I said thanks though, they were useful.

August 16th 1977, Elvis Presley died; I had all his records on reel-to-reel tapes. I knew the lyrics of them all and had always played them loudly, singing along whilst doing my housework. Another dream I'd never have come true, to meet the man. I didn't fancy him like his fans or want to get him in the sack, just to be like a sister to him, to do a duet with him, not on release or anything. I had interests in other artists and particularly liked country music. Dan had always thought that I was odd; his preference in music was Pink Floyd, Black Sabbath and that sort of thing. Other than Elvis, I was always more interested in the particular songs and lyrics, rather than the artists singing them?

Chapter 20

September came and Dan was laid off again. Money soon became an issue, made worse because soon afterwards I became ill with an infection in my fallopian tubes and was unable to make love, much to Dan's annoyance. For three weeks I could hardly walk, so Dan looked after Lee, with the help of his Mum and when I had to go into hospital for tests, Lee was cared for at her house, very well cared for and thoroughly spoilt and I didn't have to worry about him. Dan spent his nights in the pub; he'd always gone out at least three nights a week anyway, so in or out of hospital, if I were ill or otherwise, it made no difference.

It wasn't until November, three weeks after I came out of hospital, that we made love again, it was over quickly and I was grateful. He was often rough, especially when he'd been drinking, on this particular occasion he hadn't been drinking but I still suffered for a week. The doctors found that I had a hormone imbalance; also, at some time or other, I'd had two miscarriages. I was told it might be difficult for me to have any more children because of the scarring of the tubes. Dan was quite happy with that idea, as he liked to remind me, he hadn't wanted children anyway and it was enough that Lee had taken my attention away from him. I wanted more children, I didn't want Lee to be an only child, and the idea of never being able to have more was devastating. My hormone imbalance made me depressed too, I had anxiety attacks and hated being alone, I was convinced that I would die. It was worse still when Dan took a job working nights, as a taxi driver. On the two nights he had off a week, he usually went to the pub. You know how most people have pots of paint? Half empty pots? Well, we also had a few and during one of my many attacks I mixed all those odd pots of paint together, came up with a very dark plum colour and painted the walls of our hallway with it. The hall ran the length of the centre of our flat and had no windows, it was naturally dark anyway. When Dan came in at 3:30am he was really angry, I told him why I'd done it, how I didn't do it to aggravate him, I needed to occupy myself, I was afraid. He turned to his whiskey, I knew what was coming. I tried to think of a way to placate him and went to bed, checking to make sure everything was tidy, hopefully he wouldn't find another reason. At 5:30am, it came, the hand across the back of my head, he punched me around the kidney area, screaming at me to get up. I did as I was told and tried to slip by him, he kicked me and I stumbled out of the room,

"Get me some breakfast," he hollered,

"What would you like?"

"What do you think?"

He called me all sorts of names - slut, slag. He stood at the kitchen door as I cooked him bacon and eggs, telling me how useless I was. I turned and gave him a warning look,

"Oooh I'd better go and sit down before you lose your temper."

He laughed and walked away. I took him in his breakfast and walked back into the kitchen, he followed a couple of minutes later and threw his plate on the draining board,

"I'm not eating that shit, I'm going to bed!"

Much to my relief he did… it was over. I cleaned up and went into the lounge. I lay on the settee and dozed off thinking about what I had done; I had asked for it, I shouldn't have painted the hall, it had seemed a good idea at the time, but I regretted it now.

Lee had slept through it all as usual, he was a very good baby and loved his sleep; he would go down at 6:30pm and not awake until 9am, except when he was ill, which was just as well given the circumstances. There were no visible bruises so nobody, other than Terry, knew what was happening, not for a long time anyway and Terry wouldn't say anything to Dan, if he did, he'd end up falling out with him, then he wouldn't be able to be there, to 'support me' and he said it could get worse. I was prescribed hormones pills but unfortunately they didn't have the desired effect, I was prescribed different ones. It took a further 8 months for me to feel anything like normal, either mentally or physically, I had a lot more whiskey beatings too.

July 1978 brought on yet another pelvic infection and I had to go into hospital for a laparoscopy. The results confirmed that of the previous diagnosis, it was thought that I had had a few miscarriages, though had probably been unaware of them, they were very early. It was therefore assumed that I possibly wouldn't be able to carry another child to full term. Dan said it was for the best;

"Lee will be at school in a year or so and we'll be free."

The beatings were about twice a month and with them came the apologies and the flowers, chocolates and I love you's.

To the outside world, he was a perfect husband and father; bringing his wife flowers and chocolates regularly. The perfect wife with the perfect home, always there for her husband. Weekends out with our son, visiting granny, going to theme parks or local parks. I wanted someone to see, not for us to split up, or divorce, just to say its wrong. It was one Saturday lunchtime, Dan had been to the pub and when he arrived home, I served him his favourite - egg, chips and beans. When he came in, I could see he was annoyed about something so I sent Lee into his room to play. Within minutes of Dan sitting down, he threw the Pyrex plate and contents at me, it hit me on the back of the head, spraying shards of white glass, beans and chips all over the kitchen and all over me. I heard a scream but realised it wasn't my own; Lee had seen what had happened and was standing in the doorway crying. Dan pushed past him and out of the front door; I scooped Lee up, trying to calm him with a cuddle;

"It's ok," I soothed, "Daddy's just in a bad mood."
I took him across the hall to Mary's flat and rang the bell - she now had two children and another on the way. Her husband Darren answered;

"Please, would you take Lee for a moment, whilst I sort myself out?" I asked, trying hard to play down the situation with a smile,

"Yeah, I see you've got your curlers in!" He joked nodding at my head,

"I'll be back in a minute."
I went in, cleaned up the kitchen and washed my hair; there was a lump and a small cut. I wrapped my hair in a towel and went back to get Lee. Mary motioned for me to come in and made me a coffee;

"I hadn't realised Dan was like that," she said seemingly concerned.

"Well he's not really, it was a one off and he's just having a bad time at the moment." I was trying to cover for him – although I was obviously unconvincing.

"Yeah ok, whatever you say, I'm here anytime though, you don't have to put up with it." She smiled wearily, I could see the pity in her eyes when she looked at me and I didn't want that; I thanked her, picked Lee up and left. She was right, I knew it but thought that Dan might change; deep down he was still all the wonderful things other people saw, it was the drink, that's all. I went back to the flat. Dan was back,

"I suppose you've told the neighbours how bad I am," he said, looking a little worried. I assured him I hadn't.

"What exactly did I do to deserve that Dan?" I asked, edging my way closer to him.

"You nag me!"

"Did I?" I questioned.

I hadn't said a word, had I? I tried to remember what I'd said but my head hurt. He picked Lee up;

"Daddy didn't mean it," he said cuddling him.

I truly believed he couldn't help it, he was ill, and I was in some way to blame, I should surely know the signs by now, maybe it would be the last time, he'd be more careful now the neighbours knew.

I went back to the hospital to see the specialist in November 1978, he re-iterated his previous diagnosis. I hadn't had any recurrence of the pain and my periods seemed back to normal, I was upset by his conclusion. I didn't bother to tell Dan, but decided that I wasn't going to leave it at that, there must be an answer. As it Was, I didn't need to do anything because in February 1979 I missed a period; I felt different and was sure I was pregnant. I waited 10 days and phoned the 'Life Organisation,' as I had done before; they were now situated near the central train station in town. I said nothing to anyone just took my sample of urine and kept the appointment. The lady I'd seen previously was no longer with them, I saw a much younger girl who was just as friendly. I didn't go into detail about my reasons for wanting an instant result but my delight was obvious, it was positive, who could I tell? I had to keep it to myself, for a while at least, Dan was sure to lose his temper and try everything he could to make me lose the baby. I'd have to see my G.P and the antenatal nurses as soon as possible. I made the appointments myself, telling no one of my elation and waited a further 10 days for the results. I confided in the nurse my fears about telling Dan; she said she understood why he might not like the idea;

"Children are expensive," she said, "but he'll come round, like he has with Lee."

She then told me something that I knew and she knew she shouldn't – Dan's brother's wife, Mallory, had just found out that she was expecting too, the due date for theirs was about 14th October, mine the 7th November. Maybe he wouldn't take it so bad, if his brother was in the same position… Maybe? I decided not to make a fuss about telling him, but he had to know sooner or later. He came in as usual, I let him have his dinner and I put Lee to bed, I gave him a cup of tea and the certificate from 'Life.' I said nothing, went back to the kitchen and started washing up, waiting for the fireworks to start. They didn't come, nothing at all. I couldn't stand it anymore;

"Well, what have you got to say?" The waiting was sometimes the worst part.

"Nothing!"

"Mallory's pregnant as well,"

"So what!" He shrugged.

"Hers is due three weeks before ours,"

"I'm going out, don't wait up!"

He got ready and left. I stayed awake, pretending to be asleep when he came, so that I was ready, but the beating didn't come, not then, not even in the weeks that followed, 'had he changed?' Everything was going quite well, every day I held on to the baby, I was closer to going full term. I would have to go through the amniocentesis test again, just as I had before but I was concerned this time, especially with all the miscarriages I'd supposedly had.

I was three months pregnant when I started bleeding. Dan went to work as usual. The doctor was called and he came straight out. I asked my sister to take care of Lee for me while I was being examined. I was in bed when the doctor arrived, he said he felt that I might have already lost my baby and if not, that it would probably happen in the next twenty-four to forty-eight hours;

"Stay in bed, take Paracetamol and drink plenty of fluids." Then he left.

'Was that it? I couldn't lose this baby now.' I did as I was told and stayed in bed, regardless of what Dan would say. Lou took Lee to her place for three days and my sister took care of me, with her there all the time I was safe. She was a real help for that week, we got to know each other again. Dan asked a few times how long she was staying; he was itching to get his hands on me, a source of amusement to me. Thankfully the bleeding soon stopped;

"Well, you still holding on to it or not?" Dan asked.

I was pretty sure I was but wouldn't know, for definite, until the following week. The doctor confirmed that I was still pregnant but said that he was almost certain I had lost one as well. Twins? A scan was arranged and to my surprise, Dan decided to come with me. I was sure he was only coming because he was hoping they would say it was a defective foetus... No, everything was normal, one normal baby, from what they could tell anyway, we would know for sure after the results of the amniocentesis. I went for that at 18 weeks but I was convinced that this little baby was meant to be.

The procedure had changed from the last one; it was almost 4 years since. The scans were better, but the biggest change was the size of the needle. This time it was like the needle used for a blood test, just a little longer and this time it didn't even need a plaster, I knew that the risks would be far less for this one. Dan actually came into the hospital to collect me. When we got home he even made me a cup of tea, and before he left for the pub he asked;

"Are you going to be all right on your own?"

"Yes," I replied, a little bemused, "I'm fine."

What sort of game was this? Was he up to something? I was sceptical but all the same, optimistic for the future.

At about 10am, I phoned for the results, they said it was a bit early, the results hadn't come back yet and I was to phone again later, at about 12pm. Those were the longest two hours of my life. Why had they said that? Had they found something they couldn't tell me? Please God don't let there be something wrong, not after all I'd been through to keep it inside me, not when it seemed Dan had accepted that we were going to have another child too. At twelve on the dot I phoned back and was told that everything was normal. I cried tears of relief still holding the phone,

"Are you ok?" Asked the nurse on the other end of the phone, I hadn't realised she was still there.

"Yes, I'm fine!" I quickly replied,

"Are you sure?"

"Yes honestly, it's just a relief."

"So, would you like to know what the sex of your baby is?"

I sure did...

"It's a girl!"

Finally, I had my perfect family. From then on I started buying pretty pink clothes, although Dan kept warning me not to get so carried away, things could still go wrong. He was right but I was excited. We didn't have a lot of money to spare, we never did, although things were especially tight at the time. That same week Lee had given forty-seven pounds away, he had thrown it out of his bedroom window to the kids in the neighbourhood; he said they had wanted to buy sweets. I managed, with the help of Mary, to find some of them and retrieve just fifteen pounds; it was the rent money for the flat. I was livid at the time, but not as angry as Dan would be when he got home, I had to find it before he got in. I tried everyone. I didn't want to go to Lou, again, but in the end I had no choice, it was a lot of money to lose back then. As always she came through for me, after she'd stopped laughing;

"Well yes, it is serious, but that's kids." She said.
She came straight round with the replacement money, sweets for Lee and a bunch of yellow roses from her garden for me;

"Come on," she said "lets go out for lunch!"
She often did that, she'd take us to the park, shopping or to visit her sister, Auntie Susan. It was on one of these outings that I finally confided in her; I told her how violent Dan had been in the past, I felt I could tell her now because Dan wasn't as bad anymore, he had been verbally nasty but not physically, so maybe he had changed. Lou wasn't surprised by what I told her, even though it was her son;

"You don't have to put up with it, he has no right to do that to you, if... or rather, when it starts again; walk away."

"I don't think he will do it again," I said, "he has been different this time,"

"That's the mistake I made with his father, a leopard never changes its spots."
She looked away and we both sat in silence for a time. I couldn't believe what I was hearing, could it be that my Lee would be the same in the future? No way, not in my lifetime. I made it very clear to Lee from then on that it was wrong, should he ever lay a hand on a woman I'd kill him myself. He never has and yet, he's had far more provocation than I ever gave his father. Lou had told me that Dan's Brother, Mark, had also hit his wife and it had been at around the same time. It was more confirmation that this kind of thing can run in families, I decided that it was stopping with me.

126

Lou had found a good husband in Sam, he was a 'mans - man,' a real lad, a drinker and a gambler, he could afford it though. He was loud and a joker, a show off but a real family man as well, he loved the kids around him, took them to football at the weekends or on picnics. I wished Dan could have been like that and I think secretly, he did too.

My sister and I had become close again, she was going to be married in August to Jeff, and she had been with the same man all this time. I couldn't help thinking that this was typical, she was the perfect daughter, with a perfect relationship and the man of her dreams, she would probably have a perfect marriage as well, everything in the preferred order. I was envious of her, but all the same, I truly wished her all the very best of everything.

She came to see me in June 1979. She was pregnant. She was now living with Jeff, at his mother's home, she didn't have anything but was happier there than living with Mum and Jim. She said she felt Mum was only interested in Jim; Verity didn't get on that well with him. Mum had done it again, walked away from her last daughter, in favour of a man, I considered though that perhaps it could have been that the attention, had been taken away from Verity and she rebelled. Miss perfect wasn't quite so perfect after all, pregnant before married as well... Tut tut. She was just like her big sister, regardless of Mum taking her away to save her from my influence. And So, on the one hand I was gloating but on the other, I knew what my sister was going through, how she was feeling and I think it helped her to know I was there. My baby sister was all grown up, pregnant and to be married and with Dan's brothers baby well on it's way, I'd be an Auntie twice within that year.

By the time Verity and Jeff's wedding came around, I was heavily pregnant. The whole family turned up, all except my Dad, he had declined the invitation for one reason I think... Diane had not been invited. Even though I was far from keen on Diane, she was still Dad's choice; I couldn't have omitted her from the guest list. Jim gave Verity away. Even my brother and his girlfriend made an appearance; I don't think he would have come to mine, even if he hadn't been otherwise detained. As usual everyone was chatting away to Aaron like the prodigal son and I felt uncomfortable, a bit out of place but I was there for my sister, she'd wanted me there, who cared what they thought. Lee was quite a sensation, very smart and polite. I was very proud of my son. I watched as he was introduced to family members, he shook hands and flashed everyone a big smile, his big blue eyes and blonde hair shining.

"What a handsome child."

Everybody said so, I even heard someone sound surprised that he belonged to me, and surely someone like me couldn't have produced such a beautiful child?

"...Must take after his father's side!"

Part of a conversation I over heard between two of my Aunties. I will never know what I did to deserve that treatment from Mum's family. I could have been the model child, have done everything by the book but I would still, never have been a valued member of that family. To the outside world I couldn't care less, but when you believe that nobody likes you, it does hurt. You can build up so many barriers but in the end, it gets the better of you. My Mums family aside, this was Verity's big day. I knew her Mother in law already and was introduced to all her husbands' family. They were all rough and ready, spoke as they saw, real down to earth people. They argued amongst themselves but woe betides anyone who came between them. They'd go in, in force and fight the world for one of their own, not like ours who scattered at the first sign of trouble. They were just how a family should be; I decided that was how my children would be, like them. My little sister would be happy amongst them. They've had their ups and downs over the years but for most part, she has been.

Chapter 21

My sister in law, Mallory, gave birth to a baby girl on the 21st of October 1979, Lou and I went to see her the very next day. My niece was totally bald, except for a tuft of hair, sticking up in the middle, not the prettiest of babies. My thoughts aside, I congratulated them on the arrival of their beautiful daughter. Her name was to be Marilyn. Mallory and I had attended antenatal check-ups together for the last few appointments. She had always wanted a boy as her first born; as do most people but when Marilyn arrived she was ecstatic. The baby had been a week late and after a really rough labour, coupled with a forceps delivery, not to mention a lot of stitches, she was glad to get it was over with. I still had just over two weeks to go. I had already experienced two labours; the first recorded as four hours and the second as only two hours, all the same I was anxious and couldn't wait to meet my baby.

I started getting niggly pains on Sunday 28th of October, though nothing regular. I went to my antenatal check on Monday morning, as usual, although the pains were still not regular or even that painful. I seemed to be losing water while I was at the hospital, my waters hadn't broken surely? I thought it best to visit the nurse, just to be safe; she put me into a bed on the antenatal ward for some tests. It was early afternoon before I was able to leave, they said that the baby was lying very low and they thought that it was me, my waters hadn't broken, I was wetting myself. I was so embarrassed, although, pretty positive that I would know if I had wet myself, I was confident my baby was on its way. I told Dan who'd said, if that was the case, he would have preferred I had been kept in hospital, he didn't want the responsibility of looking after me, he had a darts match arranged and it was his night out. I told him not to worry and to go and enjoy himself. He went out that night and Tuesday night too. I was losing water all the time now, but the pains were still irregular. I had, had a few weird dreams aswell, one in particular; my baby was born normally but was whisked away before I had chance to see it, the nurses told me that it was a girl, but had to be boiled for three minutes to harden, I still laugh about that to this day. I can only imagine what must have been going through my mind, all I can assume is that when pregnant, I hated the smell of frying eggs and the memory of Carl being taken away was always with me.

I was convinced that I'd give birth on Halloween, and that the baby would be a witch. I had recently developed a wart on my leg and had never had one before, it was a sign, I mused. But Halloween came; Dan and I took Lee to a model village museum and a firework display as we had promised. The pains were stronger that night but I didn't mention it to Dan. I decided that if it continued, I'd better see the doctor. I saw the GP at 3pm the following day, the 1st November. He was sure I was in labour, my front waters had fractured and he told me that I would have to go straight into hospital and gave me letter to take with me. Dan and Lee picked me up and we went to find Lou, she wasn't at home, we went to look for her, almost sure she would be doing her shopping at the supermarket. It was 5pm by the time we found her and she was only too willing, as always, to take Lee. By 6pm I was in a hospital bed on the antenatal ward, hooked up to a monitor and a drip. I had argued with the nurse, I was in labour and so should be on the labour ward, she didn't agree! Dan was getting agitated again, so I decided it would be best to do as they said. An hour later and they finally agreed that I should have gone straight to the labour ward. My contractions were now every two to three minutes apart and regular, I was well on the way. They had put a monitor onto the baby's head and a nurse sat watching. This was to be her last delivery, she said she had seen hundreds of baby's born, this was a classic boy if ever she saw one, I told her that the tests had said it was a girl but she was adamant, tests were often wrong. At one stage the monitor showed a line, nothing, my baby's heart had stopped. The nurse turned the monitor away and turned the volume down, without a word to me or Dan.

"What's wrong?" I asked, slightly dazed,

"Everything's fine," she tried to assure me with a slight smile, but I could hear the panic in her voice. She rang the emergency bell, the doctor and midwife came in, by now I was a complete wreck, as was Dan. We needn't have been worried though, the monitor had become detached from the baby's head and all was fine, a few minutes more and I'd be delivering.

"Are you staying for this?" The midwife directed the question to Dan,

"No," he replied, "I'd rather not!"

"I suggest you leave then or you'll have no choice!" She said.

I've never seen him move so quickly, he was like a rabbit, orange hair flying. I didn't mind, I had expected just this, my only concern at that time was for my baby and although trivial, I was dreading that my baby would have that same orange hair. I needn't have worried, on either case, ten minutes later at 8:25pm our daughter arrived. She was beautiful, she had long, jet black hair, it was at least three inches long all over. She was perfect, like a little doll weighing just 6lb 4oz and measuring only eighteen and a half inches long.

My 'perfect girl' was handed to me, wrapped in a towel, she opened her eyes and I knew she was going to be so bright, intelligent and sensible, an angel! Even her daddy was lost for words, he held back the tears. She was at my side every minute and was the talk of the hospital; the nurses from 'antenatal' came to see her saying,

"We hope you don't mind? We had to see this little girl everyone is talking about, what's her name?"

"Lorna Marie!" I said proudly,
I loved her name and I hoped she would. People don't usually like their own names, I know, I hated mine – Janet!! Mum had said that it would have been Jennifer, only trouble; I didn't look like one when I was born. I had long black hair too, although it was cut, straight away, it was considered 'unhygienic' at that time. All the nurses agreed that her name was perfect.

I had one scare with Lorna whilst in hospital; we were in quarantine because it was a dry birth. Either Lorna or I had picked up an infection, I was feeding her and as I winded her, she choked, milk and mucus came out of her nose and mouth, I couldn't clear it and she was going blue. I ran with her to the nursery, by now she was limp, I burst in through the door but the nurses took no notice until I said,

"Excuse me, my baby's choking!"
All hell broke loose. They grabbed her, put tubes down her throat and up her nose, within a few seconds, she was fine again, drama over.

I took Lorna home the following day. I dressed her in a pink, lace, knitted dress and coat that Mary, my neighbour, had knitted by hand. She was even more beautiful in her own clothes. Lee loved her; he kept kissing and cuddling her, telling everyone he had a sister. Dan too, was thrilled; he had taken up photography and took photographs of them both at every opportunity. Mum came to see her and also had to admit that my children were beautiful. Just maybe I had become someone she could be proud to call her daughter.

I wrote to my brother who was inside again and told him about Lorna, he wasn't pleased that I'd had a girl but congratulated me anyway. Other than the episode of choking, I had no problems with her, she slept between four hourly feeds and at just four days old, she missed out her 2am feed. By three weeks old she was sleeping 6pm-6am, this helped to keep Dan happy and we were, for a time, the perfect family that I had dreamed of.

Chapter 22

I'm not sure when it all went wrong again, exactly. Lorna was a few weeks old and Lee had just turned four. It was after Christmas and Dan had bought a new car, which he'd spent every spare minute fixing up, I didn't mind, he was happy. He was almost finished with it; he'd put in a new engine, all that was left was to put in the oil and water, but as it was now too dark to see what he was doing, he decided to leave it until the following day. The car was stolen that night – maybe that was the moment that my happy family changed. The car was found just two roads away, the engine had seized because of the lack of oil and water. Dan couldn't get to work so he stayed home with me and the kids all day. He told me I'd spent too much money on the kids over Christmas, what with the car being stolen and the neighbours coming and going, it all got too much for him and he just lost control, again. As the weeks past, the slightest thing would set him off. We soon got another car through the insurance, still he remained in self-destruct mode and it continued. To start with, the abuse was verbal, comments like;

"God, you are so fat and ugly! Do something with yourself, you're good for nothing!"

He also said that I didn't care about him, that I was only interested in the kids – an argument that always ended with him reminding me that he'd never wanted them in the first place. I had to admit it, my kids were my life and I was fat at thirteen stone. I was only good enough for him when the light was out.

We carried on like that until Lorna was six months old, then things went from bad to worse; Dan's little Gran had a stroke, he had been the apple of her eye and she was the one woman in the world he respected. We went to see her in hospital, she couldn't speak or move and Dan couldn't speak to her, he was so afraid and it showed in his eyes. He would sit, looking into her eyes, never saying a word. She looked back, pleading, but he just could not speak. We stayed for about half an hour, he kissed her cheek and a tear appeared in the corner of her eye, I kissed her too,

"We will be back tomorrow," I whispered. I knew then, she wouldn't get better. On the way home I told Dan my fears, in the most sincere way possible; I was punched in the side of the head;

"I didn't need you to tell me that, you'd like that wouldn't you?" He screamed;

"You'd like her to die!"

What had I done? I should have kept my mouth shut, I didn't want her to die, and I loved that little lady. One thing was different about this assault, it wasn't alcohol fuelled, and he hadn't been drinking! We didn't go back to the hospital, with my bruised face so very visible, I couldn't. Little Gran died two days later. I will remember the look of grief on Dan's face forever. She was just sixty-five years old, yet her twin sister lived well into her eighties.

My sister gave birth to a baby boy, Craig, on January the 25th 1980 (Lou's birthday). I saw Verity quite regularly, not though, when I had bruises, nobody saw me then. Lee had started school after Christmas; still, he didn't go to school if there had been a fight. I used his asthma as an excuse to the school, although his asthma was quite bad at times, coincidently, worse a day or so after the arguments. Terry knew what was happening and this was his cue to get his foot in the door again, who else could I talk to, he understood me! I couldn't tell Lou that it was happening again; she'd just lost her Mum and would've undoubtedly told me to leave him. I couldn't confide in Verity, she had her own life and besides, she would tell Mum and I knew she would be on Dan's side, I knew she would've probably said that I'd asked for it. I kept it to myself! Dan would go out Monday, Wednesday, Thursday and Friday nights, which put the potential for beatings at four times a week. Although it didn't happen every time he was drinking and for the most part, there were no visible bruises.

I had to do something to get my life back in order, I was the problem, Dan had said as much, that I was fat and wouldn't do anything - I started to lose weight, initially for him, maybe he'd love me again. If I had no control over any other aspect of my life, this was one thing I could have power over. I tried a calorie controlled diet to begin with, sensible eating with one thousand calories a day, it wasn't good enough and I soon cut down to eight hundred calories. I lost weight at the rate of a pound a day; I had set myself a target, to get to ten stone. Two months later, I reached it, the scales had stuck around ten stone, eight pounds for a few days so, I cut the calories once more, to just four hundred the weight loss sped up again. People were telling me how good I looked, I liked that but Dan wasn't very happy, the more I turned heads, the tighter the reign. He wanted to know why I'd started losing weight,

"Who are you trying to impress?" He had asked.

134

I told him he'd made me see how I had let myself go, with his comments about how fat I was, I was trying to be more attractive to him, he didn't believe me. Whatever I did, it was never good enough for him, at that point I decided, I was losing weight for me, I didn't care how many beatings I got. My life! My body! The more he tried to control me, the more determined I became. People were still paying me compliments – 'people' including my Mum, I was on to a winner. I couldn't see enough change and decided to continue, maybe another stone or so! I became obsessed with the scales and would weigh myself twenty times a day, always before I ate, then again after. If there was a fluctuation I would get angry with myself - All I needed to do was get rid of it, before I digested it, so, fingers down the throat and laxatives. That worked for a while, I passed the nine stone mark, and then to eight stone, ten pounds, I thought I looked great.

A few weeks earlier, I'd met with Mum and my sister to do some shopping and she'd said how good I looked. As I stepped off the bus on this occasion, the look on her face said something different;

"My God! What have you done to yourself? She continued, "I was pleased that you'd lost some weight but you have gone too far with this!"

I thought I'd looked wonderful, she was just jealous, this was the usual thing of 'lets put Jan down,' - in my mind anyway. All the same, when I got home I looked hard in the mirror and for the first time, I could see what she saw; my face was sunken in, my eyes looked enlarged, she was right! It was a hard road back; everything I ate made me feel sick. I had a problem and needed to put weight back on but not too much, I would go back up to about nine and a half stone. On occasions I slipped back but I was still in control, I could put it on and I could lose it.

Mum started coming round to the flat with Jim; she went to a local pub at lunchtimes to eat and had to pass my door to go home, usually on a Thursday. She'd say Jim had suggested it;

"Make time for a coffee," he had said.

I think though it was initially her idea, she was genuinely concerned and since the comments about my weight I had been making excuses not to meet up with her. The first time they turned up, I was really shocked to find them stood on my Doorstep;

"Get the kettle on," Jim said giving me a friendly nudge,

"What, have you come to check up on me?" I said, referring to Mum,

"Nope, Jim's idea!"

I didn't believe her, not on that day, but, as the weeks and months
went by and they turned up every week, I had to believe it. She,
certainly, wouldn't make that much effort for me. Jim and I became quite good friends; Mum didn't like it and made it obvious
with the looks she gave me. Jim would often give me a little peck
on the cheek when they left, at which point Mum would always say
things like;

"You shouldn't encourage him," or remarks like "Put him
down!"

It was never me that instigated it and it was always just a peck, but
Mum hated that we got on so well, so she made it something sinis-
ter and tainted.

I remember, Jim always loved songs by the singer Jim
Reeves and there was a country singer who sang tribute songs, regularly, in the pub that they went to. One evening he invited Dan
and I to join them. We went and I enjoyed myself so much, I wanted to go again, I would have gone along, with, or without Dan, but
there was no way he'd let me out without him, so he tagged along,
besides he and Mum got on quite well. On one occasion, Jim suggested I sing with the vocalist, performing. I was nervous but had
had a few beers which gave me a bit of courage. Besides, Jim wanted me to and it was just after his birthday too, so I agreed to sing a
song of his choice; Jim Reeves - 'Put your sweet lips.' I knew the
lyrics of a vast range of songs, which was something I'd always
been good at, memorising lyrics. Yes, me... something I was good
at!

"Bet you don't know the words?" Jim heckled,

"Bet I do!" I replied, then sang it through flawlessly, I even
got a round of applause and a few asked for more.

"Go on," the singer nudged, "do us one more."

So I did, I sang; 'I wont forget you,' another Jim Reeves number.
Jim was over the moon, and Mum and Dan had to admit, in spite of
themselves, that I was good, especially as people in the pub were
shaking their hands and saying how much they'd enjoyed it;

"You should take it up professionally!" Many advised.

Something that fell on deaf ears where Dan was concerned. Jim
was even more pleased when he and Mum went to Dorchester mar-

ket the following day, some thirty miles away and Jim was approached by two strangers;

"Was that your daughter singing last night?" They chorused,
"Yes!" He replied,
"She's very good,"
"Yes she is!" He'd said, apparently very proud. When they got back he got Mum to phone and tell me, even she had to admit that she had felt a little proud of me. From then on, whenever they visited me, the greeting was;

"Hello daughter!"
He wasn't my Dad, I only had one of those, but he was a pretty good surrogate one.

In June 1981 things were going quite well for Dan, he was working for his Step father, Sam, selling double glazing and surprisingly, he was quite good at it, he was earning a very good wage. Life was looking up for us again; Dan was still being violent on occasion, although I just accepted it. I got a little more confidence and eventually joined my sisters dart team, Dan would come with me for the most part but if he couldn't make it, for any reason, he entrusted me to Terry's care. Dan was out the most of the week and weekends too, he spent his time sailing his boat, which was moored locally. We started going out together on Saturday evenings and even some Sundays, but only when he wasn't with his sailing buddies or at the golf club. He had a very busy social life. We got to know a lot of local musicians, some became friends and would come home with us after closing for coffee, I would be expected to make sandwiches, then wash up and bed, sometimes I would get a beating before I could sleep, and still, nobody knew.

I started rebelling, as far as I could see; I was the perfect wife and housewife to him, perfect mother to my children. Where was he? He had entrusted me to a man that, every so often, would molest me on the way home and I was paying for his petrol. It was always very quick; he didn't want Dan to become suspicious. In some ways I wish he had, at least it would have stopped. On one occasion, Terry wasn't available to collect me from home, but was available to pick me up at the end of the evening, Dan couldn't take me either. I persuaded Dan to let me get the bus, he reluctantly agreed, I was needed, I couldn't let the team down, could I? He watched me dress, do my make-up, he ordered me to change my clothes, twice, saying I looked like a right slag. I closed the front door leaving him in the hallway with a look that could've killed. I

137

was to phone him the second I got to the pub, he'd checked the bus times and would know if I arrived there late. I walked out of the flat into the evening air, it was a wonderful feeling, freedom, albeit only a couple of bus rides, but it was exhilarating. An hour of not answering to anyone, although I was afraid of missing my connecting bus, if I managed to get it right this time, he might trust me to do it regularly, maybe even to come home alone, no more 'petrol payments.'

We had been on the housing transfer list since I'd given birth to Lorna and having a boy and a girl, we would be entitled to a three-bedroom property. We had looked at some new houses being built locally by the council, for private buyers who were on the list and were offered one, the second of our choice of three. We could afford a mortgage quite easily with Dan's earnings and the discount we received as council tenants helped. The only clause we could see was that if we sold it within three years, we would have to return part of the discount. At the end of July 1981 we moved into our own home and it was great. Even though Dan was possessive and aggressive, he was a good provider. I continued with my darts, seeing my sister and her in laws there. They were a family of extremely good dart players, Bev (Verity's Mother in law) had been a county player at times over the years, and Jane and Wanda (Verity's sister in laws) were also in the team. I wasn't one of the best dart players in the world or the pub, not even close; it was always more luck than skill. As Verity would say, every week without fail;

"Now we are going to play our joker!"
It was a laugh, it was company and it got me out of the house, it was just the getting home that was the problem. More and more I caught the bus, Dan and I discussed it and he decided I could take driving lessons, although he later regretted it. A couple of years later he said that it was the worst thing he'd ever allowed me to do, obviously I had too much freedom, I could get around much faster in a car and he couldn't keep track of me. The pub we played darts for was pretty rough, but because most of the patrons were friends, I never felt threatened, with or by any of them, I was much safer there than at home. I even flirted, quite obviously with the men, although it was never taken seriously. I'd kept my weight down and quite liked my appearance now, in fact for the first time in my life, I quite liked myself. Dan would come with me, on occasion, just to satisfy himself that everything was above board.

It was about that time that I met a man, who has played a very major part in my life over the last few years, Ken. He was the husband of one of our team; he chalked the score board for us, just occasionally. His wife Dorris spent her time chatting to another of our team Beatrice, so, whilst I was waiting my turn to throw I'd chat to him, nothing flirty, just about his work or how his week had been. Although looking back there was an obvious attraction on both sides, but he was married and so was I. I saw him about half a dozen times; I'd get the occasional warning look from his wife, as if to say hands off, he's mine, but I knew that already, didn't I, so there really was no need.

A few weeks later and Dan really lost his temper with me, looking back, it was obvious that the violence had taken a more serious step but, as usual, I tried to persuade myself that it was a one off. I ended up with 2 black eyes, the odd slip over the years, when he had caught me wrong, I would get a bruise that would show, but could cover it with make-up. This time I couldn't, it was really bad and intentional; I had to stay in for a few weeks and didn't see anyone, well except Terry. I had absolutely no idea what I'd done to deserve it; I guessed I must have done something. Dan apologised as usual and bought me a dog, a golden Labrador called Duke. He had known that I'd always wanted one. A few weeks after we got him, he chewed up the kitchen floor covering, we'd only put it down the day before, after Terry had decorated the kitchen for us. Lee burst into our bedroom on a Sunday morning shouting;

"Mum, the dogs ate the kitchen floor!"

Mind, after the initial shock, I had to laugh, so did Dan surprisingly. We had another incident that indirectly involved the dog that we found hilarious. It was about 3:30am, in the early hours of a Sunday, Dan and I had had a few drinks, out with some musician friends, I could hear a clip clop noise outside in the road. I woke Dan and we got up and looked out of the window to see Lee, Lorna and the dog walking up and down outside, Lee in his pyjamas, holding Lorna's hand with one hand and the dog lead in the other. She was dressed in a pink nightie, my high heeled shoes and a straw, wide brimmed hat, with pieces of fruit around it, not real fruit, Lou had brought it back from their holiday in Barbados. I tried to be angry with them, telling them how dangerous it could have been, there could have been nasty people, strangers about but they looked so funny. One of many times my kids have made me laugh over the years, they kept me sane.

139

By the same token, they were the reason I stayed with their Dad, or partly, I didn't want my children to be from a broken home, a statistic, like I was. There were other reasons; he was always generous with his money, he gave me much more than was required to keep house, besides, I really did think he was ill, he couldn't help being the way he was, it was in his genes. People liked him and for the most part, I liked him, when he wasn't violent he was really nice. He just had this thing, having to be in control, paranoid and insecure. As the beatings got worse, the presents to say sorry became more expensive and elaborate. I suppose if I'd thought about it, I could have caused even more arguments to get anything I wanted. Another occasion, he kicked me in the back of the leg and I fell down the stairs, I was bruised all over, but the worst was the injury to my back, I had slipped a disc. Once that had happened to my back, it was never the same again, even though the disc had sort of gone back. I had told the doctor that I'd slipped and fallen, I had no choice, I was warned, if I said how it had happened, I'd get worse! My gift of apology for this? A P.A system and microphone, I would set it up, sing along with records and make recordings of my voice. I'd learnt microphone technique along the way and I still had it, I had also held on to the dream to be a singer. Dan said there was no way, if I did get into a band (which he doubted), he would be staying at home looking after the kids, whilst I was out gallivanting, hanging around in pubs and clubs. I suggested that if anything came of it I wouldn't gig away from home anyway, I would never leave my children, besides, he could be my manager. Also, Sam's daughter, Abbey, had just come to live with them, she was 13 years old and sister to Alan, therefore Dan's step sister, she could baby-sit, and she had already done so a few times. Mind you, she was hard work, she had been told that her father was dead and that Sam was Uncle Sam. Her mother couldn't cope with her (where had I heard that before). When Abbey had taken an overdose and was in hospital, her mother phoned Sam to go and collect her and told him that he'd have to let her live with him, poor kid had a double whammy, especially as Sam told her that he was in fact her father and that her little brother, whom she'd carried a photograph of was in fact dead. I felt sorry for her and allowed her to spend a lot of time with me. Lou found it difficult to cope with her, mainly because she'd never had to deal with girls, especially ones who already had the emotional damage that Abbey had. On one occasion, Abbey came to see me when Terry was

140

there; I'd sort of outlined her problems to Terry. Each time I went to Terry's after that I took her with me, not on the evenings that I went to darts.

I was now driving and I passed my test on Friday the 13th September, on my first attempt. I shouldn't have done, the lesson before my test was awful, I kangarooed all over Bournemouth. My driving instructor was a lovely man, although past retirement age. Dan was happy to let him teach me because he had been Dan's instructor and had also taught his mum, (who had taken four attempts to pass) and considering his age, Dan didn't see him as a threat. About half way through the lesson before my test, at 9am on a Friday morning, my instructor said;

"Well I don't know what the matter with you is today, but if you are going to drive like this, we'd just as well pack it up and go home now."

We continued, the test that followed was through one of the busiest parts of Bournemouth, in rush hour and my manoeuvres were diabolical, I reversed around a corner and up on to the pavement saying, out loud mind you,

"Oh shit!"

The examiner gave me a sideways glance and said;

"Carry on."

I thought, I'm bound to have failed, summoning up the courage to say;

"Do you want me to do it again?"

"No, carry on."

I thought, 'yep failed!' Or maybe not? We came up to a junction, on a hill and were running backwards, again he spoke;

"Uhum, we are moving!"

"Oh yes, so we are." I replied.

He asked me rather a lot of questions on the Highway Code. I must however, have been confident and shown it or something, as he filled in the green form, he said,

"I'm pleased to tell you, you've passed, good morning."

He was out of the car and gone, I thought perhaps I'd frightened him. I waited for my instructor, as he approached I put both thumbs up, he ran to the car, threw his arms around me and kissed me. I thought, 'oh boy, I wonder what Dan would make of that.' Dan bought my instructor a bottle of whiskey for his patience; it had after all, taken almost a year of lessons to get me through. I missed

141

my weekly driving lessons and my instructor; he's dead now and has been for some years. I never told Dan about his response to my passing.

Dan had bought me a pale blue, Triumph 1300, I loved it. He'd bought it months before I passed, I could sit in it and clean it but I couldn't drive it, I wasn't insured and no way would he take me out. He had only allowed me to drive once, in a Zephyr we'd had in about 1976, I had tried to drive around a local car park one night, it was supposed to be for a laugh. After about 15 minutes it was far from funny, Dan said he would never let me drive that car again. Which was in fact true, the engine blew up a week later, and this was automatically my fault. Dan was still working for Sam, who had opened a new show room near Southampton; he wanted someone to deliver leaflets in the local area. Sam had asked Dan to ask me if I would do it for him, I could take Lorna with me, Lee was at school, he said he would give me pocket money, about £30 a day plus petrol. Well, how could Dan refuse, what could he say, I couldn't do it because he didn't trust me. I only worked for about 6 weeks in the end, I was meeting a musician friend (Bill, who lived in Southampton) for lunch, only once or twice, but made the mistake of telling Dan. Bill was a friend to both of us and Lorna was with me, I really didn't see any harm in it, however the bruises said different. He told Sam that he'd better find someone else; the travelling was too much for me. I could never have a life; I'd never be able to do anything.

Chapter 23

I was so down about being shut in, as I was, after having that taste of freedom, I couldn't handle it. I started drinking. The first of the day just after taking Lee to school, at nine in the morning, then would continue throughout the day. What started as one to get me through the day, turned into several, although I was never completely legless, my house was always spotless and my children were well looked after. All the same, the use of alcohol numbed reality.

Terry had been visiting a lot and I was sceptical about his intentions. He turned up one morning, earlier than I'd expected and found me sat on the stairs, slightly worse for wear. I'd never seen that look of hurt on his face before, he was upset to see me in such a state and for the very first time, I knew his concerns were genuine. He took the bottle from me and emptied it down the sink, Terry's mother had been an alcoholic and the booze had killed her, just before she reached sixty years old. We talked for a long while and that day I told him everything, I didn't fumble with the truth, just let it all come out, he listened and I told him how lonely I was, how I needed more in my life, outside those four walls. He said he understood but still felt I would be worse off if Dan and I were to divorce.

"Why not find your friends again? You know, Gemma and maybe even Penny? Come over and see Iris," he continued,

"you've got the car now, but you can't drive with Lorna in the car when you've been drinking, can you?"
It was a good idea, maybe if I were happier, then Dan would be too, Even if he wasn't, I would have something else to think about, something to stop me from becoming the person Dan had drummed into my skull, the person I had been for so long. Terry was a good confidant to me that day; I never told him that he was actually part of the problem. He never saw himself as a problem either.

I had kept in contact with Gemma over the last few years, but not regularly. After my chat with Terry I arranged to go to her home, once a week and have lunch with her and her children – it was a start. She now had three kids, all under the age of five. Lee, the eldest, who was now at school, Craig was three years old and then Claire, who had just turned two, was six months older than

Lorna. 'She' as Gemma had said, was an accident; Craig was only a year old when Claire was born, it was very hard for her. She and Jack weren't getting on; he was out all night and made no secret of his affairs. He would leave Gemma with no money or food and disappear for the night. So I'd take food over to her, give her money and often pick her up, bringing her to my home, a change of scenery for her too. We then started seeing each other twice a week. I really felt for her, she had done so much for me, letting Dan and I stay in her home when really, she didn't know us. Even though our first meeting was shaky we became good friends and now I was able to return the favour. I was pretty well off, financially anyway and had my own home. I should have been happy, I now had everything I had ever wanted, didn't I? I had more than most, a far cry from those early days. The only thing I didn't have was the only thing that money couldn't buy; love. Much as I tried, it just wasn't there.

Gemma and I would take off in the car with the kids to the park, feed the ducks and go to the beach. We'd take Abbey aswell sometimes. Lou and Abbey didn't see eye to eye at all, she wouldn't go to school and when she did, she would get into trouble. One morning I had nothing to do so I decided to take Lorna and go to Iris'. I arrived to find Abbey there and found out that when she should have been at school, she had actually been there quite a lot. Terry had been picking her up at the end of Lou's road in the mornings, taking her home again at the end of the school day. What was also obvious was that Terry was sleeping with her, unbeknown to Iris of course. He really did like thirteen year old girls; I was thirteen when he first met me, Iris was also that age when they first met and now Abbey. He also seemed to pick on vulnerable girls and that was obvious too. I argued with him over it and told him what I thought. He swore that nothing was happening between them and that she was just unhappy. I took Abbey back with me that day and my attitude to Terry changed completely. He was no different than all the other men I'd ever met, a user. That was it, he was a pervert, it was all very clear to me now and I would never let him use me again, no matter what the outcome. I wasn't drinking anymore, so I had my independence, my car, my children and my friends. Iris and Terry had another daughter, Anna, they now had five kids, and Dan and I were Godparents to Anna. I had a responsibility to Anna and Abbey; I owed it to Lou to tell her what was going on but I couldn't. Everyone would be hurt, I had, after all, introduced Abbey to Terry, it was my fault. I told Abbey she must never go there again without me, or there would be no choice but to tell her father what was happening, she agreed. Abbey ran away the very same week and was staying at Terry's; she had in fact moved in. Sam and Lou had collected her from there several times, but she kept running back. Dan blamed me for introducing her to them and beat me senseless. Lou and Sam were experiencing problems, fuelled mostly by Abbey, but according to Dan, I was also responsible for that. Lou never blamed me, in fact, although Abbey now living at Terry's was less than ideal, at least Lou was free of the responsibility. Shortly after Abbey left, she and Sam got back onto an even keel. Dan and I didn't, but then it didn't seem to effect me so much, I had changed.

It was about this time that I decided to find Penny again, my friend from the hostel, I drove to Blandford, I remembered roughly, even after all those years, where she had lived but had no idea if she was still there. I was a nervous driver, in areas that I didn't know, so it had taken a lot to pluck up the courage to drive the distance. I found her mum, Ruby, I'd met her just once when Penny and I had visited her, yet she remembered me. She was such a character, black, shoulder length hair, wrinkled face. I knew where Penny got her looks and character from, although she was a lot slimmer than Penny and so fit, her party piece was performing cartwheels up the road, she was in her mid fifties then.

"Penny lives in Blandford town centre." Ruby said, in her broad Dorset accent. She didn't know the actual address but it was between two buildings, above a pub, in a flat somewhere, with her husband. Well I had no chance of finding that so I left my telephone number. Penny rang the following week; she would come down for the day, if I picked her up.

We threw our arms around each other. She was still exactly the same, if a little stockier. Eccentric, telling jokes and acting the fool, she never knew it, but she was a breath of fresh air to me. She had no children of her own, though her husband had been married before and had one daughter, who lived with his ex wife. She didn't want kids anyway and liked her freedom, although she liked kids and was brilliant with my two, who fell in love with her immediately, as did the dog, Duke. I laughed more that day than I had done in years, we promised to stay in touch regularly. She remembered Dan and liked him, as he did her, although he said she was completely mad. Penny was, however suspicious of him, she had seen my reaction when he was due home, rushing around and cleaning up, getting his dinner ready on time, putting the toys away, getting the kids ready for bed.

"God, sit down woman, what's your problem?" She would ask. Dan was always sweetness itself whilst she was there, a kiss when he came in and a thank you for his dinner. He told Penny how well I looked after him, he said I was a good wife and a good mother, he couldn't wish for more. Penny phoned me the following day and insisted on the truth. I told her some of it, but held back on the real details.

"He's just very particular." I said "I get into trouble when I get it wrong, that's all!"

"Yeah ok, have it your way, if you say so." She knew!

The dog had taken to running away too. I had to pick him up from the police station twice. On the first occasion, he'd been found darting in and out of traffic on a busy road. He would eat everything, even my flowers from the garden. Tulips, he devoured, although he wasn't keen on daffodils, when the buds opened up they were all frayed around the edges where he'd nibbled at them, he tried the roses too, deciding they were best dug up... completely, the lawn to. My garden looked like the Falklands, great big potholes all over and when it rained - very muddy! One day I remember when I had just watered my garden and was in the shed, the dog had been rolling around in the mud, his yellow coat now thick and brown. I noticed a man coming up the drive; he wore a crisp white shirt, sunglasses and was holding a clipboard;

"Excuse me love, I'm from TV licensing, our records show..."

He only got as far as the gate and the dog had jumped up on him, in a friendly way of course! I told Duke to get down and as he did so, he splashed in a puddle of muddy water at the base of the gate; the poor man had muddy water all down his shirt and dripping off his sunglasses. I wanted to laugh but controlled myself. I'd heard;

"TV licence..."

"I'm ever so sorry; do you want me to wash your shirt for you?" I asked innocently, in a slow, monotone way.

"No, that's all right love!" He replied, looking very concerned at the suggestion that I had just asked him to take his shirt off. I controlled my laughter once more and shooed the dog inside.

"Our records do not show a licence for this address." He mustered,

"Oh, don't they?! (Still acting simple) Well my husband takes care of that, if we should have one, then we probably have."

"Well is he in, could you ask him?" He had taken to talking to me in the same manner.

"No, he's at work, but I could phone him."

"Could you do that, please?" he asked

"Ok, I won't be a minute!"

I went in and phoned the office for Dan, they said he was out, I went back outside. The man was examining his shirt, through dripping sunglasses, he stepped back when he noticed the dog following me... a little uneasy.

"I've spoken to my husband and we haven't got one, but he will get one as soon as he gets in," I said.

"Ok, make sure you do love." He walked away.

Four of my neighbours were prosecuted for no TV licence that day, Dan bought one on his way home and I had a really good laugh.

The dog disappeared about three weeks later, we appealed for his return in the local paper, adding a photograph of him with the kids and spent hours searching the area, and we never saw him again. We had numerous telephone calls from people saying sorry to hear about your dog but we've got one you can have. I couldn't believe people were like that and was quite rude to them,

"No, I don't want your dog, I want mine!"

He was part of the family. There were no sightings of Duke at all, I like to think that he was taken for training as a guide dog but I'll never know now.

Darts season had finished in September but I carried on going out on a Tuesday evening, Dan didn't like it but I was going to go anyway, he had the rest of the week. Mostly I'd visit Gemma or go round to one of our neighbour's, even clothes parties or the odd Tupperware party, anything to be out. I took Gemma out to meet Penny and her husband in a pub in Blandford once or twice. Penny's husband was really quite strange, a good-looking man with long fair hair and a moustache. On our first meeting he didn't say much but kept putting the song 'Free bird' on the jukebox. If

147

he did it once, he did it a dozen times and every time the song started he closed his eyes, shook his head and tapped the table to the music.

"Ignore him, he's shot away." Penny mouthed. I was a little bemused.

Gemma was a bit unnerved but then Penny was too much for her, Gemma was from a completely different background, I called her a wannabe snob, everything was 'mummy and daddy,'

"Daddy was commodore of a yacht club."

Still, she was certainly learning how the 'other half' live, the hard way. Penny didn't much care for Gemma but I liked her.

One Tuesday in June 1982, Abbey, Gemma and I went to a pub that we didn't normally go to, as usual I just had to be out. I was playing the fruit machine when two men came in, one had long dark hair and a moustache, the other was darker and shorter with short hair. The taller one was in leathers and I thought he was drop dead gorgeous, although obviously younger than us. All the same, I was married and so was Gemma. They were noticeably interested, giving the look and the eye. The taller of the two sat at the bar for a few minutes then came over and said;

"Could I buy you ladies a drink?"

Of course we said yes, we couldn't refuse that. He came back with the drinks and asked if he and his friend could join us.

"If you like!" I replied.

"My name is Gary," he said in his cockney accent, shaking us all by the hand, "And this is my brother, Ben!" Ben nodded in acknowledgment.

Abbey seemed totally mesmerised by Gary. We all chatted away; Gemma and I both told them straight away that we were married but that Abbey was single. Gary was almost twenty and his brother, just seventeen, although he did remind me that he was almost eighteen. They originally lived and were born in Hackney, London. Gary was a drummer; I thought he was full of it. We talked about everything that evening until closing. I was interested in the idea of him being a drummer; I was still in touch with Bill who had recently split with Vicky his duo partner, he still visited us regularly, usually with his guitar, we would mess around with a few ideas in my living room and had even discussed the possibility of forming a band, a drummer would be a real asset if, as he claimed, he could actually play. Gary arranged to meet Abbey the following day and

148

came to my home with her to discuss band possibilities further. He was very flirtatious and for a minute I was flattered, he was four years my junior. I reminded myself again early on that I was married! I discussed the band idea with Dan when he got home; he wasn't keen on the idea but so long as nothing interfered with his life that was ok.

Abbey and Gary were supposed to be at mine by 2pm, but turned up early at about 12pm, they couldn't wait to see me to discuss it further. They were still there when Dan came in but while they were there he seemed all right about it, I offered to give them both a lift home. When I returned Dan went out as usual but unusually he didn't come back that night. I was concerned, half expecting a call from the police or a hospital saying he'd had an accident. In a way I was quite glad because I instinctively knew I was in trouble; Abbey and Gary had still been at the house when he got in from work. I didn't sleep well, drifting in and out; I was waiting for a knock on the door or a sudden punch. My imagination was playing tricks, eventually I convinced myself that Dan must have been having an affair, why else would he stay out all night? He had been different recently, sort of distant and there were other signs, he'd been making more of an effort with his appearance, although being a salesman he had to be smart. I wasn't sure what it was, more aftershave maybe, or woman's intuition but I knew, I was upset then angry, by the time he came in at about 7am, I was so angry, livid, I couldn't have cared less what he said or did to me, I wanted an explanation. I heard his car pull into the drive and by the time he came in the front door, I was waiting on the stairs for him,

"Where the hell have you been?" I hollered,

"Sorry, had a few too many and stayed at my mates."

"What mate?" I questioned

"What difference does it make?"

I should have left it at that but I wanted an explanation, I wouldn't have got away with staying out all night. He went into the kitchen and so I followed. I grabbed his shoulder,

"You tell me who she is," I demanded.

Before I had chance to say anything else…Bang! He swung around and punched me in the face,

"Mind your own fucking business!" He spat.

I reacted by hitting him back.

"I'm off!" He said and headed for the back door.

I stood in his way and he pushed me, I lost my balance and hit my head on the table on the way down. He got out of the door but as I kicked it shut behind him, I caught his finger in it,

"Right bitch you'll pay for that!"

I knew I would but I was too busy trying to get up, I put my hand to my head and it was covered in blood, dripping onto the floor. What now? How do I get to the hospital? Luckily, the kids were still in bed! I cleaned the wound; it was only a small cut in the centre of a very large lump, just under my hairline. With all head injuries, they always look worse than they are and so I decided I would be ok. The black eye wouldn't be too hard to hide with dark glasses; it was sunny so I'd get away with that. Ok, I'm all right... Get the kids up, get Lee to school, and be prepared for him when he came back. At about 9:15am back he came to get ready for work, he said nothing, just held his index finger up to show me his wound. It was swollen and looked broken; he didn't mention my eye, even though he looked at it for a moment. He got ready for work, kissed Lorna and said bye,

"Daddy will see you later." And left.

I would face the wrath at some point. Abbey and Gary turned up again at about 10:30am. Gary noticed my eye and then the cut on my head, there was no denying how it happened, I played it down.

"Even so, any man that hits a woman should get a good hiding," he said.

"Hey, I'm used to it!" I shrugged, laughing it off; "Besides you're here to talk about drumming," I said, giving him a nudge. He should have been paying more attention to Abbey. I was quite glad that she was with him and away from Terry's clutches. The relationship between Gary and Abbey didn't last long, approximately three weeks, by that time Gary was in my band, he'd met Bill and we'd booked a local church hall to practice in. Dan even bought a drum kit, as a kind of apology for my beating, I had a little laugh to myself thinking, 'a few more beatings and I could kit out an orchestra.'

Not only could Gary play the drums, he was an excellent drummer and had an extremely good voice. Bill was less keen on the band getting too serious; it was a long way for him to travel from Southampton for practice and he'd been introduced to a local band who were already established and playing funky stuff, much more to his liking than the 'country/rock' that I'd wanted to do. I could understand it, Bill had been playing 'middle of the road' stuff with Vicky for four years and wanted a change. He would continue with us for a while, until we found someone else. Bill was also concerned at Gary's interest in me personally, there was apparently, according to Bill, an obvious change in me and my attitude toward Dan, he said the rift between us was getting worse.

On the night Gary had finished with Abbey, the three of us, Abbey Gary and I had been to a club, local to where Gary lived. I'd had a singles dart match, although I went out in the first round, I was still no good at darts no matter how hard I practiced. My Dad always played well, Verity too, even my Mum, until she was pregnant with me, apparently something else I was responsible for, she got something called darters arm, she'd go to throw but couldn't let go of the dart, she had to stop playing and hadn't played since. I think I must have been responsible for every single thing that was wrong in her life. I gave Gary a lift home that night; he sat in the front passenger seat, Abbey in the back, it was the first time that had happened, it was usually the other way around. It is amazing how, when you have lived in care and with a violent partner you notice subtle changes that, in a 'normal' person would go unnoticed. I dropped Gary off first and then Abbey at Terry's, I went in briefly and Abbey told me that she and Gary were finished. When I asked why she said,

"Don't know, I don't mind, he fancies you anyway!"
I stood in the living room making pleasantries; Terry put his arm around me,

"I've missed you, we all have, haven't we Iris?" He said,
"Yeah, where you been?"
Abbey gave me a look that could kill. I stayed long enough for a very quick coffee. When I left Terry came out to the car to see me off,

"When can I see you again?" he asked.
"You have Abbey!" I smirked. He denied it;
"She's just a child," he said.
At which point I reminded him of my age when he'd first been with me;

"That's different, you're different!"
"Well how come you never left Iris if I were so important?"
"You have Dan; he could give you more than I could offer."

"Not in the beginning though hey Terry. And now, what have I got? Oh yes, ok, beatings… Whatever!"
I left without letting him reply, the man was a pervert, end of story!

I got home late so I was in trouble again, more bruises and more sympathy from Gary. His excuse for coming round was that he wanted to discuss what we were going to do about Bill's replacement. We could still practice; we made recordings of our voices. Dan bought himself a guitar, although he couldn't yet play. He was having lessons given by another friend of ours, a Glaswegian called Timmy Stine; he played as part of a duo 'Stine and Teal.' Timmy died about 10 years ago but Rob still plays today.

Dan's lessons ended a few weeks later when Dan and I went to see Stine and Teal. Timmy came to the bar to speak to Dan, I had a black eye and when Timmy asked who did it, Dan said,

"I did," there was no brashness in his voice.

"Forget the lessons pal, anyone who hits a woman is a coward, you're lucky I don't give you a beating." Timmy said,

"I know, I deserve one, fair enough mate!" Dan replied.
It was more confirmation for me that Dan really couldn't help it and he wasn't proud of his actions. It had to be an illness didn't it? I justified it that way; I couldn't turn my back on him and walk away. Besides where would I go, who would take me on with two small children? I couldn't live on benefits, the kids would go without. We would have nowhere to live, the house was Dan's, I couldn't do that to them.

Things had been getting worse between Dan and I, Bill had been right about that. The one night he stayed out turned into several nights and then weekends too. Gary started to come over to keep me company. I had my music and my friends, Lou was there for us too, and she'd take the kids out on a weekly basis and spoilt them. If I left Dan, even though she said I should, would the kids lose her? Would I lose her too? After all Dan was her son.

The dart season started again and once again I had that to keep me occupied. September 1982 to September 1983. I missed a lot of games that season due to my injuries, the beating were worse and now the rewards were less, odd flowers or chocolates. I spent many weekends alone. The drum kit was now at Gary's, I took it there, he had more room for it and he could practice. He lived with his mum, Mary and two brothers; Tony and Ben, whom I'd already met. Tony was the youngest; he'd been sent away to school as he had been in trouble for something, although nothing serious, unlike my brother. His biggest problem seemed to be kleptomania; he stole silly things like Gary's underwear and a bead choker of mine, or the odd tape. He looked like Suggs from madness, a real character with a great sense of humour.

Ben was far more complicated, a bit of a loner and the middle child with a mental illness that manifested itself two years later. He unnerved everyone who met him, he always wore a college type scarf and smoked a pipe and was a highly intelligent man. He had dreamed of one day becoming an R.A.F pilot, in fact he'd thought he probably had already been one in a past life and that this was probably during the Second World War. He was a sad case but always tried to cover his sadness and was the main support for Mary. She was really strange but had been ill for many years; she had diabetes, the brittle type and had also suffered a heart attack in her late 30's. The first time I ever met her was when Gary had arranged for me to call round with the drum kit, as I pulled up outside the council house on an estate, I saw her on her knees, digging with a small trowel, she had her back to the gate and was wearing an old, high visibility, orange workman's jacket, her bleached blonde hair, pulled back tight in a ponytail. I opened the gate and walked behind and past her to the front door; she didn't even look up to see who it was.

"Hello is Gary in?" I asked her…

No response. I thought maybe she was just a gardener or something. Gary opened the door,

"Hi!" I said with a start, "who is that?"

"My mum!"

"Oh, is she deaf?" I asked, genuinely believing that she was,

"No, take no notice, she's always like that, she's shy!"

I learnt over the months just how shy, I'd knock on the door and she'd come out of the kitchen and open the door without showing herself or even looking to see who was calling, quickly disappearing back into the kitchen where she would close the door. She lived downstairs with her two cats and the three boys lived upstairs, although Ben spent his time with her, even sleeping downstairs with her some of the time. I thought them very strange, even quite spooky but anyway… 'Each to their own.'

I became quite fond of Gary over the following months and it was on one of these occasions when I had visited him that ended with us sleeping together. He had shown concern over a bruise on my cheek and touched my face,

"I'll kiss it better," he said leaning in.

He kissed my cheek and then looked me in the eyes, we didn't say a word, he kissed me full on the lips and I melted. One thing led to another, I hadn't wanted to at first, I was, after all, married. Then it occurred to me that I was in fact married to a man who beat me and who was, no doubt, having an affair already... Dan hadn't given me a second thought. Gary gave me back some of the self-esteem I'd lost, replaced the;

"You ugly slut!"

With;

"You are so beautiful!"

Me, beautiful? In spite of myself, I believed him, well I didn't believe I was beautiful but I believed he really saw me in a way I knew that Dan didn't. Gary was good-looking and talented, everything Dan wasn't. Our first time was passionate but I felt guilty just the same, it should never have happened and didn't again for some weeks.

Chapter 24

Early into November 1982, a Friday; Dan had gone out, as usual and I decided I needed to know where he was going, maybe it was my own guilt, I had to know for sure that Dan was being unfaithful before I could take things further with Gary. I waited for him to pull out of the drive and bundled the kids into my car, a Hillman Avenger that was rusted around the headlights but the engine was good. Dan had a Fiat 132, a much better car. I followed at a distance, right to the sailing club in Mudeford. I watched Dan walk in the door, then I took the kids and sat them at a table outside and went into the bar, Dan was talking to a man and his wife;

"Ah!" He was surprised to see me and introduced me saying; "This is my wife, I wasn't expecting her but it's a nice surprise. Where are the kids?"

"Outside at a table."

"Well go on out with them and I'll bring you all a drink in a minute."

He said it with such calm and his act paid off, the couple chuckled and Dan rolled his eyes then winked at me, tapping my bum as I turned. He came out a few minutes later,

"Well, you'll never make a private detective; in fact you will never be anything worthwhile. Did you really think I wouldn't notice you, who did you think you would find me with? I'm not that stupid, I'm not like you." He had leaned in far enough not to have to raise his voice. He drank his pint, "I suggest you take the kids home, its past their bedtime. I won't be home tonight!"

"Please Dan, come home," I pleaded.

He ignored me and went back into the bar without a second glance; I put the kids back into the car and drove home. He didn't come home that night or the next, in fact the next time I saw him was late Sunday night, after closing time, that's when it started: He beat me all over the house, kicking and punching every bit of my body and face, he was laying in punches as I lay on the floor, screaming;

"Please stop, you're going to kill me!"

And just as quick as it had started, he stopped. Just like that he sat down in the chair, put the television on and said;

"Make me a coffee and a sandwich." I was sobbing uncontrollably. "Stop blubbering, you asked for that!"

I made his sandwich and coffee. Had I asked for it? What had I done? Maybe he knew about Gary? Surely he would have said... I was certain that had he known he would have killed me. That night was the first realisation I had that Dan was capable of doing just that… Killing me. I went to bed. The following day, after Lee had gone to school, I went to Gemma's with two black eyes and bruises all over my face and body. Gary showed up shortly afterwards looking for me. I had already telephoned Lou and asked her to look after Lorna for the day, I didn't give a reason. I got Lorna ready and waited for her, when I saw her arrive I put the door on the catch and turned the shower on, she came in downstairs and I shouted down,

"Hi, sorry Lou, I'm in the shower, Lorna is all ready."

"Ok, we'll see you later, is everything ok?"

"Yes, what time will you be back?"

"I'll pick Lee up and they can stay with us for dinner, I'll bring them back after that, probably about 7pm, is that ok?"

"Yes that's Ok, have a good day," I said and she left.

I'd got away with her not seeing the state of my face; I'd find a way around it when she came back later. Gemma was shocked, as was Gary, my eyes looked far worse; the left one had haemorrhaged and as a result the white of my eye was virtually non existent, my right eye wasn't as bad. The three of us talked together for a while, Gemma echoed my thoughts that the violence had escalated and I needed to get out of there. She persuaded me to see her solicitor, one she'd used for her divorce from a previous husband. Their marriage had only lasted 10 months so she didn't even think of it as a marriage. I telephoned for an appointment at a call box, Gemma said she would come with me and Gary wanted to come too. I explained my injuries to the solicitor on the phone; it was about 11am;

"What are you doing now?" Before I had chance to respond he asked, "Have you got transport?"

"Yes!" I replied.

"Then be here at 12pm," he said and hung up.

The office was in the town centre so we all went straight there, I wasn't sure what I was doing, I didn't expect him to see me so soon, I had thought it would be a few days and I would have time to think about it, to talk my self out of it.

'Well,' I thought, 'it looks worse than it actually is, doesn't it?'

No, it didn't, that was obvious by the reaction from the secretary and even more so when I saw the solicitor. For an hour I poured out the history of my marriage, all the violence and the abuse. Horror enveloped Gemma's face; she had never known the extent of what had been happening or for how long.

"I thought you were a really happy couple, you had everything," she mustered.

At about 1pm the solicitor stood up;

"I'm going for a bite to eat, I suggest you do the same and be back here at 2pm," he said.

I did as I was told and when we arrived back he was waiting for us in the car park;

"Get in my car!" He said, opening the passenger door, "we've got to get you to the courts."

By 2:30pm we were in court, by 2:40pm we were out and I had an injunction, a non molestation order with the power of arrest, on closer inspection it had an unlimited time on it, therefore technically - it still applies today. I was instructed to dial 999 if Dan even threatened to hit me... he would be arrested.

"If he kicks off, get out, get in your car and come to me," Gary said.

"Or me," Gemma echoed.

I was slightly bewildered as everything unfolded – I was getting a divorce and Dan would know about it. Soon!

Lou phoned and said if we were agreeable the kids could stay over, she'd take Lee to school and bring Lorna back afterwards, that was quite a relief. Dan came in as usual, I couldn't tell him what I'd done, I still had the option of cancelling it all. Maybe when he realised what was happening he'd beg me to stop it anyway. I watched for the post the following day, it didn't come. Lou brought Lorna back, she was shocked at my appearance and wanted to know why I hadn't told her, she said she'd take the kids for a few days to give Dan and me a chance to talk things through, and she'd have a word with him. I didn't want her to and told her so, I didn't tell her about the divorce or the court order, I didn't want Dan to hear it from her, it would just make matters worse, who knew how he'd react?

She took the kids for the rest of the week. I decided not to go out on that Tuesday evening, I stayed in. I wanted to talk to Dan in the vague hope that he would see sense. It backfired. Since the kids weren't home and I was such a mess Dan said he was going out, he got ready and went, leaving me alone, again. I'd been here before... No kids, no husband and no dog. I wandered around, looking at my home and thinking about what I was giving up, I didn't want to be in this situation but what choice did I have? My vows were a complete sham now, Mum was right, again. I could hear her saying;

"I told you so!"

I decided to go for a drive on my own; I had to get some cigarettes anyway. I drove to Kinson, near where my sister and everyone lived. I parked in the car park behind a shop, put my glasses on and went in the shop. As I came out I spotted my sister, walking down the opposite side of the road. She called, I pretended not to hear her and kept walking, she called again,

"What's with the glasses?" She laughed but I ignored her. She crossed the road and ran up behind me.

"Oh, I see!" She said staring at me, "that would be why you didn't answer then would it?"

I didn't want her to know but she insisted on the whole story…

"Hence no darts," I said.

Her advice was don't hide it away, tell her, come to Jeff and her… Why? She liked Dan. Mum, Dad, everyone liked him, even as we talked the only question she asked was;

"What did you do? He wouldn't do it for nothing!"

Well, yes he did, he would, and he had!

The letter arrived on the Thursday; Dan read it while I stayed in the kitchen trying to busy myself;

"What's this shit? Do you really think this is going to stop me? You are my wife, this is my house, and those are my kids. I'll do what I like and nobody will tell me what I should or shouldn't do." He was waving the letter under my nose as he said it and I knew, at that moment; I was helpless. I also knew it was going to get worse, and it did. As Dan left on Friday for his night out, he pulled the telephone wire from the wall;

"Can't call the police now can you?" He said and hit me across the head.

He was gone all weekend. I managed to fix the wire but it was too late, I had no idea where he was, what was the point in phoning anyone? He had won again.

By mid December the assaults were daily. The kids were used to it by now. On the bad occasions, I'd wake them and without a question they would pick up their quilts and pillows, get into the back of my car and we'd drive around. I was still trying to find out where Dan was going all weekend. We would drive around looking for his car, sounds insane when I think about it now but I needed to know who she was, it became an obsession. One night when I got home his car was in the driveway. Without a second thought I drove straight into the back of it, on purpose.

"Mum, you hit his car!"

Yes, I had but there wasn't a mark on it, mine on the other hand was left with the headlight dangling from the socket and the bumper dented. We walked in to find Dan in the kitchen cooking breakfast, he laughed;

"Damage your car did you? Forget where the brake was? Now what are you going to do? Isn't mummy silly?"

"Will you mend it Dad?" Lee asked,

"Yes of course I will, can't have mummy driving around in the dark with you two in the car, with no lights now, can I?" He replied giving Lee a nudge and a wink. He punched me in the face and broke my nose that night, just after I'd put the kids to bed. Blood poured out all over the place; calmly he went to the freezer, took a bag of frozen peas out and handed then to me saying,

"Put those on it, I'm going out!"

He stopped and glanced round the room:

"Whoops! Must remember to disconnect the phone."

He pulled it from the wall and left. I called the kids, who came down the stairs half asleep, carrying their bedding. It had become a routine, I picked up a change of clothes, got into my car and drove to Gemma's, she looked after the kids while I went to the hospital, picking Gary up on the way, I told the kids to be good and assured them I would be back soon. I went to Gary's house and knocked the door, his mum answered. She took one look at me and said in her cockney accent;

"Oh my Gauld, wha's he done now?"

Gary came down the stairs before I had chance to answer. I hadn't seen him lately with the situation as it was; I decided it wasn't a good idea. Even so, he still agreed to come to the hospital. I had x-rays and they wanted me to stay the night; out of the question, I had children to look after. I'd convinced myself that the break in my nose wasn't that bad anyway. Gary asked me to stay with him but I declined, I told him I needed to get the kids home. I didn't though, I went to Gemma's and we chatted all night, I took the kids home in the morning with the promise to Gemma that I'd see the solicitor again... I did, but not until after Christmas.

Bill was down for Christmas, Dan and I had finally talked and I pleaded for him to give us a second chance, see if we could find a way, a compromise, anything to save our marriage, I didn't want a divorce, I didn't think he did either. Regardless of the violence, he was the father of my children, my husband and even my friend. He had a problem; I still believed that in some way... He was a loaded gun and I was the trigger, if only I could find my fault and put that right it would stop, I had to find out what I was doing wrong. Bill would be there to referee so I would be ok for the time being. It was so important to me that the children would never experience a Christmas with violence, it would ruin every future Christmas they'd have. At least the other incidents wouldn't be on a memorable date. We spent Christmas day together and it was a lovely day but by Boxing Day Dan was like a caged animal,

"Why don't you go on out for a couple of hours? You could take Bill with you whilst I clean up," I suggested.
They left together at about 8pm; Bill came back at about 10pm... alone. Dan had stayed on with some friends, it was obvious that Bill could see our relationship was over, it was nothing he said exactly, just a feeling I got. He decided to go home that night, a day earlier than I had expected and without explanation. He left and said the usual;

"Thanks for a lovely Christmas, food was good!" He kissed me on the cheek and whispered, "Be careful and look after yourself, I'll keep in touch."
I knew this was goodbye; I just couldn't put my finger on why. I never really saw him again to talk to only briefly about seven years later.

Dan came home the following lunchtime; he'd stayed with a friend and played golf early, he said Bill had gone on but he didn't know why;

"I think he just wanted to get back to you. So what time did he leave?" He questioned.

"About 10:30pm,"

"Really?"
I tried to change the subject, he didn't believe me and he was winding himself up. He calmed down again though when the kids came in. We went to Lou's for a couple of hours; there were always lots of people there so I knew he wouldn't do anything in front of them. I couldn't live like this anymore, just waiting for the next beating, he obviously didn't want it to work, I'd just as well push ahead

with the divorce, there was no point in fighting to keep him any-more.

Dan spent most of the following week away, right through to New Years Eve. He came back new years day after he'd been sailing and wished me a happy new year. Gary had stayed away as I'd asked him to, I'd told him that I was going to try and save my marriage. He was upset, he said he wanted to be with the kids and me, he loved them and me but he understood and would do whatever I wanted, if I needed him he would be there, he would wait. I did miss him, I'd been lonely and it wasn't so much him, it really could have been anyone, anyone who'd show me a little love, a little sup-port. On the 2nd of January I went to see him, it was also my Nan's birthday. With her memory came all the other bad memories of my life, they all came flooding back. The knot in my stomach rose in my throat and with it came the floods of tears, Gary said nothing, just held me and eventually we ended up making love. By the time I left to go home I felt better but looked such a mess, my eyes swol-len, my face was all red, what did Gary see in me? What was he after? He must have had an ulterior motive, I mean; I was four years older than him with two children and an abusive husband... It was an understatement to say I came with baggage. I knew he'd never last the course but I needed him and he wanted to be there for me, for now! I also had somewhere I could take the kids when the vio-lence started again, as it inevitably would and did, just two days later. It wasn't as violent but enough to give me a large lump on my head as he bounced me off the wall. I made an appointment and saw the solicitor, he was concerned that I hadn't used the power of arrest...How could I? The system wouldn't work; it was the same every time... The violence, the phone being ripped from the wall and then he'd leave. He was sent a warning letter voicing concerns that his behaviour had continued and he could be sent to prison. He tore it up, he was winning hands down.

By the end of January abuse had become an almost daily occurrence. There was something else too... A woman kept calling asking for Dan, numerous times, I asked who it was but was told it didn't matter. One night at the end of January Dan came in drunk; I was ready for bed and about to go up. He started shouting and hur-tling all the usual insults but stopped short, he then decided that he wanted sex. I wasn't going to allow it this time, it was his attitude. I'm not sure what happened, something just clicked inside me. He

161

was grabbing at my underwear whilst on top of me, I relaxed briefly and then sunk my long fingernails into his back, he jumped up
and let go. He called me a bitch but the satisfaction for me was immense, I'd won and had found the strength to fight back, to stop
being the victim. Four of my nails had broken off in his back; he
was mumbling about his rights as my husband while I cleaned up
around him, he didn't understand why I'd done something like that
to him. He never tried it again, not rape I mean.

I left the following day and went to stay at Gary's, we all
slept together in his room, Lee and Lorna in one single bed and
Gary and I in the other. I told the kids it would only be for a little
while, like a holiday. I called Lou and told her where we were, I
said then, that no matter what had happened between Dan and me,
she would always be welcome as the children's grandmother, I
would never stop her seeing them. She was very upset on the phone
and that hurt. She was a wonderful lady. Obviously she was disappointed in her son but she did, however, blame my relationship
with Gary for Dan's behaviour,

"You know that isn't true." I said
She knew I was right. I told her that I'd also had another woman
phoning looking for him. She asked when I would be back but I
didn't know; I would have to wait for my solicitor's instructions; I
had another appointment to see him on the Tuesday morning.

Dan came around on the Sunday night demanding to speak
to me but Gary and his brothers stood at the door;

"It's late and the kids and Jan are asleep, you should calm
down or you'll do yourself a mischief. Come back tomorrow," Ben
offered.
Dan eventually left saying;

"You tell her I want her home tomorrow."
I listened at the window and heard the tyres squeal as he pulled
away. My only thought was that he would harm himself, he had
been drinking, I couldn't go back to the house though. Monday
night he was back demanding to see me, this time threatening to
burn the house down, kill us all and beat Gary up.

"Do your worst, she's not coming out!" Ben intervened
again.
As Dan went back to his car, Gary jumped the wall and went to a
call box about thirty yards away, he was going to call the police.
Dan started the engine and went at speed towards the telephone
box but Gary got there first. Dan then reversed down the road and

rammed my car with his, pushing the back up onto the pavement. I was by now in the garden, and said;

"If I talk to him, he'll leave."

But Mary wouldn't let me near him. He shouted that he would get me;

"You're dead!" He spat and sped off again.

I stood in the garden a moment longer. He would be back and he meant what he said.

I was late for my solicitor's appointment the next day, Dan had been back sometime during the night and slashed two of my tyres. Gary changed one for my spare and then walked the slashed tyre to a local scrap yard to get it replaced. I finally got to the solicitor at 11:30am, one hour late but in one piece. The solicitor wasn't happy about my living conditions, mainly the association with Gary, I wanted to go home and told him so, but how could I? Eventually we came up with a guarantee, by way of an agreement between Dan's solicitors and my own, that I could return home without repercussions. Perhaps Dan would live elsewhere for a while I thought, Lee needed to be at school and both of my children needed their own beds, routine, and their own things in familiar surroundings. It was to take three weeks of living on food from take aways and café's before I could get home again. I had many visits from Dan and in the mean time I had to go home to collect various things for the children, clothes etc. The afternoon after the incident with my tyres, I'd been home and what I found sent shivers down my spine... Every item of clothing I'd had, had been slashed or had circles and squares cut out of them. It was all piled onto the floor, my shoes had the heels pulled off and every house plant had been cut up and emptied amongst my clothes. I was sure it must have taken him hours, I was also sure that if he caught me there he would, with no doubt at all in my mind, kill me! I left it as I'd found it. I had to go back again about three days later, everything had been cleaned up.

I tried only to go home, when I knew Dan would be at work, if his car was not there I could get in and out without having to confront him. One afternoon, he caught me by surprise; I was just about to leave when he came in the front door;

"You're not going anywhere!" he said.

Without a second word, he launched our wooden coffee table, inlaid with green leather and a glass top in the air, it was extremely heavy but he managed to hit the ceiling with it, we were both show-

163

ered with glass. I managed to escape and ran to my car where Gary and the kids were waiting, the kids looked terrified and were hysterical, and Dan was on my heels. I managed to get into my car and pulled away at speed but he was in his and by the time I'd reached the main road he was along side, trying to push me off the road. I pulled into a slip road and stopped by a parade of shops, he moved his car against mine so that I couldn't open the door. Dan wound down his passenger window, demanding I open mine; I did as he said;

"I want you home to talk," he said.
The children were sobbing in the back, Gary was trying to console them, I agreed to go home but he had to promise no more of this. Of course, he promised. I needed him to move his car so that I could get out. He pulled away onto the main road and I started my engine again, I swiftly took a side road and got away, I had to be more careful.

A few days later I went home again, this time it was early evening. I waited for his car to leave and kept well out of sight. As he left I was in and out in no more than five minutes. There was no sign of him. It was past the kids dinner time and they were hungry, so I stopped at a chip shop to get them some food. We were just about to eat it when Dan appeared, pulling up behind me. I locked all the doors and closed my window. He knocked the window;

"Wind it down."

"No!"

"I'll smash it," he said, through clenched teeth.
I wound it down and he grabbed my keys from the ignition, Lorna started screaming, he got back in his car and was gone. What could I do now? I Consoled Lorna and reassured her that we'd be all right, I told them to finish their food and we just sat and ate. About ten minutes later Dan came back and pulled in front of my car, he came back over to my window;

"Please give me my keys, look at what you are doing to the kids."

"Not until you come into my car and speak to me, Gary can watch the kids a minute!"

"You could drive away with me, what about the kids?"

"I'm hardly likely to do that now, am I? I just want to talk!"
Reluctantly I went with him, he still had my keys, he leaned into the back seat to the
Kids saying;

164

"Its ok mummy won't be a minute; I just need to talk to her."

He said he wanted me home, it wasn't fair on the kids and he wouldn't interfere, in fact he was thinking about staying with a friend for a while. He had had enough. Did he mean it? Could I believe him?

"Don't decide now, just think about it." He gave me my house-keeping - £100.00; "I'm sure you need that. Meet me for a meal next week and we'll talk about it over dinner."

I agreed, not sure what to think or believe. He handed me my keys and said,

"Give us a kiss?"

I did as he asked then went back to my car and watched as he drove away. I checked my mirror several times but there was no sign of him, what game was this?

I phoned Dan at work on the following Tuesday. I had informed my solicitor of the events of the past couple of weeks. I had already decided it would be best to go home; we couldn't stay where we were indefinitely and I missed the comforts of home. I explained my thinking to Gary; I wasn't going back to Dan as such, just going home. Besides there was another reason for going home, I thought I was pregnant. I had missed a period but with all that was happening I'd put it down to stress, there were other signs too that made it almost certain, like the smell of frying eggs making me feel sick. This would have to happen now, if my dates were as I thought, it could be either of them who got me pregnant. If it were Gary's, Dan would kill it and me too. I decided not to go for an immediate test this time; I needed to buy some time before saying anything to anyone.

I arranged to meet Dan at a local pub with a restaurant; I made sure it was a busy time of day. I arrived early my heart pumping, echoing in my ears… What would he say, what would he do? Through all this rigmarole, I actually missed him, well not so much him as he was but what we'd had, the security of my own home. He was waiting at a table just inside the door; he stood to greet me, kissed me on the cheek and asked if I wanted a drink;

"Please!" I said, without thinking about my latest possible development, "No! Actually, I'm driving, just an orange juice for me"

"I think I'll join you," he said.

Dan having a soft drink… 'Unheard of' I thought. We had a nice meal together, chatting just as we had in the early years.

"Where did it go so wrong?" I asked,

"I don't know but I wish we could go back..." he looked at me, "...would you come home to me?"

"No, I will come home but the divorce goes ahead. If in the future I feel that it may work I'll stop it, but for now it stays in place." I remained strong.
Reluctantly he agreed,

"Do you love Gary?" He eventually asked,

"No!" I replied. I didn't even have to think about it... I didn't! I did have a lot to thank him for but it wasn't love that I felt for him.

"So are you coming home now?"

"No, the kids are in bed, I will be home in the morning," I said. I could tell he was irritated but he accepted my decision, he wanted me home, maybe he missed me too. Gary was unhappy but he had known that eventually I would have to leave.

Chapter 25

Dan kept to his word for the first few weeks; he was trying by staying out of the way. I went to the G.P and he confirmed the pregnancy, all the tests would need to be taken again. I told Dan that night,

"So is it mine?"

"Well yes, I think so!"

I explained that I was sure it had happened during our reconciliation at Christmas. (I wasn't, but then he didn't need to know.) The dates confirmed my fears, the due date was 14th October 1984, and chances are it would be Gary's. First and foremost, it was mine.

Dan and I were sleeping together again, he had said he wasn't seeing anyone else, yet he would disappear every Friday, coming back on the Sunday and then there were the weeknights as well, I wasn't convinced. I decided to follow him again. He stopped outside a house, just round the corner from, and almost opposite Lou and Sam's house. As I pulled up Dan was just going into the house. He saw me and came back to my car, I made an excuse, I was just going to his mum's and saw him;

"So what are you doing here?" I quizzed,

"Oh I've got a mate who lives here."

"Who's that then?"

"You don't know him."

He was nervous and kept checking the windows of the house; this had to be the someone he was seeing. I asked him to come home but he said he couldn't, he had something planned,

"Something more important than me, your children, our marriage?"

"Look, I'll be home later,"

"Don't bother!" I fumed and drove away. He didn't come home for two days. In the meantime I'd opened the mail to find he'd not been paying the bills, not the mortgage, the rates, the gas, he hadn't paid anything. I confronted him when he returned, he'd said that he hadn't bothered whilst we were apart, he didn't see why he should, I was seeing Gary again and he said he had proof, I hadn't, and he was trying to make excuses.

"Well you've got someone anyway!" I said,

"No one permanent!" He said.

He then went on to tell me how he'd been with a woman who had taught him how to use a vibrator on her, he told me how much

167

she'd enjoyed it, he finished by telling me that I should get one, maybe he'd be more interested in me if I was a little more adventurous. I was destroyed and feeling physically sick. At that point I sort of shut down. It had all been a lie again. He started again;

"This isn't going to work; I'm not going to pay the bills, besides I'm not here most of the time anyway. I'll make sure you get nothing, you've never worked."

I called him a bastard and he slapped me, I went to walk away and he hit out again but missed me and caught Lorna, it was a glancing blow on the head. That was it…no more; I turned and attacked him, punching out mostly at the air as he made his getaway out of the door again. I was shouting abuse after him, things like;

"Run you coward, hitting a baby!"

My maternal instinct had kicked in and it was the strongest feeling I'd ever felt. He had always known that whilst it was possible to do anything to me, he would never get away with hurting my children. That was the final turning point for me. I saw the solicitor and told him about the bills and what Dan had said about me getting nothing, from that date his intentions were recorded in my file and I was told I wouldn't lose out. He approached the council for me and arranged for me to be re-housed, should the house be re-possessed. It would then be said that I hadn't made myself intentionally homeless, I had no income with which to keep up the mortgage repayments. I told the solicitor I was pregnant and that Dan had initially agreed that this baby was a child of the family and it would take Dan's name, which he had.

The letters from the solicitor came thick and fast, and although the violence started again it wasn't quite as bad, I was fighting back verbally now, although the abuse was awful on both sides. I was also still following him from time to time, it was still that same obsession, the not knowing who had helped wreck my marriage. On one occasion in April I went to the car park of a golf club, it was about lunchtime, his car was there and the bonnet was cold so he'd been there a while. I tried the car door, it opened, I proceeded to check the glove box and the sides of the seats, I was looking for anything that would tell me who this woman was. Then in the glove box I found an invitation for Dan to a birthday party:

'Helen's 40th' - It read – 'all my love, Helen'

Surely not? She's ten years older than him! He came home later that night and I greeted him with;

"How's Helen?" The look was enough, "I will find her and I will kill her!"

"You wont, it's nothing to do with her, this is between us."

"No," I said, "she will pay! If you hadn't of been there, you would have been here, we may have sorted it out. I'm going to see Gary again!"

I did and he was still waiting, I told him about the pregnancy which was by now pretty obvious, I told him that although Dan believed it was his, I knew it was Gary's, he was thrilled. He came with me for my scans and tests and was there when I rang for the results of the amniocentesis, it was another boy and all was ok, no abnormalities detected. I needed to get on with my life and this was the only way I knew how. I was still living with Dan on the nights he came home although we didn't sleep with each other.

Gary was at the house one night and he was just going to leave, I'd locked the back of the house and was upstairs checking the kids, suddenly there was a commotion downstairs. Gary ran up saying stay up here, as he turned Dan was behind him, he was holding a lawn edging spade. He swung it at Gary but missed.

"Come on then!" Gary challenged.

I stepped down in front of him, Dan was shouting things at us that made no sense, I told him to put the spade down and he threw it. He grabbed my hair and I was at the bottom of the stairs in a flash, he dragged me into the lounge and shut the door, wedging a chair against the handle. Gary and the kids were now outside, unable to get in and I was trapped inside.

"You stand there; I have a phone call to make." He said, pushing me towards the window. He picked up the phone and dialled 999; "You'd better get here now, I'm going to kill my wife!" He gave the address and then hung up. He then called his mum and said; "Something's happened! You'd best come and get the kids!" He then put the phone down.

"What's going on? Why are you doing this?" I whispered...

I was terrified because I honestly believed that I was going to die and my kids were on the other side of the door listening, I didn't want them to remember me screaming so I kept as quiet as possible. Dan walked over to me and grabbed either side of my head, he pulled his head back and butted me twice in the face, and the sec-

169

ond blow knocked me backwards. I could hear Gary trying with Lee to kick the door in; I could hear Lee shouting;

"Leave my mum alone! I'm going to kill you, you bastard! You wait; I'm going to kill you!"

I thought, 'he shouldn't be swearing,' just a passing thought. By now I had a chair in front of me,

"You think that's going to stop me?" He snarled.

I didn't seem to have any emotions, I felt nothing for him, I had switched off, I heard him say;

"You are prolonging the inevitable."

At which point the police were there and the lounge door was forced open. A W.P.C and a P.C came running in followed by Lou, she was shouting at Gary and then slapped his face telling him it was all his fault,

"Leave him alone," I managed, "it's your fucking son that's the problem!"

"I'd better get going, I'll see you soon!" Gary said and left. The W.P.C agreed that it was probably for the best,

"We will contact you later if we need to take a statement Mr Gosling."

Dan was being restrained;

"She's been screwing around!" He was shouting, pleading innocent, and blaming me for his insanity. I couldn't see a great deal by now, both my cheeks were swollen up, I told the police about the molestation order but they weren't interested, they believed Dan. I was told that the best thing I could do was leave, go to the hospital for a check up and then stay with a friend until he'd calmed down. I needed to show them the court order, without it they couldn't arrest him. I didn't know where it was, it was a piece of paper. Who would know in the chaos, where it was? I was watching my children's faces; Lou was saying they could stay with her;

"No way, they stay with me! Get your things kids!" I said. They came down less than a minute later with their bin liners of belongings; it was so matter of fact. I picked up my car keys and a bag with a change of clothes and left.

I couldn't believe what had happened, he'd done this to me and yet I was the one being booted out in the cold, it was our family home... Where was the justice in that? The court order wasn't worth the paper it was written on. I told the kids we'd be all right.

"Are we going to Gary's again?" Lorna asked.

"No we're not baby, but we'll be ok."

I didn't know where we were going, I just drove. I needed medical help but with what the kids had already seen I couldn't leave them, not for a moment. I ended up at a drive through park overlooking Poole harbour. The kids snuggled down.

"You all right mum?" Lee asked,

"Course I am!"

"Your face is really bad!"

I knew it was, I could feel it. I could see my cheeks over the bottom lids of my eyes. I finally decided to look in my rear view mirror at the damage; I could hardly recognise my own face, my teeth were aching and so was my head. It wasn't until the sun came up that I could see that, once again, I had haemorrhages in both eyes. I watched the sun on the water, glistening off the boats and white sails in the harbour, I was numb. I knew I couldn't go home and I couldn't let Gary see me either, instead I went round and posted a note through the door saying that what had happened was in no way his fault, I told him that me and the kids had stayed in the car park overlooking the sea for the night. We were ok and when I'd decided what I was going to do, or where I was going to be, I'd be in touch. When the sun came up, I drove to Verity's. She had already heard what had happened, or rather Dan's version of events, not mine. Obviously Dan hadn't told her how much damage he had caused to my face. My only consolation was that at least he hadn't managed to punch or kick me in the stomach, I had no idea what the stress would do to my unborn baby. But then I thought if there were a problem I would have had bleeding or something. My main concerns were my two children already here. I sat for a couple of hours with Verity and explained the full extent of what had happened. Dan had done the rounds looking for me, he'd said he was worried because of my state of mind. He'd been to my mum too who, as he told me later that day, had said she couldn't understand why he was surprised, she'd warned him what I was like in the first place, he'd do best to cut his losses and let me get on with it. Well that said it all to me; everyone blamed me for Dan's behaviour, my own mother included. Dan had told her the truth about what he had done to me too, yet she still blamed me! Maybe they were right, perhaps it was my fault, I seemed to be the only one who didn't think so. I left Verity's with the kids and went home, Dan was there. By now I couldn't care less, if he were going to kill me so be

171

it, perhaps it would be better all round. He was calm and didn't fire abuse at me, other than the usual snide remarks;

"All right ugly? See everyone agrees with me, even your own mother." "Slut!" "Slag!"
It didn't touch me, it seemed I was either going to die there in that marriage or live with him forever. Nobody could or would help, not even the law. I didn't bother with the doctors or hospital, I'd either have more bruises in a few days or they'd heal, whatever would be would be. I stayed in, Dan went out.

Terry and Abbey turned up later in the day, he said Dan had been to him too, looking for me, he then proceeded to have a go aswell, telling me how it was my fault because Gary had been Abbey's boyfriend, I'd taken him off her and if he saw Gary he'd kill him. I protested the truth, I never stole him, Gary had told me that Abbey had talked of nothing but suicide, they'd walked by the river and she'd threatened to jump in and drown herself, she was going to take an overdose, she wanted him to screw her and he'd refused. Abbey convinced Terry it was lies, she believed that if it weren't for me they'd still be together.

"What are you both concerned about anyway, you've been getting it from each other!"
I looked at Terry

"And as for you, preaching to me!"
He apologised, denying for the hundredth time any involvement with Abbey, saying I should know how much he thought of me, he'd been showing me for years. They finished their coffees and went, I didn't bother to go out and say goodbye, just shut the door. The kids were playing upstairs as if nothing had happened, I sobbed alone in my kitchen.

By chance, a week later I saw a friend, June, she lived on our estate. I'd met her in passing several times over the years and had had an occasional coffee with her. We had been at the same secondary school, my second school. My face was still a mess; she too had recently split with a violent husband and became the rock I needed to steady myself. I told her my story and she went through hers.

"Well, if you want to come here and stay for a while, you can."
I took her up on the offer. Her two daughters got on with my kids, just as well really since the four of them had to share a bedroom. Dan had asked me not to leave again but I said I felt it would be best, just for a while. The house was being sold and we had no gas

172

because it had been disconnected, I didn't have much of a choice. I saw my solicitor and told him what had happened. The letters of warning were sent, even though I said it was a futile exercise, we'd get the divorce through soon.

I didn't see Dan but he started phoning me, asking if there was anything I wanted and asking after the kids. He told me he loved me and again said he wouldn't hit me anymore, he'd realised what he'd done. For a split second I did believe him, or maybe I wanted to believe him, he seemed very depressed but I couldn't take that risk. I told Gary where I was and he visited once or twice. I was advised by the solicitor that I still needed to be living at home when the house was sold;

"The local council will not house you."
I couldn't go back, not yet, I needed more time and we'd have to go to court together anyway to arrange the custody of the children before the divorce could be final.

I had been at June's three weeks when hell broke loose again. The kids were in bed and Gary had come round to visit, as had one of June's neighbours Mindy, we were all having a quiet drink. At about 8:30pm the phone rang, it was Dan, he poured his heart out saying how unhappy he was and gave the usual spiel. In the end I suggested that he come round and talk, I told him Gary was there but he said that it didn't matter, he believed me now that we were friends. I said we were just having a few drinks, June didn't mind. At first he said no but then said,

"Ok then, just for a while, if you don't mind?"
He turned up a few minutes later. Gary was still there but he was to my mind now a visiting as a friend, in fact he was sat next to June when Dan arrived. Dan sat next to me, we were there like that for about three hours, laughing and joking, there was absolutely no tension at all. At about 12am, Dan had had a few drinks too many and said he should go, he was driving so I suggested he stay but he declined as he only had to go around the corner. He kissed me goodbye and I watched him drive away, I went in and shut the door. About five minutes later there was a knock at the door;

"Who is it?"
We'd thought it may be June's husband but it was Dan;

"Only me, I've forgotten my cigarettes." He said.
I opened the door, and smiled... BANG! Punch in the face:

"Got a hard on has he?"
"What?" I was in total shock,

173

"You heard!"

He picked up a pickaxe handle that was by the door and swung it at me. I tried to get away into the kitchen, he missed me and hit June's door, smashing the glass all over the floor. June and her neighbour ran upstairs and got the children out, I shouted for them to call the police. By now Dan was holding the handle to my throat, from behind, pulling it with both hands, it was strangling me.

"Let her go!" Gary stepped in, he was holding a hammer.

"Careful, you'll hit her!" Dan laughed.

Gary swung the hammer hitting Dan on the head, he narrowly missed me, I'm not sure how. I was now on the floor and Dan was hitting the glass in lounge doors, the glass was shattering all over me, he was then hitting me with the pickaxe handle, with his free hand he reached and felt his head, he was dripping blood,

"Look what he's done to me!" Then hit me again.

The next thing I knew, the police were there,

"Mr.......?" the officer said, walking towards Dan

"Nope!" Dan answered, "Right house, wrong person!"

An ambulance was already there, the police wanted us to get into the same ambulance, I refused so they called another. I asked for Gary to go with me but the policeman wouldn't allow it.

"We need to talk to him first," he said.

June said not to worry and that the kids were fine with her, I was whisked away. At the hospital they took X-rays but nothing was broken, there were just superficial cuts from the glass all over my legs and a few bruises, the baby was fine..

"Where's Gary?" I asked but nobody knew.

They told me that my husband was in another cubicle and asked if I wanted to see him? After what he had done, I didn't think so; I was surprised that they had even asked. I was discharged but the police officer said I would need to go to the police station in the morning to make a statement; they had arrested Gary.

"For what reason, exactly?" I quizzed,

"G.B.H, possibly even attempted murder; he did hit your husband with a hammer!"

"He was protecting me; Dan attacked me, what is wrong with you people?"

I was dumbfounded; these so called peacemakers didn't have a clue about what was going on. I left and ordered a taxi, June said she'd pay it when I got back, we'd sort it out later.

"June, I'm so sorry, what about your house?" I asked.

"Its just material things, the important thing is that you are all right and so are the kids."

We talked about the nights events and about the things that Dan was saying, he told her that he had planted a bug down the side of the chair and had heard me and Gary talking. We were both completely bewildered. June told Dan that nothing had been said and that she was with us the whole time. We sat and questioned further what we may have said that even remotely sounded like 'he's got a hard on' but nothing. It was another unprovoked attack. June and Mindy had already cleared the glass but three of her four doors were without any glass at all and the other one had just one panel left.

I went to the police station as I'd been asked where I learnt that both Gary and Dan had been arrested for breach of the peace; they were to appear in court later that morning. I went through the details of my marriage, I explained the non-molestation Order but it was dismissed. The D.C who interviewed me said that Dan had a serious injury requiring seven stitches, whilst Gary was unhurt. No but I was,

"So, if I'd have hit him with a hammer that would be different then would it?"

Well yes, apparently that was exactly the case. I left the kids with June and went straight to the court, Lou was already there and she burst into tears at the sight of me

"My God, what has he done to you now?"

She apologised for blaming me the last time and for all the other things but Dan was her son, she was there to pick him up and support him

"Are you here to meet Dan aswell?" she asked,

"No, I don't want to know after what he's done to me, to June's home and to
my children."

"So you are here for Gary then?"

"Yes, what did you expect? He just about saved my life...
Again!"

The court usher came out, we'd been waiting a while so I asked about the case only to be told it had finished and both Dan and Gary had been released, via the police station. I went to the police station. As I was leaving Lou pulled up outside, she was told they had been bound over in the sum of £200 for a year but had walked out together and got into a taxi... Together. I was absolutely livid

175

again, I thought, 'I don't believe this, Dan had done it again.' Now Gary and he were friends so where did that leave me? I drove back to June's. Lou was already there with Dan. Dan would pay for the damages and Lou gave June some money for the trouble that he'd caused. Gary was sat in June's lounge, I asked him what he was playing at but he said Dan had approached him and suggested they share a taxi; it would be cheaper as they were going to the same place. Lou and Dan left; he said he was going home to have a shower. Lou suggested we all go to her home for dinner and talk about things, the kids too. Sam would be there and he'd play games with them and keep them amused. I drove the kids there after taking Gary home, he asked what I intended to do, I said he'd got into enough trouble because of me but he wasn't bothered. He laughed about the fact that Dan had cried all night, saying over and over

"What have I done?"

Until another prisoner had shouted at him to shut up. I didn't find it funny, It was Dan's money that paid for the taxi, I said I'd ring him in a couple of days. I wasn't going back to Dan.

I got to Lou's at about 5:30pm, the kids were so thrilled to see Grandad and he took them off into the other room. Lou was in the kitchen and Dan and I chatted, it was decided that the kids would stay with Granny and Grandad overnight, Dan and I would go back to June's and collect all our belongings and I would go home with him. For the most part he would live with his 'mate', during the week and come home weekends. There would be no more violence,

"Yeah, yeah! Ok!"

He said he had learnt his lesson... Again. I could see who ever I wanted but until the house was sold and I was re-housed, he didn't want anybody there with me, male or female. I really had no choice, here I was six months pregnant and homeless, or soon to be and no money. Dan would continue to pay me maintenance and housekeeping. That was how it was.

Quite a few weeks passed and then in mid august the buyers came to look at my home. The first ones who saw it bought it, it broke my heart to be showing people around my home. The solicitors and the housing department sent letters back and forth but nothing was finalised, the people buying my home said I would have to be out by the 15th September 1984, just four weeks before my baby was due.

It was mid august, Dan didn't come home on the Friday night as I'd expected, especially as he was due to pay me. He'd missed a couple of Fridays since his promises at Lou's but he always came in on a Saturday morning. I waited all day Saturday but he didn't turn up, I called Lou and asked if she knew where he was? She'd heard nothing. She called me back on Sunday morning.

"Any sign?" she asked,

"No, I'm going to take the kids and see if I can find him."

"Ok!" She told me to let her know.

I drove to the sailing club, checked the mooring, the boat wasn't there, he must be out on it. It was sunny so I walked with the kids along the prom, I was heavily pregnant, wearing a bright orange bikini top and navy blue dungarees, and I looked a real sight.

"There's Daddy!" Lorna said and headed off towards him. He was walking towards the sailing club having just landed the boat, there was a woman sat with her back to me, on the groin.

"Come with me," he said to me, "I'm going into the club."

"No, you go," I said looking over his shoulder, "I'm going to have a chat to your friend."

"Please don't make a scene," he piped.

"Me, why would I?"

Why shouldn't I? Was more the point. As I walked up behind her I studied her, she still had her back to me and looked slim. She was tanned and well kept with long curly hair, everything I certainly wasn't. Well, I had an excuse! I approached her.

"So, you are my problem are you?"

As she turned around I got the shock of my life, she was old and all wrinkled, I suddenly felt quite good about myself.

"Sorry, who are you?" She asked – well spoken,

"Dan's wife!"

"Oh right!" she said glancing past me in search of Dan.

I noticed she had scarred wrists, so she was obviously suicidal as-well. Dan came back over, as I sat down on the groin. The kids were playing in the bit of sand close by. Dan sat between Helen and me, silence descended…

"Boy, you are really scraping the barrel this time! Surely you can do better than that?" I said, breaking the silence.

He was angry, I could see it in his face but what could he do to me though with her watching? He handed me my money;

"Don't worry love, you're not the first and I'm sure you won't be the last"

177

"Dan, can we go? I don't have to put up with this!" Said Helen,

"Yes Dan, off you go!" I butted in…

Who or what did she think she was? I called the kids and we went home, I laughed most of the way, if nothing else I felt better about myself than I had in a long while.

I phoned Lou when I got home and told her I'd found him, I explained where he was and that he was with another woman, she came straight round. As we talked, I gave her the description of the woman I'd met, the recognition began to grow in her face,

"Do you know her name?" She asked.

No, I didn't for sure but I explained the invitation I'd found earlier in the year,

"Helen!" I said, "I followed him one night to a home in the road opposite you."

She looked horrified,

"It's not my friend is it?"

"I don't know, you tell me,"

"It sounds like her!" Lou was hurt by the thought, "either I go round to her or she comes round to see me every Friday, she hasn't said a word. How long do you think he's been seeing her?"

"Well over a year." I replied.

"I'm so sorry, I really didn't know, she's been working for Sam too, as his secretary. I really didn't know, do you believe me?" she was mortified,

"Yes, of course!" I did, her face had said it all,

"You wait until I see the pair of them; I'll put a stop to this!"

"No, it doesn't matter anymore Lou."

I was hurt and upset, not for myself but poor Lou, he'd betrayed me, that I could take but to have done this to his mother and then what sort of friend was this Helen person? She made sure Dan had been out, knowing Lou was going round every Friday, for over a year. I found out later the following week that poor Lou had been so upset when she'd left me; she went straight to her sister in tears and told Susan the story. Susan called me, she said how upset Lou had been, she had thought I would think she had lied when she said she hadn't known and I would stop her seeing the kids, she had stood by Dan, even through every thing he'd put me through. I called Lou, I told her I believed her and it wasn't her fault, I re-iterated what I had said before,

"I would never stop you seeing your grandchildren, not the two I have, or the one due." To which she said,

178

"It is Dan's isn't it?"

I still didn't know for sure but I said,

"Yes of course it is."

She never knew, although I'm sure she always suspected. Even though, she always treated him as one of her own. We were friends, I loved her, and she was the best mother in law I could ever have had.

Dan was very different when he came home that night, sort of sheepish. He apologised for something, I'm not sure what. I was angry with him, not because of me, I'd known for ages but for his mum, I told him so but I didn't really need to say anything, he knew. Dan suggested ending his relationship with Helen, telling me he'd be the perfect husband and father, we'd move away and start again but I didn't want that. He cried that night, I had never seen that side of him although I never knew whether it was real, did he regret what he'd done to us and his mum or was it just total self pity? He came out with the usual tit for tat, 'if you hadn't done this I wouldn't have done that.' He had to take responsibility for his adultery. Finally he went to bed and I sat alone in the lounge.

About an hour later he burst in through the door, I didn't even flinch. There was no violence but he looked terrible, white as a sheet;

"What's the matter?"

"I've had a nightmare!" he said, looking absolutely terrified,

"What about?"

"I've just seen Gran. She warned me about someone with the initial B."

I didn't know anyone with that initial, other than Gary's brother but why would she say anything about him?

"It's just your mind playing tricks, go back to bed!"

He was so child like, it was quite unnerving especially as Dan was a total atheist, ghosts, the afterlife were all complete rubbish to him, yet he was totally convinced that he had seen her.

I slept on the settee that night but took his tea in to him in the morning. He woke straight away which was very odd. I usually had to put the tea down, call him from the door and run before he launched something at me. He hated mornings, my son Lee is exactly the same. He asked me to talk for a while and I agreed, he was still trying to change my mind and convince me that we could make it work.

179

"Dan we've done it all, we've tried, I love you but I don't like you, its over."

He cried again, "Please don't do this to me!"
I thought… 'Stay strong, don't give in.' After about an hour he said something I'll carry with me always, whenever I have doubts. He said;

"We may have had our problems but I've always loved you and I could never wish for a better mother for my children!"
There was the Dan I knew but I knew he would never be that Dan for long. We had a few more harsh words towards the last month in the house but 'we' were over, there was no need to fight anymore. I had too much to think about anyway, I still hadn't heard where or when I would be housed after the sale of my home.

Dan didn't fight me on custody of the kids; we agreed to have joint custody. He admitted that he'd never be any good at bringing the children up anyway. He'd pay maintenance and wanted to see them, I would never restrict that, He was their father after all and the problem wasn't theirs, it was ours. I am a firm believer in that and still stand by it.

I saw Gary regularly, although I didn't feel the same about him as he said he did about me. I really didn't want to be alone; I would be a single parent, which in hindsight would probably have been better. The baby was due in just a month, I had kept most of my antenatal appointments, I had missed a few but all had been well on the scans and the amniocentesis. He was still in the breech position but had time to turn; my son was safe inside me.

Chapter 26

The one area I didn't want to live in was where I was put but I had no choice. I was allocated a three bed roomed, terraced house, just three days before the new people were due to move into my home, at least it was a house with its own garden and not a flat. Dan hired a van and helped with the removals. We collected everything, packed it up and closed the door on my home, all the perfect, ideal family ideas were left on the doorstep. I knew nothing could ever replace that ideal, though the reality was quite different. I looked at Dan; somewhere through everything, fighting back the tears, I did still love him. He smiled back and said,

"You'll be fine, I know you will." We drove away.
By the time we had got to my new house, Dan and I had exchanged a couple of harsh words, being civil never lasted long. The only remark, the words that cut so deep and will stay with me always were:

"You're where you belong, back with your own kind, where I found you!"
I couldn't help thinking that he was right although, maybe he had said it to hide his own hurt. Perhaps I had read him wrong all these years, maybe everything he'd done to me was to cover his true feelings, lashing out to protect himself. I couldn't afford to have feelings and thoughts like that, taking risks, my life had been truly at risk and if I considered it as anything more than a passing thought he would, without a doubt, at some point have killed me and I had to keep that thought.

The kids weren't happy in the area we had to live in either. They had to go to a different school and had lost all of their friends, they had lost everything. Even as we were moving in there was a knock on the door, it was the neighbour;

"Would you mind clearing up the mess your children have made!" He ordered.
We had a communal alleyway between his and my house, I looked out,

"What mess?"

"They have dropped crisps all over it!"

"Ok, thank you for letting me know, I will see to it in a minute." I said as agreeably as I could,

"I would like it done now!" He replied. I wasn't best pleased,

"Yes mate, I'll drop everything just for you! Hold on while I rush and get my dustpan and brush. Now… Which box would it be in? Eany… Meany… Miney… Mo!" I replied, sarcastically, pointing to the boxes that scattered the whole ground floor of my new home. I called the kids in; "What have you been doing?"

"Nothing," Lee said, "it was a crisp, that's all and I've picked it up. That man had a real go at us."

"Oh did he?"

I stormed round and knocked the door. My new neighbour opened it and was quite taken aback;

"The crisp was picked up and I apologise if there was a mess but I tell you now, you ever shout at my children again and I'll rip your heart out and stick it where the sun doesn't shine, you got that?"

I walked back down the path; Dan was stood on my doorstep watching me although saying nothing. My neighbour protested,

"I just like it kept tidy!"

I carried on walking, the kids were laughing hysterically.

"Well that told him. Yep, you'll be ok!" Dan said smiling.

Before Dan left he asked me if he could have a key, just in case there was an emergency, I didn't see why not, I would double latch the door at night so he wouldn't be able to get in unless I wanted him there. I gave him the key and asked for a contact number, which he gave, he left saying,

"I'll be over to see the kids on Saturday, ring me if you need me."

I walked to the call box just up the road and called Gary,

"I'm in and Dan's gone."

"Ok, I'll be there shortly."

An hour later he arrived and stayed that night, he helped unpack and put everything where I wanted it. Lou visited the following day,

"It's not that bad is it?" She said, looking around.

"It will have to do," I replied.

It could have been worse, although not much. I told her about my neighbour and how we were off to a really good start. I really missed my home and my friends. My new home was now nearer to Gemma and Iris, Mum, my sister and even my Dad. I tried to look at the positive. I was even closer to Gary's family but it wasn't my home.

Just a few days later, Lee came in looking really upset, not crying, just sad;

"What's up honey?" I asked.

"Nothing." But his face said different, his lip started to quiver.

"Come on tell me, you know you can tell me anything." I said brushing his hair away from his face, he burst into tears and said through his sobs,

"I want to go home, I hate it here!"
It broke my heart to see him so distressed.

"It may only be for a while."
I promised him and myself that we would find a way back to where we used to live, we wouldn't be able to live in the same house but I would somehow put it right for my children. It took three years of hell but I kept that promise.

I received my part of the settlement from the house, a mere £2,500, which was all that remained after deductions for legal aid. Much more than Dan though, my solicitor had kept to his word. Dan had intentionally run up the bills and it was deducted from his share. By the time they'd finished he only had £700, out of which he had a personal loan to pay, finally ending up with about £200, he wasn't pleased, he'd said as much when he came round. Gary always stayed upstairs when Dan came round, so as not to upset him, he was also brilliant with the kids and even bought them a kitten. I had never liked cats, I've always been more of a dog person but I let them keep it.

Verity lived just two roads away and now had three children, two boys and a girl. I loved them all but with everything that had happened I hadn't spent enough time with them; I felt it might be different now we all lived so close. Her daughter Kirsty was six months old, martin was just three years old and Craig now four and a half years old - three months younger than my Lorna. My third child was almost due.

The pains started on the 10th October 1984. The cat had an appointment for treatment at a vet in a part of town about twenty minutes away from me, the appointment was at 5:30pm. I had been ill in bed for three days prior to that, maybe the stress of moving, or a virus, or both but I was constantly sweating, Gary had called the doctor out but he couldn't find anything wrong other than my baby was still in the breech position. I had driven to the vets but Gary had to take the cat in for me, the pains were getting very strong and regular. I drove home like that, getting back at about

6:30pm. Verity had looked after the kids at hers, so Gary rushed around there to see if they were ok. Verity came back with him and the children, I wished she hadn't, I didn't want the kids to see me like that, it was obvious by now I was well into labour, I heard Lee ask Gary;

"Is mummy going to die, should we get my Dad?"
I called him over and cuddled him,

"I'm ok honey, the baby is coming."
He didn't look very reassured but I did the best I could to make him feel at ease. Gary phoned for an ambulance which arrived very quickly, I couldn't drive in that condition. Verity offered to look after the kids. I kissed them and said,

"Granny will bring you in later to see your new brother."

"I think we may need to get there pretty quick," said the paramedic, "maybe with a blue light driver!"
We drove the twenty-minute journey to the hospital in about eight minutes. The paramedic was amazing and relaxed me by making me laugh, he kept saying,

"Don't push or anything."
As we whisked past the end of Dan's road I thought, 'someone should tell him' but there was no time now and when we arrived at the labour ward everything happened very quickly, it was 7:00pm and all hands were on deck. Gary came running in just as my baby boy, Matthew was being delivered, the midwife said;

"Oh, it's a bald one!"

"I don't have bald babies!"

"Oh my God!" She corrected, "Nope, it's a bottom!"
He was there in seconds, no stitches and no time to think, at 7:25pm it was over, a perfect baby boy at 6lb 4oz. Three out of four of my babes, were all the same weight, Carl, Lorna and Matthew, Lee however weighed an impressive 8lb 2oz.

From the moment I saw Matthew it was love again, relief as well, through it all, he had no side effects. The other thing that struck me was how like Gary he looked; he had a likeness to the others too, especially with the mass of black hair.

"Well, I'll go and finish my supper, it should still be hot. I wish all deliveries were as quick as that." The midwife said.
She was very surprised, especially as he had been a breech delivery. A new baby, a new home, a new partner and new beginnings, I wondered was it possible that finally I could have found a form of happiness?

No such luck! My happiness was short lived, Dan came in at visiting time the following day, ranting and raving about how I should have told him and gone round to get him, I'd let him down yet again. Eventually the nurse came in;

"Please, would you either keep it down or I will have to ask you to leave," she said, he glanced at Matthew and said,

"Don't worry, I'm going!"

I had tried to explain the timing of it all but he wouldn't have it, he just left. I felt better when Lou came in a little later with Lee and Lorna; they looked so big against this little bundle and were also really pleased with him. I thought how beautiful they all were, Carl too, he should've been there aswell, and everything would always be tinged with sadness at his loss.

I decided that as I was well and the baby was well, I would go home, I wanted to keep all of my children close. I didn't altogether trust that Dan wouldn't use his key whilst I wasn't there, who knew what he might do then. I arranged to go home by taxi, Lou had offered to keep the kids overnight but I wanted them home all together, I had preferred that they were with me, the first and only time I refused her, though I assured her that she was very welcome to be there too. She seemed happy at that suggestion, she would give them their dinner first for which I was grateful, at least I wouldn't need to worry about what was at home to feed them with. When I arrived home Lou had sorted everything for me, filled my cupboards with food, sweets and milk for the baby. As she left she handed me another £100 saying that I had to buy something for myself or the baby and once again she had crocheted a shawl.

Saturday arrived and the kids sat at the window waiting for their Dad to come and visit, he didn't show. I rang him and he'd said that didn't feel he could face it. I persuaded him to come round just for an hour or so, the kids had been really looking forward to seeing him. He sat with Lee and Lorna and I made him a cup of tea, Matthew was in the carrycot, although Dan didn't even acknowledge him. It was said that him paying no attention was my fault; he had no connections with this baby because he hadn't been there at the hospital, again I explained the circumstances of the birth but he said that if I had wanted him there, I would have found a way. He left soon afterwards telling the kids he loved them and that he would see them the next Saturday. He didn't turn up then or for quite a few weeks after; he would put my maintenance in an envelope and put it through the door.

My money from the sale of the house came through and I was able to carpet my new house, my Dad came round and fitted them for me. I rarely saw him, he was still with Diane but I still didn't really get along with her, I phoned him every couple of weeks or so. He never knew what I'd been through with Dan, not then, I only told him recently and even then I never told him any details, what could he have done anyway? What had been, had been. Aaron never knew what had happened with Dan either, although Dan thought he did and was frightened enough to borrow a shotgun and put tin cans above the bedroom door, just in case. My brother was in prison at the time anyway.

Mum popped round just after I'd brought Matthew home, which was one of three visits in the three years that I lived at that house. She had been going to my sisters, around the corner, twice a week; I was used to it by now. Jim died a year later, in October 1985 without ever seeing Matthew.

I'd given up on my music aspirations, just another dream down the drain; I'd had to sell my P.A to pay for car repairs, to keep mobile. Gary still had the drum kit though and part of my money went on financing his new venture; he had decided that he'd like to form a band, with me as his manager. In the whole year that 'The Keep' were together I didn't make any money, just paid out. I even bought them a cheap van; Gary didn't have a licence so it was driven by one of the other members of the band. I arranged gigs and paid for studio recording time.

If I'd had any doubts about Matthew's parentage at the start, by the time he was just four months old it was confirmed in my mind who his father was, when we put music on, or the band practised he would get up on his knees in the pram, rocking backwards and forwards to the rhythm of the music, sometimes so violently his pram would move from one side of the room to the other. Gary didn't work, he signed on for benefits and was (on paper) still living at his mum's house, although he stayed with me most of the time. When I suggested us becoming a proper family and he claim for all of us he didn't want to, he said he wasn't ready. What if it didn't work out? I did question that many times over the whole of our relationship; we'd stayed together through some really bad times. Things were much calmer now; didn't he want to be with us? There was no way I would be going back to Dan, what was the problem?

Dan had moved in and was living with Helen by then but we still saw each other regularly. On one occasion, when Matthew was about three months old, I'd been out with Dan for a meal, Gary babysat. We went out to the New Forest, to a restaurant where we chatted away about everything. Dan had said that he'd wanted to talk about his visiting rights and maintenance payments, the divorce hadn't been finalised yet and Matthew now had to be included in the custody issue. He played a Paul Young tape in the car the whole time we were out, 'I want you back' kept playing, each time it played he'd say,

"This is what I want!"

Well, somewhere inside, so did I! Even though I knew it could never work, the way he was that night it would have been so easy to give in and say yes, Gary was all right but he wasn't Dan. He echoed my thoughts;

"Helen is very nice but she's not you!"

When we got back to the house he kissed me and his hands wandered but I stopped him saying,

"I'm sorry! This isn't going to work; we can't go back this time."

There it was again, he got angry and then said I had led him on.

"Just get out," he said.

I didn't need telling twice and he sped off, tyres squealing. I watched him disappear and waited for a few minutes before going indoors, waiting, expecting him to come back but he didn't. I told Gary what had happened;

"Did you get your maintenance?"

"Yes!?" Only, I didn't know what the hell that had to do with anything,

"Only we need petrol for the van," he said…

Aah, I see! I gave him the money, was that all he was interested in? I had a few hundred pounds left in the bank but had to get another car. Aaron had started dealing in cars and persuaded me to buy a V.W. Golf from him,

"An economical little car, ideal for you," he had said.

I bought it and Aaron disappeared into the background of my life again. The money from the house was spent; I'd have to rely on the maintenance payments and social security to keep us going now. Dan had been pretty good up until our 'night out,' after that I ended up having to phone and ask for the maintenance. He reduced it too, he didn't see why he should subsidise Gary, I could understand his thinking and he was quite right but ultimately it was for his children's keep. I would have to go and meet Dan to collect it at 1pm on a Friday, usually outside a pub in the car park. I turned up one day as arranged and he wasn't in the car waiting but his car was there. I waited a few minutes and decided he must still be in the bar so I went in. He was there talking to a couple of friends, when he saw me he told me to get back to the car park,

"…I'll be there when I'm ready!"

Instinct told me to get in my car and go but I couldn't, I had no money, I would have to wait. Dan came out about ten minutes later and went to his car,

"Come and get in then," he said.

I got out of my car and walked round to his driver door behind him. He grabbed me, pinned me to the car and held his left arm across my throat, his right hand holding a Stanley knife to my face;

"I could kill you now, couldn't I?" he said.

I spotted a man across the other side of the car park, going into a house and shouted to him;

"Help!" He looked across, "phone the police… Please!"

Dan shouted;

"Go ahead mate; she'll be dead before they get here!"

At the same time he released his grip. He threw the knife back into his car, put his hand in his pocket, pulled out the money and threw it at me saying,

"There's your blood money!"

I picked the money up off the ground as he sped away. There was no sign of the police, I waited, shaking and crying for at least twenty minutes. I went home and called my solicitor, I told him what had happened and he wrote to Dan's solicitor telling him that his behaviour was unacceptable. I would never meet him on my own again and I never did. If he saw the children I always arranged for someone to be there, or for someone to be with me if I took them to Helen's house, Gary would always collect them.

The 'Decree Nisi' was through by September, I didn't push for the 'Absolute' until the following year and there really wasn't any hurry, it wasn't as if I was intending to marry again. Lou carried on seeing the kids, taking them for weekends, though not Matthew at first, not because she didn't want to, she just felt she couldn't deal with nappies and things. She always turned up laden with food, sweets and presents for Matthew and he was treated exactly as the other two.

Lou had bought Lee's first ever school uniform and did so every year, Lorna's too when she started school, and when they had to change schools, she bought the new one's for them. Lorna had settled well into her new school, which was situated just at the top of our road, Lee though never settled in the school, the other children bullied him and things were made worse by one of the teachers who did the same. Lee had wet the bed and I had always put it down to what was happening with me and Dan but it continued, even after he'd gone, I then decided that it was just one of those things. Lee came home from school one day saying that he had been beaten up by three boys on the teachers say so;

"What?!"

I was horrified by what I was hearing. Lee explained he had been late by two minutes, so the teacher had kept the whole class behind for ten minutes and then told them all that if they wanted to know why they had been punished, they could blame Lee and get him on the way home. Three of them did! I was out of the door and up the road to the school within minutes. Gary stayed with Lee. When I reached the school gate the teacher was just coming out;

"Oi you, you bastard, don't you go anywhere, I want you!" I shouted.

He stopped in his tracks, suddenly the old Jan had returned; hurting my kids is like a red rag to a bull. I charged towards him and pinned him to the wall, as big as he was and as small as I was, I found the strength.

"Who the hell do you think you are?"

I threatened him with all sorts; the head master came out and demanded that I put the teacher down,

"Release him!" He boomed.

"No chance!"

"I'll call the police," he said.

"Go ahead, we can tell them how your teacher has had my son beaten up," I said. Finally I released him and said, "Actually, on second thoughts, I'll go to the police and the education office, I will have your job."

I did, I took Lee to the doctors and the bruising to his face and back were registered in his medical records. I reported the incident to the education officer and told them that if I didn't get satisfaction I would report it to the police. Mr Trent was later suspended and out of the school for three months. He left shortly afterwards, a relief, not just to us but quite a few others; it seemed, as I learned from many of the parents and children, that this was far from being an isolated incident and this teacher had been a bully, and had even locked a number of children in a supply cupboard for minor misdemeanours, one little girl was quite traumatised and scared emotionally by this man.

Gary was rather shocked at this person in front of him, what had happened to the battered wife he'd first known? Vulnerable... A victim! This was different, this was my son, I'd fight to the death to protect my children, a lesson many people in authority learnt over the years. I would like it known though that I am a firm believer of discipline, children should respect their parents, teachers and each other but equally, it is a two way street, they should be shown the same respect. I wanted my children to have the best education I could get them, something I was not afforded.

Gary's mum and his brothers came to see us at least once a week, Tony the youngest more often. I didn't mind, he was such a joker. Ben on the other hand, rarely came around on his own, he was becoming very strange, he spent hours alone in his room, sometimes days, writing words that made no sense, just words that came into his head, there was no order, just pages and pages of words. His mother too was becoming unstable, her diabetes was a cause for concern and she'd had a lot of 'hypos.' The latest one was at my home, whilst holding Matthew in her arms, the boys were there and so was Gary, I was chatting away about nothing in particular and hadn't noticed what was happening. Gary nodded at Ben and calmly said,

"Take Matthew."

Ben took him from Mary and handed him to me; Mary was sweating profusely and was just looking at Matthew. Even after I had him, she was sat still looking, as if he was still in her arms. Gary rummaged in her handbag and pulled out a mars bar, he started putting it in her mouth piece by piece,

"Come on eat this," he said.

Tony had the kettle on and was piling sugar into a cup,

"Tea's made, drink it!"

Mary was sort of giggling but a few minutes later she came round. It was a very peculiar experience for me but obviously something that the boys were very used to dealing with and I was very impressed by the way they had dealt with it. Gary told me some of the stories of these 'hypos.' On one occasion he'd found her watering a wall in the garden with a watering can, swinging it back and forth, it was empty. Another time she was stuck under a bed, kicking her legs and giggling. She'd had a serious head injury when she'd fallen in the bathroom; she had also fallen into a main road whilst waiting for a bus and into a freezer whilst shopping at the co-op. On the latter two occasions she had been hospitalised for a couple of days, it was no wonder Ben felt he had to devote his life to her. Looking back these stories were very amusing, they were equally serious and alarming to someone who had never experienced it before. The strain on Ben was obviously far too much and early in 1986 he attempted to take his own life with an overdose of his mother's insulin. After hospital treatment, he was sectioned in a mental hospital, initially for twenty-eight days. This was the start of a catalogue of events that lasted about two and a half years.

During 1986, I had called Dad several times and spoken to Diane more than I'd ever done before, she too was having severe mental health issues, and convinced people were persecuting her, threatening her. She claimed that even the dustbin men were following her and stopping behind her as she walked up the road, obviously just emptying dustbins but there was no convincing her or consoling her. Dad didn't seem to know what to do to help and so did as he always had, he ignored it or made light of it,

"It'll go away," he'd say.

He'd been with her a long time although they'd never married, it was obvious that she was going to be Dad's choice of partner and I'd have to accept her. Verity never felt the same though and to this day has no time for her. But then she never accepted Jim either, even though Mum had married him. I had liked Jim even though I didn't see him very much at all in the last two years of his life. Verity wasn't biased though, she had equal contempt for our Dad too and the same remains so today.

So it seemed I was now surrounded by mental illness in one form or another. I didn't have much problem with Dan at that time, though he was still threatening, with a look or a comment but, for the most part, he hadn't been too much of a problem. I had had a conversation with Helen, relayed via Dan, she said she'd like to meet me sometime for a coffee and sort things out, she wanted to be part of my children's lives. No way would that ever happen! I told Dan in no uncertain terms that "she" would never be part of my children's lives, we didn't need to meet, and he could also tell her that;

"One day I will be in her rear view mirror."

191

He didn't like what I'd said although did look slightly amused by my eloquent phrasing. Another occasion was a conversation with her, when I'd phoned Dan and had a go at him, something he'd said about me that came back via Terry. I can't remember exactly what it was but it wasn't very nice. It ended with him putting the phone down, something he did regularly, in particular if I'd managed to hurt him with the things I'd say, this was something I had learned to do now, simple use or sarcasm was usually all it took. It was a weapon I used to pay him back a little for the abuse he had inflicted. I was very bitter and extremely angry but as my brother always said;

"Revenge is a dish, best served cold!"

A few seconds after Dan had hung up the phone down it rang back, it was about 11:30pm;

"What have you done to Dan?" It was obviously Helen.

"What the hell has it got to do with you?" I asked,

"We have just been out, it's my birthday and we've had a lovely time. You've spoilt it!"

"Well into your forties now then!"

"Yes and don't I look good on it? If you look half as good as me at my age you won't be doing too badly."

I laughed out loud and said;

"You've been looking in the wrong mirror missus! Don't ring here again unless I give you permission to do so. If Dan is upset you make it better, you are after all almost old enough to be his mother, bye, bye."

I put the phone down thinking, 'God that was bitchy' but even so it made me tingle with satisfaction... Poor Dan my eye!

Chapter 27

1985 to 1987 were a bit of a blur in one way or another, I'm sure at some time, early in 1985, I'd had some sort or breakdown. I was functioning, going through the motions of life, dealing with the many problems that arose, Lee being bullied at school, the continual arguments with my neighbour, who complained about everything, my children playing, chimney soot on his car, I had the chimney swept several times to please him but it wasn't enough, his car was still getting soot on it. I used to watch him clean the car, he even cleaned the door struts with a little brush, the size of a nail brush, with a light on the end, it was only an old mark 4 Cortina. He suggested I get a gas fire to stop the soot;

"You buy it and I'll have one!" Obviously he didn't.

He once spent a week cleaning that car and when he'd finished it wouldn't start, I had to laugh. He was always knocking my door, complaining about something. I'd, had enough when he said that my car was parked in his way, it was parked directly outside my house, even so, he claimed that when he came down the road he couldn't pull into his drive;

"Well, I suggest you drive around the block and come in the other way then." I said slamming the door in his face.

I also had two cats by now, another reason for him to complain, they had apparently messed in his garden, it was said as if I was the only one in the neighbourhood that had cats! Almost every house had one or more… Both my cats died from being poisoned and I believe he did it, strong accusations I know but he kept creosoting the fence between our gardens and the cats kept licking it, it obviously tasted of something. I sat with my cats and watched them die, first the older one 'fluffy' and two days later my kitten, who was only about four months old. My neighbour denied it of course, but I said it wouldn't work; I would just get more cats. I did, I got three more and dared him to touch them.

I already had a dog, a collie cross spaniel named 'Toddy,' he was such an intelligent dog. We'd had several break-ins in the area but no one had got into my home, we didn't have much worth taking but my Todd made sure no-one got in. One night someone got into my car but obviously decided that it wasn't worth taking, though they had smashed the windows on mine and my neighbour's cars that night. I could hardly believe my eyes when, the morning after, I looked out of my kitchen window to see him

193

sweeping the shed roof; it was about 9:00am and there he was, I decided then that he was completely nuts. I opened my back door and shouted,

"Are you completely mad? You will fall through that!"

"Someone has broken into my car," he said "I've had to call the police."

"And you need to sweep the roof, why?" I asked,

"It's got to be kept clean!"

"Boy, you need help!" I laughed.

I did feel sorry for his wife and children, later on him too, his wife was diagnosed with cancer, just after she had had their youngest child, he was just two years old when she died, we moved just after.

Gary and I weren't doing so well; I paid for driving lessons for him and paid for him to get a private hire licence, to drive a taxi. I needed him to work, I didn't want to stay on benefits, I wasn't used to it and I didn't want the kids to go without like I had. Besides, it was about time Gary started paying his way, if it hadn't been for Lou's constant donations and Dan's maintenance we would have drowned in debt. I worked part time at a sweet factory for the six weeks before Christmas, to get the kids their Christmas presents. It seemed to me though that all the time I was solvent, Gary was there, when I wasn't, neither was he. I bought Lee a keyboard and Gary taught him to play the basics, it was good a grounding for Lee's interest in music. Matthew too, you could tell from his early head banging in the pram that his timing was spot on. I bought him his first drum kit when he was just about 18 months old; he is still a drummer to this day. I don't remember much about Matthew's early days and I've always felt guilty about that, I do know I loved him as I did the other two, I just think that I was so busy trying to make things perfect for them and everyone else, I didn't have time to notice the changes in him, that's why I say I think I had some sort of breakdown.

Matthew was about a year old when I was rushed into hospital with severe stomach pains; at first they thought it was appendicitis, then maybe an ectopic pregnancy. Neither turned out to be the case but I was in hospital for three day, under observation and given two large doses of anti-biotics, although nobody seemed to have a definite diagnosis. Lou had told Dan and on the second day he came to visit me, not out of concern but to have a go at me;

"You're pregnant aren't you?"

"No I'm not."

"Yes you are!" He yelled, "Well I'm going to the house and I'm going to take the kids, I'll kill him and there is nothing you can do about it."

I was in pain and in floods of tears. Dan hadn't noticed, with all his ranting, that my Mum was stood behind him, when he realised he turned;

"Oh, hello Betty, how are you?" Ever so friendly,

"Don't you hello Betty me!" she yelled, "What do you think you are playing at? I never believed her (meaning me) when she said what you were like but I certainly do now, I've just heard every word. You won't go to my daughter's house and you won't be taking the children, anywhere! Now get out and don't come back!" Wow mother, where did that come from? She really did tell him. When he'd gone she looked at me, I was crying again.

"You can pack that in," she said calmly, "you're all right and he's not going to do anything, I will make damn sure of that. I'm sorry I didn't believe you."

It was a side of my Mum I had never seen before, my Mum was sticking up for me, I had real trouble believing what I'd witnessed but I remembered it. It didn't really change anything though; I didn't see her for several months after that.

During the months of 'The Keep' I felt I was quite a good manager, I secured regular gigs for the band, we even went to London trawling the record companies but without success. I sent tape after tape to various D.J.'s, including Alan Freeman, a radio one DJ but he responded as did most of the others;

"They have good potential but are not what we are looking for at the moment."

I even nailed a half hour interview on Solent – a local radio station that had played some tracks on air and an interview with Kerrang magazine but it brought nothing. The band split after about a year, frustration and a clash of personalities I suppose. The other thing was that my money had been subsidising the band and it was running out. Gary was and still is a very talented musician but luck definitely hasn't played a part in his life. The final gig the band did was as a support band for 'The Sweet' in Bournemouth, Gary had been a fan when they were at the top in the early 70's but they were pretty well forgotten by this point. 'Wig, Wham, Bam' and all those tracks will remain but the band as it was, were pretty much gone. I would loved to have gone along to watch and give support but was suffering with back problems and ended up lying on the floor for seven weeks, a disc in my spine had popped, I had no idea how it happened, obviously I had a weakness from my back injury. I'd had a few days of similar symptoms a few years earlier, after Dan had pushed me down the stairs, this time though I thought that I would never walk again; my left leg went dead from my hip to my toes. Hospital and chiropractor treatment had no effect, that was until I went and saw a remarkable woman; Mrs Bushby, she was an osteopath. I travelled there lying flat in the car, in absolute agony but after one treatment I walked out upright, although I've never regained complete feeling in my left leg.

The band went without me but when Gary came home he was very disappointed and disillusioned. 'The keep' had played well but the lead singer of 'The Sweet' was out of his face, he could hardly stand let alone perform. Gary knew then that it would never be the same again and neither was he. He tried to form another band firstly with a young guitarist called Ryan, another very talented young man, who was just sixteen years old. His claim to fame was that he had been on TV with Jimmy Saville: He had wanted to be 'Shaking Stevens.' I think Ryan was about five years old when he had appeared. He was good at writing material with a classical vain although rock was the main objective. I still have recordings somewhere of his early writings. Cliff, a bass player, joined and they did a few gigs but that soon ended too, I just couldn't afford to fund them anymore. After the band split, Gary spent most of his nights out working as a private hire driver.

Later in the year of 1986, Gary's Brother Ben's mental state deteriorated as did his mothers health, things were failing again. Then in early 1987, Ben attempted suicide again with the aid of his mother's insulin, once again he was admitted to hospital and sectioned under the mental health act for twenty-eight days. Gary had to keep an eye on his mum, as well as working nights on the taxis and it took its toll on his health too. The cracks were showing in our relationship, Gary's other Brother, Tony wasn't really any help either, he carried on living his own life and doing his own thing. He'd decided to move out of his mums and in with his girlfriend, putting more pressure on Gary to care for their mother, he was tired all the time. Ben decided, with a lot of persuasion, to stay in hospital for a while longer but then changed his mind and discharged himself. March came, along with another overdose, and he was again committed but this time when their backs were turned, he got out. He was missing for two days but was found and returned once

196

more to the hospital. Each time he did this he got worse and each time, Mary's health deteriorated, putting more pressure on Gary and our relationship. We argued constantly when he was awake, (which wasn't a lot) or in the few minutes we spent together each day. Gary then started taking pills to keep himself awake, caffeine ones to start with, although, unbeknown to me, he'd started taking other things too, I don't know what.

He had always been a little effeminate but that was part of his charm, though I really did start to wonder, especially when he started using my eyeliner, he had worn it before, when gigging, I thought most musicians did, although I hadn't noticed it with the rest of the band. I woke him up one evening, he was about to start his shift as a taxi driver, it was then I noticed the black smudges under his eyes... 'Panda eyes.' I asked him why and how long he'd been wearing makeup to work, his response;

"It makes my eyes look brighter!"
I have to admit I was pretty confused, what do you say? I decided to let him get on with it but from then on there were several things that concerned me, little things, like carrying a handbag or as he called it, a shoulder bag, he needed it to put his bits and pieces in, like his taxi book, his cigarettes, makeup, 'normal things' you expect to find in your male partners handbag.

At the end of April I went to see Ben in hospital, he'd phoned and asked if I could take him some tobacco. Mary was there when I arrived, they were sat, talking in a corridor and Mary was obviously upset by something Ben had said so I suggested we go for a walk in the grounds. Ben was acting very strangely but that was sort of expected now, he was skipping and running up and down the hills. It occurred to me that he might be acting; perhaps he wasn't quite as mad as he'd made himself out to be. I found out from Mary why she was so upset, he had apparently told her, as they'd walked near the cliff top at the back of the hospital that he could push her off the top, kill her and no one would know.

"He wouldn't do that, he thinks too much of you," I said.
She wasn't convinced. I just think he wanted a life away from her and was torn between duty and his own needs and by the time I left, I was almost convinced that Ben was play-acting, at least some of it. He walked out to my car with me;

"I've got a knife in my pocket!" He said in his most threatening voice.

"Have you got a fork to go with it?" I replied calmly, he laughed, we both did,

"You know too much," he said, "You're too clever for me!"
I left waving goodbye; although Ben unnerved a lot of people I was never afraid of him. Two or three weeks later he got out again, he went home and although he shouldn't have left when he did, Mary claimed to the doctors that he was much improved, as far as I could see, he was far from it. He would shut himself in his room hardly eating and only drinking whiskey, and then he started missing his medication and hoarding the tablets in stacks. At the end of the third week Mary came to see me, she said Ben had flipped. He'd come out of his room dressed only in his underpants and gone into her room,

"His eyes were like the devil," she'd said.
She was standing in the middle of the room and he was pointing at her from the doorway, as he pointed at her he said,

"Now go!"
And with that, using only the movement of his finger, he flew her up in the air where she hit the light shade, then she came down and ended up sat on the floor with her back against the wall, she claimed he had been no where near her;

"If you need confirmation you can check the light shade, the tassels are still up in the air." She said.
I wasn't sure what to say, Mary was very unstable but she believed this had happened. She was wearing a neck brace and sort of crying, almost howling, that in itself was quite disturbing for me. The whole conversation seemed to have no effect on Gary; he was look-ing for a telephone number in the yellow pages for a car parts com-pany. I finally said;

"Gary do something, she's your mother!"
"What do you want me to do?" he asked, he turned to her,
"Are you all right?
Do you want a cup of tea? Where's Ben now?" She seemed to calm down,

"He's at home,"
"Well, you need to call the doctors again!"
She did, on my phone but only after Gary had made his call, which was apparently far more important. Ben was admitted back to hos-pital later that day but again discharged himself; it wasn't until dur-ing the school holidays that he was re-admitted once more. He'd been sat in my house the day before and had shown no indication

that he was planning his next suicide attempt though his mental state, according to the doctor, was worsening.

In July 1987 I managed to secure the move I'd promised my children. Mary, who had been one of my neighbours in the flats, told me that her mother, who lived in a council house less than a quarter of a mile from the house I'd owned with Dan, wanted an exchange for a smaller property, she only needed two bedrooms now as her four girls had all left home and she was rattling around in a large, much larger than mine, three bedroom house. My problem was that my house too had three bedrooms and she only wanted a two. I really wanted that house, there had to be a way and I found it. My sister was living in a two bedroom house but needed a three, she wanted to stay in the area, Mary's mum didn't like the area I lived in either, but Verity's brother in law and his wife, Robert and Meryl, wanted to exchange their two bedroom home, a relatively new property, smaller again than my sisters but ideal for Mary's mum. So the exchange became a four way swap, we all went to the council, we took a diagram showing who was going where and a mutual exchange was agreed, we were over the moon, the kids could go back to their old school, though Lee only had six weeks left before going to secondary school, at least he'd be able to find all of his old friends again. Lorna would have to start again but she was very adaptable, independent and made friends very easily. The one thing that gave me the most satisfaction was that Dan had to eat his words, now I really was going back to where I belonged. He tried to keep me down and had failed miserably. Even though he said that he was pleased for us, the expression on his face said just how gutted he was. Not only had I got back but I'd done it without him, I'd proved that I didn't need him.

Mary's mother had a husband, who she was trying to get away from, he was an alcoholic and about twenty years younger than her, and he had become abusive and violent. Now, where had I heard that before? He lived with her some of the time, and then he'd beat her and leave for weeks at a time. As luck would have it, for me anyway, the weekend we moved he had one of his violent outbursts and left. She hadn't given him her new address. I went to my new house a day early with a few things, pretending to have already moved in, she'd said she thought he may be back but he wouldn't stay if we were there, we were meant to be moving in the following day anyway. Anybody else would probably have said;

"Sort it out for yourself!"

199

But I had been there and I knew what it was like to be with an abusive partner, there was also the possibility that she may change her mind about the move, I didn't want to lose the chance of getting my new home and it was just that, my home, from the moment I saw it. Just as predicted he came back, opening the door with his key, Gary and I were in the kitchen,

"What the hell are you doing here?" He asked

"Well, more to the point, what the hell are you doing here?" I returned, "This is my home now!"

"Since when?" He asked.

"Since yesterday!"

"So where's she gone?"

"I don't know," I lied, "she wasn't exchanging with me."

"Oh right. I'll just get my things and go if you don't mind." He looked broken and I did feel quite sorry for him but then that was a dangerous pattern of emotion so I had to curb it, especially given my past experiences. The only time I was worried was when he said,

"Excuse me, I need a knife!"

He reached into the cutlery drawer right next to me and took out a carving knife; he needed a piece of washing line to tie his bag up. I'm pretty sure my heart stopped for a second, he put the knife back and said,

"I won't be a minute, and then I'll be out of your way."

Then he disappeared back upstairs, he was gone for about fifteen minutes but came down with his bags. He put his keys on the side in the hall and asked;

"I don't suppose you have a cigarette do you?"

"Yes sure." I gave him a cigarette,

"Thanks!" He said putting it behind his ear. "There are some weights there if you want them." He was pointing to a bar bell in the corner of the hall, "I can't carry them, so if you want them, you can have them!"

"Thanks," I said, "and good luck!"

He returned the gesture and left. I took a very deep breath; it was a real relief that that was over. I really don't think that I had been breathing properly in the half hour or so that he'd been there.

The following day we moved in for good, it was a very chaotic day given that four families and the contents of four homes had to be moved in one day. We all started at 8:00am and finished at 10:00pm, a total of thirteen people, five dogs and six cats were moved that day and boy, what a day! That night, Gary and I slept on a mattress on the floor of our new bedroom. I was in pain with my back and absolutely exhausted, but I was elated, this was my home and I loved it. I still do, eighteen years later.

The children settled almost immediately as did the cats and dogs, the only one that wasn't settled was Gary. He had further to go to work and was a lot further away from his family. If he couldn't settle then he'd have to do whatever but this wasn't about him, it was about my children, even if our relationship suffered, then so be it, my children were and always have been my number one priority.

Young Ryan, the guitarist, was still on the scene and often came round, even though the band had come to nothing. Gary liked writing material with him but that didn't last long either. The three of us were sat in my car, outside a local supermarket and Ryan announced from the back seat, completely out of the blue, that he was in love with me, he said he needed to be near me. I looked at Gary and he at me, though he said nothing. I told Ryan that I was flattered but of course it could never be, I was with Gary and much, much too old for him, I told him he would be better off finding someone his own age, he started crying, saying that that was the problem,

"You think I'm just a kid!"

"How do you think I feel, you announcing that to my girl-friend?" Asked Gary, "I think you're out of order!"
Well it was almost farcical; at least he'd said something. All the same, Ryan stopped coming round.

I couldn't reach Gary at work on several occasions but I wasn't really surprised... I should have been. Christmas day came and went, Dan came to see the children, on Boxing Day we all went to Lou's, Gary included and when we arrived Helen was there, Lou was in the kitchen so we went straight in there, I really wanted to rip Helen's head off but it wasn't the time or the place. Sam came in and offered us a drink, in his usual jovial way, he said to me,

"So what would my favourite daughter in law like to drink?" Draping his arm over my shoulder.

"Vodka please!" Helen said,
Sam snapped;

"You're not now, nor will you ever be my daughter in law!"
Ouch.... I looked at Lou, who by now was disappearing into the sandwiches she was making, I turned to Sam,

"I'll just have a beer please!" He went to get it,

"So Helen, have you had a good Christmas?" Lou asked,

It broke the atmosphere, as was intended,

"Not bad," she said, "until now!"

"Take no notice of Sam; you know what he's like!"

Yes 'he's great' I thought, I had to control the urge to laugh for Lou's sake. Helen was destroyed in one line, even more surprising was that Dan didn't say a word in her defence; he didn't even seem angry, instead he went and talked to the children. We stayed just a couple of hours then walked home again.

I spent New Years Eve 1987 with the kids, Gary was working but the kids stayed up and saw the New Year in with me. Lee put his arm around me;

"Happy New Year Mum!"

I said the same, kissed them all and put them to bed. I phoned Gary and wished him happy New Year but he was too busy to talk. I knew, even though I wanted our relationship to last, it was coming to an end. The money had run out and the only reason he was staying was because of Matthew, who was now over three years old. We had bought him a real, half size drum kit for Christmas, Lee already had his keyboard so we had bought him an electric guitar and amp, they would, without doubt, be musicians. Lorna didn't seem to have the same interest in music, drama was her forte and she certainly was dramatic. She knew exactly how to twist everyone around her finger, in particular her Grandad, Sam. He would give her the world, Marilyn too but it was obvious that Lorna was his favourite; she'd only have to say,

"Grandad you know how much you love me?"

She would sit on his knee and he'd empty his pockets of cash and give it to her, Marilyn didn't have quite the same way with him. Lou often had them to stay; they now lived in a big house with a swimming pool, walking distance from where we lived. Lee and Matthew stayed too but not as often, although they'd go over in the day and swim. Sam had taught all of the children to swim almost as soon as they could walk, all because of what had happened to Damien. Matthew had fallen in the pool once and Sam went in fully clothed, pulling him out before he'd even touched the bottom, I had never seen such fear on a man's face before. Matthew was none the worse for the experience and within three or so weeks could swim like a fish. On Monday's, Sam always had his friends round to play cards and both Lorna and Marilyn would be the waitresses, fetching and carrying. Lorna would tell Sam what cards his friends were holding and he'd slip her a pound for each bit of information, in time she caught on and would do the same to his friends, telling them what cards he was holding and they in turn, gave her money. She made an absolute fortune, not exactly the way to teach children about money but it was all in fun.

In the spring of 1988, I started work at a Pontins holiday camp with my old friend Gemma, as chalet maids. Jack had long since gone and she too had transferred to a house on an estate close by. The job was part time: 10:00am to 2:00pm, Mondays, Wednesdays and Friday and 10:00am to 4:00pm on a Saturday, the beauty of it was I could take all the children with me; they could use the facilities, swimming pool and amusements, although the older ones were at school during the week. We loved it and Gemma and I renewed our friendship.

Chapter 28

It was September 1988: Gary's mum and Ben came round, Ben asked if he could stay the night, just to spend some time with us, it was Gary's rare one night off. I was concerned but I agreed as long as he was searched first, to prove he had nothing on him that he could harm himself with, Ben was fine with that. I took Mary home and said I'd be in touch and bring Ben home again in the morning, she was grateful for the break, even if it was just overnight. We sat with Ben all evening laughing and joking; he really was very funny and seemed more relaxed than I'd seen him in years. He suggested then that I should try writing poetry, mind you it was something I'd already tried with a little success, it was something other than my music that I had taken an interest in. Given my hectic existence to date, I hadn't really had much time to think about anything other than survival.

That night I went to bed before Gary, he came up at about 3:00am, not that it made any difference, its not like we had any physical relationship to speak of, besides, I had an aversion to sleeping with a man who was wearing make up. At about 7:00am I heard a sort of grunting noise, I listened for a minute thinking it was the one of the dogs, we now had an Alsatian too, it was then that I remembered Ben was there. I woke Gary and asked him to listen; he jumped out of bed and flew down the stairs,

"Phone 999, Ben's done something!" He yelled up the stairs.

I did as he asked, telling the operator we needed an ambulance and that I thought Ben had overdosed, he was on my settee and was having a fit, foaming at the mouth. The ambulance arrived in minutes but had to send for another, Ben couldn't be put on an ordinary stretcher, he was still fitting and his body was convulsing so much that it took four medics, carrying him in a canvas sling to get him out. He was very seriously ill but there was a funny side and I had to laugh, he was wearing a t-shirt with Donald Duck's three nephews on it and underneath it read 'stoned again', very apt. It was exactly the sort of humour you'd expect from him, somewhere along the way, I think I must have gained a similar warped sense of humour.

We phoned Mary and told her what had happened, she started weeping;

"I'll be there in a few minutes to pick you up!" I yelled over the howls.

Gary waited for Lou to collect the kids, he would go to the hospital after, so off I went, again. When I got there Mary was in a terrible state, I checked she'd taken her medication, she said that she had. She had suffered from angina and was complaining about a pain in her chest. She just wanted to get to Ben; I could understand that, he was her son, although I think she was more concerned about what would happen to her if he didn't pull through. Her chest pains were becoming worse and I put my foot down, speeding all the way, I couldn't have cared less if I was stopped, besides the police would understand, one look at Mary and I would have probably gotten a police escort anyway but as usual, when you want one, there's none about.

When we arrived at the hospital I ran in for some help, Mary was taken from my car on a trolley into emergency outpatients where she was put on a heart monitor. I explained to the nurses what had happened and that Mary was really anxious about Ben, they phoned up to I.C.U and assured her that he was stabilising, they also informed Gary of where we were. Here I was, one in emergency treatment and one in intensive care, I think I was losing the will to live myself but then I'm too nosey to end it all. I looked up to the sky;

"You keep throwing them, I'll keep handling it!" I said, I wasn't at all religious but something about talking like that, helped. Later the phrase changed to…

"You keep throwing them pal!"

A couple of hours later Mary was released, her angina had stabilised so we went to see Ben, I waited until she went in to see him then I left, I had to get home to my children, Gary stayed at the hospital with his mother then took her home when she was finished.

On the Tuesday Mary phoned to tell me that Ben was being released, it had only been two days, surely he was going to be hospitalised? No, he was being released into her care but she needed a lift to collect him and of course I said yes. I waited outside in the car park whilst she went in, about ten minutes later they came out. Ben sat in the front with me and Mary in the back; I noticed he still had a drip needle in his hand;

"Why is that still there?" I asked, "They wouldn't have left it in!"

According to Ben they had told him he could take it out himself, I knew then that he'd discharged himself, I questioned him but he denied it. We pulled up outside Mary's house she got out, thanked me and went to open the front door, whilst she was out of ear shot, I asked Ben;

"Why Ben, what is wrong? Why do you keep doing this?"

"I love you, you know? You know me better than them!" He replied.

"Ok," I said, "but why?"

He smiled and said;

"It's my life and if I want to end it, I will!"

"You're not going to do it again, are you?"

"It's my life and there's nothing you can do about it."

He got out of the car and I followed, Mary was waiting at the door, I had to tell her.

"Ben has just told me he's going to do it again!" She turned to him,

"Your not going to do it again, are you Ben?"

"No, course not!"

She turned to me;

"See, he's not so don't worry about it."

I had to do something so on my way home I called into the taxi office to let Gary know what was happening. He was out on a drop so they called him on the radio to come back to the office, I waited, he returned about thirty minutes later. I told him what Ben had said and that I knew he was going to do it again, I was worried, Gary said;

"What do you want me to do; I've only just started my shift?"

When he realised how distressed and convinced I was that Ben was going to do it again, he told me to go home, he'd see what he could find out and ring me. He rang about an hour later, he had phoned his own G.P, who had also been dealing with Ben and what he said was frightening; basically nothing could be done, Ben was 'schizophrenic' but until he had reached a point in his illness where he could cope, he would continue like this and if he was intent on killing himself, nothing any of us said or did would change it. The doctor had also said that people in mental hospitals, under supervision, would still find a way to end their lives, if that was to be their sole intention. I had to accept that what would be would be. Just three weeks later my worst fears were realised.

Gary left me just two days after Ben discharged himself, I'd found out that he had been seeing a girl who was just seventeen years old. I had been concerned about his health, given the problems with Ben and his mother. He was also putting in extra hours but not really earning any extra money. I decided to speak to his boss, the 'Judge' as they called him,

"What's up?" He asked, "Gary playing away from home?"

"No, I don't think so!"

I was a little taken aback by his assumption, and then he said,

"Well, he's never where he's supposed to be and he's always off air when he's called, no wonder he's not earning."

It was then that I realised what was going on, he was doing the dirty and cheating on me? I wasn't playing any games this time so, when he came home I asked him. First of all he denied it but in the end he admitted it, I realised that this had been going on for well over a year and not just the one, this young girl was the latest in a long line. I did consider the possibility that it was a man, I only had Gary's word that it was a girl, either way I said he had to leave, not tomorrow, not next week but now. I watched as he packed a few of his things, he could come back for the rest later. I was hurt and very angry; I just couldn't believe that it had happened again. He left that night and I went to work the next morning as normal. I hadn't slept that night, I was so upset and my mind had been working overtime. It had started with thoughts of Gary being with someone else, imagining him touching another woman, then the thought of another man and then my thoughts turned to anger, he knew exactly what I'd been through with Dan and still he did the dirty, he had managed to spend all my money and use my car too. I'd got him everything he wanted and he left me with a little boy of four years old and two kids that thought the world of him.

The kids went to school, I'd decided not to tell them that he'd gone, I'd wait until later when I would have time to sit them all down and talk to them. While I was at work Gary came back with two men, who had decided that it was a good idea to kick my dogs all over the house, granted my Alsatian could be a little vicious and unpredictable with strangers but he was wonderful with the kids, particularly Lorna, besides that what he was for, protection. Also, Gary knew what he was like and so should have locked him in the kitchen. As a result of the beatings the dogs received, they messed all over my furniture and carpets, even my bed, they must have been petrified. Gary ripped out the stereo and speakers;

in fact he'd taken everything he could get his hands on, guitars, stereos, microphones, even my leather jacket, what he hadn't taken was left covered in dog crap.

I got home at 2:30pm and was shocked by the devastation. There was no way that I'd have been able to clean up before the kids came home. I rang Gemma and told her what had happened, I'd only just dropped her home but she said she'd come straight round. I then called Lou to see if she could take the kids for the night, she too came straight round and was there by 3:00pm, she took Matthew with her and offered to stay and help clean up but I said no, I didn't want Lee and Lorna to see the mess. We were all horrified that he could have done this to me, if I'd ever needed confirmation of the reason he had been with me, this was it… He was only in it for what he could get and one thing was for sure, he'd be bringing it all back, especially the things that belonged to the children, including Lee's guitar and his stereo. I really found it hard to believe he could be so heartless. Gemma and I spent the next three or four hours just cleaning, all the furniture, all the carpets. When we were finished Gemma went home and I was alone, no children, no partner, just alone and crying, again. Was I really so bad that he felt he had to do this to me? I tried to watch the television but I couldn't concentrate and finally decided I would feel better if I contacted Gary, face to face, I wanted to know why he'd done this to me, to the kids and the dogs. If I phoned he would be able to hang up on me and there was no way that I'd let him get away with this one. I drove to the taxi office, he wasn't there, he hadn't turned up for his shift. I drove to his Mum's; she invited me in but claimed that he wasn't there, although he had been in a bit earlier. Tony and Ben were there too, they said that he hadn't brought any of my things there but if he did turn up they would phone me. I could tell from Ben's actions that I was being lied to, although he was agreeing with Mary and Tony verbally, he was motioning with his head towards the ceiling as if to say; "He's upstairs!" Ben was lying on the settee, obviously very mentally ill but what was more obvious was his loyalty to me. He kept repeating, over and over again,

"Jan wants to get a gun, Jan wants to shoot Gary!" Almost sort of singing it. When I went to leave he motioned again to the stairs but said,

"Don't be a stranger, we still love you!"
I said goodbye. That was the last time I saw Ben alive, the following day I had a call from Mary saying Ben had gone missing;

"Is all your insulin there? Has he taken any with him?" I asked,

"I don't know," she replied, "I don't think he has taken any of it!"

I couldn't help thinking, 'why isn't she certain?' Surely, given Ben's history, she had kept it locked away and would be aware at all times of how much she'd had there. No, apparently not, I had hoped he would head for my home but he didn't turn up or phone. I knew then that I was clutching at straws. The police were notified and all the hospitals were checked but there was no sign of him. I went out with Mary the following day looking for Ben through the woods, Gemma came too. Mary seemed to think he might be hiding, camping out somewhere. I instinctively knew that he'd died; he had succeeded this time, though Mary wouldn't have any of it. Looking back, I would say she had been, even from his first attempt, in denial.

I took Gemma home, we had found nothing, I then went back to Mary's, we were going to check a few more places, around the grounds of the hospital close to where they lived and around the scrap yard. Mary thought that maybe he had slipped, unseen, into one of the vehicles being dismantled. Again we found nothing. As we looked out from the hospital grounds, towards their home, I had a feeling that he was close by and that he could see his home and us from where he was, I said as much to Mary. We called his name for a bit, mainly just to please her but in the end we went back to Mary's house, still nothing. I went home, I suppose it had taken my mind off Gary but now I was alone again. I tried to phone him again but he hadn't turned up at work, I sent a message via Mary that if she saw him to ask him, firstly to bring our things home and secondly that we needed to talk.

The following day, just after I'd taken the kids to school Mary phoned, a man walking his dog about two hundred yards away from her home had discovered a body, it was lying in gorse bushes next to the dual carriageway, that ran through the estate where they lived. She would have to identify the body to confirm that it was Ben but Gary was going to take her to the morgue. So, Gary had been there all the time, how else would she have been able to contact him? This wasn't the time to be saying anything. I had been right about Ben's actions, I was right about him being dead and that his body was close to the hospital grounds overlooking his home, I had been right about pretty much everything. She came around to see me later that day, Gary had brought her but dropped her off outside, he wouldn't come in, he left saying he'd be back to pick her up. She was very strange, very matter of fact, as if she was talking about the weather. She described Ben in detail, how he'd looked like he was asleep, he had marks on his face, she said, made by the bushes. They were probably doing the post mortem at that time, she would let me know the results and what had killed him. At twenty-three years of age, Ben was dead. While Mary spoke, I kept thinking; 'Is she for real? Is this really happening?' I wasn't sure who was madder, her for talking and acting as she was or me, for listening to her and looking for bodies around scrap yards. She'd lied about Gary's whereabouts, even though he'd stolen my stuff, broken my heart and left the children who, I thought, he'd accepted as his own and to add insult to injury, my belongings were hidden in her home, along with Gary. When Gary came to pick her up he said that he couldn't come back that night but would be round the following day, agreeing we needed to talk.

He came round at 10:00am, I asked him what had happened to my dogs, he'd said that Pups had attacked his friends.

"Well you knew that he had to be shut in! Why didn't you do that before letting them in?"

"I forgot!"

I told him that he'd ruined my life and the kids lives and that I wanted him to, at the very least, bring back my children's things,

"And If I don't, what are you going to do... Put a hex on me?"

What was he talking about?

"If you like!" I replied, with a little sarcasm and didn't really think anymore of it. We talked about how he felt and about how this girl that he'd been seeing, didn't mean anything to him, she was just one, in a long line. It seems they'd met, as with most of them, when he'd taken her home, essentially customers. He'd said that he was sorry but he couldn't cope with the responsibility of all of us, he'd never wanted to settle down. The list was endless but it was all about him. He was willing to try again; he didn't want to live at his mum's. I don't know where my head was but I agreed, I guess I didn't want to be alone. He stayed the night, although I wouldn't sleep with him and went to work the following night as if nothing had changed… There wasn't even a mention of Ben, nothing; it was as if he'd never existed.

Later that week, it was around the third week in September but I can't remember the dates exactly, we had the results of the post mortem... Ben had injected enough insulin to kill an elephant, he'd injected it and just walked until he dropped down dead, they were surprised, on account of the amount he'd used, that he'd walked as far as he had before he'd died.

By the end of September Gary was 'unreachable' on the radio again, and then he didn't come home at all for a couple of days. Inevitably, when he did, we'd have a massive row and to cap it all, he'd missed Ben's funeral, which had taken place with just Mary and Tony attending. Poor Ben! He'd had the right idea though and was well out of it now. Gary finally went for good on the fourth of October 1988, just six days before Matthew's 4th birthday. We'd had another argument just after he had gotten up for work. I had wanted him to stay home, at least that way he could get away from a girl who, he claimed, was following him around and wouldn't leave him alone, even though he had told her that we were staying together, or so he said. I drank a couple of cans of beer and argued with him some more. I went upstairs, whilst there I heard him talking to this girl on the phone;

"She's gone off on one, she's completely nuts," I presumed he meant me, "I'll get there as soon as I can!"
He obviously didn't realise I was in ear shot of the whole conversation, I walked in mid sentence and told him to,

"Get off my phone!"
Then I punched him in the side of the face, I wasn't entirely sure where it had come from but I felt better for it all the same. I picked up the rest of the cans of beer and headed for the car, I didn't drink them but I needed to go, get away. I drove to nowhere in particular and just sat. I then stopped at a call box about 15 miles from home to say that I was coming back but there was no answer. Now I was frightened, I'd only been gone about 45 minutes. What had Gary done with my kids, had he left them alone? Lee was very capable but he was a child none the less and I was pretty damned sure that he'd have answered the phone. I phoned Gemma in a panic but she stopped me before I became hysterical;

"The kids are here with me, they're fine!"
Gary had told her I was drunk and had gone out in the car. He was right, I was out in the car but I was far from drunk. He'd also told her that he was leaving and that I had beaten him up. He couldn't

211

cope, so was leaving the kids with her... She said he'd dropped Matthew off to her with no shoes or socks and none of them had coats, he had also told Lee that I wasn't coming back. Gemma had phoned Lou and Sam, she didn't know what else to do and they were on their way to pick up the kids,

"Gemma, don't let them take 'em until I get there, I'll be about 10 minutes!"

I got to Gemma's to find them waiting, Lou said,

"I'll take them all home with me; at least they will get a good night's sleep. Sort yourself out, and then you can come round when you're ready. Can you bring their coats?"

I couldn't believe Gary had just dumped them; I cuddled the kids and re-assured them that I was fine, I'd just needed five minutes peace, I would never leave them and they should know that by now. They waved goodbye and I went in with Gemma.

Gemma came with me to my house, it was in darkness, Gary had gone and no way would I ever allow him back. We collected up the children's shoes, coats and pyjama's and headed to Lou's. When we got to there the kids were all tucked up and fast asleep. I told Lou and Sam everything that had happened and they echoed my thoughts, that I would be far better off without him, he'd never been any good, I'd just needed someone to lean on after all that had happened with Dan;

"I'm not saying Dan will come back to you but you will see a lot more of him now Gary's gone," said Sam,

"I don't want that again, no way!" I said.

There was no way I was going to go through that again.

"Please yourself, I'm just saying it's an option."

Not an option for me, I left the kids sleeping and went home.

Gary's friend Ben, yet another Ben, was waiting when I got back. He'd been a long-standing friend of Gary and had been around quite a lot, he loved the dogs and had heard what had happened. I told him of the recent events and whilst he was there Gary came back, he shouted through the letterbox;

"Let me in!"

To which Ben replied;

"Go away, she doesn't want you anymore!" He looked at me, "do you?"

"No but he can leave his key!"

He did as I asked and dropped it through the letter box calling Ben names and saying things like;

"Would you jump in my grave as quick?" And "you're welcome to my cast offs!"

"Thanks, if she wants me I would love to oblige!" Ben said laughing.

Gary punched the door and left. We thought he had come back when there was another knock on the door. Before I answered it I pulled the curtain back to see who was there. It was the police; I opened the door and let them in. It seems they had had a report that I was driving while under the influence of alcohol, Gary had alerted them saying that he thought I would do something stupid. I assured them that I was fine, I was not, nor had I been drunk. I told them that we had had a row and that he was off his head, delusional;

"It's him you should be concerned about, does she look drunk?" Ben interrupted.

"No, she looks fine," the policeman said, "We just have to follow these things up."

I apologised for wasting their time and they left, I shut the door and totally fell apart. I was sobbing uncontrollably, how he could have done this? Ben put his arm around me,

"Come on, I'll make you a coffee but only if you stop that!" He was a strange one, thought much more of animals than humans and he was a loner but his heart was in the right place. I remember him having a bit of a warped sense of humour, his remarks, quite often, offended people but he really made me laugh. And oh how the man could draw, his artwork was absolutely fantastic. He offered to stay;

"Not with you in your bed of course, but just to keep you company," he said
and winked, "I really wouldn't mind!"

"No, that won't be happening Ben" I said

"Well think about it, if you change your mind just call, I'm a light sleeper."

I laughed and said goodnight. He had to be at work by 8:30am but before he left he said that he'd pop in again on his way home.

Dan turned up the following day saying how he had heard what had happened and said how sorry he was, he even asked if I wanted him to stay for a while.

"Yes, you can stay for the kids but not for me, Ben will be here soon,"

I said the words praying that he would be and that he hadn't changed his mind. I need not have worried; I was only alone with Dan a few minutes when Ben arrived;

"Everything all right? Is my dinner ready?" He asked, wandering into the living room.

"Ben, you remember Dan?" I gestured,

"Ah yes, how could I forget?" He said smiling.
He obviously made Dan very uncomfortable because a few seconds later he stood up and said;

"I'll be in touch!" Then he left.

I cooked Ben and the kids some dinner but couldn't eat anything myself, I hadn't really drunk anything either, I was in a sort of dream state. I didn't go to work, I couldn't face anything. Lou kept taking the kids back over night, but Dan kept coming in too. By the end of the week Ben had decided that he needed to get home but he didn't want to leave me on my own. I thought I was all right but he had been watching me, I had lost nearly a stone in that week. In the end he phoned my Mum, he told her how I was and asked if she'd just take over for the night, the kids were all right so she didn't need to look after any of them. I argued with him saying I would be all right but Mum agreed with him and said that she wanted to see for herself.

It was 10:00pm when I got to Mum's; she was waiting for me with a cup of milky coffee, as only my Mum seemed to make;

"You haven't eaten I'm told?"

"No," I mumbled,

"Since when?"

"I don't know, I can't remember." Food had been the last thing on my mind,

"Right, well you need to eat something and you'll not be sleeping until you do!"
Cream crackers it was then, once I'd started eating and drinking my coffee I felt a bit better.

"You're sleeping with me in my bed," Mum said,

"Well…um, I think I'll be ok on the settee," I replied,

"No, Ben was absolutely right to bring you here, so don't argue. Get your head down and get some sleep," she said, "you have really been through the mill over the last few years girl!"
I was grateful for that night with Mum, even though I found help hard to accept from her, I slept like a log. The one night was enough though and by teatime my kids were home with me and I

was back to normal again. I had to pull myself together for my children, who else would be there for them if I fell by the wayside? It was definitely touch and go, it didn't get any easier either. I had Matthew's birthday the following day, which Mary came down for, she had asked if it was all right and of course I said yes, Matthew would be pleased to see her anyway. Gary turned up with a present for Matthew so I allowed him in, I had to. I felt for Matthew but I found it so hard to deal with, he still hadn't bought all of my things back, including my leather jacket and I wanted it back, he said he felt that he was entitled to it and a lot more as he had, after all, been my common law husband. So, as was inevitable, it ended with him leaving under a cloud. All the time Mary was there, she talked about Ben and how she'd believed he was trying to talk to her from the other side, the following week she was going to see a medium, I thought, 'please leave the poor boy alone, he's dead and still he can't get away.' I was relieved when she left, I had had enough.

Dan came in on Matthew's birthday too but had left as soon as people started arriving, he too had stopped bothering me so much, although he started turning up on a Saturday, when I'd just finished work, on a regular basis and so I arranged for him to see the kids at his mum's house, inevitably he soon started finding excuses to be late and eventually not turn up at all.

Mary called in again the week after Matthew's birthday, after her visit to the medium. Apparently the medium said she had seen Ben stood in a bright light, Ben had said that he was happy and that the lights were so beautiful but he couldn't describe them adequately. He said he would also be with Mary, always. This started another catalogue of events, constant phone calls and two days later Gary turned up with a lot of the things he'd taken, jacket included. He pulled up outside and put them on the pavement, he said just one line;

"Now take this hex off me!" He stammered.
Was I hearing things…? A hex? Through my laughter I managed to tell him that I'd thought that he must have lost the plot, he was doing this to himself, he sped off. At least I'd got my things back, mind you; thoughts of his demise were constantly in my head, so maybe there was some truth in it after all.

I was getting calls from Dad's partner, Diane aswell, complaining about people following her. According to her; people or 'they,' had been in her garden and had cut through her rotary line. She called almost daily with a new catalogue of events, coupled with Mary's calls about how Ben was coming through on a solar powered calculator, even after she had accidentally stood on the calculator which she carried around in her shopping bag, she said he was still getting through and it was spelling out words, even my name had been spelt, he obviously had a message for me. I wanted to cut the ties, this was getting completely out of hand and Diane had phoned the very same day at 9:00am, she was laughing as I answered the phone,

"I've done it, I've done it!" She said.

"What Diane, what have you done?"

"I've taught them a lesson they won't forget!" She said, still laughing a little disturbingly.

"What have you done?" I was thinking she'd finally flipped and killed someone.

"I've smeared dog shit on my fence, the dogs got the runs! When 'they' jump my fence they'd be plastered in shit, bye!" Laughing away, she put the phone down. Had I heard right? I mean, I hadn't been up long… No, I was definitely awake, this was ludicrous, I was living in a world full of deranged people. I was also getting numerous calls that I believed were Gary saying nothing, initially quick calls and the phone would go down but then they started lasting longer and longer, after a while I decided to stop waiting and listening for the phone to be put down the other end so, before hanging up, I'd go off and do my washing up or hovering, saying things like;

"It's your money you're wasting!"

Some of these calls lasted over an hour. This went on for almost two years.

Chapter 29

Two weeks after Gary left, our Alsatian – 'Pups' - bit my neighbour. To this day I don't know the circumstances but like with the previous house, I shared an alleyway with next door and they had claimed that Pups was loose, I had been at work and had just got in when my neighbour came around, he showed me his coat which had a small tear in the sleeve and was saying that the dog was vicious, well, he had been since the break in, from that moment my dog had become very unpredictable. Even so, he was always inside, secured and I still believe that my neighbour had opened the gate into my back garden, for reasons best known to himself, the dog was most likely defending our property but I had nothing to substantiate my thoughts. Our neighbours reported the matter to the police. I really couldn't deal with this on top of everything else so I asked Ben if he would consider taking Pups for a while, I would keep my collie cross, Todd, he agreed to give it a try. Pups loved Ben and Ben loved him but unfortunately he couldn't cope with him, Pups barked constantly and what made things worse was that Ben lived in a ground floor flat and so every sound disturbed the dog.

A police officer called around the following evening and asked if he could see both my dogs, I tried to explain that I'd given the Alsatian away but he insisted he would have to see him all the same. I was expecting Ben to turn up at some point, although I was praying that it wasn't whilst the police man was there, sadly this wasn't to be. I'd just introduced Todd to the policeman when Ben turned up, with Pups, luckily seeing the police car outside he'd left the dog in his reliant (or 'black hedgehog killer' as Ben called it) and came in, telling the policeman that he now had the dog. The policeman asked him to bring him in but Ben insisted that they had to go out to the car. As the policeman walked towards the car the dog went completely mad, snarling, growling and trying to get at him, to the point that the reliant was rocking backwards and forwards, moving across the road. The policeman came back saying;

"That is one vicious dog; I've dealt with dogs all my working life, that's what I do. Believe me when I say nothing can be done with him."

He also said that I would have to go to court, the outcome of which would determine the dogs future but he also felt that the report that he was obliged to turn in would seal the dog's fate. After the policeman left I talked to Ben about what had been said, Ben said that he would try for a few more days to see if he could get Pups to settle, if he didn't then he'd take the dog to the vet himself, there was no way that he was going to let Pups go with strangers.

Just over a week later and my dog was dead, he was only sixteen months old. Ben brought him home to be buried in my front garden, next to my neighbour's fence. While Ben was digging the grave the next door neighbour appeared;

"Oh, I didn't want that to happen."

"Piss off mate, what did you think we'd have to do? His blood is on your
Hands!" Replied Ben.

I had to go to work and leave Ben to it, I'd already taken a lot of time off and I couldn't afford to lose my job, it was my only source of income. That night I put the Pups' metal bowl, his collar/chain and his lead in a bag and drove to the taxi office. Gary walked towards me; I swung the bag at him…

"This is your fault, Pups is dead! He'd never have turned like that if your friends hadn't given him a kick in!" I was screaming at him.

He had nothing to say for himself, I got back in my car and drove home in tears, something else my children had lost. But, once again, they seemed fine, like me they seemed to accept that this was the way our lives would always be, everyday something seemed to happen to us, it seemed the whole world was trying to bring us down. It was my determination to protect them and keep us together whatever it took, that kept us going.

I wanted to be at work, I could relax there in that holiday atmosphere, something we had never had… A holiday, although I suppose the kids did fair better than the average child, if they had to come to work with me then there were facilities available to them at the holiday camp like amusements, swimming and park areas, when they were with Lou they would go swimming at her house or she would take them out to places like Paultons Park or the New Forest picnicking. They would even go away for weekends with Sam and Lou on their boat.

After a while Gemma and I started getting involved in the evenings on the camp. We'd go down to the camp to see the cabarets, we had done it a few times when I was with Gary, and he was working on the taxis at the time so I thought, 'why not?' He'd said he didn't mind either, well, now I know why, don't I? Dan didn't like much though but then it had absolutely nothing to do with him, as I told him when he mentioned it. In fact the same applies today with every relationship I've had, or ever will have with a man. Not long after I'd started going out in the evening, I met a man who also worked on the camp, as a kitchen porter. Everyday as he headed for the kitchens and restaurant he'd shout up to me;

"Hello darling!"

I never answered him at the time but was flattered all the same. About a week before the season had come to an end, Gemma and I had been in the restaurant for a coffee, it was a few days after the dog had been put down and I was feeling particularly low, we'd decided to take a break for a chat. He came in, also on a break and came over to our table;

"Would you ladies mind if I join you?" He asked,

"No, we've got to get back to work anyway," I said standing,

"Perhaps I'll see you later?" He asked and smiled at me.
As we left I said,

"Perhaps you might!"
We walked back to work

"You've got a problem there, he's really keen!" Gemma said as we headed back and she was right. His name was Pete and over the next few days, each time he passed our chalet block he'd stop and speak, I would always be polite, stopping to have a natter, general chit chat. On the 31st October there was going to be a staff party to celebrate the end of season, Pete asked if we were going…

"Yes!"

"Ok, I'll probably see you there," he said and winked.
He was already there when Gemma and I got there, chatting to the girls. He wasn't bad looking, 6ft 1inch with dark hair, although a bit thin to my way of thinking. When he saw us he came straight over. We chatted all evening, he told me that he would be unemployed and homeless from that night on and so had decided to go back to where he had come from – Portsmouth, he would have to if he couldn't find another job in Bournemouth. We went for a walk and I told him about my life and the recent events, the phantom telephone calls, the break in, the dog, well pretty much everything. He seemed unflustered by what I'd told him. He'd had problems too, with ex partners although he had never been married and was just three months older than me, 'well,' I thought, 'at least he's old-

219

er!'. He told me that he'd been doing martial arts for many years and that he was qualified as a security guard, he'd taken the job with Pontins for a laugh, a change.

The evening ended and the camp closed up, Gemma and I ordered our taxi home, Pete was going back to a room he had in a family's home which was local to where we lived, I suggested he could take the taxi with us, it was about 2:00am;

"Why not?" He said, "I've got to get home somehow!" When we pulled up outside my house I offered Pete in for a coffee, he jumped at the chance. Ben had been babysitting for me, I'd told him that I would be late, so he could sleep in my bed; he had suggested that when I got in I could share it too. He seemed to be putting pressure on me to sleep with him constantly, even though he had done so much for me over the few weeks prior to that, I didn't want that sort of relationship with him, I valued his friendship too much, he was my security, if and when Dan turned up again. I decided that if Pete came in I'd have an excuse not to go to bed, even though I had intended to sleep on the settee anyway but at least this way I had a valid excuse. On top of that, it was Lorna's 9th birthday the following day and I still had cards to write, presents to deal with and her birthday cake to finish.

Pete and I chatted all night and when Ben got up he wasn't very pleased, he didn't say anything other than goodbye and went to work. Lorna was a little nervous towards the stranger in our house at first but was soon more interested in her cards and presents, the boys too were apprehensive, I could see it in their faces. I explained who Pete was and that he had nowhere to live after that day, I then asked them how they would feel if I let him stay for a while, just until he'd decided what he was going to do and found somewhere to live and work. They agreed that he could stay with us, just for a while and on the condition that he did look for somewhere else, and that if it didn't work out, he wouldn't hurt me. I relayed this to Pete, he agreed and moved in, and other than to collect his belongings he never went back to his previous lodgings again. When he brought his things in I noticed that he had a lot of clothes which had all been dry cleaned and neatly hung in the cellophane covers, most of his trousers were too short for him, just an inch or so but enough to be very annoying, he also brought a small piece of cheese and half a lemon, I questioned why he'd bothered,

"Well, I hadn't thought about it," He said, "you never know when you might need it."

Pete was there the next time Dan came around to visit, I introduced him as my new partner and Dan stopped bothering me, the one thing that really upset me about this was that he didn't turn up for his children either. Pete started answering the phantom phone calls too but instead of stopping, as I'd hoped they would, they got worse. Then other things started happening… My car tyres were let down and someone, on several occasions, had also been sitting in my car, the radio station would get changed aswell as my seat and the interior mirror would get moved. It was annoying but I tolerated it, besides Pete was there, I'd seen some of his martial arts moves and they were really quite impressive. Ben had stopped coming around as much too, the only time you were guaranteed a visit was on a Sunday… He liked my roast dinners. It's something I've always considered important and one of the great British traditions; A Sunday roast and a family altogether around the table. I also feel that that one meal of normality kind of helped us to face the daily problems that seemed to plague us.

Pete and I were together a week before attempting any physical intimacy, he had already told me that he'd always had a problem and had never really had successful intercourse with anyone. We attempted it just twice during the November but weren't too successful;

"Still, there's more than one way to skin a cat."

Even though I had said several times that it wasn't a problem to me, Pete was concerned. He didn't manage to find a job and at Christmas we both went back to work at Pontins, just for three weeks and had quite a good Christmas out of it.

Pete met Lou and whilst she seemed to like him at first she did voice concerns as she left to go on holiday;

"Be careful," she whispered, "I don't care who you are with but if anyone ever lays a hand on my grandchildren I'll swing for them!"

"You and me both and I guarantee I'd get there first!"

I smiled, hugged her and said goodbye. Off she went on her annual holiday, usually to Barbados; they would always go around the 10th of January for two or three weeks. I really missed her during those weeks.

Pete went to the doctor to see if anything could be done about his problem and he discussed his options with the doctor. They didn't get very far though, especially when Pete mentioned my thoughts. He said that the doctor started laughing, threw his pencil in the air and exclaimed;

"Oh boy, I give up!"

I missed a period and had a feeling that I was pregnant. Pete eventually found a job as a security officer; unfortunately it was a temporary contract whilst some shop improvements were going on. He started the job in mid January, 1989 and it had ended by the March. By then my pregnancy had been confirmed and I had returned to Pontins, although I would have to leave again in the July because the baby was due around the 25th of August, I was determined that I would return for the end of the season, I would be able to take the baby with me. I went through the same old tests but this time Pete was with me all the way through. My old back injury gave me a few problems but I soldiered on.

Pete was only out of work for a couple of weeks, he got a job working for another security firm. I knew by now that whilst I thought a lot of him, I was unsure if I loved him. What would I do? No way would I cope with yet another baby and the other three, alone! It sounds gutless, to stay with someone for the children but I thought I was doing the best for my kids and that was all I'd ever wanted. Besides, Pete and I seemed to get along with each other. Then little things about Pete started coming to light, things that made me realise that he was of less than average intelligence. Although he was a real gentleman in most things, he'd open doors for me, he was attentive and very protective, I had the nagging suspicion that I'd fallen into the same pattern again. Pete was adopted and didn't get on well with his adopted father, who was an ex-policeman. Pete had claimed that his father had physically abused him, had beaten him as a child in favour of their natural daughter. I had got on well with his parents when I had met them but given what I'd been told about Pete's father, I remained suspicious of him. Pete had also claimed that at thirteen years old, a stranger in a car had assaulted him on his way to school, I did feel very sorry for him, he too had had a bad childhood. To top it all off he'd had a nervous breakdown early in 1988, before I'd met him. Eventually I managed to replace his clothes with ones that fitted him properly and bought him a cheap car, he hadn't had one for about three years but had a full licence... He would have had far more chance of securing employment further a field if he had his own transport and I wouldn't need to take him to and from work either. He continually bought me cards, flowers and chocolates and even some maternity clothes that he'd seen whilst working as a retail security officer. Unfortunately, unbeknown to me, he was using his credit cards for those purchases... So, that's how we were.

I had the amniocentesis test and the results came back that, once again, everything was normal and that it was to be another boy. I really had hoped for a girl this time but just as before I was far more relieved that it was going to be healthy than worried about it's gender.

This was a somewhat quieter few months, other than the anonymous nocturnal activities around the cars, which wasn't too much of a problem, I suppose the average person that worries about the price of baked beans might have found it stressful but it had become sort of normal to me.

We had a good time when the weather warmed, on at least one night of the week we'd all go to the beach. We usually left it until about 7:00pm to avoid the holidaymakers in Bournemouth. I loved the beach, especially then, being pregnant my feet were always swollen from the heat of the day and working, the salt water made them feel better and the sea air would clear my head, we could just relax for a couple of hours listening to the waves as they raced in and out washing over the pebbles, the giggling children and the occasional cry from a seagull, it was happiness itself. Pete would sit with his trouser legs rolled up, lying on the sand next to me and my great big bump, watching the children play. It was on an evening like this in early July, I was seven months pregnant, we had been on the beach for a while when a man came out of the water a few yards away from us and suddenly collapsed, he wasn't moving and I could see that there was a problem;

"We need to check him out!" I nudged Pete.

As I moved closer I could see that he was dead, I knelt beside him and felt for a pulse, there wasn't one. I screamed for Pete to get help, he ran up the beach to the nearest phone, it was at a café some quarter of a mile away. A girl in her early 20's was running towards us crying, she too was heavily pregnant. She was screaming;

"Dad, Dad!" Whilst beckoning to two men in the water. There was nothing I could do. Another woman came over, said she was a nurse and tried to revive him. Luckily my children were too

223

engrossed in their playing to notice what was going on and when they did come towards us I told them to just stay away. I led the girl away walking up and down the beach whilst the two men, her brothers, stayed with the nurse and their father. Some ten minutes later the ambulance arrived but they couldn't get onto the beach, the emergency gate was padlocked, so they had to carry a stretcher down onto the beach some 200 yards from the ambulance. I'd managed to calm the daughter down and found out that her Dad had recently had major heart surgery and that it was her parents' anniversary, he'd had a heavy meal and a few too many drinks. It had been a very warm day and he had wanted to go swimming with his children, even though her Mum had asked him not to. This was the consequence, he was forty-nine years old and his first Grandchild was due a few weeks later, he was confirmed 'dead at the scene' by the ambulance crew. Pete and I watched them leave, I felt so sorry for them and I realised then how fragile life really is.

We didn't go to the beach again that year, my place of peace was gone, I just didn't feel I could face it. It seemed that I wasn't affected as much as I would have expected, though that in itself worried me. I went to work as usual, though the housekeeper and the other staff were quite surprised I had come back when I told them of my experience but then, what would I have gained from staying home? At least at work I had something to occupy my mind.

Sunday August 20th 1989, Pete's Dad's birthday: At about 6:00am the pains started, Lou was once again to have the children for me but being a Sunday I felt it was far too early to phone anyone, my waters hadn't broken yet so there was no real rush. We'd left it until about 8:00am before phoning Lou, by 8:30am she was there. I arrived at the hospital at about 9:30am where it was the usual routine; jump into bed for an examination. Michael, as his name would be, was diagnosed as breech and with all diagnosed breeches they like to do an episiotomy, to stop you tearing. I hadn't needed one with Matthew and nor had I with Lee and Lorna, I didn't see why I should have one with Michael and if I could avoid it, I would. At about 11:00am a man came in and broke my waters, he had difficulty doing it but after the second attempt, it worked, Pete had stayed the whole time. This labour seemed slow and I regretted going in so early, I had thought that this one could very well be quicker than Matthew. Full labour with my other children had been four hours, two hours, one hour and just about half an hour with Matthew, this labour was definitely different. By 1:00pm Pete was getting on my nerves, with every pain I had he'd say;

"Are you all right? Shall I call someone?"

It was 1:30pm before the doctor came back and examined me again, this time the midwife and a student midwife stayed. I was offered gas and air, I had been offered other painkillers but as with the others I refused it. The doctor left leaving instructions that he should be called should I progress suddenly. Right, that was it, I knew that when he came back he'd be cutting me; I needed to control this and pick my moment. So, with the help of gas, air and Pete's hand I did just that. Pete's hand was a deliberate act, I kept thinking if I could squeeze his hand hard enough I could cut off the circulation or maybe snap his fingers one by one, he cried out in pain each time I squeezed it. That was a source of great amusement to me, I actually laughed for the last twenty minutes or so of the delivery and the midwives had started laughing too. Pete looked quite perturbed, I think that he thought I'd lost the plot and the strange expressions on his face were funnier still. At 2:20pm, the midwife left the room to call the doctor, that was my cue, I'd have this baby out before he had chance to get near me with his scalpel, the poor student midwife didn't know what to do and by the time the doctor and midwife came back I had delivered the legs and the body, just the head to go.

"God, how long has she been like this?" Shouted the doctor.

"She just did it!" Yelled the student.

The doctor eased Michael's head out. There he was… Another perfect, dark haired baby. Pete was trying to separate his fingers and had tears pouring down his face, not because of his fingers (so he said) but the joy at the sight he'd just experienced. I on the other hand was still laughing at what I had done and also had tears running down my face.

"I've seen some births recently," the student said, "but this was my first breech."

To which the midwife replied;

"This is the funniest birth I've ever attended, one for the book!"

What was also funny was the expression on the doctor's face when he entered the room and the obvious disappointment that, 'Mr Scalpel happy' hadn't got his way. I did apologise to the midwives saying that I had done it on purpose, for that reason;

"It could have had serious consequences!" Said the senior midwife, though she didn't elaborate.

It didn't though and Michael was fine although he did have, as I discovered, an enormous scratch down his thigh, about three inches long. I questioned it and the doctors examined it, it was decided that the instrument used when they'd broken my waters had caused it… Cue Pete;

"If that leaves a scar I will sue whoever is responsible, for everything they've got!"

This was another one of his traits and I didn't like at all, his over reaction to almost any incident. I felt that threatening wasn't the right way, my way was calculated and calm and to only ever say what you needed to. In fact all of my children had learnt that if I shouted at them they were relatively safe but the moment I spoke quietly to them they'd run.

So here we were, Sunday the 20th august 1989 at 2:30pm, my youngest child was born. I knew instinctively then that this little one was different, even though he had weighed exactly the same again as the last two, six pounds and four ounces. The midwife handed Michael to Pete whilst I went for a bath and when I got back they had cleaned Michael up. He was handed to me where he had his first bottle, and then we were all moved to postnatal. Pete left, I had to ask him to, I had said that he needed to let everyone know. He was like a kid with a new toy, beaming from ear to ear, I had trouble dealing with this childish excitement but then it was his first and definitely going to be his only child, especially if he stayed with me. Although, I suppose I would have considered another, if I'd had some guarantee that it would be a girl. He was back at visiting time that evening laden with flowers, cards and congratulatory messages from everyone, then without warning he popped the question… would I marry him? He'd asked before and I had kind of skirted around it, I hadn't taken it seriously, though this time when he asked, it felt different somehow. Now we had a child together, now we had Michael, aswell as the other three of course. He had promised me that this child would be treated no differently than the others and I had to admit it, he had been very good with them so far.

"Yes!?"

An answer I was apprehensive about from the moment I gave it and from that moment on everything happened very quickly.

He had phoned both of our families and told them our second lot of good news and by the time I had left the hospital, Mum had already said that she wanted to pay for the reception and had been asking when and how many we would be catering for. I don't think it was so much that she liked Pete; she just wanted to do it, maybe to try and make up in some way for the past. A task that unbeknown to her and to my mind would never make amends for all that I'd been through. Over the years, try as I might, I could never understand her or forgive her. Having children of my own had, to a certain extent, helped me to understand the difficulties of bringing up children but it also added to my frustration at how she, as a mother, could have ever have left us. No matter what, I would never leave mine.

Chapter 30

Michael was a crying baby from the first night, in fact for the first ten months of his life that's all he did, he was a sickly baby too who didn't seem to need sleep. The daytimes I could handle, it was the nights that were stressful; the longest he actually slept for was just two hours. He also had a problem with his bowels and so was constantly constipated; he wouldn't take his feeds properly either and seemed to suffer with colic relentlessly. I called the doctor out so many times that in the end he warned me that if I called him again after hours he would charge me twenty pounds for each and every visit… Or he'd take us off his patient list.

Pete was still working as a security officer and was getting up at 4:00am to get to work for 6:00am, where he'd be until 6:00pm, which meant, so as far as was possible, I stayed up with Michael, pacing the lounge floor, trying to calm his crying. I could tell that something was wrong with him.

In the meantime the wedding date had been set for the 25th of November 1989, I had always wanted a church wedding so Mum had arranged to have the ceremony at a Methodist church near where we lived, and they were the only ones that would marry us as I was a divorcee. I bought myself a white lace skirt and top and Mum made me my veil, from a lace tablecloth of all things, I have to admit that it did look just like a veil too and wasn't half bad either.. Good old Ben offered to be the photographer, he hired top hat and tails for the occasion and made up an 'Official Press' card for himself which was tucked into his hat band throughout the whole day. I made my own bouquets, all the buttonholes and the posies for Lorna and my niece Kirsty, who were my bridesmaids, all from silk flowers. This was another thing I'd learnt to do, flower arranging, I hadn't had any formal training but then I guessed that it must be in the blood. I had made the flowers for Gemma's wedding too. (She had married a man ten years younger than her just six days after I had had Michael and although Pete and I did go to the wedding we'd had to take Michael with us and decided to leave soon afterwards because he wouldn't stop crying.)

Dad gave me away and it was the best thing about my wedding day; him walking me down the aisle.. Pete had tried his best to be traditional and do things properly by asking him for his permission to marry me. I had to laugh;

"If you want to, take her on!" Said Dad.

On the day I had got ready at Mums flat, her hairdresser did my hair and Dad came there to meet me. When Mum and everyone had left for the church, Dad and I went and had a beer together, I so missed those day's in the pub with my Dad, we were picked up by Verity's brother in law, Simon, who was driving the wedding car. Pete and I were married at 3:00pm and being as it was in November it was getting dark when we came out of the church, we still managed to get a few photographs though. Pete's sister wouldn't have her photograph taken and wanted to get away persuading the rest of Pete's family to do the same, this followed on to the reception... Pete's family sat one side of the room with mine on the other and none would mix with or speak to the other, and other than a couple of photographs of Pete's parents sat at the top table there were no photographs of his family at all. Ben said that he had tried to but Pete's sister had refused. I also heard later that she had asked if she was allowed to go home, I never did find out what her problem was with me. The one person, other than my Dad, that I was most pleased to see at the church was Lou; the kids had sat with her throughout the service. I'd invited her to join us for the reception aswell but she had declined saying that it didn't feel quite right, I knew what she meant and I felt exactly the same... I didn't want another mother in law and no one could ever live up to or replace Lou.

All of Mums family had turned up, 'What hypocrites,' I thought, all but one of course... Mums eldest sister, she had never been judgemental; though I'm sure that she had her thoughts and opinions she never voiced them. She also sent cards for every birthday and Christmas and still does and was the only one who had sent a birth card, condolence card and wreath for Carl all those years before.

For the evening do we'd had a disco but the D.J. didn't have anything that anybody knew which had put a dampener on things. I had found a song that I'd taped and wanted it played for Mum, I thanked her for all she'd done and the D.J played the song for me; 'Pal of my cradle days.' Almost immediately Mum had burst into tears, as I knew she would.

'Pal of my cradle days, I needed you always,
When I was a baby, upon your knee,

229

You sacrificed everything for me,
I took the gold from your hair,
I placed the silver threads there,
Try as I may I could never repay,
Pal of my cradle days.'

Verity was angry at my choice but before she could say anything Michael had started crying so I took him out of the back door and sat on a beer keg with him for the rest of the evening. Pete came out a few times with a drink for me but other than that I didn't really see anyone. The guests left and I was just glad it was over. I went home in the back of a transit van with Michael in his buggy surrounded by the wedding gifts; Pete was in the front passenger seat next to the driver and best man, his friend from Portsmouth. Pete had been unwell; he'd had flu the week before and was still feeling under the weather, mind you he did look ill, very pale. I'd even thought beforehand that… 'We may be able to…' Or should I say… 'Have to cancel the wedding!' All the same, it was done now!

Pete had further investigations into his erectile problems at a Local hospital, it was decided that he would need a 'Nesbit Procedure,' this meant cutting a 'V' shape out of the side of his penis and sewing it to straighten it up, they'd also said that a circumcision should be considered and as if that weren't enough they also decided that it was best to do a vasectomy whilst they were at it. I had told him that I didn't want anymore children, four was enough and he agreed saying that one of his own had fulfilled his wishes and he didn't want anymore. So it was decided, the only problem was; he'd have to have the operation in London. It was January 1990 and he was booked in for the operation, I had been nervous about being alone even though it was only going to be for four days at the most, as it turned out I quite enjoyed it. We had still been getting the phantom calls, though not as bad. Dan didn't know I was on my own either, we saw almost nothing of him anymore, apart from Christmas day when he would pop in for an hour to see the kids. I'd decided that he must have resigned himself to the fact that he couldn't come back now, especially since I had remarried.

The operation was done and Pete travelled back from London on the train, I picked him up from Bournemouth station, he was in a lot of pain and could hardly walk. A week later and he had an infection in the wound, obviously very painful, but then he never did have a very high pain threshold. It was three and a half months before he returned to work and his mental state also took a turn for the worse, I couldn't put my finger on the problem so I made excuses for him; I blamed the operation, I would say he'd had a hard day, I tried to compensate for everything he'd been through by buying him everything that he wanted and keeping the kids quiet but nothing worked. He kept all his belongings, clothes, records and everything he owned in boxes, he even kept his toothbrush and toiletries in a wash bag away from our things. He continued to isolate himself from us more and more and as if that wasn't enough he would talk incessantly about leaving me. I tried all ways to change things, to make it easier for him but nothing worked. So, just as with my first marriage, I would once again take my vows seriously and persevere. Pete finally went back to work but took a lot of time off due to illness; he always seemed to have something wrong with him.

At ten months old Michael got whooping cough, he hadn't had the vaccine because of a fear that the convulsions Lorna had had may have been a result of the vaccine and given his other health concerns I decided, wrongly as it turned out, not to allow him to have it. We had six very worrying weeks, day and night of coughing spasms, I was exhausted. Michael then spent his nights sleeping with us in our bed, it was the only way he seemed to settle and I could then grab a couple of hours sleep, at the very least. Luckily Michael showed no sign of brain damage and recovered, though there were now concerns about his eyesight, although that wasn't due to the whooping cough. I had mentioned my concerns on his development check when he was six weeks old and again at ten months but I think they thought that I was a neurotic mother. I had no faith in health visitors or doctors and least of all in social services so, for obvious reasons, I'd developed a tendency towards not asking for help, I would rather muddle through and cope, draw on my own experiences and the information that I've digested over the years which, given my educational background, has been surprisingly extensive. 'The school of life!' Although every child thinks they know what is best, there's no substitute for a decent education and although I haven't had any kind of real schooling it has always been something that I've tried to impress upon

231

my children, the best education available is what they need and I have striven to ensure that they get it. I had concerns about Michael's physical development too, he was nothing like the others, although Matthew had been slower than Lee and Lorna so far as walking was concerned, he hadn't started to until he was fifteen months old, he had been about average in all other ways. Michael on the other hand had no interest in shapes or colours whatsoever, he didn't reach for anything and seemed basically disinterested in everything other than music. Finally at eighteen months old he started walking but he didn't talk until he was two and a half years old, he would just point and make noises and everyone knew what he wanted and would get it for him, the health visitor had said that Michael didn't talk because he didn't have to but I knew that there had to be more to it.

Gradually, Pete got worse, the operation had done nothing for our sex life, which didn't have a chance of improving all the time that Michael was sleeping in my bed, not just whilst Pete was working but with both of us on his nights off too. I decided to give up on the idea of sex altogether. I amused myself with D.I.Y. projects instead and I made up my mind that that was how it would be from then on. Pete was absolutely no help with anything at all; least of all anything D.I.Y. his only interest was in Martial Arts. I encouraged him to go for his black belt in Shotokan karate, which he eventually got but then he decided that something wasn't right with the instructor and changed to another style, that didn't work either so he changed again, throughout the years he must have changed a dozen or more times and would always use the same excuse: That it was someone else's fault. He had started eating his meals in our bedroom too, the deterioration continued and it was obvious that it was going to be permanent. I had also noticed that he was changing towards the kids' aswell, in particular Matthew who, Pete had once told me, reminded him of Gary. This problem wasn't helped by the fact that Gary had continued to cause us problems which always became worse a few weeks before Matthew's birthday and would continue until just after Christmas. I had also had a reoccurrence of my previous back problems and was referred to hospital. It was in fact upon returning home from one of these appointments that we realised that someone had been into our house, as I walked into my house I had sensed it straight away... Call it intuition, call it whatever but I knew that something wasn't right. Although nothing had been stolen things had been moved around, someone had eaten sandwiches and a few drawers had been opened in my bedroom. On the edge of my bed lay an old taxi book, it had been left open with a note written in Gary's hand writing, it was a description of Pete;

'Male, 6'1, slim build, dark hair.'

It was obvious that Gary had been there. We rang the police who duly came out to investigate the report, initially they had said that they would take fingerprints but then changed their minds saying that as nothing had been taken and no damage had been caused there really wasn't anything that they could do. Therefore, (if that was the law as I saw it) it meant that anyone could walk into my home, help them selves to my food, go through my personal belongings but as long as they didn't take anything… There was nothing we could do about it.

"If I catch him he'll get a good hiding!" Pete ranted at the police,

"If you do that Sir then you will end up in court on an assault charge!"

We were advised that if we did catch him then we were allowed hold him until the police arrived, as long as we only used 'reasonable force,' a term used loosely.

"Well, when I go out I won't bother locking up," I said, "I'll leave sandwiches and a note for all to come in and help themselves though I will say please don't leave a mess. In fact…" Pause for a breath "…Why don't I open my home for the public to use as a thorough fare?"

They apologised and left whilst I was still talking, or rather ranting.

So things carried on and we carried on; we carried on getting hassled occasionally by (we suspected) Gary, who had even loosened the wheel nuts on our cars and let the air out of our tyres, the funny phone calls carried on too. At the same time as all this was going on we were getting the occasional visit from the ex-husband of the woman who had been the previous tenant and had exchanged houses with Robert and Meryl. One night at about midnight, just as I was dosing off I heard someone shouting so I started listening, it was a male voice and it was coming from down the road. The noise had gradually gotten closer until it was right outside my house, so I got up out of bed and looked out of the window where I saw a man swaying in the front garden slurring things like;

"If you didn't like it as it was, then why did you fucking take it?" And "I'll teach you for changing my home!"

I hadn't realised who it was until he walked up my drive, Mary's Mum's ex-husband. He was obviously very drunk and when he knocked the door my heart shot into my mouth but I went to confront him all the same; he was going to wake up the whole street and from what I'd heard he was threatening my children too. As it was Pete had seemed reluctant to go and answer the door so I left him upstairs where he could phone 999. I stood behind the front door and decided that my best form of defence would be to attack; I opened the door and started shouting;

"What do you want? This is my home! You know where your wife is, now go away!"

He had looked very shocked and calmed down almost immediately;

"I... I just wanted to see what changes you had made." He whimpered.

"That my friend," I answered, "is none of your damn business!"

Just as he turned away saying that he was sorry to have bothered me three police cars pulled up outside, he was interviewed outside my gate and taken away. When we had spoken to one of the police officers he had said;

"This guy is well known to us and is actually considered to be quite dangerous, hence the three cars!"

We had two further visits from him over the years; the last was in 1992... I had just finished a twelve-hour day shift, working on a builder's clean for a new Tescos, (it was a casual contract that had lasted for just two weeks but I had needed the work as the season at Pontins had finished.) I was just relaxing in the bath when Pete came running up the stairs saying;

"He's here again, I'm phoning the police!"

I jumped out of the bath, wrapped a towel around my head and ran down the stairs in my dressing gown, shouting;

"Tell him to go bother someone else! Go see your ex wife, or even Mary! Just fuck off!"

He was walking away and apologising again before I'd even reached him and once again the police arrived almost immediately… This had become quite unnerving now! The officer talking to him had said,

"You see Sir? These nice people don't want you here!"
He was calm but there was I swearing like a fishwife, I think that the officer had decided to take him out of the area for his safety as much as ours. In a way I did feel sorry for the bloke, I learned later that he had been evicted from his home and had obvious alcohol addiction problems. He had knocked the door a few weeks prior to this last incident saying that he lived under the bridge on a local roundabout and had asked if I could spare the price of a bag of chips? I had said no, mainly because I really didn't have the price of a bag of chips. Then again, if I had given it to him I would most likely have encouraged him to bother us even more, so it was just as well I didn't have it. I later heard that he had held up a local pub, for a drink of all things and had been locked up in prison… Needless to say, we didn't get any more visits from him.

Gary though was a different kettle of fish altogether but then I always was a soft touch, giving in, feeling sorry for everyone. I had looked for dead bodies, listened to demented people talking about haunted calculators, taken years of abuse and heartache but, after all that Gary had put me through, I still felt sorry for him. He became obsessive and the trigger was, I believe, an incident just a couple of months after he had left me… He had phoned me saying that his girlfriend, Lisa, had stabbed him, he was calling from a telephone box and needed me to pick him up and of course I went straight there. When I arrived I found out that she had attempted to stab him and not actually stabbed him. He showed me a small hole that she had made in his leather jacket but she hadn't even reached his skin, let alone broken it. I dropped him off at his friend's house and thought that that was it, it had been the only civil contact we had had since we'd split up and I'm pretty certain that the strange occurrences had started shortly afterwards. I was and still am convinced that it was him that used to come and creep around in the garden, so convinced that whenever we had our prowler I would call the taxi office where he was working and tell them that he had been here, again… He was usually recorded as being on a job and had either been dropping off or picking up locally or in the town. These 'jobs' would have given him the perfect opportunity to stalk us as we lived on the main route through from the taxi office into the town, he would've been able to stop off for five minutes, do whatever he wanted to and still be on time for his pickup. Our only choice was to either; catch him and hold him, or put up with it in the hope that he'd get fed up, the latter seemed to work and it did stop… For a while. There was one time though, while we were getting all the trouble, that we had seen Gary… Pete and Michael were with me and I was out driving at the time when we spotted him coming out of a local shop. I stopped the car, on Pete's instructions, right next to him at which point Pete jumped out of the car leaving the door open, grabbing Gary by the throat he pushed him up against the wall;

"If you keep tampering with my car, I will punch you so hard in the face that even your mother won't recognise you!" Well, that was really very good for Pete, quite an amusing quip and it made me laugh, I congratulated him on it too when he got back in the car.

Chapter 31

Early in 1992 Gemma had started to have serious problems with one of her daughters, Claire. Gemma's most recent marriage had only lasted a year and all of her children were playing up, all that is except the youngest, 'Bub' as they called her, she was the child of a relationship that Gemma had had after Jack. I had never really liked Bubs father; when Gemma had fallen pregnant to him he had told her to have an abortion and on his say so she did which is something that she really regretted doing and still does to this day. Then, within a couple of months, he had gotten her pregnant again and left her for another woman. – Ah, same old story, where have I heard it? - Gemma had decided to keep the baby, 'Bub' who looked just like her father, Blonde hair and blue eyes, just like Gemma's more favoured son, Craig. Claire, the poor girl, was dark haired and born when Craig was just eleven months old and though for a while she'd had a position as the youngest child and the only girl, Bub came along and as if that wasn't enough Gemma's eldest daughter got in contact. So in a matter of a few months poor Claire's life was turned upside down, she never knew where she fitted in and this predictably resulted in rebellious behaviour. It really couldn't have been worse timing for Claire, was looming and she developed an unhealthy interest in men… Far too much like me at that age! Gemma, having been such a good girl when growing up had never dealt with this sort of thing, she really could not cope with Claire, every time things got really bad she'd call on me for help and I'd go and talk to Claire. On one occasion when Claire was 12 years old she had stayed out all night, Gemma had called on me for help so I went straight there only to find that the other children were calling Claire names, even the eldest one kept calling her 'a little slut!' I was furious with Gemma, first of all for allowing her children to do this to one of their own and then for allowing this stranger; who had only just come into the family and didn't actually know Claire or have an understanding of her life so far, to be calling her things like that in front of Bub, who was obviously taking it all in, a fact that I had pointed out to Gemma. I went to Claire who was, by now in another room sobbing her heart out;

"They all hate me, I wish I were dead!" She sobbed.
I turned on Gemma and the others;

"Just look at what you're doing to this girl… How you dare treat her this way!"

They were all pretty shocked by my outburst and I didn't leave until they had apologised to Claire. I gave her a cuddle, which was something that she was obviously in need of, especially given the way that she held on to me. Even so, a couple of months later Claire was put into care, Gemma, (who had moved into a house three doors away from me a week before it happened,) had insisted on it, saying that it would only be for a few weeks, just to teach her a lesson. Social services had said that they too thought that it would be good for her. I stood with Claire when they came to collect her, she was crying and pleading with Gemma saying that she'd be good and begging for her to let her stay but Gemma stayed firm, only until the car had pulled away, then she fell apart. I promised Claire that I would go and see her wherever she was sent. How Gemma could have done that I'll never know, or for the life of me understand.[1]

I kept to my promise and three day's after Claire had been taken into care I went to see her. She had been placed in the Reception Centre, which was on the same site as the girls hostel that I had lived in all those years before, although it was now being used as offices by the Youth Justice Service. Gemma had come with me but Claire wouldn't speak to her although she had greeted me with a cuddle. When it was time to go I promised to keep in touch and told her to behave and she'd be home before she knew it, her response was as I'd expected to be but at the same time quite heart breaking;

"She..." She said as she pointed a finger towards Gemma

"... Won't have me back now! She's got her precious ones and got rid of the one that she never wanted!"

I knew at that moment that this was the start of a downward spiral that Claire was to inevitably take and I was right. Within a few days she had been sent to a foster family... The family had three young children all under 5 years old and through no fault of their own were the wrong placement for Claire; they'd had no experience with teenagers at all. She was only with them for one week and in that short time she had threatened the children, had made a play for the foster father by flirting with him and walking around half naked, and then she ran away with a girl that she had met at the reception centre. She ran away several times after that and each time they caught her she was taken back to the reception centre. The main problem was that each time she absconded she managed to get into some kind of trouble with the police; she stole a car, was involved in credit card theft, had got in with the wrong crowd and was taking drugs. By the time she was 13 years old she was very well known to the police and regularly taking drugs. I kept in touch with her as much as I could, in between looking after Pete with his increasing mental problems, the odd visit from Gary at night, cleaning at Pontins during the holiday seasons, office-cleaning in the evening, it felt like I was constantly on the go and it was all I could do to stay sane myself but I managed to stay on top of it all.

In late 1992 there were discussions between Social Services, Gemma and I about the possibility of Claire may be coming to live with me, that I fostered her... I had hated the idea of her being in the centre and was very concerned at the escalation in her troubled behaviour, obviously I needed Pete to agree and then we would take the foster parenting course. I spoke to the kids as I had with everything else and they were all ok with it, Lee had just turned 17, had left school and was training in electronics, Lorna had just turned 13 and was at secondary school. Matthew on the other hand was having his own problems, I'd had to move him to a different school, he was being bullied... That turned into a troublesome time: I had to go and see the headmaster one day after having a call from the school to say that my son, Matthew had head lice, they had pulled him out of class and he had been made to stand in the corridor until they'd contacted me. I was so livid I cannot put it into words, I said to the head that if Matthew had head lice then there would be a lot more in the class that did too, how dare he pull my son from the class and single him out. It then degenerated into my telling him that he and the majority of his teaching staff were a waste of time, Matthew couldn't read properly and had no idea of his times table, I informed the head that I would be moving my son;

"And if you have the same problems with bullying and his ability's after you've moved him?" He questioned,

"I'll apologise, but I think you'll find it may well be you that does the apologising."

He was 7 years old when I moved him. I started him at a school a little further away which was more structured and disciplined in its teaching methods, something that I knew would be better for Matthew. I had amused the Education Officer with my comments aswell when he had asked;

"Well, why do you want to move Matthew?"

I then told him of my conversation with the head, he then asked;

239

"I take it you don't like the headmaster very much?"

"As a hairdresser, he'd be wonderful but as a headmaster, he's bloody useless!"

There it was… My sarcastic side, my one liners, which always became more apparent when I was stressed and at the time, I sure was stressed. I know that most parents see their children as beautiful and intelligent but Matthew was, he was a very bright child, from about the age of 4 or 5 years old he was telling me the distance of certain planets from the earth or wherever, usually when I was doing the washing up;

"Yes, ok Matthew." I'd say with each ounce of information he had to tell me… Its not that I wasn't interested, I was completely astounded that this little boy knew all this. It turned out that he was a very able musician as well and at the beginning of 1992 he joined a church choir, by the end of the year he was singing extremely well. Lee had also become a talented musician, he had won a talent show in 1991 when we'd had our first holiday ever at the Camber Sands Pontins and as his prize he had won us a free weekend to the finals at the Blackpool Pontins. Unfortunately he didn't win that although he had deserved to, he had played his own composition on his keyboard. He had also made me a scroll of the song which I keep it in a cabinet to this day. I suppose that was something to thank Gary for, he had taught Lee the basics of playing the keyboard.

As it turned out I was right to move Matthew because as soon as he'd moved he began to excel; in his reading, his writing, his maths, he'd even understood Shakespeare; he would sit and digest the story, then tell me the basics in terms that I, or anyone else would have understood. He was still being constantly bullied though, he was considered by others to be odd; he wasn't really into sports and he didn't like football, he had always preferred to read a book. Michael too seemed to think that Matthew was 'put on this earth for his benefit' and if Matthew didn't do as he wanted then Michael would tell his Dad, Pete and then Matthew would really be in trouble. Pete had picked on all of the kids with the exception of Michael, and so as far as was possible I tried to be there at all times whenever Pete was in order to protect them… Still trying to keep everything together and making the same old excuses for Pete's behaviour. I also had a promise to keep to Claire and just before Christmas 1992 I managed to convince Claire's social worker to allow her to stay with us for Christmas… I remembered all to well the feeling of being alone especially at that time of year. They agreed and said that I could pick her up on Christmas morning but she'd have to be taken back by Boxing Day evening. I had also arranged for Gemma to come for dinner too, add in with that some friends of Lee's who also didn't have anywhere else to go and we ended up with sixteen people for dinner that Christmas.

At 9:00am on Christmas morning I went to collect Claire, it had snowed a little at some time during the night, just a sprinkling but with the frost it made everything look pretty and as I drove to collect Claire, driving down the roads I'd walked as a child, so many memories flooded back and although it was painful, I felt somehow at peace with those roads. Claire was waiting at the door when I arrived and ran out to meet me, begging that I take a little lad home with us aswell but I couldn't, Social Services wouldn't allow it. It was very hard and terribly sad looking at his little face as he waved us goodbye and Claire made me feel guilty, all be it briefly, for leaving him, as was her way but she soon settled down as we drove home. On the drive back I noticed that all the snow had gone and with it so too had the feeling of peace.

I had worked hard to give everyone a decent Christmas that year, I'd bought a present for everyone who was invited to dinner, to try and make their Christmas a little more homely and welcome. My present; was to see them all so happy, knowing that they didn't have a moment of loneliness, although Pete had chosen to be on his own and had stayed upstairs away from us. Still, it was only for Christmas day because he had opted to work on the Boxing Day anyway and in some ways that was a relief. I took Claire back the following evening and promised her I'd do my best to arrange for her to come and live with us but with Pete's mental condition getting worse I wasn't sure that they would allow it. To top it all off my health wasn't what it should've been, I knew that I was going to have to have a hysterectomy sooner rather than later but for all their sakes I had to put it off as long as possible.

I had taken the kids to see Lou on Boxing Day for an hour; Sam and Lou had been having problems in their marriage... Lou had found out that the previous year Sam had been having an affair with his secretary and there had even been talk of an illegitimate daughter, something that was later confirmed as true. Rumours had been rife for sometime before Lou had found out for definite, on the day she did she marched straight into Sam's office where the secretary was actually sat on Sam's lap and in typical Lou style she walked straight up to the woman, slapped her around the face and ordered her out of the room, then turning on Sam she said that she was leaving him and demanded money, he begged her to talk but still handed her a cheque saying;

"Wait until I get home before you do anything."
Lou walked out of the office and headed home. On the way she called in on her sister then popped in to see me and the kids, she told me all that she had found out and what she'd just done, she also said that although she had threatened to go she wouldn't be going anywhere and if anyone would be leaving it would be Sam. Needless to say he didn't go and they stayed together although she did cash her cheque. Things were never quite the same between them after that and Lou made him pay in everyway, although she wasn't nasty about it and neither was he, they were just so good together and always the perfect grandparents and Lou was so much more my friend and always there for us.

In January 1993 they were off on their annual holiday and just as in previous years Lou came in to say goodbye, they were off to St Lucia for three weeks. Business hadn't been so good, neither had the situation between Sam and Lou. Her parting words to me were;

"I don't really want to go but I'm going to, it might be the last holiday I get." She was waving as she left;

"Look after yourself and the kids, bye!"
That was the last time that I saw her.

It was the day after they had arrived on the island; Sam had said that they were on a golf course and Lou had just hit a really rotten shot, as he turned to tell her how rubbish it was she collapsed. She was flown by air ambulance from Barbados to Tampa Hospital in Miami; she'd had a brain haemorrhage. Dan had phoned to tell me what had happened and a few days later he flew out to Miami promising to keep me informed; which he did daily. They did an operation to re-inflate the veins that had collapsed in her brain but hadn't held out much hope. I prayed like never before, the kids were inconsolable, pleading with me not to let her die, begging me to reassure them that she wouldn't. As the days went by I began to think maybe she would survive, she was in a coma but not on life support, just asleep. Lou had always said she would hate to be in a wheelchair dribbling, unable to control herself, dependant on whoever to do everything but we all just wanted her back, we didn't care what the damage. On the 7th of February 1993 she was flown home to England. She was taken to Southampton hospital; although she was stronger she was still in a coma. Matthew and the church choir had made a tape of their hymns to play to her and the rest of us had taped messages, I had even been in touch with Neil Diamond's agent asking if there was any chance that he may have been able to visit her and although he had recently been in England, when I phoned he had already returned to the States. So we'd missed him but even so his music could be played to her, we were willing to try anything to bring her back. On the 10th of February she was moved to Bournemouth hospital and even though she was in a private room they wouldn't allow the tapes to be played.

In the early hours of the morning on Valentines Day, 14th February 1993 I had a dream; Lou was stood in front of me and her mother 'little Gran' was stood just behind her, in my dream I remember saying;

"Please Lou, either wake up or go with your Mum!"

"I think I'm going to go with Mum" she replied, turned, walked away and joined her Mum; I woke up very distressed and looked at the clock, it was just after 3:00am. At about 6:30am I got the call I had been expecting;

"Mum's gone, she died sometime in the early hours..."

She was just 59 years old; her birthday was the 25th of January. I truly believe she came to me that night and that she has done on many occasions since. Valentines day would never be anything but a sad anniversary to all of us, although it must have been much harder for Dan's stepbrother, Allan because it was also his birthday. I suppose in a way though it is still an anniversary of celebration of love, not in the romantic way but the love and remembrance of a wonderful Mother, Gran and my dearest and best friend.

The days up to the funeral which was on the 18th of February were a haze for me. We'd all spent that time in tears, the pain was unbearable and my children's pain was so obvious on their little faces; they wanted an explanation but I had no answers; I was supposed to protect them wasn't I? I really felt that I'd failed them instead. Even before the funeral had begun the chapel had filled to overflowing with mourners and all around the graveside there were so many of her many friends and family, all with tears flowing but the saddest sight of all for me was my children: My Lee was hugging both Lorna and Matthew, none of them making a sound as the tears bulged and fell from their eyes, I thought that they would never stop... God has so much to answer for. Sam seemed to have been numbed by the whole thing, he really had loved her, although the truth did come out that on the night Lou had died, Sam had apparently spent the night in a hotel with his ex wife; the hospital had been unable to find him and one of the men who had worked for Sam, who was also his friend and drinking partner, had known where he was and gone to inform him. As it turned out Sam had been having an affair with his first wife, Abbey's Mother, for some weeks, ever since Abbey had invited them both to her flat for a meal. Abbey had also had a child with Terry and although Iris suspected as much she stayed with Terry all the same. Abbey's wish to have her mother and father back together had worked.

The wake was held at Lou's home where Susan, Lou's sister, slapped Sam around the face. It was said that Lou hadn't made a will, although she had told me that she had and that it was in the wall safe at the house but Sam denied it and it couldn't be proved... As a result the contents of her bank account were shared between her boys and they got just £1000 or so each. Lou's wishes had also been that Marilyn and Lorna be given her jewellery, though not all of it was as Susan had taken many pieces herself, I didn't feel I could say anything because Lou was after all her sister and as if that wasn't enough Helen had sent Dan to the house with an inventory of items that they had bought Lou as presents over the years and had been given instructions to collect them all, he had ticked off each item as it was located and found all but one, then he spent his time questioning everyone as to the whereabouts of 'the missing bird ornament,' finally accepting Sam's explanation that it must have been broken at some point over the years. They were like a venue of vultures picking over bones and I was reminded of my Nan's funeral. There were all these arguments over the material items yet the most precious thing of all was Lou and they didn't seem to care at all that she was gone, absolutely no thought for her... I took the children and left.

Sam had promised to see the children regularly and be just as he'd always been but he didn't and he wasn't... My children had lost them both the day that Lou died. Lee went off the rails, not in terms of breaking the law more on the road to self-destruction, I knew that he'd had such a hard time dealing with Lou's loss, we all had, but he would spend many hours sitting by her grave, I had hoped that it may have been helping him to come to terms with her death but truthfully, for the first time in his life I had no idea what he was up to, or that some 18 months later he had started using drugs. Whether it was my own grief, the fact that I was so preoccupied with keeping Pete from losing the plot completely or even my concern for Claire, I just didn't see it.

Chapter 32

It was early April 1993 and Claire had to appear in court, I had promised to go too. She was on a charge of Grievous Bodily Harm against a young man: The report said that she had stabbed him in the thigh, rolled up a magazine and ordered him to open his mouth, rammed the magazine in and hit it with her hand into the back of his throat. The reason, as she had claimed, was that he was going to rape or had raped her friend. The story was sketchy but the photographs were real enough and although, to a degree I understood the provocation, I found it very hard to believe that Claire at just 13 years old could have done this and acted alone, as was the claim. She did admit to me later that others were involved... The girl whom it was claimed had been raped and a young man of twenty, who Claire had been seeing since she had run away and she had by then absconded many times, she had told me that the young man had also been in trouble for various offences, the latest had been while he was with Claire; G.B.H. and a charge of: 'Taking and driving away a car.'

I took Michael to school and headed to the courts; at that time Michael only attended school in the mornings which meant that I had to be back from the court in time to pick him up at twelve. When I arrived at the courts Claire's social worker asked to speak with me about the possibility of Claire being able to stay with us at weekends, just to see if things worked out... She told me how she thought that if the courts felt that Claire had someone who was willing to help her, support her and give her a second chance they may go easier on her. I agreed to try it, especially as Claire was saying;

"Please, please? I'll be good, I promise and it would only be weekends to start with!"

I'd had to leave to collect Michael from school before the case was heard, I left with the Social Worker promising to let me know the outcome, and she didn't. It was in fact the Reception Centre who had let me know what had happened when they called me at 5 o'clock that evening... Claire had been placed on curfew from 7:00pm to 7:00am and bailed to my address. I was then told that because of this bail condition; if she was still at the Reception Centre after 7:00pm she would be arrested, I was then asked if we would take her immediately, at least until the papers could be sorted out in the court. What choice did I have? I couldn't let her be arrested; besides they'd promised that it would be dealt with the following morning. They delivered all her things to my door at 6:30pm, I had no bed for her yet so she had to sleep on a lilo on the floor in Lorna's room; a prospect Lorna wasn't too keen on but there wasn't any other choice. Claire was as bewildered by the sequence of events as I was, especially when they had said that it couldn't be brought back into court. I told the Social Worker that Claire having to sleep on the floor was unacceptable and that she needed a bed immediately; it took two weeks to get her one. The court papers didn't get sorted out and Claire didn't move on until March 1996. Three years and an awful lot of heartache and strain on us as a family.

Pete and I had only gone to 'Foster Parent Training' twice so in the eyes of Social Services we weren't qualified, therefore weren't entitled to be paid anything towards Claire's keep, it took 6 months before we finally got the payments sorted out... Once again a Social Services cock-up, just confirming the beliefs I'd always had; that these so called experts didn't have a clue. That girl had come to me as a mistake on the court papers with nothing, not even a bed and it was one fiasco after another. Once again I was a victim of their incompetence and it wasn't until September that we were considered before a panel in Dorchester to be foster parents; the first application was refused, the social worker had made yet more mistakes on the paperwork. Obviously I questioned their decision, saying;

"We have been acting foster parents for Claire for over 6 months, yet according to the panel we are not suitable to be foster parents." Then the comment; "Claire is known as a runner (a runaway), for all you know we could say that she's run away when we have actually murdered her and buried her in a shallow grave in the garden."
This was the comment I think that made the Social Worker get her act together and three weeks later our application was accepted.

In the meantime I had decided that I could put off my hysterectomy no longer. I arranged for Matthew to stay with my Mother, although I wasn't keen on the idea, I felt that it was the better option, that or leave him in the house with Pete, besides Mum actually seemed quite keen on the idea. I felt that the others would be fairly safe with Pete; Lee was old enough to help if needed, Lorna and Claire would speak up and indeed stand up to Pete and Michael being his son would be more than safe with him. I prepared and froze all their meals for the week, left instructions for everything with each of the kids and made a rota of chores for each of them too. On the 12th of May 1994 I went into hospital, I was to be the first on the list the following morning and I was scared; especially as the operation day was also the anniversary of my Nan's death… What if I didn't survive…? What if I woke up during the operation…? What about my children…? What if Pete couldn't cope…? I was very tempted to discharge myself. The anaesthetist came and put my mind at rest about waking during the procedure anyway, guaranteeing me that it couldn't happen. I took a shower at 8:00am and got back into bed, I was doing a word search, still thinking I could change my mind when the anaesthetist appeared, he handed me two little pills and said;

"Take these it'll all be ok."

Two little pills, I could still change my mind…

Next thing I knew it was 6:00am the following morning and I was connected up to a drip and being administered painkillers at the touch of a button. It had been done, it wasn't as painful as I'd feared either and the nurses were wonderful. Especially when at just after 9:00am one of the nurses came in and said;

"Your husband is here to see you."

I knew at that moment something had to be wrong, I felt that it was highly unlikely he'd be visiting out of concern for me but then I thought; 'I could be wrong!' …Nope, my first instinct was right: He said that he couldn't cope, that Claire and Lorna were playing him up, that Michael wasn't very well and that I'd have to come home now. I told him how ridiculous the idea was so he threatened to leave, he would leave the kids on their own and he would go, I was reduced to tears. The nurse came in on hearing the conversation and raised voices;

"What are you doing to her? Have you any idea what your wife has been through, how serious the operation was?"

Pete calmed down a little and apologised to the nurse.

"I'll contact Mum or Verity," I said.

I begged him not to leave the kids on their own and he agreed to stay if I promised to speak to the them. The nurse said;

"I think you'd better go." He left and she turned her attention back to me, saying; "He will have to cope, you need to concentrate on you!"

All the same, I asked if she could bring me the phone. I had decided that I needed to get out of there as soon as possible. I spoke to the kids and asked them to please stay out of Pete's way; it would only be for a few days. From the moment of Pete's visit I stopped using the pain machine and didn't use it again, I needed to be able to think straight and by lunchtime the machine and the drip were removed, by teatime I was out of bed. I was warned several times that I needed to slow down but how could I?

Mum came in to see me on the Saturday; she told me that Matthew was fine and that she was very surprised by my recovery. So was the doctor, I had asked when I could go home and was told;

"Be patient, probably Tuesday but not until the stitches come out."

My sense of humour kept me going, as it did many of the other patients' aswell; I would wander about in my towelling dressing gown and big fluffy wolf slippers singing; 'Like a virgin!' One day after the visitors had gone the woman in the opposite bed said that her visitor had asked what I had been having done, when she was told that I'd had a hysterectomy she was dumb struck. As far as I was concerned it had to be done and my determination and fear for my children's safety had made it impossible for me to do anything else. On the following Tuesday morning, five days after my operation, the stitches were removed and I was going home. A week later and I was at the life organisation again but this time with Claire and from there I had to take her to the hospital clinic for sexually transmitted diseases. She wasn't pregnant, thank goodness but she had contracted a mild disease which was treated with anti-biotics. I had been told that I wasn't supposed to drive for six weeks but I managed to get behind the wheel again in two… A week after that and I was laying new tiles on the floor in my lounge. Pete had tried his best to be helpful but there was no way that I would ever forgive him for what he'd done and things would never be the same again. Nor would I; mentally or physically. Pete's attitude towards the kids had improved briefly after Lou's death and I had even thought that he may have finally realised what he was doing but it didn't last long and he got worse again, far worse, it became quite obvious that he really didn't want Claire there either, so I now had to keep them all apart and hold down my jobs.

In the July I was offered a temporary job working for the security company that Pete worked for; it was a three week contract doing bag searches at Bournemouth Law Courts during the

Conservative Party Conference and although it was only for the duration of the conference it was a job and as Pontins had closed I needed the work. I had to wear a uniform; not since the days of school had I been required to do that and somewhere inside me there had been a rebellious teenager trying to get out; I just smiled to myself and suppressed it, I really did feel that I'd come a long way since being in care myself. I was now the carer and wearing a uniform too... Whatever next? I enjoyed the experience.

I'd had to work with another security officer, he was quite young and I managed to have a little bit of fun with him; especially when the prison bus had arrived one morning and it turned out that I knew three of the detainees on board.

"Hi Jan! What are you doing?" The first had asked.
Another one had said
"Long time, no see, how is everyone?"
And the third asked;
"Ok Jan? Got a fag?"
I gave him a cigarette and we had a brief conversation, laughing and joking and when he had to go I said;
"I hope they lock you up and throw away the key."
We both laughed and off he went, my security partner had looked at me totally bemused;
"I really don't think that I should know you, let alone work with you... You know all the criminals!"
I had to admit that he did seem to have a point but work with me he did, right up until the end of the contract and even though Pete hadn't liked me working with him we had needed the money so he didn't get a choice in the matter. The contract ended and I was out of work again but the security firm promised to find me something else. Then Pete took yet another turn for the worse and took a lot of time off work and Lee's friend, Steve, had been made homeless; he had fallen out with his father and had been thrown out... I couldn't see a youngster on the street so I told him that he could stay for a while; besides he had offered to pay keep which helped us out a lot with Pete taking so much time off sick. Steve had stayed in the boy's bedroom with Lee and Matthew, he slept in Michael's bed; Michael had moved into my room on a z bed that he rarely slept on still preferring to sleep in my bed. So now there were 8 of us!

I had heard that Sam was having tests because he'd had a very bad cough and that he was living with his first wife again; though not in Lou's house; he had said that he'd never let her live there, it was and always would be Lou's house. They were living in his mother's bungalow, by then Sam's mother had been put into a nursing home. Within months of Lou's death he had got rid of all of Lou's possessions and rented out the house and even though I had tried to keep him in contact with the children his partner had limited the amount, there was always an excuse, they had been away on holidays a lot of the time although Pete and I had been invited to Sam's 50th birthday party at a restaurant where his ex wife had presented him with two tickets to New York inside a balloon. I had never liked her from the outset, I mean; she had left her own children, she had robbed my children of their Granddad not to mention sleeping with Sam on the night that Lou had died and when we had visited the bungalow it had been decorated how she wanted, there were no photographs or ornaments either, which to my way of thinking had showed just how cold and callous she actually was, trouble was Sam couldn't see it. I did feel better though when Sam had said to me, referring to her;

"She's not bad but she's not my Lou!"

In late May 1994 the diagnosis came that Sam had lung cancer; it was said that the shock of Lou's death had in some way caused it but it could've also been the fact that Sam had always smoked about 80 cigarettes a day. Either way Sam's ex-wife made it her life plan to keep us all away from him. She had then divorced her other husband and in August 1994 she and Sam were re-married, we didn't get invited to that one. She then got Sam to change his will and unfortunately he couldn't see past his illness, something that she used it to its full advantage. The estate in all its entirety was worth some £3,000.000 with the many properties that Sam owned; the factory, the business, six houses in Salisbury that had been left to him by his father, Lou's house, another bungalow in Bournemouth and his mother home where he was living. I really had to hand it to Sam's now 'new wife,' she knew exactly how to manipulate everything to her advantage.

We did manage to see Sam briefly on Christmas day 1994 and even the presents that she'd chosen for the kids seemed cold; all in cardboard boxes wrapped up in matching plain paper, all clothes and no toys. I just could not understand how Sam could have chosen to be with someone so different from Lou; Lou's house had been all photographs, 'The Rogues Gallery' as she had called it… Pictures of all the children, ornaments, nick knacks, plants and flowers. This woman had none of that, she had known how close I'd been to Lou and had made it known that she didn't approve. She was now in charge and any contact with Sam would have to come through her. After that, even if we had been invited to the wedding I don't think I would have gone; my life was difficult enough as it was and I really didn't feel the need to have any more conflict or confrontation.

Sometime near the beginning of August 1994 Pete had gone to the doctor, returning a short while later with a letter addressed to me, in it the doctor had written:

'As Pete has expressed a wish to get away for a while, I feel that he should be allowed to go and stay with his sister in Portsmouth.'

Apparently, Pete had told the doctor that I wouldn't let him go unless the doctor had asked me to; I was totally gob smacked, not by the letter but by the fact that I'd had absolutely no idea that Pete had even wanted to go to his sisters, sure he had spoken about leaving on more occasions than I could care to remember and his belongings were still kept separate, he had even taken to packing it all into his car so that he could leave on a whim and then he would take everything out again; it was as if his things were on elastic. I handed him the telephone;

"Phone her, go if you want!"

He rang her up and asked if he could stay at hers for a while but she had said no, she had told him that she didn't have anywhere to put him up so he stayed with me. I then found a letter, it was the reply to a letter that he had written a few weeks earlier, to some friends in Emsworth, asking if he could live with them; they too had refused him but said that he was welcome to visit. I confronted him with the letter and he told me that it had been a few weeks earlier when he'd been really down. To be quite honest; I really hadn't noticed an 'up' since he and I had been married. He then said that he didn't want to leave but felt that he really needed help. I had to agree, I should have thrown him out there and then but I felt sorry for him, I did warn him though; that I wasn't well enough myself to deal with all his problems and then reminded him of my priority - my children.

Two weeks later Pete went and saw the doctor and this time it was suggested that a psychiatrist should be sent to see him at home later that day, Pete agreed. When the psychiatrist had arrived he'd asked me if I could go out for a bit and take the children with me, he needed to speak to Pete alone. I had needed to get some petrol anyway so agreed and proceeded to pack all the kids into the car; Lee was already out somewhere at the time which was just as well really because with Lorna, Matthew, Michael, Claire and Steven all squashed in the car was absolutely packed. When I had re-fuelled the car and was going in to pay I realised that I knew the girl working on the cash desk; she had been neighbour of Terry and Iris'. She had recognised me too and had asked how I was and what I was doing in the area;

"I only live down the road." I answered.
Then, as she looked at my overloaded car she asked me;

"They all yours?"

"No..." I replied and then proceeded to explain who everyone was, she then asked;

"Are you still with the ginger one? Oh no... The one with the long hair? Drummer isn't he?"

"No, the ginger one turned to drink, beat me up and left... The one with the long hair, Gary, started taking drugs, wearing my make up and then he left..."

"And now?"

"... And now; I'm out because my current husband is with a psychiatrist asking to be hospitalised... Committed!"

"Boy, you can pick them! Are you sure its not you?" She questioned.

"Well there's a thought, it could be!"
I laughed and said goodbye but her words had echoed far too close to my own thoughts... Maybe it was me.

I took us all on a long drive along the seafront before going home, when we got back to the house the Doctor was just about to leave; which meant that he'd been assessing Pete for over an hour, but he then said that he now needed to speak to me before leaving so the kids had to leave the room again, I had been left wondering what the hell Pete had been saying, obviously something detrimental judging by the tone of voice the Doctor had taken with me and he wasn't about share whatever it was either. He had told me that he felt that Pete needed to be hospitalised for a while, then he used our phone to make arrangements for a bed in a local mental hospital and off we went again. As it turned out it was also down to me to take him there... Well, I'd just about had all that I could stand. On the way to the hospital Pete had talked about us separating and him finding a bed-sit when he came out. I didn't know if it was all just talk to get a dramatic reaction or what anymore and to tell the truth; I really didn't care. I didn't love him, all I'd felt was pity for the man but I kept up the pretence all the same… After his operation Pete had threatened suicide, on more than one occasion, mainly because he knew of the effect that Ben's suicide had had on me; especially my feelings of failure and how I felt that if only I'd tried harder to make people listen Ben may have still been alive. I had felt guilty and Pete had known it… But what if he really meant it? What if I missed the signs? Maybe it wasn't an empty threat!

On that night, while driving him to his hospital bed I had actually hoped, albeit briefly, that he would carry out the threat after all; he was no good to me, himself or most importantly, my poor children, he was cruel, selfish and self-centred but deep down I had felt that I was in some way responsible for his state of mind too. I had gone into hospital and onto the ward with him where I kissed him goodbye and left. Talk about contradiction and adding to my increasing confusion; he said that he loved me and had made me promise to visit him the following day, reminding me not to forget the cigarettes! This man had just been telling me how he was leaving me and almost before he'd even drawn another breath he was asking me to do this, that and the other for him; what I should of done was say, No! But as usual I said that I would do whatever he wanted me to. That was a week before Michael's 5th birthday.

I had thought it best not to tell Social Services that Pete had been hospitalised; they may have insisted that Claire be placed elsewhere and she wouldn't have been able to cope with that, she was having enough trouble dealing with the rejection of her family and had said that she felt somehow responsible for Pete's state of mind too. I spent so many hours trying to convince her that it wasn't her fault and that it was more to do with how Pete had been treated as a child; his being adopted, claims that his father had beaten him, being assaulted by a man in a car on the way to school... It seems to me that that was the fate of a lot of people from my generation, all assaulted or abused by some pervert who was lurking around the corner. It didn't help that everyone was reluctant to talk about such things back then and they probably wouldn't have believed you when you'd told them anyway; there wasn't television as we know it today and those sort of offences didn't get the publicity or the media coverage that they do now and although it seems as if there's far more of that kind of behaviour nowadays, I don't think that there is, it has always been the same, the only difference between then and now is that it gets publicised today, we're shown that it goes on and we have no choice but to believe. The best thing is that children are encouraged to talk about it now, to tell someone if they're in danger and they have people that they can talk to; Child Line, Child Support teams, even their teachers. All we were given was a warning; "Don't talk to strangers!" Although the warning was clear, nobody would ever really say why not to talk to strangers... Then again, I cannot help but wonder how many more kids are out there now, too afraid to ask for help; for every one that is reported there are probably another ten suffering in silence. I know that if I had my time again I'd shout it from the roof tops at the very least. I also know that my children have never been afraid to tell me anything and everything.

Claire had started to open up a bit. It was hard work and mentally draining; talking to her and getting her to talk or sitting with her and talking at her usually reducing her to tears. I'd always use the same pattern; she'd go out and do something that she shouldn't, (sleep with some low life, take speed or stay out all night.) I'd then have to go out looking for her, find her from the clues that she'd leave and bring her home, she'd shout and scream at me and I'd laugh at her, then she'd calm down and we'd talk, she'd cry and I'd give her a cuddle and tell her how important she was, then I'd crack some kind of joke and make her laugh and at that point I'd know that she was ok again, for a while at least. When she had first moved into ours she'd gone off the wall every few days but as time went on the outbursts became fewer and farther between; although when Pete deteriorated and had to be hospitalised Claire's outbursts began to increase once again. I knew that it was the insecurity and uncertainty of her future that was that was the problem so I'd stay up talking with her until 3:00 or 4:00am, until I got a result.

There was still the daily diary of events to keep up with and Steven; he was self-harming by cutting his arms with a scalpel blade, something that Claire had seen and decided she should try but had soon realized that it wouldn't work with me and had stopped. I had to spend many hours talking to him aswell but when he realised the effect that it was having on Claire it had encouraged him to stop. My children had needed my re-assurance too; Lorna had become resentful of Claire and the time that I spent with her.

255

My daughter has always been so sensible and she knew what I was trying to do and even though she didn't cause me any real trouble, she did make me realise just how she felt;

"I think I should go out and stab someone, and then I'll get £7.00 a week pocket money and a clothing and hobby allowance from social services. It doesn't pay to be a good girl does it?" I then asked her if she would really have wanted to go through all that Claire had been through and have Claire's mother as hers.

"No thanks!" She answered, "I wouldn't!" She loved me and I her and although it wasn't said every hour or everyday, I knew it and most importantly she knew it, I have always been so proud of her and always will be.

Onto Matthew, he was being bullied on a daily basis; he was rather overweight, partly because he would eat to compensate for the hurt that he was feeling... Being intelligent has its down side. I visited and complained to the school too many times to remember and to the choirmaster aswell, it had been happening there too; an adult male chorister had been getting a little too close to Matthew, far closer than Matthew, or indeed I were comfortable with, I had voiced my concerns very strongly and the man had kept his distance. If I'd ever needed to know whether or not my children would tell me if they were having problems here was my answer, it's just sad that my theory even had to be tested and proved and unfortunate that it was on Matthew.

Michael too was suffering at the hands of bullies; he had very bad eyesight which didn't get diagnosed or treated until his 4 ½ year pre school check up and even though I had tried to point out that there was a problem so many times before then, nobody listened. We knew that he'd had a squint but were told that he was almost blind in his left eye too; from then on he had to wear a patch/excluder over his right eye making it virtually impossible for him to even see a hand in front of his face. Michael had also been very slow in his development and had made erratic noises and hand movements and had very bad hand to eye coordination aswell, we were told that it was due to his poor eyesight; I knew there had to be more to it than that and had tried time and time again to draw attention to as much and to have maybe have gotten him the appropriate help but still no one listened. So Michael, like Matthew was different, an outcast, he couldn't kick or catch a ball and the other kids wouldn't include him in their games, so he inevitably spent his time alone. He couldn't dress himself properly or as quickly as they had wanted either and was ridiculed for that too. Then he was isolated further still when a teacher had drawn attention to him by saying that he had dirty hands;

"Look at your nails; nobody would want to hold your hand would they?"

He was made to go and wash them, all the while he had tried to explain that he hadn't noticed that his hands were dirty and that he was sorry but that someone had pushed him over, the teacher wasn't about to listen.

He was the only one of my children though, who'd managed to lose every item of clothing, including his socks, within his first year of school... One day, after spending a lot of time looking for one of his socks, he had told me that he thought he'd lost in his classroom so we went looking for it but couldn't find it and gave up. When we got home we found it in the toe of his shoe;

"Wasn't that uncomfortable?" I'd asked,

"No!" He'd replied, he hadn't even noticed it was there. Despite it all, he was so loveable with his big brown eyes and he did have quite a sense of humour aswell, although he didn't seem to understand jokes, at all. He did make my life seem worthwhile, always looking up at me saying;

"I love you mummy"

Chapter 33

The main source of light relief and entertainment had been Penny; she had tracked me down again and had taken to coming to see me on Friday nights, we'd sit and drink a few cans and then a few more. (She still had a drink problem but would never have admitted to it.) She'd get a lift down early in the evening with this real odd ball called Ozzy. Before Pete had gone into hospital he and Ozzy had been going to martial arts together whilst Penny and I sat and drank. She had known that things were difficult but hadn't realised how mentally unstable Pete really was, or quite how unstable I had become either, I had learnt to cover it well but it all inevitably came to a head: It was a Sunday afternoon and Pete had been in hospital about a week, I went to see him as I had done everyday and as I walked in I saw Pete and his sister standing out on the balcony having a chat so I headed out towards them. As I joined them Pete had said hello;

"Hi, how are you today?" I asked, then turning to his sister I said, "Hello, how are you?"

"Don't bother," she replied, "I've got nothing to say to you!" I walked away having absolutely no idea why she had spoken to me like that, although I had known that I wasn't about to leave it, not until I'd found out what the problem was but it was neither the time nor the place. I headed into the visitors room and sat down, Pete had followed me followed by her, and he looked across;

"Would you like a coffee?" He asked, then he turned to his sister; "Tea?"
All I had wanted to do was leave but how could I? That would have upset Pete even more...

"Yes please!" I answered,

"Why?" His sister questioned, "Are you stopping then?"

"Any reason why I shouldn't?"
I was getting extremely annoyed and I think Pete could tell because he looked at me and pleaded;

"Please don't, I'll make a drink!"
The second he left the room it began, in front of a number of patients and visitors she started ranting, loudly;

"You are nothing but a slut, it's your fault my brothers in here. Keeping that girl at your house, (I could only assume that she meant Claire,) drunk all the time and sleeping with that kid!" (Presumably Steven.)

258

That was it, my cue;

"For your information lady, Pete has said, as has the doctor that him being in here is due to an assault that happened to him when he was a boy, and also because of your father abusing him, and you 'the dear daughter' caused a lot of those beatings… Some sister you are, you wouldn't even find the room to put him up. For your information, I am in fact the only person who has stood by him and I'm not going to justify your outburst about Claire and Steven with an answer."

She stood up to take a swing at me and I was ready for her, almost too ready;

"Just once lady, I'll drop you where you stand!"

At that moment the door had opened and a doctor who had heard the commotion came in and said;

"Do you mind? If you wish to do this would you kindly leave, this is a hospital and you are upsetting the patients."

I apologised to him and the to rest of the people in the room, at which point Pete came in with the drinks, he had heard some of what had been said and was obviously upset. I, on the other hand, was extremely angry;

"I'm sorry Pete but you have obviously been telling her a pack of lies about me."

He said that he hadn't said anything but then how else could she have known about Claire's troubles, or that Steven was living at my house? So I said;

"Either she goes or I do!"

Pete looked at me then he looked at her, she had then turned to me and said;

"Well off you go then, we don't need you!"

"Well Pete, looks like you've got to make a decision for once in your life."

He had then turned to his sister, who'd said;

"Its ok, I'm going anyway, just come and see me off."

But I told Pete;

"You do that and that's it! She found her way in, she can find her way out"

She did and Pete stayed with me. I had only stayed for a short while after his sister had left, just enough time to chat briefly about what had been said, to tell Pete what was happening at home and to ask the doctors their thoughts about him and how long he'd be in there. When I left he had walked out to the car with me where I gave him his cigarettes and the money that I took him everyday. He was still saying that he was going to find a bed-sit and that he wouldn't be coming home either, I had to agree that it was the best idea. He'd then suggested that; once he had found a bed sit or flat, maybe we could start seeing each other, go out together like 'normal people!' We'd never had that, he'd just moved in. I responded with;

"Maybe?"

I knew then that with the mood I was in at that time and with our previous history together it would never work, I pitied him and that was something that would never change, I could never look at him in any other way. At least he'd be out of my home though and I decided that when he'd got himself settled, I'd tell him how I felt.

I was still angry when I got home but luckily Penny had stayed that weekend so I had her to talk to but whilst I'd been telling her what had happened at the hospital Lee and Lorna had been listening in and had decided that they were going to Portsmouth to sort out Pete's sister, as did Steven and Claire. I eventually managed to calm them all down by assuring them that she would pay for the things she'd said but for time being they needed to leave well alone, meanwhile I had a Sunday roast to cook for which Penny had done all the preparation for me, she was a Gods send. Ben came round for dinner as he often did on a Sunday and we all sat down to my usual roast dinner, family and extended family talking about the week they'd had. Ben gave me my birthday present; an appointment with a medium for a reading the following Saturday. The medium lived quite close to the hospital so I was able to go and visit Pete beforehand. I had mentioned to Ben that I'd wanted to see someone; I needed to know if the trauma was ever going to end and it was, to my mind, a choice between seeing a medium to find out if there was an answer on the other side or booking a twin room at the hospital with Pete, I'd even said jokingly, on many occasions, that I wanted to wear a jacket backwards and sit in a nice padded room, rocking back and forth in the corner... Many a true word spoken in jest.

So Saturday came and I went to see Pete, as was the daily routine by now. I sat and listened to him waffle on about how he was feeling and what the doctors had said, how part of his therapy was writing his feelings down and how he was making me a surprise present, he'd said that although he wasn't meant to tell me what it was, he was going to anyway because he'd known how much I had wanted one. He was so excited, almost childlike;

"Guess what it is..."

I had no idea, I thought; 'do I really care' but I was trying to look pleased all the same;

"So, what is it?"

... Finally he told me;

"A wooden toilet seat!"

"Yes Pete you're right, something I've always wanted!" Yep, that had just about summed it up! It was a far cry from the presents that Dan had bought for me; the flowers and the chocolates, yeah I'd had to take a beating or two but at that moment, I'd rather have had that than the mental torture I was suffering and for what? A wooden toilet seat, whoopee I couldn't wait!

All the way to the medium I kept thinking; 'Toilet seat, I'd never have guessed a toilet seat; a basket maybe, or even a plant trough a picture frame at a push but never a toilet seat... Imagine the splinters!' I'd seen his attempts at D.I.Y and feared the worst. By the time I reached the mediums home I must have looked totally mad, I just couldn't stop myself from laughing and I couldn't tell the medium why I was laughing until after the reading because I felt that would have been coaxing her, I mean; it wouldn't have taken much guess work on her part if I'd told her why now would it? She invited me in;

"Please come in, have a seat."

Her greeting had caused me to smile again; she gave me a puzzled look and said

"You seem a happy person; it's nice to see someone smiling"

She soon changed her tune when she looked at my palms. Although she got it straight off;

"My goodness my dear, what a terrible time, your husband is in hospital but not for anything physical. You don't love him though you will take him back for a while but it wont work, its not what you want and you shouldn't blame yourself you've done all you can."

She touched on my previous violent marriage aswell and said that my eldest child was having trouble too, she'd also said that I would meet a man I had already known; someone who drove a lorry or is a driver of some sort by profession. There were also a few other insignificant things that did however happen to be true.

As I left I had wondered; 'could she be right...' The only person I could think of at the time that drove for a living and that I'd known for some years was Nick, he'd also recently divorced from a friend of mine and had taken to calling in occasionally, late in the evening. I must admit the thought was quite appealing; he was a man's man, all leathers and motorbikes, my sort of man. I'd quite fancied him and I'm sure that the feeling had been mutual. Unfortunately there had been the morality issue; I was still married and Nick had himself been betrayed by his wife and his best friend. Even so he invited me out to the pictures and for a meal and we had a good evening, I did make the mistake of offering to pay for my own meal and much to my surprise he'd been quite insulted at the suggestion and had said;

"No way! Besides it's your birthday present; to say thank you for being there and listening to me with the break up. You've helped me more than you know!"

I was pleased that I'd been able to help in some way, besides he'd helped me too, also by listening and with the evening out and being treated like a human, a lady, it enabled me to step back from the life that I'd been living albeit for a few hours at least. Nick was a real gentleman; he'd opened doors for me and made me feel really special. When he took me home I'd invited him in for coffee and he accepted. The kids were all upstairs and had come down to say hello. We sat and had a coffee and he rolled a joint; something that he always did at the end of his day, I never really had an objection to it. Nick had offered me the joint saying;

"Go on, give it a go."

I hadn't smoked it since the days staying at Jo's house and then it hadn't really had any effect on me, so I thought; 'why not? It may help me to stay relaxed for a little while longer.' Boy was I wrong, one drag and my head was swimming. Nick had then bent over and kissed me, I was so caught up with the effects of the spliff that I hadn't seen it coming but luckily at that moment Steven had walked into the room; I think he noticed that I was grateful for his presence and he sat down, saying;

"Skinning up are we?"

Nick handed him the spliff. Steven and I somehow created an unspoken connection; he instinctively knew that I needed him and he was there. Nick had left after about an hour, he'd obviously hoped for more but I'd told him that with all the kids around I had trouble finding time for one to one contact of that kind, even so I thanked him for a wonderful evening. Nick continued to come round, usually after or during his taxi shift; he owned his cab and so could do as he pleased but he never really made any other romantic advances after that night... Maybe the Medium had got it wrong; it certainly wasn't going to be Nick.

Steven and I also became very close after that night; though I had to keep reminding myself of his age, he too had problems of his own and they would've been worsened by confusing the boundaries. Even so I enjoyed his company, he was amusing and did the stupid things that young men do. He was really good looking aswell and when he suggested that we go for a drink with his Mum and Stepfather one evening in Poole I'd jumped at the chance, besides with all the daily visits to the hospital to see Pete, backwards and forwards to the opticians to get treatment for Michael's eyesight and then the visits to various different schools in different areas of the town; complaining about the bullying of Matthew and Michael; being summoned to Lorna's school because one of the teachers had confiscated her leather jacket and a ring that Lou had bought for her (I'd demanded their immediate return) and then visits to the school, social services reviews and not to mention the pschycologist every other week with Claire, I was at breaking point. I needed to get away from it all for a few hours, a little light relief, this night out with Steven was possibly it and it's not like I was going out with him on my own, I mean his Mum was there. Penny had agreed to baby-sit, she'd been around most of the time while Pete had been in hospital although she was still drinking too much. I even told Pete that I was going out with Steven and his parents too and about my evening out with Nick and he didn't seem too bothered... He didn't have a lot of choice as I saw it; he and I were separated. I'd also taken the kids (all that is with the exception of Lee, he didn't want to go and I didn't push the point), including Claire and Steven to visit Pete at his request; he'd said that he missed them. We had all walked down to the beach with Pete and they'd messed about in the sand, play fighting, even Pete joined in briefly. He had laughed like I hadn't seen him do for sometime and had even admitted to enjoying himself, so there was some positive too.

Steven had arranged for us to meet his Mum and go and see a band that were playing in a pub on Poole Quay; it was a Tuesday night and I'd had a particularly bad week and didn't really feel like going out but Penny had agreed to baby sit for me and everything had been arranged, so reluctantly I went. Mentally I was falling to pieces: Claire had run off on the Sunday evening and I'd had a call from the police station in the early hours of the morning; they had picked her up for trying to buy alcohol and cigarettes on a stolen credit card;

"Would I please collect her?"

Dutifully I went straight to the police station. Claire was half naked, wearing just a see through top and a very short skirt;

"Where are your clothes?" I asked,

"I've no idea!" She replied. "Still the pigs don't mind, do you perv?"

She was shouting at a nearby Police officer. I apologised to the officer and Claire apologised to me, telling them all how wonderful I was; loving her no matter what she did. She was charged; this time with theft and fraud and so the process of court appearances, Youth justice, and Social Services would begin all over again. Michael had also been taken ill with an asthma attack and as if that weren't enough I found out from one of Lee's friends that he had been quite heavily into drugs. I took him aside for a long conversation; the why's and the wherefores. He said that it had started after Lou's death, he couldn't cope, he'd even attempted suicide; he just wanted his Gran, so did I. My baby had been through all of this alone, why hadn't I seen it? I was at bursting point; I'd been too busy dealing with the houseful of lunatics to notice the pain that my own son had been going through. He assured me he had dealt with it; he was all right now but he had decided that he wanted to move out;

"Just for a while Mum."

It wasn't going to be until a few weeks later. I didn't want him to leave and I couldn't sleep at all. The Monday night was spent questioning and reassuring Claire and worrying about how many more signs I'd missed in my own children, poor Lorna was always so good; other than the occasional run in with her teachers. If anyone had the right to rebel it was her but she never did. She was funny, sensible, pretty and clever, even so I had decided that I would need to watch her closely, especially after missing the signs with Lee, I wasn't about to make that mistake with her.

So, albeit reluctantly, I went with Steven and his mum to see the band on Poole quay but I'd realised that I had to put a stop to the attraction that he had to me and my growing feelings for him, maybe Pete's sister was right. I had tried to tell Steven during the evening how I felt but the music was too loud and I wasn't sure that he could hear most of what I was saying. He chatted away to his Mum seemingly oblivious and I decided that I had to leave, to get away. So saying nothing I stood up and walked out. My anxiety was growing and I knew that I'd have to walk home but I just couldn't stay there any longer; I needed to be with my kids, so I started walking. As luck would have it, Nick had just dropped off a fare in Poole, seen me and had pulled alongside; by now I was in tears and looking a complete mess, he told me to get in, he would take me home;

"Have you been attacked? What's happened?" He'd asked.

"Please wait," I sobbed, "I'll tell you in a minute, I just need to get home!"

We drove the long way around, along the sea front and eventually, when I had managed to control myself, I explained the week I was having, about Steven and how I'd just needed to get away. He said he that understood and then reminded me that he was there anytime if I needed to talk. He dropped me home and went straight on, Penny was waiting;

"God what happened to you?" She asked, "Steven phoned asking if you were home yet, he's looking for you, I'll ring him!" Ten minutes later Steven came in, he was saying he thought that I'd jumped in the quay or something; he was worried, angry and upset. I then explained how I'd been feeling, starting with the fact that I'd told it all to him earlier in the evening but, as I'd suspected at the time, he hadn't heard me but did say that he understood. He listened to what I had to say, calmed down and then said that he was going out for a while.

The days that followed were a blur, just the usual routine. Although Pete had decided to ask for a weekend out, telling me that I would have to pick him up on the Friday evening and take him back on the Sunday by 10:00pm. Steven and Lee were staying with Steven's sister at her flat, so Penny had told me that she would be staying with me for the weekend; she'd said that she wanted to just in case he started and I needed to take him back to his padded cell in a hurry, she knew how to amuse me.

When I went to pick Pete up for his weekend at home I couldn't help feeling apprehensive... Why did he want to come home when he'd been trying so hard to get away and move out? I'd asked him why and he told me that moving out and leaving was still the plan... So what on earth was I to make of it all? What was

265

this game he was playing and what exactly was my role in this relationship? Even so, Michael was pleased to see him, running up and hugging him before he'd managed to get in the door but he was the only one who was; Pete received a very cold hello from the girls and Matthew just stayed upstairs away from him. For his part, Pete acted as if he'd never been away; we got into bed and he kissed me goodnight, once again the thought; 'what the hell sort of game is this?' I had no idea. Michael then climbed into bed, in between us so I made the excuse that I wasn't comfortable with Michael's fidgeting and couldn't sleep then went and slept on Michael's 'Z' bed. It was the same on Saturday and on the Sunday too. After our roast dinner, Pete decided that he'd like to go back early, which was a huge relief to me; he had said that although he felt the weekend had gone well, he was tired and feeling as if he had over stretched himself... 'He'd over stretched himself?' I thought; 'he should live one day in my shoes!' Well, I didn't need asking twice and as Penny helped me pack his bag for him she said;

"I don't know about him but I've had enough and I'm sure you have too!"
At least she'd noticed, he'd said his goodbyes as if nothing was wrong and off we went.

I had asked Steven to make my apologies to his Mother and he came back saying that she'd said that she really would like to see me again. I wasn't keen; I was sure that she would think I was a complete nut case but Steven said that he'd explained a bit about what I'd been through and that it would just be for an hour and if I wanted to go home again she'd understand. Steven assured me that he'd bring me home as soon as I'd had enough. In the end I agreed to go, only because it was the anniversary of Steven's friend's death and he was struggling with his emotions. The boy had been Steven's school friend from his first day but had been quite ill and had lost his fight for life at just 15 years old, Steven had been deeply affected, I realised just how deeply later that night. Claire had been acting up again; threatening suicide but I'd felt that it was an attention-seeking thing. Penny wasn't able to come down and baby sit for me but Lee had come home for the evening, he'd insisted that Claire would be fine and she too had agreed that I should go out. So off I went with Steven to his parents' house and his Mum and his Stepfather were fine with me. Although she did ask me about what I'd been through, about Pete and his illness but

I didn't really want to spend the whole evening talking about my problems and I think she must have sensed it because she said;

"Anyway forget it all tonight you are out to get away from it all, relax and enjoy yourself!"

It was good to talk to someone, albeit briefly and get a bit off my chest and for a while I actually enjoyed myself... How wrong could I be?

Chapter 34

Steven and I got back home at about 11:30pm and Lee and Lorna came running out saying that Claire had taken an overdose of paracetamol, they didn't know how many she had taken but it had been about an hour ago. So we bundled Claire into the car and I drove straight to the hospital. Once again my children were left to take care of themselves but as I left I told them that I'd phone as soon as I could. Steven was in the front passenger seat, seemingly calm at first but then he suddenly flipped out and started shouting at Claire; telling her how she was selfish and ungrateful.

"That's enough!" I yelled, "We will deal with all of this later. Claire, how many did you take?"

"About ten or so," she muttered, thankfully still conscious.

"Why?" I questioned,

"I don't know!" She sobbed.

It was obvious to me that this was nothing more than a cry for help and more attention.

By the time we'd arrived at the hospital Steven was very angry and upset, so had opted to stay in the car whilst I went with Claire into accident and emergency. They took her straight in; her stomach had to be pumped, although they thought that she'd be all right if, as she said, she'd only taken ten. She was put into bed, made to drink a solution of some sort then told to wait. As I sat there I'd felt my anger rising up inside me; I was angry with her because she had no reason, no explanation as to why she'd done it but I was angry with myself too; for leaving her and for leaving my children with such a responsibility. I told Claire that I would be back then left her to go and make sure Steven was ok. I had found him sat in the waiting room and he seemed as if he'd calmed down so I asked him if he could go and sit in with Claire whilst I telephoned my children, I was sure that they would be worried. Satisfied that all was ok with my kids I headed back to Claire but when I got back Steven was sat on a chair, next to her bed, hitting the back of his head really hard against the wall and Claire was being sick. I only just managed to calmly say;

"Steven, please, not now!"

What I had really wanted to do was scream at them both. Steven had then exploded again at Claire, screaming at her about how his friend hadn't wanted to die;

"Yet here you are, you selfish bitch trying to kill herself. You deserve to die, he didn't!"

He'd then told her that he could kill her and do the job properly. I couldn't believe what was happening; one in the bed, suicidal and being sick, one flipping out and beating his head against the wall and Pete, my husband in a mental hospital… My kids, what about my kids? If I could've walked out of that hospital at that moment and left them all to it, I most certainly would have. Eventually a nurse came in and asked Steven to wait outside;

"You going to make me?" He snapped,

"Yes," she replied, "I'll call the police!"

She said it so calmly and without any hesitation that I couldn't help but think that she must have dealt with people like him a thousand times.

"I'm sorry!" I said to her, "Please give us a minute?"

She left us to it, pulling the curtain closed as she went; I had then turned back to the other two and stammered;

"Steven, please?!"

By this time Claire was crying again and once again I told her that I would be back, I had then taken Steven outside and pleaded with him not to make matters worse at which point he burst into tears as well;

"Take my keys and sit in the car," I'd said handing him the keys, "let me see what's happening with Claire and then we'll leave."

He agreed to do as I'd asked and I went back into the hospital to see Claire and asked her again why she had done it. She still claimed that she didn't know but felt that nobody cared about her;

"Well what the hell have I been doing all this for then?" I whispered, trying to keep my cool. "Certainly not for my own health!"

She apologised saying that she shouldn't have done it and certainly on that day, she hadn't known about Steven's friend but he'd told her whilst I was phoning home. Claire apologised again and again. She had said that she thought Steven would hate her after what she had done, I tried to convince her otherwise;

"No, he won't Claire; he's just worried about you that's all!" I put my arm around her, "You silly girl, you know I love you!"

She had then asked if she would still be able to come back home to which I'd replied;

"Yes why wouldn't you?"

What I had really wanted to say was 'No!' but I couldn't do that to her; she was frightened and vulnerable and needed me to be there for her, I just wanted to give this problem to someone else and concentrate on my own kids, I also wanted Pete to stay in hospital forever aswell.

"… I'll be back in a minute," I said, "I just need to talk to the nurse."

I then walked outside and started crying myself. Once I'd regained my composure I went and found the nurse who had told me that Claire was ok but they wanted to keep her in over night for observation and that they were going to get someone to talk to her before she was discharged, although she felt sure she would be all right. I then explained Claire's history, the fact that I was fostering her and that I would notify the social workers the following day. With that done I returned to Claire;

"Ok, you're all right but they want you to stay overnight." I had said the words as cheerfully as I could but her smile faltered and I was stopped in my tracks as on came yet another outburst;

"You've told them you don't want me haven't you?" She yelled, "You're not letting me come home!"

The nurse came running in and reassured her;

"Claire, you're only staying in for tonight, Mum will be back to pick you up in the morning!"

"You see?" I asked as I looked at her.

More apologises had followed, I'd cuddled her and asked if she was all right now, I told her that I had to get home to the others but I would come back and see her first thing, I'd then told her to behave herself and there it was… The smile; the, 'I'm ok' smile, she was back on an even keel again and I knew that I could leave her, for the time being. Her drama was over for the night but mine had only just begun… Now it was time for Steven and his 'emotional fireworks.'

I braced myself and walked back to the car, when I got there I found Steven sitting in the car, crying and going on about his dead friend and what an ungrateful bitch Claire was. He told me that he wanted me to take him to the cemetery; he wanted to be with his friend and if I wouldn't drive him, he'd walk. I then noticed that his knuckles were all cut so I asked;

"What have you done to your hands?"

"Punched that wall…" He replied, shrugging, "Why?.. It doesn't hurt!"

"But why did you do it?"

"I just want to be with my friend. This is nothing to the pain that he went through!"

And then he went on again with his tirade of abuse about Claire. It was now 2:30am and I was very tired so I agreed to take him to the cemetery; it was the only way that I could persuade him to stay in the car and leave the hospital grounds with me. I did drive but instead of taking him to the graveyard, I drove us home. As I turned the corner into the road where we live Steven decided to open the car door and jump out, slamming the door behind him; the house is only a few yards from the corner so luckily I was slowing the car anyway and could stop before he hurt himself. I shouted after him to come back but he wasn't about to stop, he just continued on down the road, shouting and swearing at me for tricking him, he then got into his own car and skidded away. By now I couldn't care less if he lost his licence that was his problem, he was as selfish, if not more so than Claire; he was now putting other people's lives in danger, not just his own. As I was getting out of the car Lee was coming out of the house having heard the commotion but I ushered him back indoors saying;

"Don't worry about it!"

I'd had just enough time to explain to Lee why Steven was kicking off and about Claire being kept in hospital overnight before Steven came back; as he came in the door he'd been yelling, calling me a lying bitch and slag but before I'd had a chance to respond Lee had picked up a golf club and was threatening him with it. I started shouting at Lee to put the club down and he did but began fighting with Steven using his hands instead. The fight continued into the front garden where they both lay scrapping in my neighbour's hedge, the neighbour called down from the top window next door;

"Enough! I'll phone the police!"

Lee let go of Steven and came back inside the house and I turned to Steven;

"How dare you attack my son?" I shouted.

Although Lee didn't seem to have a mark on him, I then told Steven to go and cool down;

"I won't be back!" He spat,

"Ok, whatever Steve!" I spat back.

He really had lost it, Lee told me that he was concerned for me, he'd seen Steven like this once before and he was dangerous, I said;

"Lee you shouldn't have got involved!"

"No ones going to call you names and get away with it Mum, after all that you've done for them."

He knew and I knew that he was quite right and there was no going back; Steven would have to go, Claire though was a different story; she would have had to have gone back into residential care if I had given up on her so I explained to Lee that as much as it pained me, I really couldn't do that to her at that point.

Steven had appeared outside the house again a few minutes later and just sat there in his car. I watched him from the window for a while and he'd eventually climbed out of his car and started walking backwards, he'd moved a few feet away from the car before he began running very quickly back towards it where he smashed his head into the side, wobbled backwards and fell to the ground... I wondered if he'd knocked himself out but I couldn't see him, I guessed that he would have landed on grass and waited a few moments but he didn't get up. I asked Lee to go and check on him for me and a few minutes later he called me; Steven wasn't moving and had a really large lump on his forehead that was noticeable even in the dark. I came outside and checked him; he was ok and I knew instinctively that he was pretending to be out cold... He was just someone else wanting yet another piece of me, a little more of my attention but I had nothing left to give;

"Just leave him there Lee!" I said and walked away.

After a while Steven came indoors;

"So... Are you better now? Look at what you've done to yourself!"

I told him to go and sleep it off and that although I didn't expect him to leave until he'd found somewhere else to live, he did have to go. (That was the only thing I was certain of.) He agreed with me and apologised for everything that had happened... If I had to hear one more apology at that moment I think I would've screamed, if I'd had the strength that is. I went to bed deciding that a couple of hours were better than none.

The following day I got up and took Michael to school, as per the normal routine, came home and rang Social Services to speak to Claire's social worker but as usual she wasn't available so I told the person who was about Claire's overdose and they agreed to get a message to the social worker, then asked if I was requesting for Claire to be taken out of our care; this seemed to be their only concern.

"No," I said, "I'm just informing you that she is in trouble and of what she has done."

This, I reminded them, was an agreement and a legal requirement. I was annoyed that nobody was ever available when they were needed, their only concern always seemed to be the same; did we want to get rid of Claire, if we didn't want her then she'd be a placement problem for them. Another thing that always seemed to be the same was that there was never any support either, I was just supposed to manage. So I did what I felt that I had to and that was cope, although I couldn't help but wonder how quickly Claire's social worker would've called back if I had said that I'd wanted her removed, all the same, I wasn't prepared to risk Claire's welfare to test my theory, not to mention what sort of effect such a test would have had on Claire's state of mind at the time. So I just hung in there. Next I had phoned the hospital to ensure Claire was to be discharged and asked if they could tell her that I'd phoned and that I was on my way. Lorna and Matthew had taken care of themselves, as was the usual and got themselves off to school and Lee had gone to work but Steven still lay in bed so I went in to check his head and see that he wasn't unconscious or anything worse but he was fine, just bruised, he told me that I shouldn't worry about it and that he was ok but before I left for the hospital I had reiterated what I'd said the night before; that he would have to find somewhere else to live, just in case he thought that I'd had a change of heart.

I went to collect Claire from the hospital and was told by the doctor to keep an eye on her, he'd said that although he felt that she was ok there was always the risk with paracetamol that the kidneys had been damaged and the effects wouldn't show for a few days afterwards but if I had any concerns then I should take her to the doctor for a check up… Great, so she could still be damaged? I took Claire home and we talked for a while, when we were done I was satisfied that she had learnt a valuable lesson, at least for the time being although she was very upset that Steven was leaving until I'd explained that it wasn't her fault and that he had his own issues to deal with.

A little while later Pete had phoned, the moment that I answered he began ranting about how he had tried to call earlier and no one answered;

"Where were you? Out as usual!" He quizzed.

Without really waiting for answers he continued and told me that he wanted me to pick him up at 2.00pm and take him to see his boss at the security office so he could find out about his future within the company; he wanted to know if he'd still have a job and he had to be there for 2:30pm.

"Ok, I'll be there!" I'd answered.

"Not if it's too much trouble for you." he said.

The man had absolutely no idea at all; in his tiny mind I should have been sitting there just waiting for his call because of course I had nothing better to do.

"No, that's fine, I'll be there!"

Steven came down the stairs as I was saying goodbye to Pete with his bags packed;

"Where will you go?" I asked in spite of myself and to my surprise, after everything, I felt guilty.

"I'm going to stay with a mate," he replied, "he's got a flat and has said I can doss with him for a few weeks."

"Well there's really no hurry!"

"No, it's for the best," he said shame faced,

"So, you will let me know how you are. We are still friends?"

He promised to phone me and come round regularly and regardless of the events that had happened during the few weeks leading up to that moment I still felt that I'd miss him all the same. We said our goodbyes, Steven left and I had another problem to resolve; I didn't really want to leave Claire alone whilst I picked Pete up from the hospital, I didn't really think that it would've been a good idea. 'Who could I call on?' I'd thought, 'I know... her Mum!' Gemma didn't exactly do much for Claire but I'd thought that if she knew of Claire's overdose she may feel otherwise so I popped round to see her and told her about the events of the previous night then asked if she would do me a favour and watch Claire for a while; she told me that she didn't want to but if there really was no one else then she supposed she could, on the condition that I wasn't going to be long. I just couldn't quite comprehend what I was hearing, I had just told this woman that her daughter had taken an overdose and this was her response; I suppose so? Unbelievable! I had decided it best to ask her not to question Claire, or rise to the bait if she decided to exaggerate or lose her temper, as another favour to me. Gemma was obviously disturbed by the prospect so I'd said;

"If she starts just send her back to my house!"

I then spoke to Claire about the arrangements and she'd told me that she'd be all right on her own so I said that I'd feel better if she wasn't alone...

"So as a favour to me?" I asked,

"Ok, but only as a favour to you!" She replied.

Well, it was better than nothing, besides she knew it was an inconvenience to her mother, which she said she'd enjoy.

"Don't wind her up!" I told her.

"Me?" She said trying to sound surprised, "Wind her up... Would I?"

She laughed and I had to laugh too, she may have been hard work but she also had her endearing side and was so like me in her attitude it was uncanny.

So with Claire at her mothers I went to pick up Pete and take him to his meeting, my problem now was that if the meeting with his boss went on too long I'd have to go and collect Michael from school and then go back for Pete. I pulled up outside the hospital doors and Pete was stood there waiting; he'd obviously had another change of plan aswell because he was holding his suitcase... Now what?

"What's going on?" I'd asked,

"I've discharged myself!"

"I thought you were getting a bed sit?" I questioned,

"Yes, I will but I want to come home for a while, I can look for one just as easily from there can't I?" He'd pleaded... Oh boy! Here we go again.

"What about your job?" I asked,

"I've still got an appointment to see the boss but if I had told you I was coming home you wouldn't have let me, would you?"

"Well of course I would!"

I lied and he was absolutely right, I probably wouldn't have let him had I known his intentions.

"Still, you never know," he said, "we might be able to work things out now that my heads a little more sorted, isn't that what you want?"

"I don't know, we'll have to see how it goes!"

'Still the control freak,' I'd thought as we pulled away though I said nothing. I should have told him where to go there and then, I should have seen it coming and I should never have told him what the medium had said about him leaving, he'd obviously decided that he had to prove her wrong, whatever the cost. I took him to see

275

his boss; the meeting took all of five minutes and wasn't pre-arranged as he'd told me at all. Pete was told to pop in when he was feeling better and able to return to work again so yes, he still had his job, his boss then said that he could return on the Monday if he wished but Pete declined saying the following week would be better; he wanted to settle in at home again, spend some time with us, his family and even had the nerve to say that I had needed the help. So with everything agreed we left and went to collect Michael from school but when we got there we were a little too early so Pete suggested that we go for a coffee at a café close to the school, he'd always loved café's and still does. I didn't feel that I wanted to sit in a café with him, I didn't really want to sit anywhere with him; he asked why I was being so off with him. He just didn't seem to get it, his assumption being that I didn't want him back because I'd found someone else and began ranting on about as much until I'd said;

"For God's sake Pete, shut up!"
Then I'd blurted out the events of the previous forty-eight hours, to which he'd said;

"Well good, I'm glad Steven's gone and if you had any sense you'd get rid of Claire too."
'Yes, and you my friend!' I'd thought while saying;

"No Pete, she isn't going anywhere. I'm not about to give up on her!"

"I hope that Michael didn't see any of this?" He snapped,
"No!" I snapped back, "he was asleep!"
There was no mention of or show of concern for my other children, the three he had promised to take on as his own, which I'd just thought of as typical Pete behaviour and there didn't seem to be a thought or a concern for me either; well, if he had thought it he certainly didn't say anything. On the other hand Michael was thrilled to see his Daddy, especially when Pete had told him that he was coming home for good. Well at least my little baby was happy, as was Pete; two happy out of eight wasn't bad going. Claire too had seemed all right when I had gone to pick her up from her mothers and Gemma had no complaints either… So we were making more progress there aswell.

Nobody from Social Services had bothered to contact me until the following week and when they did it was suggested that perhaps Claire should have weekly counselling instead of fortnightly… It was hard enough to get her to go once every two weeks and bring those feelings forward; which in itself was very difficult for her and always resulted in some sort of outburst and given the recent events I wasn't even sure that the sessions were actually doing her any good either but they were a condition of her supervision order, along with the monthly visits to Youth Justice and part-time school in the mornings; initially a taxi had been arranged to take her to school but then Claire had decided that she wanted me to take her instead and wouldn't go by taxi anymore; this was a big problem as Michael was at school on the other side of Bournemouth to Claire and there was no way that I could drop him off early and leave him there on his own so I'd made arrangements with Claire's school for her to come in either earlier or later each day. As it turned out later was better for them, I think that it was their preferred option as Claire was very disruptive; in the short time that she was actually at school each day she'd have special education in a small group where she'd tended to either cause a disturbance or go into what was called 'the quiet corner' and go to sleep and by mid morning I would've had a call to come and collect her early.

When I was sat thinking about the events in my life to write this book, I realised that for two years all I seemed to do was run around after people.

Pete had only been home a couple of weeks when Lee left; he too was going to stay with friends. We had discussed his reasons for leaving and he'd said that he felt it was time he moved out. It wasn't easy; my eldest son leaving home... Where had the years gone? I knew that he had to leave eventually and I knew that I had to let him go if he was ever to come back again. He needed to find out for himself how hard it was out there and I wondered if he was going to miss me like I already missed him. People had warned me of this feeling but unless you have been there you can't understand it; it felt as though a part of me was taken away.

"Love you mama!" He'd said as he always did when he left and still does.

Then he was gone although he promised to be back for his Sunday dinner as normal. The family dinner; the only remaining stable and unchanged part of our family's tradition. He'd kept to his promise and had seemed fine and quite happy which he'd said was due to the peace and quiet he was enjoying and very grateful for;

"Can I swap places? I could really do with the break!" I joked, knowing that I wasn't going anywhere; I just had to hang on in there.

Pete had seemed to have been keeping his head down since the moment that he came out of hospital; he wasn't any help but then he wasn't really a hindrance either, he was just there; I think he thought that if he didn't make any waves then I'd forget about the idea of him moving out. I decided not to mention it for a while, things were far more peaceful that way. Besides we still had no physical relationship to speak of, (which was a relief to me,) mainly due to Pete having to work nights; he'd sleep all day, have his meal in the evening and leave for work so I didn't even have to share a bed with him most of the time and Michael was still in my bed most nights anyway.

I found that I was busy most of the time but somehow, with the help of the kids, I retained my sense of humour... The week after Lee had left home I'd had a call from Lorna's school; they'd asked me to come to the school and see the head mistress as they believed that Lorna was having problems. So I made an appointment and went to the school. When I'd walked into the office I was confronted with the head mistress, the deputy head and Lorna's form teacher; now I was fearing the worst, I thought, 'something's wrong with my daughter and I've been too busy to notice!' Actually, no! The teachers said that Lorna was fine and doing very well considering what she'd been through...

"Been through?"
I started panicking, 'Oh God, she's been badly effected by the recent events.' I let the head continue;

"With having had glandular fever and all."
It took all the strength I had not to laugh out loud, 'What glandular fever? Surely I would have noticed that?' I said nothing, merely nodded.

"We find she is very tired!" The head continued, "so we let her sit out of games, although I wonder whether the fresh air and exercise might be ok now, it has been almost a year now hasn't it... What do you think?"
Oh boy, they really didn't want to know what I thought; my darling daughter was sure in trouble, with me, she could've at least warned me of what she'd been saying, I smiled sweetly;

"Yes she has had a rough time with this," I'd said, "bad throats and generally feeling under the weather, perhaps we'll leave things as they are for a little while longer, (Luckily I knew a little about glandular fever, mainly the length of time it takes to get over it and that people who have had it do get tired; but for a year?) I'm sure that she's over the worst now though!"

"So how do you find she's been at home?" The head had asked.

I had the feeling that they'd suspected that there were possibly some untruths being told;

"Well as you say, she's very tired and it doesn't seem to matter how early she goes to bed either."

"Well, thank you for coming in so promptly and may we say that Lorna is a credit to you and a valued pupil." They all shook my hand and I left.

Lorna was waiting for me at the bottom of the stairs when I got back home so I gave her the look, the 'Oh boy are you in trouble' look but I couldn't stop myself from laughing at her... The nerve of this child!

"Sorry mum," she'd said, "not for lying to them but for not telling you. I didn't think they'd call you in!"

I punished her by grounding her for a week and realised how good at drama she really was; she had made up the excuse so that she didn't have to do P.E, had written and signed letters excusing herself from games and had convinced all of the teaching staff that she was truly ill. I'd had another call from Lorna's school a little while later saying that she was smoking at school, something I knew couldn't be true, she'd hated it, she had even hated the fact that I smoked. I was told over the phone that a number of girls who Lorna had been with, were caught smoking at lunchtime, then they said that Lorna had smelt of smoke but had denied smoking herself... That really got my back up;

"I smoke," I snapped, "are you saying my daughter smells because I smoke too? I'll be there in a moment to talk to her!"

When I arrived at the school, Lorna was outside and came running over to meet me;

"I swear I haven't been smoking mum!"

I could tell then that she was telling the truth;

"Tell the teacher I want to see her!" I said,

"Why?" She asked, a look of horror creeping across her face, "what are you going to do?"

Without another word or an answer she fetched the teacher, bringing her back to where I was waiting. I knew that the girls called this particular teacher; 'cauliflower breath!' The poor woman obviously had a problem. She shook my hand;

"How can I help?" She asked with a big smile in her face.

"Well as I said on the phone, I smoke! It's like me saying to you that your breath smells of cauliflower; insulting don't you think? My daughter will not be doing any detention as she did not and does not smoke!"

The teacher had excused herself saying that she needed to speak to the head. Lorna looked at me;

"Mum… I can't believe you said that!" She said with a very shocked look now on her face.

"Well it's got you off detention hasn't it?"

It had and she didn't have to do a detention, although I did feel a little guilty about my insensitive remarks and thought that the teacher had taken it well. (Lorna did say that she'd thought the teacher had gone off to cry even though she didn't look like she had.) Besides, I was standing up for my daughter, as I always have for all kids, mine or otherwise.

As did Lorna, so Claire too also amused me; usually with her attitude to authority. Whilst at a review at Central Social Services, she had sat with her feet on the table calling them all;

"… A waste of space!"

Claire had then decided to crawl across the table which made her social worker and the review board quite agitated.

"Get down and sit properly!" Claire's social worker said through gritted teeth,

"Don't speak to me like that…" Claire replied, laughing.

"...Make me! What you call properly isn't what I call properly and I'll do what I want to!"

When I felt that everybody disconcerted enough I said;

"Oh Claire, that's enough!"

She stopped what she was doing in that instant and sat down next to me;

"Yes, ok!" She said, "I'll do what Jan asks because she does care about me and doesn't tell me what to do, she asks nicely."

I couldn't believe the nerve of the girl; in the end she'd also refused to talk to the counsellor and had sat playing with a small tea set asking him if he'd like a cup of tea;

"Sugar? Milk?" She knew just how to wind them all up; a great source of amusement to me.

Then at the other end of the scale of humour we had Pete; always confirming his total lack of basic intelligence. One very memorable occasion was when our telephone had broken and he'd started panicking;

"What are we going to do now?" He asked,

"We'll go up the garage and buy a new one!" I said trying to calm him down, "they're only about four pounds each."

"How can I do that?" He said looking confused.

"What?.." My sarcasm was bubbling to the surface "Well, you go in and buy one... What's the problem?"

"Will they be able to get one?" He was now becoming irate.

"What are you talking about? Just buy one!" I too was getting annoyed. "They've got loads, all different colours."

"Yes..." He said, like I was totally mad, "but will they have one with our number?"

That was it, I completely fell apart laughing until tears were running down my face, the more annoyed he got the funnier I found it. Once I'd calmed down I'd had to explain why I'd found it so funny and after a few attempts he finally got it;

"Yes, the number is on the line and not the telephone!"

That moment will stay with me forever but it was also confirmation that both Pete and Michael had a real problem, a problem that I would need to get to the bottom of; for Michael's sake.

Then there was Penny; she was the funniest of all and the things that she said and did were, without doubt, stupid on every level. She was the main person who'd kept me sane. She was still coming down on Friday nights, even though Pete hadn't gone back to martial arts again yet and on one particular evening we'd managed to persuade Ozzy, or 'chauffeur' as we called him, to take Pete up the pub whilst Penny and I sat drinking our cans, playing records and having a laugh, reminiscing about old times. By the time the men came back I was really quite the worse for ware and had fallen asleep on my settee. The next thing I knew; Pete was waking me up saying that the police were on the phone;

"They want to know if Penny can stay the night."

It was about 1:00am.

"She's already here, isn't she?" I asked sitting up. "I thought she was upstairs!"

I kept thinking; 'Why would she get the police to ask if she can stay? Why could she not just ask me herself? She must be frightened of me!'

"Yes of course she can stay!" I'd said. Now that I was sat up I was feeling unwell, drunk; "Pete, I need something to eat!" He went to the kitchen and brought back a fresh cream cake that I'd bought earlier in the day. Now as far as I was concerned Penny was still hiding out upstairs, so imagine my surprise when, plastered in cream cake, I answer the front door to a policeman and Penny.

"Are you Jan?" The policeman asked with a look of confusion on his face,

"Yes, that'll be me!" I answered with custard and cream all over my face.

"Thank you for taking Penny in, we couldn't take her back to Blandford."

It turned out that Ozzy had been arrested for drink driving, no licence and no insurance.

"That's ok." I managed

"I'll leave her in your capable hands then," he said and left.

"Yep, ok!" I'd said as he walked away.

I felt more than a little embarrassed by the state that I was in but even so Penny and I did have a good laugh about it, especially when I'd explained to her that I hadn't actually known she'd gone, that I had thought she was upstairs, she said;

"You looked like you had rabies or something!"

Penny and I started going out together regularly again at weekends, just like the old days. It was the welcome break in my week and I'd developed a taste for it; going out with Steven had seen to that, albeit only a few weeks. Pete would baby-sit for me and when he couldn't do it Lorna and Claire did.

Chapter 35

Christmas 1994… I had heard how ill Sam was and that he only had a few weeks left, (he had responded well to treatment initially but I just knew that he was nearing the end,) so I'd arranged for the kids to see him for a couple of hours, although I didn't get invited; I was kept at arms length mainly because of my friendship with Lou and the fact that I couldn't betray her memory by accepting Joan.

Sam had re-married Joan the previous August and none of us had been invited; I wouldn't have gone anyway but Joan had taken advantage of my absence and of Sam's illness too; she had managed to get a rushed divorce, had arranged her marriage to Sam almost immediately and had gotten him to change his Will. The contents of which were contested later by Sam's son, Allan; who claimed that his father had been mentally incompetent because of the cancer. I felt that he should have challenged her right to the contents of the Will, needless to say Allan lost the case and there was nothing I could do being divorced from Dan. So Joan inherited everything, including all that had belonged to Lou. I do take consolation in something that Lee and Lorna told me; that during their last visit, Sam had kept repeatedly calling Joan by Lou's name. She wouldn't answer him when he did and had tried desperately to ignore him but it proved to me that he was still thinking of Lou… It may have been the lack of oxygen to his brain that had caused his confusion but I like to think that Lou was still his number one, more importantly I feel that Joan must have known it aswell. Sam finally died March 7th 1995, just two years after Lou had passed and on the anniversary of my baby Carl's death.

Joan had written to Dan's brother and me telling us both that we would not be welcome at the funeral; I didn't realise that you needed an invitation. I didn't go and it was just as well because by all accounts a number of people had walked out of the funeral in disgust, including Allan: It seems that during the service the speaker had been saying what a loving husband and devoted partner Sam had been to Joan for many years and how he'd done so much for charity. (The only charitable thing Sam ever did was to buy a mini bus for Romania or somewhere like that.) Everyone had said that they'd thought they were at the wrong funeral and as Allan had walked out he'd said aloud;

"My Dad was a womaniser, a drinker and a gambler and my Mother was Lou, not her!"

She'd never be his mother in his eyes, blood or otherwise. I heard later that Joan had tried to bribe Allan with money saying that if he would apologise and accept her as his mother then she'd give him his inheritance but he'd refused. My kids though had had to deal with yet more loss. Lorna said that she felt as though when Lou and Sam had gone away for that fateful holiday, neither of them had come back and to her they were still on holiday… The end of an era.

A couple of months after Sam died I found a wooden cannon in a Salvation Army shop that I'm sure had belonged to Lou; I had wandered into the shop without realising where I was going as if I'd been guided and when I stopped, there on a shelf in front of me was the cannon. I picked it up, examined it closely and discovered a piece chipped from one of the three balls on the back of it. That was the Confirmation I'd needed that it was the very cannon Lou and Sam had bought whilst holidaying in Spain years before; Lee had been playing with it when he'd accidentally dropped it and the piece had chipped off, he was about four years old at the time. The cannon had always sat in Lou's fireplace and I was forever telling her that I wanted it and she had always joked saying that when she died it would be mine; well, she was true to her word and it only cost me £2.00. I searched around in the shop for a while longer; just in case there were other things I may have recognised but couldn't find anything else. The cannon now lives in my fireplace. Joan sold or disposed of everything that Lou and Sam had owned, within about three months of Sam's funeral. She had even written to Lou's sister Susan saying that; as Sam was dead, she felt she could no longer be expected to pay for the upkeep of Lou's and little Gran's graves anymore, as Sam had always done, so Susan had to pay for it from then on. Sam's Mum had also died within a few months of him and Joan became the executor of that Will and inherited the majority of that too. She was the first and third wife and she inherited everything; in total over three million pounds, then she'd quickly moved back to London, as we all knew she would and remarried the man she had divorced so that she could marry Sam… One thinks that it was all very well planned. Although there is or was talk of some off shore accounts that Sam and Lou had held together which Joan was unable to get at; for all we know they could still be sat there now. Still, if my beliefs are correct; one day she will have to answer for all she has done and I hope that day will come to pass. Meanwhile I have my cannon and every time I look at it, a part of my best friend is here with me.

Penny was staying with us more frequently and it wasn't long before it became every weekend, which was just as well as I had been offered a job working for the same security firm as Pete; on their reception during the week and as a perimeter guard at weekends. Pete was on his way down again and Penny had offered to take care of the house and kids for me, I couldn't have gone to work otherwise, I still couldn't leave Matthew alone with Pete; Matthew was safe when there were other people around, Pete would never do anything to him then. Claire too had decided to take a step backwards; she was hanging around with the wrong crowd, getting heavily into drugs and had decided that she preferred the company of black or Asian men as opposed to white men, she had also taken on the Afro Caribbean slang too; terms like 'baby mother' which were silly, annoying and false but it all created the desired effect; it gave her the attention that she craved.

It started again around January of 1995; Claire was back into drugs and as a result she'd decided that she was an addict and had to be treated as such, although she still had a choice. So here we were again; the many nights of talking, the angry outbursts, the tears, the "I hate you's" and apologies, the "I love you's" that followed after, it was very draining emotionally but by the end of April she was almost back on track. On one of her nights intoxicated she'd had a tattoo of a bird done on her right hip; although it was quite pretty I couldn't help but hope that it would remain out of sight of the majority of the population. She then started seeing a man from Bangladesh who was very pleasant but had caused a lot of conflict because of his beliefs; Claire was expected to change to accommodate him and his culture, the trouble with that being; she'd expected him to change to suit her. This union was therefore; doomed from the start, I had long conversations with them both separately but it finally ended with Claire lashing out at him and damaging his car and him being very confused by the whole experience. It wasn't long after they'd parted company that Claire found out she was pregnant and in June of 1995, I had taken Claire to the Life Organisation for a test and it was confirmed; yes she was pregnant, she was confused, she didn't know what she should do;

"What would you do?" She questioned, "Will I have to leave your home?" "Will you insist on it?"

I was reminded so vividly of my own feelings and confusion when I'd found out that I was expecting Carl. Claire was just over Fifteen years old when she'd found out she was going to be a mother and although she was a year older than I had been, it was no less difficult for her emotionally; in some ways more so given the child's mixed parentage, which I told her wouldn't make any difference and that if she did want to go through with the pregnancy I would stand by her, whatever the decision but she had to make the decision herself. I remembered how lonely I had been and there was no way I would allow Claire to feel that way.

"Well at least this baby will be someone who loves me," Claire had said, "and be someone that I can love back!"
It was the very same thoughts that I'd had all those years before. Perhaps this was all part of some master plan for me that the experiences of my past were meant to enable me to deal with Claire's problem now. If so it was a very cruel lesson to have to learn at the expense of Carl. I'd had doubts as to whether or not I'd be able to cope; with whatever Claire's decision happened to be, with Pete and his problems and with our home already bursting at the seams… Where would I accommodate a baby? I figured that I'd just have to and did precisely that. Gemma's reaction had been exactly as Claire had predicted it would be;

"She should get rid of it!"
And Claire had reacted exactly as I'd expected; she dug in her heals and said,

"No way!"
Even if she'd had every intention of having an abortion up until then, Gemma's reaction had definitely ensured that Claire would do completely the opposite; she was keeping the baby and from then on she'd have the ability to say,

"She (Gemma) would have liked for me to have gotten rid of it just like she got rid of me!"
I tried to justify Gemma's attitude by telling Claire that it really wasn't her mother's fault, she really didn't have the experience to deal with Claire's problems, cocooned as she was as a child to the realities of the 'real world'. In some ways I think that Claire did try to see her mother's position but Gemma would inevitably say something insensitive and Claire would revert to her previous way of thinking. The Social Services were also trying to encourage Claire to have an abortion but she stood by her decision to go through with the pregnancy and I stood beside her and her decision as prom-

ised. When I was asked by social workers how I felt and how disappointed I must be after all my hard work I'd said;

"At least she's not taking drugs anymore!"

I wasn't disappointed in any way; I was just glad that she hadn't succeeded in taking her own life, or run away, or worse! For their information I was proud of Claire's achievements and that most of the work had been done by Claire, against the odds. Whilst I was defending Claire and her decisions I couldn't escape the feeling that I was also defending the decisions of my own past. Later I thought about my life experiences, asking myself; if I could relive my life again, would I do it differently? Well in some ways; yes I would but then weren't these experiences the very reason I am the person I am today? Probably for the first time in my life I had to say that I quite liked the person I was. It was something I'd been trying to get through to Claire; that she should love herself or if not at least like herself as much as I liked her... How could she expect others to like her if she didn't like herself?

Lorna had been quite angry at the prospect of having a baby in the house again; it was bad enough that she'd had to share her bedroom with Claire but with a baby aswell? Disturbed sleep and everything else that goes with it but as usual she just grinned and bared it! What choice did she have? Claire had already taken over her room and she wasn't the tidiest of people, had taken and worn many of Lorna's clothes, had even tried to take Lorna's boyfriend but Lorna had said that he wasn't interested in someone who had slept with anything and everything in trousers. The fact that they had shared and slept in the same room for almost three years never influenced my daughter to become like Claire at all but then Lorna was confident, sensible, independent and happy with herself, equally sociable and comfortable in public; very different to Claire.

Claire's now ex boyfriend was told, via his cousin, that Claire was pregnant, he came around to see her; he said that he didn't want Claire to be his baby's mother and when it was born he would apply for custody. I'd asked him how he intended to take care of the baby and he told me that he'd get a wife and that would be her job.

"And what if this wife doesn't want the job?" I'd asked,

"She would have no choice," he responded, "it would be her job and she would respect my wishes, it is her place to look after my children!"

'Well,' I thought, 'no wonder it didn't work out with Claire, she would never be able to agree to those ideals.'

"I'm sorry," I'd said, "but Claire will be keeping the baby, she will fight to keep it and I will be supporting her but it is of course your choice to apply for custody if you wish to do so!" I was angered by his attitude.

We didn't see him again after that and Claire had been a little upset at the prospect of being a single parent, although I had a feeling that she wouldn't stay single for long and I was right because by the time she was five months pregnant she had met and was with a Syrian man; Lamar was much older than Claire at thirty-six and had recently divorced but he wanted to stand by Claire and was really quite nice. He even seemed to relish the challenge; although he was warned beforehand what he would be up against, he felt he would be able to stay the course. I didn't really approve of him at first but he certainly seemed to be good for Claire and had taken a lot of pressure off of me, leaving me with more time to concentrate on my own kids again.

Matthew and Michael were both being bullied at school, I decided to move Michael from the school he was at which was the same one as Matthew was attending and although Matthew had needed the more formal, structured education, Michael needed the more open, relaxed atmosphere of the local school that I'd moved Matthew away from so I went and saw the headmaster and asked to enrol Michael, he agreed to take him on. They enrolled him into year two, although he was meant to have gone into year three but given his problems and that he was so behind, backwards in his education, I felt that it would be better for Michael if I didn't mention the mistake until it was too late to change it. It was only a couple of weeks before the headmaster realised that there was a mistake and had asked me about it: I admitted that I had done it on purpose because of Michael's obvious educational needs and it was agreed that he would stay in that year, although the headmaster said, quite rightly that I shouldn't have done it;

"I know!" I'd laughed,

"I've got to hand it to you," he'd said, "You really have got a nerve!"

"I'd do anything for my kids!" I replied.

And so began the years of assessments, statements and government changes that are still going on to this day. Michael settled well into the new school, although the bullying continued. I went to see his teacher on the first open evening and will always remember his comments; when I had asked how Michael was doing; he'd smiled and said,

"Well he knows the grass is green and if you say to him; Michael could you sit down, he can be surrounded by thirty empty chairs and he'll still say where?"
It wasn't meant as an offensive comment but it summed Michael up exactly, so much so that I had to laugh. Unfortunately it would be another four years before any kind of specific diagnosis was made and a lot more heartache watching him struggle every single day... I had known from the start that there was a major problem with Michael's development and intelligence and no matter how hard I tried it appeared that I was unable to protect my last baby from the cruelty of the average or 'ordinary' people.

Matthew too was still having problems, he was now at secondary school and being constantly bullied, both at home and at school and it was taking its toll; when your eleven year old son comes to you and says that he really feels he wants to die, to end it all; you sit up and you listen... What else could I do? I sat him down and talked to him telling him that; no one was worth him even considering taking his own life and that I, his mother, was there to help, to put things right but for his part he needed to fight back. I'd then contacted the school and told them about the conversation Matthew and I had had and of my fears for Matthew's safety; they didn't seem to be listening until I said,

"Have you any idea what it is like when your son of eleven stands in front of you and tells you that he wants to die because bullies run the school and the teachers do nothing about it?"
That saw the beginning of the arguments; the school had claimed that they knew nothing about any bullying incidents, even though Matthew said he'd been telling them whenever it had happened. I told them that; if I have to send my son to school then from that moment on every minor incident would have to be reported and written, any more serious incident would have to be reported to the staff, whereupon I wanted to be phoned immediately and I would collect Matthew from school, then I would require the names of the bullies and I finished by telling them that if they wouldn't protect my son then I would contact every agency at my disposal in order to put a stop to the problem myself.

Next it was Pete's turn to be put in his place. He came in from work, grabbed his dinner and disappeared upstairs; he was still eating in my bedroom away from us. I decided that regardless of his mental state he had to be told to leave my son alone. Although Matthew hadn't complained about any physical violence, it was the constant threat and the fear of it that he had been living with and it was this that was getting him down; it was mental abuse, something that Pete was very good at. I hadn't realised until then what Pete had been saying to Matthew, he'd told him that if he left it would be Matthew who was to blame, solely Matthew, he'd said that I had agreed and that I'd said I wanted Pete to stay and how I'd be really miserable if he left, especially as he'd take Michael with him. Did he, Matthew, want to be responsible for making me that miserable? 'How dare he?' I'd thought. I waited for him to finish his dinner and it took everything I had to contain myself and wait that long. I went to collect his plate as I always did and for once in his life he must have realised that something was wrong because he asked,

"Who's upset you?"

That was my queue;

"So you think you can threaten my son do you? By using me?" I was seething. "It isn't if you leave, it's when and that'll be because we don't have a marriage! Because of you and solely you and if you threaten my son in anyway again, or any of my kids for that matter, I will physically remove you from this house! Oh and you'll not be taking Michael with you when you go, you won't be taking Michael anywhere… When you leave you'll be alone. Now you can apologise to Matthew, right now or you can leave and believe me; it'll be the happiest day of my life when you do go!" Cruel to say but true.

I felt that I'd been biting my tongue since his release from hospital, making excuses for his behaviour; poor Pete was ill, he'd never cope alone. Unfortunately for Pete, at that point the welfare of Matthew was my priority; the maternal instinct in me was so strong that I was prepared to fight to the death to protect him from this bully who lived in my home.

"Matthew?" I called

"Yes?"

"Come here please!"

He came upstairs and stood in the bedroom doorway, obviously nervous;

"What have I done?" He asked,

"Nothing!" I replied, "Pete has something to say to you."

Pete motioned for him to come closer,

"Come here." He'd even said it quite nicely,

"No, I'll stay here." Was Matthew's reply.

He just stood in the doorway and I found myself quite taken back by the obvious fear he was feeling in Pete's company; it was written all over his face and he was almost hiding behind me for protection;

"My God! What have you done to this boy? You sick bastard!"

Pete was obviously shocked by my outburst and Matthew's reaction;

"I am really sorry, I didn't realise but you wind me up!"

"No Pete," I interrupted, "he's a child and you are a man and you are blaming him once again."

"No, I'm not; it's just that I'm ill!" Another excuse. "Ok matt, I'm sorry! It isn't your fault, it's mine!"

It was obvious that Matthew didn't believe that this was the end of it and neither did I but he'd done what I'd asked and apologised. Even so; there was no way that I could leave Matthew in his care unsupervised ever again. Matthew left the room and Pete asked if I still wanted him to leave and said that he would go if I did. I had wanted to say;

"Yes, go, get out now!"

I just couldn't, he had behaved as a child would; 'I promise I'll be good!' Was the impression that I got and my reaction was like that of a parent;

"Ok, you can stay but if it happens again; you will have to leave!"

Somehow in his madness he seemed to know exactly how to manipulate me and even though I thought about it many times and wondered how he did it… I mean I have always felt that I am intelligent and strong willed so what was it about him? I never could figure it out! He gave me nothing; he didn't help with the kids, the house or the bills and he was forever buying himself silly things; ornamental swords, videos, body armour and bandages. Yes, bandages and tubi grip! He wore them most days on various parts of his body; he'd pulled this muscle or sprained that one, he even wore them in bed along with his socks and his underwear. I had joked many times saying that it was like sleeping next to a mummy with all those bandages and if I'd ever had a sexual urge, something that I couldn't really visualize happening, it would certainly have worn off by the time he'd unwrapped himself. Then there was his smell; deep heat, liniment and muscle rub coupled with a mixture of B.O. and various body sprays. He was very untidy aswell and would leave dirty clothes and part eaten food on the floor of our bedroom. The only thing that he was really particular about was his hair, almost to the point of obsession; he would wash it over and over again, sometimes two or three times a day and he'd definitely had an obsession with toothbrushes; he collected them, all different types and colours and he had kept them all in his many various soap bags.

Michael had inherited similar obsessive behaviour patterns from Pete: His shoe laces had to be tied exactly right; the loops had to be the same size and both of the laces ends had to be exactly the same length, he would get very frustrated if I did them even slightly wrong and so would I after undoing them and then tying them up again at least five or six times in the morning. Another of his traits was to remove all of his clothes whenever he used the toilet, when I'd asked him why he did it he'd told me that he didn't know, he just had to. Then there was his little plastic man which he still keeps with him to this day; he would hold the thing by its arms and twizzle it back and forth between his fingers, in front of his face, as fast as he could, making very odd noises and again when asked why he did it, he'd said that he didn't know. Penny also had a couple of obsessions; she had to have her clothes pressed with the creases exactly right and she always sniffed soap. I used to joke and say that if I went shopping at the supermarket with Pete and Penny; I could leave Michael in the crèche, while Penny sniffed the soap, Pete looked at toothbrushes and I could get the shopping done in relative peace and quiet... Maybe there was something wrong with me, perhaps their behaviour was normal and I was the odd one; perhaps all of the population did this sort of thing, although I must admit; I've never really noticed hundreds of people loitering in the toothbrush aisle or standing around smelling soap, I never really noticed anything like that in my other children either; Lee has a thing about dirty hands and likes to keep them clean but not to the point of obsession and Lorna still has a silky piece of material like the sort you find on the edge of a baby's blanket that she calls her sleep and she rubs it on the side of her face when she's tired or poorly, something she has done since she was very small; is that obsessive? Anyway, Pete was better for a few months after our 'chat,' which was just as well for him really, I'd had enough!

Claire had been staying out rather a lot with her Syrian boyfriend at his flat until I'd told her Social Worker, who had told Claire that it would have to stop. This was something that Claire hadn't liked at all because she wouldn't have been able to keep tabs on Lamar and had thought that he would go off and sleep with someone else; she was jealous, possessive and insecure and no matter how hard Lamar and I tried, we couldn't convince her that he wouldn't do that kind of thing; I'm sure it didn't help that I didn't have the courage of my convictions; as I was telling her, I was thinking of my past experiences with men and of how I was sure that all of them, without exception, would cheat if given the chance but there was no way that I could let those thoughts be known to Claire and her already none existent feelings of self worth. Claire had been nearing the end of her pregnancy around that time and I had felt that she would be better off closer to home anyway so when the labour started I could be with her; she had wanted me to be at the birth but had also wanted Lamar and her mother there too, although she'd told me that she only wanted Gemma there because she'd suffer watching Claire go through childbirth and so that she would be one of the first to see the child she had wanted Claire to kill. I didn't tell Gemma the real reason for Claire wanting her there, instead I told her;

"Every daughter wants her mum to be there!"
Even though she was apprehensive about it at first, Gemma finally agreed to be there.

Claire had gone into labour whilst out at her boyfriend's house, as soon as the contractions had started he'd brought her home. The contractions were mild to start with, though Claire managed to make the most of the attention, saying how much it hurt whilst bending forward over a chair until eventually I called the hospital. Although the contractions were still ten minutes apart and not at all regular, they agreed that we could take her in so they could see how she was progressing. We went in at around 10:00pm and were back at home two hours later. I had then informed Gemma that she should expect to go back in sometime during the early hours of the morning and she'd told me that she needed her sleep but to give her a call when we went back to the hospital; she'd probably come down later if Claire hadn't had it by then. 'Here we go again,' I thought. If it were my daughter there's no way that I could even consider sleeping, let alone allow someone else to be with her at a time like that, especially given that Claire's was just sixteen years old. Claire hadn't been surprised at all by her mother's reaction, saying that it was exactly what she had expected. We went back into the hospital at 7:00am, by then the contractions had become closer together, were lasting longer and were noticeably more painful; it was obvious by now that Claire was having 'real' pain. She was also becoming quite aggressive and I remember thinking that perhaps it was better if Gemma wasn't there after all but Claire's boyfriend had decided to go and collect Gemma anyway at about 11:00am. Claire didn't want him to leave, but he promised her that he'd be back quickly and to his credit he was back within the hour, I was there the whole time anyway. Lamar came back with Gemma and a selection of sandwiches saying that he thought we might need them. Claire refused the painkillers, then she was going to try a water birth but immediately changed her mind the moment the bath had been filled and just like Claire had been doing her whole life, she tried running from the situation and I do mean literally running; with each contraction she decided to run, out through the bathroom into the various connecting rooms, luckily they were all empty because she was stark naked and kept screaming;

"Get it out of me!" And how she... "Hated everyone and everything!"

The midwife had tried to connect Claire up to a monitor with a belt around her waist and almost immediately Claire had ripped it off and thrown it across the room, kicking the midwife and screaming at her, I shouted at Claire;

"Pack it in! Running is one thing but kicking the midwife is something else entirely different!"

Surprisingly she apologised but was gone again as soon as she felt the next pain. At first I had tried to keep up with her but had eventually decided I was tired of running around and that she would be back between contractions anyway. It was very hard to watch this little girl who had already been through so much and who I really did care for going through this, we were all helpless. Gemma was quite apparently disturbed by what she was witnessing, saying over and over;

"I really don't want to see this! I really don't want to be here!"

Then in the next breath she was saying that she couldn't leave her that way, finally showing some compassion for her daughter... Too little, too late. I'd tried to make light of the situation, where at all possible;

"You know that little tattoo you had done Claire?" I asked, smiling. "Looks like a damned Pterodactyl now!"
The tattoo had stretched where her abdomen had grown to quite an immense size; what was once a pretty little bird was now something almost prehistoric looking, even Claire had laughed when she'd seen it and then she was off again. The midwife brought us all tea so we'd decided to eat the sandwiches that Gemma and Lamar had brought with them.

"Want a sandwich?" I offered Claire,

"Fuck off!" Came the answer,

"I'll take that as a no then shall I? Should I leave?"

"Don't you fucking dare!"

"Claire, language!" I demanded,

"What do you expect?" She said, waving her arms in the air. "Just get it out!"
We laughed and Claire ran. The midwife had tried to run with her, attempting to keep up and do an examination to see how close to delivery she was... Talk about funny; the midwife was in rubber gloves chasing around after a naked girl. Eventually the midwife gave up aswell, sat down and waited with us. Then, all of a sudden Claire climbed up onto the bed saying that she wanted to push; so with me one side, Gemma the other, the midwife in position and Lamar watching and rubbing her leg, a beautiful baby boy was delivered safe and sound, he had beautiful olive coloured skin and dark hair, then the tears flowed. I only stayed for a few minutes afterwards; I felt that I'd done my bit, as hard as it was to do. I told Claire that I'd be back later and left. In truth I had wanted to stay, to hug her and the baby (she'd named him Ashton.) but in reality; this wasn't my daughter or my grandchild and I figured that if I left Gemma with Claire, maybe they could rebuild a little of the mother and daughter relationship that I thought they should have and believed they both craved, for that moment at least.

I needed to compose myself; I was dealing with so many thoughts and emotions, I'd felt like I was going to explode so I left the hospital, drove down to the river and sat watching for a while as the moonlight danced on the ripples of the water flowing past, it was 9:30pm, I knew that I should have felt far more tired than I did... 'Just five minutes peace!'

Chapter 36

Feeling a little better I'd driven home from the river, gone inside and had been greeted by Pete, who'd made it blatantly obvious that he was annoyed;

"Why did you stay with Claire?" In his opinion I shouldn't have. "You have your own children and me to think about! What about their dinner, what about mine? Gemma was there with her wasn't she?"

I started cooking the dinner as I replied, calmly and quietly;

"Well Pete, I was there because that's where Claire wanted me to be and now I'm here because it's where I want to be, with the rest of my children."

With that he walked away, I think that for once he knew he couldn't fight me; no matter what he said or did to me on that day, he would have absolutely no effect on me at all. The kids had been the complete opposite to Pete, they were excited;

"What's the baby like?"

"Is Claire all right?"

"When can we see her?"

Everyone was pulling together for once, all that is except for Pete but then he really didn't matter any more; something that was hard for him to accept but had been surprisingly easy for me. We'd made room in Lorna's bedroom for the carrycot, had prepared the steriliser and made sure that everything was ready and two days after the birth, Claire and the baby were home. It was strange having a baby in the house again, with all the paraphernalia that goes with them; the pram, the cot and that unforgettable 'new baby' smell.

Pete had opted to go back onto a night shift at work; something that I'd considered to be a good idea. Then he'd decided that at weekends he was going to Portsmouth to stay with his parents; 'also a good idea,' I'd thought. Occasionally I had allowed him to take Michael too, although I had considered the possibility that Pete might not have brought him back but of course he did. Pete would've never have been able to cope with Michael, not on his own and his parents wouldn't have been able to help him a great deal, if at all as they were well into their seventies at this time; in fact Pete's father had become quite frail and the prospect of losing him had caused Pete to become depressed again and had also forced him to question his roots again, he'd wanted to know if he would ever be able to trace his birth mother. He had tried to trace her once before, through the Salvation Army when he was about eighteen years old and he'd claimed that they had told him his mother was from Singapore; he had always felt that his flair for martial arts had come from those roots. Well, as the story goes... No! I'm not sure how but I just knew that he wasn't of Asian descent, it was yet another of his obsessions; Bruce Lee, Pete mimicked Bruce Lee's head and body movements, even down to the facial expressions, he had all the videos and watched them continually, usually with Michael who was also very good at martial arts. Pete had been taking Michael with him when he went to his training sessions and Michael had shown real flair, remembering the patterns with ease; he only had to be shown something once or twice, would pick it up almost instantly and was able to do it very well. It was suggested by the sensei that if he trained at it and stuck to it, Michael really could be very good, although Pete appeared to have a lot of difficulty dealing with this idea; on the one hand he was proud of Michael's ability but on the other he seemed to be jealous of Michael, fearing that his son would outshine him.

Social Services had put Claire's name on a waiting list to get a flat, designed for unmarried mothers in a purpose built block, she was still with Lamar and the baby was thriving and even though she came home most nights, she was either out somewhere or at Lamar's flat during the day. She seemed to be coping very well although I kept a watchful eye on her just the same. It was as if she had transformed the moment Ashton had been born; her involvement with drugs had stopped, she'd started seeing more of Gemma and it even looked as though they were getting on aswell; maybe the worst was over; Claire had become a young woman and was a far cry from the confused child she had been when she'd arrived on my doorstep, it looked like the suicide attempts were also a thing of the past.

With Claire on an even keel, I had a little more time on my hands and had decided to try and trace Pete's mother for him, I contacted Social Services to ask how I would go about tracking down his records; it turns out that on the day Lee was born, 11-11-1975, the adoption law had changed and it became the right of adopted children to have access to their birth records and to be able to trace their biological parents if they so wished, the same however did not apply to the parents. It was explained that the first thing Pete would need to do was speak to a Counsellor; giving his reasons for wanting to trace his mother, to talk about his expectations and to discuss any possible outcome should he find her. An appointment was arranged and the counsellor came to see Pete at home and it went well, she took all the information from Pete that she needed; date and place of birth and his adoptive parent's names, then after a lengthy chat about the why's and wherefores, she seemed to be satisfied as to Pete's motives and left saying that she would see what she could do. Two weeks later she'd phoned to say that she had traced Pete's birth records and asked if she could come around and talk to us again. Another appointment was made, I had tried to explain to Pete beforehand that he shouldn't build his hopes up, we still had a long way to go and that all the counsellor was bringing was records from almost forty years earlier but in his usual childish way he just couldn't contain his excitement.

After chatting to Pete for a while, the counsellor had handed him two sheets of paper with his details, the circumstances of his birth and how he came to be adopted printed on them: Pete's Grandfather had insisted on the adoption, his mother had been sixteen at the time, she was one of eight children, living at home and her name was Joan… 'Not another one!' She was described as being five feet, four inches tall, dark hair and blue eyes (like me) but it also said that she was below average ability, "slow," as were two of the other seven children. (Not like me!) Her sibling's names, parent's names and the address at the time of adoption were also given. Pete's father was claimed to have been an Irish man named James Ogan who had worked on a building site in the London area, he was described as being five feet, seven inches tall, with blonde hair and blue eyes but nothing more was recorded on him… I had my doubts that this was Pete's father; Pete was six foot one with black hair and brown eyes, Michael like Pete also had brown eyes which is said to be the dominant gene, so if his mother was supposed to have blue eyes then his father had to have had brown eyes, simple genetics. Before the Social Worker left she had told us that we would need to go to St Catherine's House in London, where all the birth, death and marriage records are kept, if we wanted to know anymore. Unfortunately we couldn't afford to make the trip to London until a few weeks later and believe me it was hard enough waiting for that long; once Pete had made up his mind that he wanted something, he would keep on and on until he got it, just like a child but I'd still felt that I wanted to help him, regardless of our relationship or rather lack of one, so I put up with it; to my way of thinking; if we were successful in tracking down his biological family there was always the chance that Pete may well be able to get the answers he so desperately craved to shed some light on the confusion over his past; something that I'd felt could've been another of the major causes for his mental illness but equally; if we didn't succeed in finding anybody, or if Pete was upset or unhappy about anything that we did find out then the opposite could be the case and the whole experience could tip him over the edge. Although, having taken everything into consideration I'd felt that it was probably worth the risk... 'Who knows,' I'd thought, 'it could even make him easier to live with for a while!'

Claire was offered a flat and in March 1996 she moved out of our home and into her own; I knew that I was going to miss her and the baby but at the same time I was also relieved that finally, after three years of struggle and stress she was on her way to independence. I must admit that I was quite proud of myself for getting her through it and gained a great deal of satisfaction from that fact... I had achieved something. All the baby equipment was gone and Lorna's room was back to precisely that which was also a source of happiness; my daughter's relief at the prospect of having the room to herself once again, smiling and happy, planning what to do with all the space, finally her friends would be able to come round and possibly even stay over, we were becoming normal again. Claire's social worker called around two weeks later to ask if I would take on another girl but I'd really felt that I had to say no, it was very hard to do and I'd felt a little guilty; the girl was a heroin addict and had recently come out of care, they were looking for after care support for her but I really didn't want that sort of influence around Matthew and Michael, not only that but Lorna would've had to have gone back to sharing her room again. I told the Social Worker that Claire had been different; it was easier to care for her because I'd known her since the day she was born and also said that I needed some space to sort out my own family. Rather than take 'no' for an answer she persisted for a while, giving me a contact number in case I changed my mind and had even offered extra money for the placement; which was a little unfair but rather than influence me to take the girl on, it made me all the more determined not to give in. I felt that Social Services wanted to rid themselves of this girl without any real consideration of the impact on either her or us. I did miss the income however, I only had my weekend security job and the occasional shift, as a chamber maid in a hotel where the housekeeper was a friend of mine; whenever they were short staffed she would phone and ask if I could cover; fortunately, as luck would have it, the week after Pete had found out that he needed to go to St Catherine's House she'd phoned me and said that she needed cover from Monday to Friday; my first thought was 'this'll pay for our coach trip to London and maybe a couple of birth certificates too.' So I booked the tickets for the following Tuesday and Penny had agreed to come down, stay over and look after the kids for me; as it was she'd come down on the Friday night and had stayed for the next ten days. I enjoyed her company and had suggested that she come and live with us, saying;

"You just as well, you're here more than you are at home anyway!"

I had then pointed out that she would also have far more chance of finding work in Bournemouth than in Blandford or rather the village near Blandford where she was now sharing a cottage with her sister and her three children; which her sister had been talking about giving up anyway as the rent was too high so Penny would've been homeless and had told me that she really didn't want to go and live at her parents house so she'd give the offer some thought.

It was the Tuesday of the trip, Pete had finished his night shift, come home, changed his clothes and almost immediately we had left to catch the coach to London. To have said that Pete was excited would've been an understatement, so much so that it was quite embarrassing being seen with him at times, so I had decided to try and sleep part of the way, at least then I could've ignored him for a while and I must have dozed off because I'd had one of my 'premonition dreams,' as I called them, similar to the dream I'd had the night that Lou had died: The year after Lou had died, Verity's mother-in-law, Bea had also died, she had been just fifty Two. Although I'd been quite close to her and her death had affected me, adding to the grief I was already feeling at the loss of Lo; had Lou not died I would probably have been devastated but at the time it was easier to deal with, I guessed I didn't have that far to fall. In my dream, Bea was standing, surrounded by darkness and she turned to me saying;

"All right, how are you? Don't worry you'll find her. I'm not saying that it'll be a good experience but you will find her!"
I jumped and woke up.

"Are you ok?" Pete asked,

"Yes" I'd answered and then proceeded to tell him about what had just happened and what had been said, finishing with; "It was probably just a dream but I guess we'll find out later won't we?"

At least I would know if these dreams were real or just my imagination.

Pete didn't seem to have any trouble finding his way around London, even the underground with its escalators; I hate escalators, I have a dim recollection of being stuck on one as a child and will normally do anything to avoid them but you don't get a lot of choice in the matter when in London, escalators are everywhere. Once we had made it off of the tube system, we caught a bus to St Catherine's House and began sifting through the records for the names that we'd been given. By the end of our search we had found two possible matches; both marriages to someone who had his mother's name but we could only afford one certificate and had to make a choice as to which one. Instead I wrote down the details of both of them, I had to do something, I could see the disappointment all over Pete's face and his mood was changing rapidly. I'd also suggested that we should go and check out the old family address; chances were that they wouldn't be there but someone might've known where they had gone to. We jumped in a black cab, gave the driver the address in Wood Green and off we went. When we got there although the majority of the road was still there the number we were looking for, the number that should have been right on the end of the road was gone; it had been demolished to widen the road. The meter was still running so we'd decided to get out of the cab and ask around, maybe someone had known them, we paid the driver and he wished us luck; obviously Pete had felt compelled to tell his story during the journey. We watched the taxi drive away then went and knocked on the door of the house at what was now the end of the road; two doors away from where Pete's families address had been. The people who'd answered had only lived in the road for two years and didn't recognise the name, so we'd tried knocking on a few more doors but came away empty handed.

"Come on!" I said, "Lets head back, we'll have to take the bus."

We were running out of money quite quickly but it only took two buses to get back to Kings Cross and it looked as though we had found something that Pete could do after all; he could find his way around London… Not a lot of use if you live in Bournemouth. By the time we had made it back to the coach station Pete was really down so I'd tried to reassure him by promising that I'd find his family and as I was thinking; 'There must be a way!' I couldn't help but wonder whether my dream of Bea and worse still my dreams of Lou were, just my imagination.

When we got home Pete had gone straight up to our bedroom and there he'd stayed, he phoned in sick, telling his boss he couldn't work and went to bed. Penny was very puzzled until I'd explained what had happened, I then went to check on Pete and he was asleep, he stayed in bed all that night and slept until the following lunchtime. The next day I'd decided that after I had taken Michael to school and dropped Penny at the job centre I would go to the Central Library in Bournemouth and check London telephone directories to see if there were any instances of the name that Pete and I had found; it felt like I was clutching at straws but at the same time, I had to do something. I managed to find one entry with the correct spelling of the name and the right initial so I wrote the number down and resolved not to Pete until I was sure that there was a connection. When I got home Pete was up and about, he said he was feeling fine but didn't want anything to eat; I could already see that this was really going to be a problem;

"Don't give up, there maybe news yet..." I said reassuringly,

"...I've got to pop out; I'll be back in a while!"
I had to try the number and our phone had been cut off temporarily because I hadn't had the money to pay the bill, although it would be back on forty eight hours later, I couldn't wait that long, so I'd opted to use the telephone box around the corner from my house and as I really didn't want Pete to know what I was up to it was better this way, he had been annoyed that I wouldn't tell him what I was doing or where I was going but I asked him to give me half an hour at the most and I'd be back.

I stepped into the callbox, picked up the handset, put in some money and stopped; I was just about to dial the number when I'd thought; 'How am I going to explain this?' I really didn't know! What if this man didn't know about Pete? I may have been causing a real problem, putting the cat amongst the pigeons and ruining a marriage and what if she really didn't want to know either; 'If that is the case,' I thought, 'At least I can tell Pete that I've found her.' I dialled the number and a male voice answered;

"Hello?"

"Hi, sorry to bother you, do you know a person called Joan?" I'd asked,

"Yes, my ex wife," came the reply

"Ex- wife?"

"Yes"

"Well, I don't know if you know this but I believe she may be the mother of my husband... He was adopted as a baby!"

"Ah yes, I know all about that!" He said.

Much to my relief he actually seemed thrilled and said;

"I still have contact with her; she lives on the other side of London. I don't have a contact number for her anymore but I do know where she will be. Do you have a number I can contact you on?"

"Yes," I replied, "I'll give you my sister's number!"

"It'll take me a little while," he said,

"Do you think she will want to know?" I questioned,

"Oh Yes, that's all she's talked about for years!"

"Well thank you and maybe I'll speak to you later."

I put the phone down and rang Verity almost straight away; I updated her on the situation and told her that I would call back later. I then went home and told Pete that there was a possibility we would have to go out later, at short notice later; he was starting to get wound up because I wouldn't tell him why so to keep the peace I said;

"I've been making a few inquiries and may have a possible lead to your mother. Please, just be patient and wait a while!"

His mood brightened a little bit after that and at 6:00pm I went to the callbox and phoned my sister; Pete's mother had called, leaving a contact number for a pub and instructions to call there at 10:00pm, she would be there. Verity said that Joan had sounded very excited, overly so and like she'd had a fair bit to drink aswell, I started to have doubts as to whether I'd done the right thing but the wheels were set in motion... We would have to wait and see. I went back to Pete;

"Ok, we need to have some dinner and then we've got to go out!"

"You've found her?" He asked,

"Yes but please don't expect too much!"

Fed and watered, we drove to Verity's, picked up the telephone number and then went to the phone box at the end of her road; I really couldn't have waited any longer for Pete to make that call,

303

the two hours I had spent waiting for that moment had felt like two days with him constantly waffling on about the what ifs and why's of it all and giggling in that childish way that he did… But hey, at least it was better than the depression. Pete dialled the number and the landlord answered;

"Can I speak to Joan please?" Pete had asked,

"Joan phone!" The landlord shouted, then he asked; "Is this her son?"

"Yes!"

A cheer went up in the pub; I would have heard it if I had been stood outside the phone box. Joan came on the line and Pete chatted to her for quite a few minutes, it was like they'd never been apart, 'I needn't have worried after all!' I'd thought, but then I still felt worried. During their conversation Pete had arranged to meet her at Kings Cross on the coming Friday; it was already Wednesday; I'm not really sure how he had expected me to find the money for that one but then I don't really think that he even gave it a thought, just assuming as always that I'd manage it somehow and I knew that somehow I would have to. We went back to Verity's and she asked us how it had gone; I'd told her what had been said and asked her if she could help out. She managed to find the money but said that she really would need it back the following week as she was borrowing it from her rent money.

On the Friday we travelled back to London but this time I had asked Gemma if she could come along too, partly for moral support but mainly for company; Pete had a lot of catching up to do. So off we went again but this time we had instructions; Joan would be wearing a pink top and Pete would be holding a bunch of flowers.

We got off of the coach in Kings Cross and stood watching the people passing by for a moment and it seemed to us that everyone was wearing pink. Then two women came around the corner and it was immediately obvious that one of them was Pete's mother; it was like looking at a small female version of him. She started running towards us and was sort of howling with joy as she went, 'that's really too much!' I'd thought and put it Pete on edge, Gemma and I too, especially when she started kissing and hugging him, poor old Pete didn't know what to do.

"Come on Joan." Her friend intervened. "Calm down, you agreed you wouldn't do this!"

"I can't help it!" Replied Joan.

Pete handed her the flowers and said;

"It's thanks to my wife Jan that we've found you."

"Thanks!" She'd said, glancing at me briefly, then, slipping her arm through Pete's, she said "Come on!"

We headed towards a café and I tried to explain to Joan that we couldn't stay for long as we had to catch the 2:00pm coach because we'd needed to get back for the children;

"You're not going are you John? Sorry Pete! I called you John; you will always be John to me!"

"Well I can understand that," said Pete, a little defensively, "but my name is Pete now!"

"Ok but you are staying aren't you?" She pleaded, "I have arranged a party at the pub, everyone's waiting for you and then you're staying overnight at my place!"

Pete looked at me,

"Maybe next time!" I said

She became quite aggressive at this point and responded with;

"He's my son and I haven't seen him for forty years! You go back if you want, you don't need to stay!"

"Well that's down to Pete!" I said

"No, I'm sorry I can't stay, I have to work this evening." Said Pete.

Once again Joan's friend intervened;

"Now Joan, come on, we talked about this."

By now I was very concerned and it was only 10:45am. I got up to go to the counter and buy the coffees,

"I'll give you a hand," Gemma said and followed me, when she'd caught up she said, "I don't like her!"

"No, neither do I!" I replied. "Something isn't right is it?"

When we got back to the table, Joan was holding Pete's hand and stroking his face, I could see he was really uncomfortable.

"Isn't this lovely?" She said "Just like courting!"

Now I was uncomfortable too and I struck up a conversation with Gemma, thinking that 2:00pm couldn't have come quickly enough and then things got worse; we'd only been there about five minutes when Joan stood up and said,

"Come on lets find a pub, I need a drink!"

"They're not open yet are they?" Asked Pete,

"I'll find one," she said, "being as you're not coming back to my local!"

We then followed this woman around the streets of London whilst she tried the door of every pub she came to, getting more and more agitated as she went along. When she'd started banging on the doors it became quite obvious that she had a serious drink problem and if I'd had any doubts about it, thinking that maybe it was just the excitement and expectations of this first meeting with her son, my fears were soon confirmed. We finally found a bar that was open and everybody except Joan asked for soft drinks, she ordered a lager and a double gin which she had polished off before we'd even started our drinks and was going back for more saying as she went that she didn't have a drink problem in case we were thinking she did but from the looks that her friend was giving to Pete and me, I was fairly certain that there was an issue of some kind, that the friend was aware of it and slightly embarrassed by it all aswell. She'd then told Pete, while Joan was out of ear shot, that she felt they should probably get the early train back to North London rather than wait until our coach had left and not a moment too soon as far as I was concerned. By 1.00pm there was no denying that Joan was getting rather drunk and although she was begging to stay in the pub;

"Just one more drink?"

Her friend had insisted that it was time to leave. Poor Pete, his disappointment in this woman was quite apparent and he was very quiet as we left London, I tried to think of something positive to say;

"At least you have found your roots! You have a brother, aunties, uncles, cousins, a grandmother and a grandfather."

Pete's mood brightened a little; I think it was the prospect of having a brother; it was something that he'd always wanted. I then reminded him that the whole Family, brother included wanted to meet him, that he now had their addresses and telephone numbers and promised that as soon as we could afford it and the arrangements could be made we would go back and meet them all, although his brother Shane would have to be first and even though that cheered him up a little more he still asked;

"Why couldn't she have been more like...? A Mum?"

I understood what he meant but felt that at least we no longer had any illusions about the woman and when we got home I managed to persuade Pete to phone his brother early that evening before his shift and he did. They chatted for almost an hour and Shane had been thrilled to speak to Pete; he confirmed that their mother was indeed an alcoholic and said that he had lived with his father, (the man that I'd spoken to on the phone,) since he was twelve because Joan had left them. He really didn't have much to do with her, although he did have regular contact with and lived opposite one of the aunties, an uncle and a cousin, their Nan lived around the corner and was divorced from their granddad who lived just three doors away and all of them were only one road away from the address that we'd been given by the Social Services and had visited four days before. Shane was married for the second time; he had one child from his previous marriage and a sixteen month old child from his current marriage. He was an H.G.V driver so was away for a lot of the week but had said that he would try and phone Pete the following week and maybe even arrange for Pete to be able to come and stay with him and his wife for a weekend, that way Pete could meet everyone else too; although he'd said that he preferred it if Joan wasn't included in that weekend because he didn't really want her at his home, Pete agreed... This just compounded my thoughts and fears about this woman. Was I going to regret this meeting? I knew that, at the end of the day it was me that was going to have to deal with the aftermath anyway and this was after all about helping Pete; if he still wanted to leave, as he continued to claim, there was a possibility that he'd have somewhere to go other than Portsmouth. Shane and Pete talked to each other on the phone every week but didn't actually speak face to face until the August of 1996, when a meeting was finally arranged.

Chapter 37

Even though, once again, the relationship between Pete and I became a little easier for a while, mainly due to his gratitude for my efforts in finding his family, I knew that it was only a matter of time before we would finally divorce; I was just about hanging in there but I really didn't know why, something in me had changed; my kids had all but grown up and were emotionally scarred at the hands of Dan, Gary and Pete, my youngest child, at seven years old, seemed to have some sort of genetic problem which had obviously been inherited from Pete, Matthew was now twelve years old and being bullied at school and home, a seventeen year old Lorna had been pushed aside to accommodate Claire and had grown up into a young woman, even though she was very stable I knew that she had suffered over the years and being as headstrong as she was, she'd also been bullied by Pete, on top of everything else but had always held her ground well; she should never have had to and somehow along the way I'd missed that transition from girl into woman, she was going to college, studying law and was something she'd enjoyed doing but had to give it up in the end because I couldn't afford to fund her.

Then there was Lee; he was now twenty one and living away from home, he'd been involved in drugs, heavy drugs and had managed to get through it by himself, he'd also gotten involved with a woman who was mentally unstable, fourteen years his senior and had a four year old daughter. I really had felt that she was far too old for my son but it was Lee's decision and no matter how much I'd wanted to interfere, I couldn't, it wasn't my place, I would just have to be there to pick up the pieces when it all went wrong. All I could do was sit back, watch and wait as my son was twisted mentally and physically in front of my eyes... Very hard to do! Although I did reassure him that I'd always be there;

"Just say the word and you can come back home!"

After a little deliberation Penny came to live with us; she had found herself a job working in a local laundry and the extra income her rent money brought to the household proved to be very helpful. Especially when the telephone bill had arrived and it was almost £300; all calls to other continents like Africa. I queried the numbers with the telephone company only to be told that they were

"Premium sex lines of course!"

I argued the point saying that no one in my home would be making such calls, I then went and confronted Pete, who swore that it wasn't him, saying;

"It must be Matthew!"

So I confronted Matthew and he said that he'd never phoned any numbers like that and I believed him. I went back to Pete and told him as much and eventually he admitted responsibility for the calls... More hurt, it wasn't enough to yet again blame my son for something that he hadn't done and run up a bill that he knew I would be unable to pay because he hadn't thought that they would cost so much but to cap it all; he had no interest in any kind of physical relationship with me always saying he couldn't and yet could talk to strangers about it on the phone. The excuse; 'he was inquisitive!' He'd wanted to know if his inability to perform was purely because he didn't want me;

"And it took you three hundred pounds to find out, did it?"

I then asked him how he'd have felt if I'd done such a thing and he said that he'd be upset but still didn't seem able to consider my feelings about the whole thing. I had to get away from him, I needed a break.

"C'mon Pen, we're going out!"

Penny never needed to be asked twice when it came to going out for the evening and was out of the door, quick as a shot. We had really good time that night and enjoyed ourselves so much, that we decided to make it a regular thing and as it turned out; Verity was the captain of a ladies darts team at the time and Mum was also in the same team, so Penny and I decided to join up and Tuesday nights became darts night and even though I wouldn't drink anything alcoholic because I'd be driving, it still felt good to get out of the house once a week.

One Tuesday night though, we arrived at darts only to find that the game had been cancelled and someone had neglected to tell us. I really didn't want to go home and miss out on my night out, so I racked my brains trying to think of something else to do;

"What about the country music club?"

There was a country music club that also happened to be on a Tuesday night and they had live bands playing every week, Penny liked the idea so off we went, we had intended to check it out one week when we weren't playing darts anyway.

We got to the club, paid on the door and went in, Penny headed to the bar whilst I looked for somewhere for us both to sit down and I found a table with a raffle ticket machine on it, thinking that it wouldn't be a problem I sat down but I was wrong and as Penny came towards the table, so too did this old chap; (who we later learned was the organiser of the club.)

"You can't sit there" He said,

"Why is your name on it?" Asked Penny, in her usual belligerent way,

"Because…" said the man looking quite un-amused, "… I said so!"

"And, who are you?"

"I say who comes in here and who doesn't!"

I thought to myself; 'that was quick we've barely had a chance to sit down and were about to be banned!' At that moment another man walked over and said;

"Its ok Perry, we'll make room on our table." He then looked towards Penny and I; "Hello, I'm Jim!" He offered.

We thanked him and followed as he led us back to his table, I took a moment to look around the room at the people who were there and they were a strange bunch, some were dressed as cowboys and there were a few that were obviously 'special needs' but everyone seemed nice. It looked as though Penny and I would have a really good time and the real bonus was that I could finally listen to live bands playing my favourite music whilst having a real good laugh with Penny. Jim introduced us to everyone on the table, there were ten of them in total and all were very friendly. Jim was "normal" and had a good sense of humour. Penny was her usual self, testing the water and telling jokes, usually with rude or sexual content to see how far she could push her luck. At the end of that night we apologised to Perry for the incident that started the evening;

"Apology accepted," he said, "hope to see you again"

'Yes we'll be back' I thought and we dropped the darts in favour of the country music club. Penny and I started going out at weekend's aswell as our Tuesday night country club sessions, we would go to various social clubs and hotels following different bands, anywhere there was live music you'd find us. Penny was such good company, flirting as she did with all the older men, dancing with them and around them and usually managing to remove a tie or undo a shirt, always very close to the mark. Then there were continual jokes, the more she drank, the worse she got and the funnier everyone including myself found her. When there were no men to play up to or if we went somewhere new we would dance together playing off of each other. As a result of our antics and with my interest in music we became friendly with band members and more often than not they'd come and sit with us during their breaks. We had taken to following a particular band called The Echoes. I was particularly fond of the drummer Ernie, although he was happily married and we were only ever friends. On one occasion, in one of the better social clubs in Poole, the band had sat with us before the start of the gig and we were all talking amongst ourselves, when somehow we had gotten onto the subject of underwear, suddenly, more loudly than I think she had realised Penny announced;

"We wear crotch less knickers!" (Total silence.) "They are not supposed to be Crotch less, they've rotted!"

The band and I looked at her and the whole place including us erupted into laughter. By the end of the evening there were people who'd normally have been quite reserved, aged from thirty to eighty, that were up dancing and thoroughly enjoying themselves, telling Penny and I that they had enjoyed themselves so much and asking if we would please come back again. This seemed to happen everywhere we went. Very occasionally there would be one male that wanted to take things a step too far but we were very good at defusing such unwanted attention. One particular occasion at a social club, a man who had been playing up to both of us; we'd seen him before and on a few occasions had danced with him, he came into the crowded ladies room where myself and several other women were stood at the sinks, Penny was in the toilet. He stood next to me, smiled, undid his fly and took his penis out, laying it on the side of the sink saying;

"What do you think of that then?"

"Yeah very nice" I said which it wasn't. "Put it away!"

At that point all of the women without exception were laughing so he put it away very quickly and left but Penny wasn't happy just leaving it at that; she went out into the main club and at the top of her voice, whilst pointing at him, announced to everyone what he'd done and everyone was laughing. He was so embarrassed by it all that he left immediately. That really should have been humiliation enough, but when we hadn't seen him for a few weeks I asked where he was and was told that he had been brought up before the Club's Committee and banned for three months. Penny and I had felt rather guilty but it certainly proved a point; as women we were far safer in the clubs than we were in pubs. The bands would take good care of us aswell; The Echoes always introduced Penny and I, saying that we were the fan club, they'd tell the audience that it was ninety seven pounds to become a member and that we met once a week in a telephone box if anyone wanted to join. More often than not Ernie would ask me to sound check for them too and it was nice to feel that I was involved in music, even if it was in a small way and more importantly that I was valued for my opinion. I still had my dream of being on the stage that had been formed so many years before but I still had my Mother's words echoing around my head too; that I would never be any good at anything!

My marriage was a complete shambles; I'd fallen into the same old cycle of staying in it because my partner couldn't help what he was doing, he was ill; Dan with his drinking and the violence, Gary with his drugs and the need to wear my makeup, both of them had cheated on me and both had made me feel worthless; like I had to do everything they asked for, exactly as they wanted and give over everything that I had of myself to them. Precisely what I was doing all over again with Pete and even though he was never violent towards me, I feel that what he had done was far worse, he had abused my psyche for so long that I was mentally defeated. It was at that point I'd stopped feeling guilty about enjoying myself and decided that I would stay in the marriage and do what I could for him, albeit in a small way but should the chance arrive; I would cheat on Pete. I'm sure that Penny and the band could never have hoped to know how much their company, or the fact that they valued my opinion meant to me at that time in my life; if it hadn't been for my children and them, I have no doubt in my mind, I would have ended it all there and then... It would seem that I was having a severe bout of depression and poor Penny usually had to bear the brunt of it; unfortunately for her, she didn't know when to shut up or when to leave me alone. The most memorable example of Penny not knowing quite when to quit had been one weekend when Pete had gone to stay in Portsmouth: Penny and I had decided to stay in and drink but the more I drank the worse I felt, I couldn't stop thinking but at the same time, the more that Penny drank the more she kept on;

"What's wrong? Talk about it!" Over and over, on and on, her voice slowly grinding away at me. Then Steven had wandered in talking and laughing but had realised something was wrong and followed on with Penny's line of questioning;

"What's wrong? Do you want to talk about it?"

I had to get away and walked into my kitchen, I thought 'maybe there's something out here I can take to make me forget for a while.' I turned around and Penny followed;

"What are you up to?" She asked,

"Leave me alone!" I replied.

She headed back to the lounge and started talking to Steven; I couldn't hear what they were saying but could tell that Penny was quite drunk; I knew that there was no way she was ever going to shut up in that state and had thought that it was probably a good idea to go out for a walk and get some air. So without uttering a word to the other two, I left the house and started walking up the road. All I was wearing was a skirt and a t-shirt but it was a fairly warm evening and I hadn't planned on going very far. I'd also had on some wooden sandals which weren't particularly easy to walk in but then I wasn't in any major hurry; all I'd needed was a few minutes alone, a little breathing space but I stopped briefly to look behind me and 'déjà vu;' there was Penny about five hundred yards away and Steven, who was running, almost behind me saying;

"Come back, where are you going?"

"Please go back," I'd told him, "and take Penny too! Give me a few minutes and make sure you don't let her near me!"

I could still see Penny, as relentless as ever, coming up the road towards me, I took off my shoes so that I could walk faster but still she kept coming;

"Seriously Steven, take her back, if she comes near me I'll deck her!"

He just argued and then she was there, as her hand touched my shoulder she'd said;

"What are you doing?"

By that point, it was all too late; I swung around with my shoes in my hand, connected with the side of her head and she hit the floor.

"I warned you!" I snapped, at both of them.

She was just laying there and as Steven bent down to help her I continued walking up the road. I hadn't gone very far before I turned back again to see if she was ok, she appeared to be and she and Steven were walking back towards the house… Good, she was ok, I hadn't meant to hurt her. I walked around the block before heading home myself and somehow I'd managed to get back first, so I sat in my car and as they walked up the driveway I got out and went in the house behind them. Penny turned and looked at me,

"Better now?" She asked,

"You should have left me alone" I'd told her

"Why, what's the matter?" She continued

"Don't start again!"

"Well I want to know what I did to deserve that."

"Please Penny, leave it!"

I could feel myself losing it again but luckily this time Steven intervened;

"For Gods sake, will the both of you shut up?!"

It worked and the both of us did indeed, shut up! The following day, Penny had a very large lump on her head and was a lot quieter than normal. She'd asked me if it was her that had caused my outburst and if so did I want her to leave? I told her of everything that I'd been feeling and all that had been going through my mind the night before, assuring her that; No, I did not want her to go anywhere, that her being there was one of the few things actually keeping me sane and that she was my saving grace;

"Well I'm so glad I could help!" She said. "Only, next time, could you give me some warning? Oh, and not wear clogs!"

And there it was, just what I needed; laughter… She's always had a knack for that!

At the end of August, 1996, the final arrangements had been made and we were going to London again, this time to meet Shane and the rest of Pete's family. Penny agreed to take care of the house and the children for me. I'd decided against taking the kids for that first meeting and to be honest I'd rather not have gone myself; it was looking like it would be two very intense days and I can't really say that I was relishing the idea of spending that much time in Pete's company, I'd grown quite accustomed to not having to be around him much and I really wasn't too interested in listening to his incessant talking or the childishly, over-excited demeanour. I was far more nervous about what to expect this time aswell, especially with the experience of meeting his mother still so very raw in my mind, although having actually spoken to Shane on the telephone I knew that he was of a totally different character to Pete and Joan; he was intelligent for a start and had also confirmed that my opinion of their mother was correct and not, as Pete had claimed, mostly in my mind; Pete had said that he felt I was jealous, threatened by the prospect of his future relationship with her and his new family; he had this odd notion that I was afraid of losing him… I'm afraid he couldn't have been further from the truth; I wanted lose him, for him to leave, he'd have been doing me a favour and the sooner the better as far as I was concerned, although I never said as much aloud. Shane had explained that Joan was, as I'd suspected; trouble! So much so that he wouldn't let her into his home or allow her to be around his children; he didn't want his kids to see her drunk and couldn't remember the last time he'd seen her sober. It appeared that Shane now had even more reason to resent the woman too; he'd told us that from the day Joan and Pete had met each other he'd been getting almost daily phone calls at all hours from her, demanding that he let her know as soon as he knew when Pete was going to visit, he said that she'd actually threatened him aswell, her own son, over the phone, saying that he and his children (her grandchildren) would pay if he didn't tell her. That particular call, he'd told us had been at about ten o clock in the morning and even then she'd sounded as though she was in a drunken state. Shane told me that he had no intention of letting Joan know that we were coming and to say I was relieved is an understatement.

"She'd never wanted to see me over the years anyway!" He'd said, "Why start now?"
I knew what rejection had felt like and had a lot of sympathy for him; I'd felt it was my fault and apologised for inflicting the whole sorry state of affairs on him but he'd told me not to worry about it, although he did say he'd hoped that Pete hadn't been expecting too much of him; as far as he was concerned, he'd been an only child and he wasn't really sure how he was going to cope with it all but was willing to give it a try; "We'll see how it goes!" He'd said.

Pete and I were stood by a tea bar underneath a bridge, as had been previously arranged, when a car pulled up next to us, a man jumped out and shook hands with us both;

"Hi, I'm Shane, you must be Pete and you must be Jan!"
There were rather distinct differences between Pete and Shane; the first being that Shane was Blonde, he was quite a bit shorter than Pete aswell at five foot eight, although they both had very similar builds. I thought to myself; 'now this is the son of the Irish man that Joan had claimed was Pete's father.' We all hit it off straight away and I think that Pete would've liked to have hugged him but Shane was definitely not the type. Another thought flashed through my mind; 'if only Pete could have been more like him!' After the initial 'hello's and intro's,' we loaded up Shane's car and were driven back to his house. When we arrived his wife, Bea was waiting with their children and all of them had been very friendly and wel-

coming. The plan was that we would spend the evening with them getting to know them first and meet Pete's auntie, uncle, cousin and grandfather the following morning. Shane told us that his auntie and uncle would come in to see him at some point everyday and that they'd been more like parents to him than Joan ever had. Pete's auntie had been too excited to wait until morning and within a few minutes of our arrival was knocking at the door and it was obvious that Shane had a really good relationship with his aunt and uncle and that they were very nice people too. Something else that also became pretty clear though was that everyone seemed to be a little concerned about the introduction to Pete's grandfather, who lived a few doors away, that was arranged for the following day; it was mentioned several times that none of them were particularly sure what sort of reaction Pete was going to get at the meeting and I'll not deny that I was a little unnerved by this obvious concern and started to worry about what we were walking into. I did feel a little better about the situation though when everyone agreed that Pete's grandmother had seemed very keen to meet him. When Pete's auntie and uncle had left the original plan resumed, we got to know Shane and Bea a little better and everything went well.

I'd had trouble sleeping that night and Pete had attempted to be the sensitive husband, putting his arm around me as we were about to sleep but I'd shrugged him off saying;

"I'm too hot!"

While thinking; 'get away from me!' But from his reaction I was fairly certain that he had no absolutely no idea of what I was thinking;

"It is a bit warm isn't it?" He'd said "Goodnight love!"

I needn't have been concerned about the meeting between Pete and his grandfather, he'd seemed to be pleasant enough: As arranged, we'd arrived at exactly 11:00am, something Pete's grandfather approved of immediately, looking at Pete he said,

"I like punctuality. So, you're the one I'm supposed to know then are you?"

He then shook Pete's hand. We only stayed about half an hour but still, long enough for Pete's grandfather to have explained his thoughts, his decisions and the motives surrounding Pete's adoption, saying that he still felt he'd made the right decision and that he wasn't going to make any kind of apology for it. I have to admit that I was a little annoyed by some of his comments;

"Did you have a good childhood?" He'd asked. "Your adoptive parents were good to you?" Pete had nodded. "Well, that's all that matters, isn't it?"

The last thing Pete's grandfather had said before we left had left me somewhat puzzled, he shook both of our hands and said,

"Goodbye, nice to have met you both. We probably won't meet again!"

'What did he mean by that?' I'd thought and decided to ask Shane his opinion;

"Take no notice," he'd said, "that's just the way he is, abrupt and straight to the point."

Pete's grandmother was completely different; to celebrate Pete's homecoming she had made a great big Victoria sponge, which was by all accounts her speciality and she seemed lovely, a real granny, just like they used to be. She gave Pete a big kiss on arrival and welcomed him in saying how she had longed for this meeting, how she didn't want him to be adopted and that that bastard had made her, he was an evil man and she was glad she had divorced him. With that said she asked;

"How did we get on with him?"

"Well, ok!"

"That's a surprise!"

Another two more aunties had appeared while we were at Pete's grandmothers and both seemed to be pleasant enough, although one had a very bad squint and it was then that I realised where Michael had got his from, along with his learning difficulties; all were undoubtedly inherited from this long lost family of Pete's. 'My poor little boy!' I thought. 'It's in his genes and he'll never be cured!' Hopefully he had gained some positive genes from me and I've prayed and prayed that he wouldn't turn out to be too much like Pete.

By the time we left his grandmothers any fool could've seen that Pete, as he was promising to see her again soon, was completely taken with her. They'd kept in touch by phone but it wasn't until later in the year, at Christmas, that he managed to see her again. Although when his auntie and uncle had gone camping in the New Forest in the October, they'd visited us and then in the November Shane, Bea and the children had come to Bournemouth for the day, it was then that we'd arranged to go back just before Christmas, this time we'd take Michael too.

317

We'd decided that we were going to drive to London this time but it had meant that I'd had to buy yet another car for Pete: One of some eleven cars I'd bought for him over the years, from 'Ford Cortinas' to 'Mitsubishis' and every single one had some kind of problem, some sort of fault;

"It doesn't feel right... The brakes are faulty... There's something wrong with the steering... It's making a strange noise..." The list goes on, he was never happy and yet he managed to drive to London with no complaints and succeeded in negotiating his way around very easily; that's something I'd never even contemplate attempting but then I would never want to, I feel that London is such a cold, callous place, where the pace of life is much too fast, for me anyway and it is the only place that I've ever been where I've seen people dressed in furs, pull up outside posh hotels in their Rolls Royce's and are totally oblivious to the poor, homeless people that they have to step over to get to the hotel doors. I am aware that there are many thousands of people who suffer the same plight, but nowhere in Britain is it more obvious than in London.

We arrived at Shane's house without incident. Shane had told us beforehand that he'd agreed to allow Joan to call around briefly to see us, as long as she didn't drink any alcohol prior to, or during the visit. He'd also said that she'd been very upset when she was told that we had already been there once before, although she did apologise to him for the drunken threat. I had dreaded that second meeting with her but she was sober and a totally different person, all except the possessiveness of Pete, that was still as prominent as before; she'd insisted on sitting next to him and holding his hand the whole time that she was there and you could see that Shane was very hurt by this show of affection and once again I really felt for him. Joan had given us a Christmas card with a fifty-pound note inside, the card had read:

'To John (Pete) and Jan'

It was pretty clear that she'd had no intention of dropping this 'John' thing and it was getting on my nerves a bit, it was also getting to Pete aswell. Joan had given Shane a Christmas card too, he'd told us that it was the first one he'd had in years but there was no fifty pound note inside his card and again he was very hurt, only this time it seemed that Pete had felt some compassion for the way that Shane had been treated... Maybe he wasn't totally devoid of feeling for anyone but himself after all, who'd have known! After that visit we didn't go again, it was Pete's choice; he'd told me that he would probably go back and visit at sometime but he'd met them all and was happy enough with that. But it's never that simple and Joan it would seem, had other ideas, she felt that I was to blame for the fact that Pete didn't want to go back and took it upon herself to continually ring me up, usually drunk and accuse me of keeping her son away from her, telling me that I was being jealous of her. I'd told Pete about it, he promised to put her straight the next time he spoke to her. I wasn't prepared to listen to the abuse anymore and intended to put the phone down on her in the future. I did feel a little guilty about taking this course until I'd spoken to Shane and he agreed that it was the best way to handle her. I then told Pete what had been said and he agreed with Shane; that it was probably for the best.

Pete still had his job; working nights in a barrier security box on an industrial estate at Bournemouth airport and on occasions Penny and I would pop down to see him. We would go for drives into town aswell; usually to the taxi rank where we'd chat with Nick. I still kept in touch with him and he and I had remained good friends and whenever Penny and I went out anywhere, all I had to do was ring him and he'd be there to take us to our various Saturday night clubs, or the Tuesday night country music club and he was always available to return us home again at the end of the night.

I don't remember a great deal about 1997, other than the usual catalogue of problems, bullies ruining my children's lives and visits to schools: Michael was now eight years old and I was working on finding an exact diagnosis of his problems. Thanks partly to my insistence on my child's right to a decent education and in part to the support of the Education Welfare Officer at Michael's school, Michael was finally statemented and given seven and a half hours extra support in special needs a week; tests were also carried out to find out what the specific problem was and for the first time it was suggested that Michael may have had an Autistic Spectrum Disorder; there was no doubt in my mind that whatever was wrong with Michael would almost certainly be the case with Pete too, especially given the various character traits that they shared and the obsessive compulsive behaviour that I'd observed in them both. When I'd suggested my theories to Pete, he'd misconstrued what I was trying to say and had accused me of calling him 'mad!' He'd said that I was making excuses and blaming him for Michael's problems, saying I only blamed him because I couldn't admit that I was at fault and that I was failing because I was a useless mother; always out, never at home where I was supposed to be. Then came a period of name calling and losing his temper with Matthew and/or me, whereupon all his belongings would be piled into the car for a quick jolly around town and then after about half an hour, he'd come back. After that followed months of him not speaking to anyone, just shutting himself in the bedroom; eating all his meals in there and spending a lot of time sleeping, he only ever really came out of the room to go to work. If we did speak, it was usually for one of two reasons; either his mother had made yet another abusive phone call to me or; Michael had told him that Matthew had done something to him, this would prompt Pete to threaten that if I didn't do something about it, he would and my response was always the same;

"You lay a hand on him and see what happens!"
The trouble was; it wasn't so much the laying hands on him that was the problem most of the time, it was the fear of it and the constant verbal abuse that we were all subjected to, including Penny. The only person who seemed to escape Pete's wrath was Michael. Even the school were getting the sharp end of Pete's tongue and as far as possible I'd tried to discourage Michael from telling Pete about anything bad that may have happened during the day. The only problem there was that almost everyday Michael had been bullied by someone and the teachers had neglected to do anything about it, so Michael would come home and let something slip, Pete would kick off and take it upon himself to go and do something about it; I'd had to phone the school on several occasions and warn them that Pete was on his way there, they'd then lock all the doors. Michael had instigated most of these outbursts in the beginning but as time went by he, like me would get very embarrassed whenever Pete kicked off and each time it happened I felt obliged to apologise to the school staff on Pete's behalf. I'd even suggested to the Education Welfare Officer that Michael might've stood a much better chance if I'd been on my own and that maybe I should've divorced Pete.

The E.W.O. was a lovely man, He'd said;
"Well, whilst I can't say either way or encourage you in any way, I would think that it must be very hard for you living with two of them with such similar problems and that perhaps having just the one would be easier!"

Once again my thoughts were confirmed and I really couldn't see how I was going to be able to live like that any longer but as soon as I'd reached the end of my tether, told Pete that I'd had enough, suggested that he find himself a bed sit; to stop threatening to go and just do it; he'd turn everything around again, apologise for his behaviour and be quite normal and nice again for a few weeks; constantly playing with my mind... How could I see him homeless? I'd tried so very hard to help him and keep him happy, all the while attempting to protect all of us from him, keeping everybody separate and everyone happy.

Chapter 38

Christmas day, 1997 and Pete had had to work, so as a surprise I'd decided to take his Christmas dinner to him, complete with a cracker and a can of beer. Lee informed me that he'd given Pete a 'spliff' with instructions to take it to work with him and celebrate Christmas… I must say that I was a little concerned as to what kind of effect a whole joint may have had on Pete, he had never really had more than a few puffs at any one time and although it did relax him quite a lot, at the same time he would always get very giggly and silly after a puff or two. I left Matthew and Michael under the supervision of Lee, his girlfriend Bonnie and her daughter and said that I'd be gone for about half an hour, it would depend on how relaxed Pete actually was;

"I may have to bring him round!" I'd joked.
Penny came with me and held the tray whilst I drove and when we got there, it turned out that Pete had smoked the majority of the funny fag and although he was still conscious he was, as expected very giggly. He'd told me that he was grateful for his dinner because he was beginning to get really hungry, then he'd started laughing and continued to do so as we pulled his Christmas cracker. He was still giggling to himself as he put his paper hat on and we said our 'Merry Christmas's!' Then Penny and I headed for home and as I was driving away, I looked in my rear view mirror and saw one of the funniest sights I'd ever seen: In the middle of a lonely quiet road, sat in a security box was Pete, wearing his security uniform topped off with pink paper hat, poised with knife and fork in hand, smiling to himself and staring out into space. (Luckily his boss didn't turn up at that moment.)

We had quite a good Christmas without Pete there; just me, Penny, my four children, Bonnie and her daughter and with the absence of Pete, Matthew was far happier than I'd seen him in a long time, in fact we all were, 'if only it could've been like this all of the time and not just Christmas day.' I'd thought. Nick popped in with his children so I could give them their presents, which I bought for them every year and Nick gave me a gold locket and chain which I still wear to this day. Dan had also popped in as usual to see the kids; although he never stayed for more than an hour and I would stay out of the way for most of the duration of his visit so that he never really knew who was at home and who wasn't, that way I'd felt relatively safe. A feeling that was bolstered by the fact it had become obvious that Dan was a little intimidated by Lee, who was six feet tall and towering over his Father and I knew that Lee would never let anything happen to me while he was around. Helen never came with Dan and even though they had been together thirteen years my children had never accepted her; on the rare occasions they had seen her, she'd always managed to say something rude about one or the other of them, their partners or even me and much to my amusement Lorna had by now taken over where I'd left off; bringing whoever was on the receiving end to their knees with her sarcastic wit and was really good at it too, the torch had been passed and there was no real need for me to say anything to anyone anymore. Dan had left a little sooner than usual, even though it was the one day of the year he missed the most and I think the reason he didn't stay very long was in part because he couldn't answer Lorna's sarcastic remarks but also because Helen didn't celebrate Christmas although she had children, whether by choice or because she was Jewish, I was never quite sure and perhaps Dan didn't want to either because of the memories of all that he'd lost; the wonderful Christmases we had spent together, being around his children and Lou... Every year I put up the last Christmas cards that Lou sent us all and every year we include her in our celebrations, raising a glass to her memory.

It was obvious that Lee and Bonnie's relationship had become strained; all day she kept sniping at him and it irritated me but I could tell that it was the beginning of the end, for which I was thankful, although I knew it was going to be hard for Lee and had hoped it would happen sooner rather than later, for his sake. I waited until I could find a quiet moment with him and spoke to him;

"You can always come home, you know?"

"No, we're all right." He answered.

"Well, the offers there."

"I have thought about it, more than once. At least I'd get fed decent food, I'm sick of pasta and lentils!"

Bonnie and her daughter were vegetarians and since being with her, Lee had become thin and very pale, always ill with continual chest infections. It didn't help that he'd also abused his body with drugs over the years and was still smoking marijuana... I was however more concerned about the affect that smoking tobacco was having on his chest, at the same time as being relieved that the days of cocaine and ecstasy were now behind him. I'd asked him to come home for a few weeks, just so I could build him up a bit but he wouldn't agree to it, although a few months later he did return home anyway, to live.

In the May of 1997 Lorna met Barry and even though I liked him instantly, I couldn't help being more than a little apprehensive, due solely to my own experiences of men but she'd seemed really happy and I, in turn was happy for her; if anyone deserved happiness it was Lorna and it looked as if she had found 'Mr Right!' Even so, I was afraid that my little girl would get abused as I had and I'd watched Barry like a hawk, trying to find something wrong, some fault but found nothing. Lorna had no illusions about life anyway and from the outset she was in control but it still pulled on my heart strings just the same; the realisation that my little girl might be leaving home, just like Lee had and, as with Lee, I knew that I'd have to just let her without saying or showing her how much I really didn't want her to go. I'd asked her if she was going anytime soon and she'd laughed saying;

"Are you trying to get rid of me?"

"Yes of course!" I'd responded and laughed too.

"No way!" She'd said. "Not yet anyway, you can't get rid of me that easily." She would stay with Barry on occasions at his parent's house but only really during the weekends and I always knew she'd be back. Penny too was talking about finding herself somewhere else to live, saying that even though she liked being with me, like me she was fed up with Pete and found it so difficult to stay neutral, especially when he'd shout at me or in particular Matthew. She was constantly telling me what she felt I should do and questioning my decision to keep hanging in there; this sadly caused a little conflict between us and usually ended with me telling her to mind her own business.

Then one evening Lee phoned;

"Mum, she's gone mad, she's just hit me and she's threatening to kill me! She's just thrown a lamp and its hit me in the head; I think I've got a cut!"

All I could think was; 'I have to get my son out!' I could hear her in the background, screaming at him, things like;

"That's it, run to mummy!"

"Ok, I'm coming now." I'd told him, "Never mind your belongings, just get out of there!" Then I hung up.

If I'd had any concerns as to whether I was being an over protective mother or that my instincts had coloured my first impressions of this woman, this call certainly removed my doubts and confirmed that I was right all along, that coupled with the cruellest thing I'd ever known a woman to be capable of: Two days before that phone call, Bonnie had come to my house to see me with her six year old daughter and Lee and announced that she was pregnant; Lee was over the moon at the prospect of becoming a Daddy and she had told her daughter who was also excited at the prospect of having a baby brother or sister, yet at the same time Bonnie had made an appointment for a termination the very next day. She went through with the abortion and then told her daughter what she had done; that poor child would remember forever that her mummy had killed her baby brother or sister. Lee was heart broken, as was I it would have been my grandchild, although I wasn't as upset as I would have expected. At least my son still had the chance, when the time came to make a clean break; he was however concerned of the affect his leaving would have on Bonnie's daughter.

When I arrived at Bonnie's house, Lee had already packed his belongings and was waiting for me by the door, so Penny and I went straight in and moved what we could; I'd already given Penny prior warning that if Bonnie had said one word, or if she had really hurt my son, I was going to crucify the bitch;

"Don't be too surprised if I get arrested" I'd told her.

"Well I'm coming with you then!" Penny replied, "Why should you have all the fun?"

Lee had pleaded with us to leave Bonnie alone; he knew how I would react and was afraid of what Penny might do; there's never been any doubt that Penny would protect my children and me, no matter what and Bonnie, obviously realising what a very dangerous position she'd found herself in, passed very few comments or criticisms of Lee but rather blamed her hormones, her depression and her medication for the outburst. As far as I was concerned, it was too late and my decision had been made; my son was coming home with me, at least for the time being and once home I knew that I'd be able to get him back to his old self... That was now my priority. I really did believe that lee was well on the road to total self-destruction and that death was a very real possibility, something that would, without doubt have killed me too; there's no way that I could ever withstand the loss of another child. It wasn't very long though before Lee was well on the road to his old self; he'd put on weight, the colour was back in his cheeks and he was smiling again, much to my relief. Bonnie did try once or twice to get him to go back; using her daughter as emotional blackmail, telling him how hurt the child had been and how she'd missed him but Lee managed, with a little persuasion from me, to stand his ground and I was proud and relieved at that, although he was still going off on his weekend binges, staying out for days at a time and worrying me sick but he always came home again, when he was done.

On June the 10th 1998, four days before Pete's birthday and whilst he was at work, I received a telephone call from Shane saying that Joan had died of liver failure; she'd finally succumbed to the alcohol and was only fifty-seven years old. Apparently the doctor had warned her a few weeks earlier that she would die if she had another drink, she didn't heed the warning and now she was dead. I really didn't have a clue how I was going to tell Pete; just two weeks prior to her death, he had finally plucked up the courage and told Joan to stop phoning and abusing me. Every call she made to me over the two years that we'd known her; she had been drunk and Pete had told her that he wanted no more to do with her, that she would always take second place to me and my children and even though she cried, begging him not to give up on her and promising to stop drinking, he'd remained firm and had ended the conversation with;

"If you're ever sober then maybe we can talk again, in the mean time we'll be changing our telephone number!" Then he hung up.

That was the last time that Pete spoke to Joan, although I heard from her one more time: She had phoned me again a few days later, whilst Pete was at work and the call had been pure venom; I was all the slag's and sluts under the sun, she'd told me that she was going to kill me and my bastard children for keeping her son away from her and had finished her rant with;

"You'll find out what it's like to lose a child!"

That hit such raw nerves with me, on the one hand I already knew what it was like to lose a child, so could understand her pain to a degree but more importantly, she'd threatened my kids and as with any threat to my children, I became like something possessed and even though logically I knew that it was an empty threat; she didn't know where we lived, nor was she capable of finding us, it didn't stop me from telling her what was going to happen the next time I saw her. That was the last time that I spoke to Joan and as I drove to give Pete the news of his mother's death, I couldn't help but think how well she had chosen her moment through the drunken madness; it was the final turning of the knife... Perhaps she had planned for it to happen on the day of his birthday but it had gone slightly wrong. I'd pulled up near the security box and Pete came straight over to the car;

"What's up?" He asked,

"I've got some bad news"

He'd just looked at me;

"Its Joan isn't it," he said, "she's dead right?"

"Yes!"

He'd told me that he knew it was coming, that he'd had a feeling something had happened and wasn't surprised when I'd turned up to tell him. I'd suggested that he radioed for someone to cover and then come home but he'd declined saying that he'd be all right. He headed back towards his security box;

"Ok, as long as you are all right?" I'd called after him, "I'll see you in the morning!"

Checking in my rear view mirror as I left, he was watching the television as if nothing had happened and I was confused by his reaction. When he got home I was waiting for him.

"Are you ok?"

"Yep fine"

"Are you going to ring Shane?"

"No, I'll ring my Gran about nine, before I go to bed"

"Do you want breakfast?"

"No, just coffee!"

That was all he said, he rang his Gran at nine and they spoke for a minute after which I'd asked;

"Is she ok?"

"Yes, fine!" He'd replied.

With that he went to bed. He seemed to have taken it well; I'd expected the usual, over the top display of 'poor Pete' talking to anyone who would take pity on him but surprisingly, it didn't happen. I'd also expected the blame to be placed solely at my feet, waiting for him to say that his last argument with her had been caused by me, I was fully expecting it but that didn't happen either.

Later on in the week he called Shane and then his Gran again to discuss the funeral arrangements but she'd told him that it wasn't worth him going up for the funeral, it would be a small service with just a few members of the family, that caused a reaction;

"Well that's nice," he'd declared, "I'm obviously not family then!"

I was a little taken aback by what she'd said myself and thought; 'maybe she's a little too good to be true!' The instincts were right again and that Christmas I sent all the cards to London, as I had done in previous years and a few days later a card arrived for Pete from his Gran. On the front it had read; 'to my grandson' but the shock came when we read what she'd written inside:

> 'To Pete,
> I'm glad to have met you,
> But I don't want to see or hear from you again,
> Love from Gran.'

Nobody could've prepared for that one, it hurt Pete and I felt for him, I could not understand why she'd done that and didn't think that I ever would. Then, a few months later I was watching a program called; 'Neighbours from Hell' it was the last episode in the series and who should appear? None other than, Pete's Gran and she was making some poor girl's life a living hell; the girl had lived in the flat above Pete's Gran and the poor thing was a complete nervous wreck. I really couldn't believe what I was seeing; that seemingly dear, little, old lady we had met, famous for making her beautiful, Victoria sponges, who we'd thought wouldn't have said boo to a goose, had a very dark side and if the story were to be believed was as I'd previously thought: 'Too good to be true!' Suddenly it became clear that Joan had actually been honest in her rants about how she'd been treated by her mother. Joan and her drinking had been blamed for so much when in fact; her Mother had played a major part in driving her to drink in the first place and it was also true to say that the same flaw had been apparent in Joan's character too; obviously the venom that had spilled from her mouth during those drunken telephone conversations had been inherited and though I could never forgive her for that, it went an awful long way to understanding why she'd behaved the way she did. I'd relayed my thoughts to Pete, who seemed to understand Joan just as suddenly as I had, he'd told me that he was enlightened, that he could see the same behaviour patterns in himself; I had hoped that this would help him to realise that the way he'd treated us was similar to the way his Gran had treated his Mother, hoping that now that he knew it, he may change. The only thing that did change was; from then on he justified his behaviour by saying he couldn't help being that way and I shouldn't expect him to change, it was in his genes… As far as I was concerned it was yet another reason to give up trying to revive our relationship: Pete could now justify himself and if anyone had to change it would have to be me, I'd have to accept whatever he chose to do to me but more importantly; to my children and although he wasn't much of a threat to Lee or Lorna because they were out most of the week, Matthew was the one that I feared for. Pete promised to try a little harder with him whilst he was staying in my house; he still talked of leaving but it was said so often that it became old hat, empty threats, Pete didn't seem able to make any decisions and stick to them. He did however start to realise, with a little persuasion from me, that Michael had been manipulating everyone, including myself but especially Matthew and using Pete as a threat to get what he wanted.

Matthew was now fifteen, a fairly big lad and not quite so easy to bully or control anymore. Like Lee, he had metamorphosized overnight from a little boy, almost into a man and also like Lee had finally fought back, turning on one of the bullies that plagued him at school: He had been lining up with the other pupils in his class, waiting to go into a lesson when a particular lad began calling him names, the boy had then decided to take it a step further by punching Matthew in the back, only this time Matthew turned around and hit the bully back, the boy fell and caught the side of his face on a radiator, was badly cut and needed to have several stitches. Although I didn't condone the use of violence, it looked like the only way to boost Matthew's confidence and convince him that he didn't have to put up with it or be the victim anymore. Matthew was firmly told by the school that the only reason he wasn't getting expelled was because it was completely out of character for him to react this way, if it had been anyone else, they would have been out and should it ever happen again, so would he. It never did, not at school. I had told Matthew that I was proud of him for finally fighting back and that even if he had been expelled; I would have stood by him. He continued to feel guilty about what had happened though, not the fighting back but for the permanent scar the boy had;

"I didn't mean to do so much damage," he kept saying, "I just wanted them to stop!"

Eventually, with a lot of talking from me and the teachers at school, Matthew's fear of his anger and losing his temper eased and unlike other children who are bullied, Matthew's grades remained unaffected throughout, giving credence to my belief that Matthew thought it was just a way of life, that he was put on earth to be treated like this, bullied and beaten by Michael, Pete and the pupils at school, ignored most of the time and just there, apologising for everything, always thankful for his food, for his clothes, grateful for everything and expecting nothing in return. If you were to ask most children, my own included, what they want for Christmas or their birthday they'll give you a list as long as your arm, not Matthew, he would say things like;

"I know how hard things are for you Mum, if you can afford it I'd like this book, or a C.D, or a jumper, not all, maybe just one of them but if you can't afford anything it doesn't matter." Obviously I'd treated him exactly as I had the others, buying them all anything and everything they'd wanted but no matter what I did for Matthew, I couldn't seem to get him out of that cycle of guilt and feeling as though he wasn't worthy of anything. Even so, he gained a little more confidence at school and appeared to have more friends too, although he had no illusions about any of them, he'd said that even though it was nice to have friends, he felt that the majority were only hanging around him because they felt safer after what he had done to the bully and that they seemed to think that he was going to protect them should they be picked on. They could've been right but he really didn't think he'd be able to live with himself if he ever hurt someone like that again. Extremely likeable, very polite and always so considerate of every ones feelings at the expense of his own, something that has, without doubt been a disability for him; always putting everyone else before Himself. To this day Matthew is an incredibly good looking, very intelligent and highly motivated individual, he's a very gifted drummer, (according to some; one of the best in the south.) a talented vocalist with a natural presence on stage and he played the lead in his last two school productions. He plays in a group with Lee, who is also a very talented musician but is happy to be playing in a band, if he makes it; all well and good. I do feel that Matthew's loyalty to Lee has held him back a little but I pray that one day he'll be recognised by some sort of talent scout and get that one real break he so deserves... Most people reading this will probably think that it's all just a mother's bias but one day you'll be able to judge for yourself.

At the end of August, 1998, Lee came home with a very young looking girl, or so she appeared to me and I'd had a bit of fun with Lee about it saying that she'd looked about twelve; she wasn't, she was eighteen and just a little indignant at the suggestion.

Whilst I joked in my usual way I could tell that I was very keen on Carrie right from the start, she was and still is a very attractive girl and as with Lorna and her boyfriend Barry; I felt that my son had finally found the right one: She was the right age, she didn't take drugs and didn't have any mental hang-ups, I'd even wondered what such a lovely girl could see in my hippy son, looking like a derelict with his hair down to his waist and a long 'ZZ Top' beard... I couldn't have wished for better partners for my children or parents for my grandchildren!

Chapter 39

Over the course of two or three years prior to 1999, my Mum had become increasingly frailer and Verity had to go and see her everyday; looking after her and all her care needs. I visited Mum more frequently, not that I'd wanted to, or that she'd particularly wanted me there, Verity and her children were still the one's that really counted; it was more for Verity's sake, I could see the strain that looking after Mum had been taking on her and her family life. I'd felt guilty about my own feelings towards my Mum too, given her disability; she had Chrone's disease, Spinal Stenosis, problems with her Thyroid and she was in constant pain, I knew she was very ill but I also knew that it would only get worse. I might have hated the way I was treated, maybe even disliked the woman but she was my Mum and at the end of the day I loved her for that. As the contact between us became more regular we talked more about the past, our separate lives and where our paths had crossed on occasions, trying to make up for the lack of a relationship in a vague attempt to form some future understanding of each other, our needs and resentments past and present. I'd felt that until I had an understanding of her thinking I could never bury the hatchet. I also realised how alike we were and it occurred to me that maybe it was this likeness that had caused the majority of our rifts, although I would never understand why she'd left me and it was the one thing I could never forgive. We talked about my relationship with Pete and Mum felt as I did; that Pete was not a well man and when I'd said that I could see no 'forever' in our relationship, she agreed with me, though not completely;

"Is there anything else you could do to turn things around?" She'd asked and of course the same old question, "Was it your fault?"

I was annoyed by the suggestion;

"I've tried everything Mum!" Feeling those old resentments rising, "Just remember, you didn't believe me about Dan!"

I then reminded her of how she had taken his side over all the years and of how she had changed her tune after the things she'd heard in the hospital and she apologised;

"Yes I know, I just worry!" She'd said.

'About me?' I'd thought, although it was easier just to say;

"Yes I know!"

"I suppose your marrying Pete was my fault?" She'd asked. "Going at it like a bull at a gate and arranging it all. I'd thought it was what you wanted."

I didn't tell her what I'd really thought, it was better to just let it go, it wouldn't have served any purpose and as far as I was concerned; that was all in the past, although it was nice to know that we had reached a sort of mutual understanding.

In the weeks and months that followed Pete and I grew further apart, Lee left again, this time to go and live with Carrie at her Mum's house and Lorna finally left home and went to live with Barry and his parents; I was lost without her, although she still came home one night a week to be with me. Penny made an escape aswell and moved into a shared flat near to where she worked, I missed her too but at least we still went out together on Tuesdays and at weekends. My home seemed so empty; I was lonely and felt as if I was losing everything that I'd worked so hard to keep. I still had my job as an evening office cleaner, just to get out and about after the security contract had ended but I needed something more in my life so Penny and I decided to join another social club; it was quite cliquey to start with but after a few weeks we'd been accepted. It helped that Verity's in laws were all members too, in particular her father in law, big Jeff as I called him although he wasn't all that big really, it was just that Verity's husbands name was also Jeff. I'd always joked that one day big Jeff would come and live with me and stay in the cupboard under my stairs, it was a joke that had been on going for some twenty years, ever since the days of darts and Dan. I always gave big Jeff a kiss whenever I went in the club and he'd giggle, he was a real character and by 1999 he was almost seventy. He and Bev had had quite a rocky relationship but somehow they always managed to keep it together, even when they were living in separate houses. Bev swore that she hated him and big Jeff swore that he hated her but I loved them both and when Bev died Big Jeff was devastated, he never married or lived with anyone again. He was also the Vice chairman of the club and had suggested that I put myself up for a seat on the committee; I'd thought he was joking but after a number of members suggested it aswell; saying that my connections with local entertainers and ideas for improvements would be good for the club, I decided to give it a try and in March 2000 I was elected. It was the perfect answer to my empty life; I had a purpose again, something to take me away from the problems at home. I didn't want to be there any-

333

more; two of my kids were grown up and gone, Matthew was finally holding his own and out most of the time anyway, in friend's homes, all I had left was Michael and whenever Pete wasn't working, he spent his time with him, I couldn't stand the sight of Pete anymore and somewhere along the way I'd lost the ability to cope with everyday things too, I couldn't understand what was happening; the basics of juggling money, even Pete asking something as simple as; "Do you know where my socks are?" And I'd fly off the handle.

It was around this time that the migraines and panic attacks had started and everything had seemed so illogical. I went to see the doctor who had thought it was depression at first but then suggested that it could've been the menopause as it had been six years since I'd had my hysterectomy. So I was put onto H.R.T. and initially I seemed to get better, although my blood pressure was high but it was my inability to cope mentally that was the most debilitating and it had a knock on effect on the frequency of the anxiety attacks. I seemed to spend more and more time at the doctors, I needed a diagnosis, a reason for this absurd behaviour, I became convinced that, without doubt I was going to die; with the panic came the chest pains, an inability to breathe which had caused palpitations and set my pulse racing, a constant internal fight for control, I needed to be in control. Then there was the sudden flushes that left me looking like a lobster and night sweats too, I'd thought: 'Maybe if I ended it all myself and take away the chance of sudden death, actually choose for myself.' A stupid idea but an idea that crossed my mind nonetheless, besides I am too nosey... And who knows, there may be a wonderful future ahead?

Outwardly I looked and seemed like the normal Jan, always happy, always sensible and organised; going through the motions of being everybody's agony aunt, sorting out people's finances and telling them who to call to make sure they got the right benefits, helping with advice on what to do for this injury or that ailment, or even just listening to their domestic problems. Then there were my elderly neighbours; I went shopping for them and did, pretty much whatever they needed me to. 'What would it take before someone would realise something was wrong with me?' I'd thought but then they all had their own agendas, so I figured that I'd just have to deal with it alone; I didn't want anyone to think I was weak. The one person I should have been able to turn to was Pete; you'd think that after I'd cared for him all those years he'd have returned the favour but the panic attacks he'd seen me have had, in turn, caused him to panic aswell, he'd then phone either the hospital or the doctors and start shouting at them about their lack of care, telling them that they were useless and that if I died they'd have him to answer to… So really it was down to me to deal with on my own.

Mum and Verity suggested that I go on holiday with them; a mid week break for my Birthday that they would pay for, no kids, apart from my niece Kirsty and most importantly, no Pete! Apparently Mum and Verity had been discussing me because Verity was aware that I'd needed a break and I'd have been the first to agree but I wasn't sure that a holiday with Mum was the answer; she was in a wheelchair most of the time by then aswell, although able to walk and potter around at home, she couldn't walk any distance. I was also quite worried about leaving Matthew with Pete but he'd promised that Matthew would be all right so long as he stayed out of his way and Matthew had told me that he'd intended to spend his time with his friends anyway and finished in his usual way with;

"You need this Mum, don't worry about me!"
Penny said that she'd stay for the week to make sure Pete kept his promise and left Matthew alone and Mum seemed as though she really wanted to do this so, albeit reluctantly, I accepted the offer; thinking that maybe it would be the chance for us to build some bridges, hoping that perhaps by the end of the week she would understand me a little more and even realise that I wasn't that bad a daughter after all. After all those years of trying to convince myself that I didn't want her and that I couldn't have cared less what she'd thought of me and I still craved her acceptance of me and needed her to admit that she had been wrong… Forty years old and still craving my Mother's love.

The plan was for me to drive to the holiday camp, picking Mum, Verity and Kirsty up on the way, so I packed my things into the car with Pete attempting to make me feel guilty about going, asking me all kinds of 'what ifs?' Then insisting on a rota, a menu for the week and emergency telephone numbers just in case; I remembered what had happened when I'd gone into hospital and I questioned whether or not I should forget the whole idea but Penny, in her usual way said;

"Oh just piss off will you!"

As I was leaving the kids came outside to wave me off and as I pulled away I thought to myself; 'how lucky I've been,' watching them waving and blowing kisses until I was out of sight. The three mile drive from home to Verity's house was nerve racking; ever since the panic attacks had started I had developed an illogical fear of driving and I could feel my pulse pumping in my head but I managed to keep it under control and pulled up at Verity's, still in one piece. We crammed all the belongings into the car, wheelchair included and off we went, enjoying some pleasant conversation on the way, although I'd sensed Mums apprehension aswell and had the feeling it was going to be a long week. We arrived at the holiday camp and found our accommodation; it was a chalet with a double bed and two singles, so Verity and Mum had shared the double bed and Kirsty and I had the singles. First thing was first: We sorted Mums medication and then checked what time the bingo started; something else that Mum and Verity had in common and something that I hated, so it was to be me and Kirsty together for the evening and Mum and Verity off to bingo. Kirsty and I went for a walk over to the entertainment centre to see what was there and finding only the usual amusement arcade, restaurant, café and shop, we wandered back to the chalet. We were half board so cooked our own meals and Mum and Verity had decided that if we ate our meal early they would be able to go and get their books and a table for bingo early. Kirsty had said that she wanted go too but was told that because of her age she wouldn't be able to play so with the typical attitude of a teenager she voiced her opinion;

"I think it's a stupid law and I don't know what the problem is!"

I found her so amusing and she reminded me so much of myself, she also reminded me how much I liked the company of kids; so funny, opinionated and argumentative, they think they know it all. I watched as Verity and Mum were getting more and more annoyed at the things Kirsty was saying and by the volume at which she said them; she had something to say and didn't care who heard her. Then, there it was; 'the look!' That disapproving look from Mum I remembered so well, followed by;

"For Christ's sake Kirsty, shut up!"

"No, why should I?"

I couldn't believe it, she'd even got away with answering Mum back; I found myself very quietly amused but said;

"I'm going to change for the evening and have a look around, you coming Kirsty?"

"Well I'm not staying here with them!"

"I'll see you in a while then." I said as I smiled at Mum.

"Ok, thanks!" She replied and Kirsty and I left.

I learned a lot about Kirsty that day; how she had felt about the relationship between me and Mum, that she knew an awful lot about my past and that she disagreed with the treatment I'd had at the hands of Mum as a child. Whilst it would have been so easy at that point to discredit Mum and destroy their relationship for all time, I thought better of it, Verity had said on several occasions that Kirsty had idolised me and that I was her favourite auntie but I hadn't actually seen it for myself until then.

"Well Mum wasn't completely wrong Kirs." I said, "Like you I was very argumentative and wound her up. I was a difficult child and Mum just couldn't cope with me!"

"Like me and my Mum then?" she asked.

"Yes I guess so." I answered but she had to have the last word though;

"Even so I don't agree with it, she shouldn't have left you!" We walked along in silence for a while, 'old head on young shoulders!' I thought.

The following morning Kirsty was looking through the programme of activities for the week;

"God this is boring!" She blurted, then she spotted a talent contest scheduled for later in the week; "I wouldn't mind entering that, would you go with me to register?"

We spoke to Verity and she agreed I could take Kirsty but she and Mum were going to stay in the chalet. When we got there Kirsty begged me to enter aswell;

"Go on Auntie Jan, you can sing? Please?"

So, against my better judgement I agreed, filled in the paperwork and rehearsed my song; Patsy Cline's 'Crazy', the only one I could think of at short notice and the band learnt it for me, then just as Kirsty was about to begin her rehearsal she changed her mind about entering. There was only one other entry and if I'd backed out of the talent show aswell it would've been cancelled, so not wanting to let the whole holiday camp down I felt as though I'd had no choice but to perform and I was a complete nervous wreck. We went back to the chalet, where Kirsty told Mum and Verity what she'd done, thinking it was absolutely hilarious.

"Thanks then!" I said

"Well you always wanted be on the stage." Said Mum, who seemed to find it rather funny too; "Now's your chance!"

I thought; 'Yes I did and when I do this, maybe you'll realise that I could have been something, maybe not a superstar but successful at the very least!' As usual I said nothing.

Later that week and I was standing, waiting and listening to the emcee give the introduction;

"Please welcome on to the stage, Jan from Bournemouth!" I was racked with nerves, not because of the audience but because Mum was there and although the lights were bright and I couldn't see much, I could see her, sat in her wheelchair applauding with the rest of the audience. I was thinking; 'don't mess it up now Jan!' I needed to show her that I could do it and I did. It went well, almost perfect and the reaction from the crowd was quite unbelievable, to me anyway. I took my bow and left the stage, trying unsuccessfully to see Mum's reaction as I went but as I returned to the table there it was finally, after all the years of waiting, the approval I wanted; she was smiling but there were tears running down her face;

"What's up?" I asked,

"Well done!" She said,

"Was it ok?"

"Spot on, very good, I'm proud of you!"

"What are you crying for?"

"I'm happy!"

Yes that would be it, as long as I could remember Mum had done this, she cried; she cried over lassie films, she cried over love stories, she cried over certain songs like at my wedding, she had cried many times because I was a disappointment but this was the first time she'd cried because she was proud of my achievements. She cried again later in the evening when I won too. I collected my certificate and bottle of champagne and when I returned to the table I gave her the certificate;

"There you go Mum; this is for you to keep!"

"Shouldn't you keep it?"

"No, I want you to have it."

She sat looking at the certificate for what seemed like the longest time and I think she really was proud of me that night. I was also invited back for a finals weekend in the November, although Mum said that she didn't think she'd be well enough to come back for that but hoped I would win. The next night and our last night, we were sat in the ballroom waiting for the cabaret to start, I don't know whether it was the excitement of the previous night's events or the relief of gaining, after so many years of trying just a little of my Mums love but I'd suffered with a major anxiety attack and a migraine and returned to the chalet leaving Mum, Verity and Kirsty in the ballroom. I was convinced I was going to die and when I got back to the chalet I took some painkillers and went straight to bed. I'd been alone for about half an hour when Verity appeared, she had brought mum back because she was concerned about me and wanted to make sure I was all right. She sat on my bed stroking my head.

"Are you all right?" She asked, and then said; "I'm staying here with you, Verity and Kirsty are going back over. Get some sleep and if you need me I'm just in there, call me if you want me, ok?"

"I'm all right!" I replied, "Just the usual panic attack, you don't need to stay Mum."

"Yes I do!"

Could I really have read her that wrong, all those years; had she really cared after all? Or had she just decided in these last few days that she had got it wrong, misread me. Either way it made no difference to me whose fault it was, for once we were Mother and daughter. I treasured those few days, with those memories as I drifted off to sleep and for the first time in many years I slept soundly. Mum woke me with a cup of coffee,

"Come on, get up lazy, how you feeling?" She enquired, setting down some soluble painkillers; "We've got to get out of here." She said, then pointing at the painkillers that she'd just brought for me; "Just take them and you'll be all right, they'll make you feel better!"

Mentally I felt better anyway but I have to admit it; she was right, they did help and if nothing else they had ensured that I was able to drive home without fear of another migraine. We talked a lot on the way home and Mum reiterated how proud she was and asked if I would be taking Pete and the kids back with me for the final. Then she had told me that I wasn't to put up with his bullying anymore, I hadn't realised until then that she knew and I said as much;

"You'd be surprised how much I do know!" She said.

She was certainly right about that. I dropped her home and kissed her goodbye;

"Come and see me more often eh?" She asked, "And you can phone if you want, you don't have to put up with this anymore Jan, you've been through enough over the years!"

"We will see Mum, I'll see you soon" I answered and left her, waving goodbye. Again I knew she was right; holding things together was tearing me apart and killing me, I was sure of it but at least I was going home happy and even though I couldn't bring back those missing years, I could finally move on, I understood that our relationship wasn't perfect but I had also found an understanding of this woman and more importantly of myself. I pulled up outside my home and all of my children, Penny and even Pete had rushed out to meet me. They'd hung a 'welcome home' banner and some balloons above the door and it felt wonderful to be home, I really had missed them. Pete had seemed happy to see me, although I wouldn't have been that bothered if he was or wasn't, all that mattered to me at that moment was my kids and of course Penny; she'd taken care of everything while I'd been away and there hadn't been any problems. I'd suggested that she come with us for the finals weekend and she did.

November came, all too quickly; along with it came the finals weekend. I'd had a cold and was under the weather anyway but that coupled with Pete and Penny's constant bickering, Pete picking at me because of Penny's attitude towards him and Penny complaining to me about Pete; it was just about the worst weekend of my life. I didn't win but by then I couldn't have cared, I just wanted to get home. The only saving grace of that weekend was Lorna; she hadn't be able to come with us on the first night but her and Barry had driven up for the finals show on the Saturday night and when she arrived, she'd behaved in her usual extrovert way; up on the dance floor teaching Michael the moves to the 'Steps' songs and various other party dances. Lorna always seems to be the life and soul of any party and so much like Lou, with her smile and her attitude, also very attractive. I watched her that night and it was as if I still had part of Lou; people have always said that Lorna is like me and in a number of ways she is but just there, in that moment; it was as if Lou was still here with us. Although I do believe that Lou has visited me many times over the years, I can still hear her voice and see her face. Penny too has claimed to have had two visits from her and Lou has given her messages for me, things that Penny could never have known, she never knew Lou and I didn't have any photographs of her either so Penny didn't know what she

340

looked like, or the sort of clothes that she wore, yet on both occasions she told me what Lou was wearing. I have described some visitations in this book and as the years have passed they have become more frequent... Sometimes I even think that I'm completely mad.

The finals weekend was the beginning of the final chapter for Pete and I and I'm sure that Penny had sensed it. Her flatmate had decided to give up the flat that they were sharing and move in with her boyfriend, so I'd suggested to Penny that she should come back and live with us; she was now at our home again most of the time anyway and I could've done with the extra income, with Lee and Lorna gone and Matthew and Michael still in together, I had a spare room aswell. So back she came and I spent all my spare time with her, Pete would spend his in our bedroom whenever he wasn't working, doing martial arts or staying in Portsmouth, he was also talking about leaving again but I didn't argue the point so he'd added to the threat, saying that he wanted a divorce and again, no response; I think he'd wanted me to tell him that I didn't want a divorce, that I wanted him to stay but I didn't, instead I said nothing. I wasn't too keen on the idea of being single, nor did I like the thought of going through another divorce but I was so unhappy that it didn't matter and by then all that Pete and I had left in common was the surname.

Penny and I continued to go out to the clubs and pubs, which didn't help my marriage that much but it did help me to deal with my depression and for the first time in my life I even considered being unfaithful; I'd had offers over the years but had never accepted any of them. Penny and I also talked about all the girls we'd known whilst we were in care and then more importantly; the matron (Mum), we wondered where she was and if she was even still alive. We discussed how we'd go about finding her and Penny said that she had kept in touch with her for a while, after she'd left the girls hostel. I hadn't, I'd seen her once, on a bus, when Lee was about a year old but that was some twenty four years before. Penny said she'd lost touch with Mum when she'd moved to Brighton. It was very strange that on the very evening of that conversation, we had walked into the country music club for our regular Tuesday night out, we'd gone to the bar and had both recognised a man that was working there; it was Jerry, Mum's son. We asked about Mum and he explained to us that although she had moved to Brighton for a few years, she was now back in the area and living with uncle

Don in a flat in Wimborne. He told us that she'd talked about the girls many times over the years but especially Penny and I.

"I know that she'd love to see you two again." He said, then he gave us her telephone number and his address. Penny was so excited and had wanted to ring her there and then, but I said that it wasn't a good idea at that time of night. The following day Penny and I had decided to buy a bouquet and card for Mum and take it to Jerry's house, he'd told us that she was to be staying with him for the weekend. He must have given it to her the moment she'd arrived because on the Friday evening the phone rang I picked it up and recognised her voice immediately; she sounded a lot older with a sort of sort of crackle in her voice but it was her just the same and she'd sounded as if she was over the moon. Penny spoke to her too and we arranged to go and see her the following weekend, she said that she wanted to hear all about us and what we'd been doing over all the years.

We pulled into the car park of a block of flats and a grey haired lady, her eyes filled with tears, came out to meet us, it was Mum! She hugged us both and it was the most touching moment: This little old lady, who'd had no obligation to any of us at all and had just been doing her job, taking care of us so many years before, really did care and love us both and we loved her back. She was the reason I'd found it so easy all those years before. All the heartache I'd gone through, she had felt it too, she had been there beside me through it all and she was still there, quite a bit older but still just as genuine; in my mind she is without doubt the reason that I survived those years... This was a real Mum! We talked for over two hours; Uncle Don told us how very happy we had made Mum, which in turn had made him just as happy. We sat and chatted about us, our lives, my children and managed to cover pretty much everything and as Penny and I had left we promised to keep in touch regularly... Penny still speaks to her most weeks to keep her updated on all the news and I keep in touch, though not as regularly as I should.

Chapter 40

I decided that it was a good time to buy my council house, especially as I had a considerable discount due to me for being a tenant for so many years. I'd needed Pete's income on paper to secure a mortgage but I knew that if and when Pete carried out his threat to leave, I wouldn't need his income to be able to afford the mortgage alone. He said that he would want nothing from the house, no settlement. The house was and always had been mine and my children's home and in the September of 2000 we completed the purchase and I began to feel a little more secure again; I'd been worried that with just Matthew and Michael living at home, I was going to get asked to move into a smaller property. We'd borrowed a little more money than we had needed to buy the house and had paid off all our debts; although there were some that we'd incurred jointly, most of them were solely Pete's but it was the least I could do. It also meant that when he left he could do so with a 'clean slate' and I'd have enough left over to build a conservatory.

Penny and I were outside in all weathers digging the foundations, we'd hired a cement mixer, mixed and laid the concrete ourselves, even did the brick laying and were covered from head to foot in mud and concrete, most of the time. Penny kept wiping it in her jeans until they weighed so much that they'd slip down over her hips; she'd said that it made her look more authentic with her builder's cleavage. I thoroughly enjoyed the experience and even though we were very tired and my back had been really painful for about six weeks, we laughed so much and I'd felt far better than I had in months. Even Christmas that year wasn't so bad and I'd thought that maybe we'd passed the worst but by the time New Year had arrived, I knew that it would have to be the last Christmas that Pete and I spent together. The only trouble was; I still had to find a way of getting him out and to do that I'd have to find him somewhere to go.

In March, 2001, I was voted back onto the committee at the club but I had also taken over the organising of the entertainment aswell; I was in charge of arranging and introducing the bands and running the raffle, which meant that I'd had to go out a lot more than before and of course Pete had objected but that wasn't going to stop me, I'd wanted to do it; I knew that my duties would take me out of his company for at least four nights of the week and if that wasn't enough to keep me busy; I was still working as a cleaner, I was helping an elderly neighbour who'd become housebound (I was cooking her meals and taking care of her in between the visits from her home help and the district nurse.) and I was spending more time with Mum, which went some way to taking the pressure off of Verity, so I was hardly home.

I was at the club one evening in late march when I met him: Pen was sat doing the bingo, I was watching her and waiting for somebody to call house so that I could go and check their card, as was another of my duties, when I felt someone watching me, I looked up from Penny's card and there he was smiling. There was an instant attraction and for the next hour I could feel his eyes as he watched me wherever I went in the room. As soon as the bingo had finished and I had returned to my table and Penny, he and his friend came over;

"Hello, can we join you?"

"Yes, why not!" I answered as Pen said;

"Why are we coming apart?"

They laughed;

"Hi, I'm Paul and this is Keith."

"I'm Jan and this nutter is Pen!"

Paul had an Irish accent, not strong but soft and sort of lyrical, I could have listened to his voice forever and had even thought I might. He wasn't married but I'd informed him that I was,

"Not for long," Pen interrupted, "she's not happy!"

"Is that true?" Paul asked.

I should have denied it but there was something about him, I felt I could tell him anything and in the weeks that followed, at every opportunity, I did just that. For six weeks I spent every spare moment in his company and I'd even taken to going to his flat for coffee before going home from the club at the end of each evening, although I never went there alone and always took Penny with me because, even though the attraction was so strong in my heart, I knew it was wrong in my head; Pete and I may not have had any kind of a physical relationship but we were still married. Then one evening, about four weeks after I'd met Paul, I'd had a particularly bad few days: Michael having problems at school, Pete doing his usual routine of storming in and verbally abusing the teachers, Mum was very ill and Verity had been having difficulty coping and Easter was just around the corner, so there had been extra entertainment to arrange for the club, I'd needed a couple of drinks more than usual to relax and forget and after the club we'd gone back with Paul. Paul and I had kissed and fumbled about like love sick kids before but on every occasion I had stopped it going further; not only did I have my moral issues but I hadn't had any male body that close to me, flesh on flesh for so long, I was sure that I'd make a complete mess of the situation but this time, with the mixture of alcohol and my emotional state, I let it go further, although I came to my senses at the eleventh hour and stopped him again. I was sure that it had gone too far this time and that he would lose his temper or try and force me anyway but the moment I said; 'no' he stopped and apologised for being so forward. I then apologised too, certain that I'd ruined any future relationship we may have hoped to develop but he was a real gentleman and we just laid together, him with his arm around me and I knew then that that was all I'd wanted, all that I'd missed; those male arms making me feel safe and I relaxed.

I awoke with a start and looked at the clock, it was three thirty in the morning, I got up and went to find Penny, wondering why she hadn't informed me of the time and found her asleep on Paul's settee, where she'd been watching TV. I woke her up and we called for a taxi from our usual firm, I didn't know what I was going to say to Pete but I did know that I wouldn't be able to talk my way out of this one. The taxi arrived and the driver, who we knew quite well, said;

"Boy, you're late tonight!" Laughing he continued, "I hope he's worth it!"

Penny laughed back;

"Yes, maybe for some of us!" She said.

I was a little annoyed at the comment but knew that I'd look stupid no matter what I said and so didn't confirm or deny the accusation; I just looked out of the window.

"You all right love?" The driver asked, "You're unusually quiet, you haven't been hurt have you?"

"No no, I'm fine. Just tired." I answered.

I thought; 'Well that's made it worse, why would I be tired?' And then Penny came to my aid and said;

"Its true, we both fell asleep watching TV."

We told the driver to drop us off just down the road from the house; Pen said that if Pete had waited up we could say that we'd walked home;

"It wouldn't have taken us this long, would it?" I questioned,

"Well, we'll say we walked slowly, the long way around!"
She replied.
I really didn't much care about what Pete had to say anyway and
told her so, although we needn't have been concerned, he and
Michael were fast asleep in my bed, so I went into Penny's room
with her and fell straight to sleep. We were both woken up at about
nine by Pete knocking on the door;
"You awake in there? Pen is Jan with you?"
"Yes where do you think she is?" Penny answered,
"Ok!" Came the reply and that was that.
He asked me later what time we'd got in and I'd told him 'two-ish!'
"We were busy with two male escorts that we'd picked up"
Pen said.
Pete just laughed, although I was sure that he'd suspected some-
thing but then that went some way to proving that he just couldn't
have cared less, he was happy in his own little world.

The following week, on the Saturday morning Penny and I
had been to do our key job cleaning; just a couple of hours, three
times a week and we'd only been doing it a few weeks, it helped to
fund our nights out. I'd been feeling fairly relaxed and happy after
the previous week's exploits, that was until we'd pulled up outside
home and I noticed that Pete's car was gone. I instinctively knew
that something wasn't right and my suspicions were confirmed
when I opened my lounge door to see Matthew, standing there with
his face streaked in blood and his hands bleeding. Then the panic
hit me;
"What the hell happened?"
Matthew told me that he hadn't done anything and Michael, who
was crying, confirmed as much;
"Pete was hitting him and he wouldn't stop!" He said
through his sobs.
Matthew had apparently stood up to Pete and he'd left but they
didn't know where he'd gone;
"Well something must have made him do it?" I questioned,
"Me and Matthew were arguing!" Michael admitted.
I cleaned Matthew's face and hands and once done, the wounds
were superficial and it had appeared that some of the blood wasn't
his either; I didn't say as much but I'd really hoped that some of it
was Pete's and that this time he would be gone for good, although
if he'd had any ideas of returning at that moment, after doing that
to my son, he'd have been sadly mistaken, he had to stay away.

Even so I wanted an explanation, so I called him on his mobile and the first few attempts went un-answered, it wasn't until about two thirty in the afternoon, some three hours later that I finally got a response;

"Where are you?" I asked,

"London!" He replied, "I didn't know what to do. I thought I'd better find somewhere else to live, so I've been to see my old boss but there's nothing up here at the moment."

"And Matthew?"

"I don't know, he was picking on Michael, I'm sorry, I didn't mean it."

"A little late don't you think?"

"Tell him I'm so sorry, I really am, it shouldn't have happened!" He really did sound sorry, "I want to come back and explain."

"Best you do that then!" I said, "But I'm sorry, you won't be staying!"

"I don't expect to. I'll be back in a couple of hours!" Then he hung up.

I wanted to kill him and had he been there at that moment, I probably would have but as the time went on, although I was still angry, I got myself into that same old cycle of thought: 'Poor Pete, he's ill, he's sick, he's a genetic defect, he can't help it… Why did I always follow this pattern?' This time though, the overwhelming emotion was to protect my son, regardless of my compassion and sympathy for Pete. I told Penny that I'd have to stay in and asked her if she would go to the club, explain and cover for me and tell Paul that I couldn't get there, she agreed but said that she was reluctant to leave me alone with; (in her words) 'the evil monster!'

Before Pete came back I told Matthew that I would do whatever he wanted me to do, if he wanted to press charges against Pete I would help him all he had to do was say; he said that all he wanted was for Pete to never come anywhere near him again and for a promise that he'd never touch him again. Pete turned up a little while later and for his part he made that promise but then he added;

"I know Matthew will never forgive me and I don't blame him for that."

"I should think not!" I interrupted, my anger beginning to rise.

He then went on to say he was grateful that Matthew had agreed not to press charges against him and again I could feel my temper kicking in but I knew that I had to control it.

"What do you want me to do?" Pete asked,

"I want you to find a flat and leave!"

I think that somewhere in his little mind it had finally sunk in that this time he would have to go and he agreed, although with a final clutch at the straws he asked;

"Do you think that, after a separation we could perhaps go out together as if we'd just met, like boyfriend and girlfriend, maybe get back together?"

I was stunned; he just couldn't seem to grasp the enormity of what he'd done. I agreed that he could stay until after the weekend but he was to have no contact with Matthew at all and that if he so much as looked at Matthew the wrong way, he'd be gone, there and then. I'd told him that he could stay in our bedroom and that I would sleep in Penny's room until he'd gone, that he was to leave most of his belongings in the car, after all they wouldn't be there more than a couple of days and in so far as the deposit on a flat was concerned, I'd take it out on my credit card; he'd run his up to the hilt again and had also accumulated yet more debt on our joint account.

"What about my tax on the car, would I get that too?" He asked

"Yes, anything, just leave!"

He told me that he'd buy the local paper and see what was available, then said that he wanted to get a proper flat, I drew the line there;

"You will take whatever is available!"

He agreed, disappeared off to the bedroom and I was left questioning my decision; 'Was I being unfair? Had I overreacted?' Penny came in a bit later and it was pretty clear that she'd had a few to drink;

"Still here then is he?" She asked, then announced, rather loudly; "He's just a bully!"

"Ssh, keep it down!" I'd tried to hush her but she'd refused,

"No, why should I, it's the truth isn't it?!" She said.

I knew it was the truth but I'd thought that Pete would've come out to confront her and I'd dreaded that because I knew that after a drink Penny would, without a doubt have beaten him to a pulp, I'd seen her in action. Luckily for him, Pete didn't appear and once

348

Penny had calmed down a little and I'd explained what had been agreed, she was a lot happier, although she did say:

"He's completely mad you know? And so are you if you think any of this is your fault!"

Once again, she was right and it was the confirmation I'd needed... This time I would stick to my guns!

Pete took a room, in a large house, in a good area of Bournemouth, he'd wanted me to go with him and see it but I'd refused, I just gave him the money; one months rent as a deposit and a months rent in advance and at seventy-five pounds a week I had thought was a little extortionate for a room but I wasn't about to say as much, I was sure that that's what he was expecting me to say so that he'd have an excuse to buy more time. I said nothing and Pete moved out and everything was blissful for a time; every-one was getting on so well and I didn't even miss him at all, I had my own clean bed, in my own clean bedroom again and I scrubbed the house from top to bottom. I even told Mum what had happened and that he'd gone.

"About time!" She said, "Perhaps if you're settled now and on your own for a while, I might see a little more of you?"

"Yes probably but I still have the committee work and my oldies! (My neighbours.)" I replied.

The peace was short lived and soon shattered, just two weeks after Pete had left, he was on the phone;

"Can I come back? The landlady has accused me of stealing a stereo and a shirt!"

"Who's shirt?" I asked, trying to find some logic in the con-versation, "You've got shirts!"

He then told me that the landlady had thrown him out and wouldn't give him back his money, what could I say other than;

"You'd better come round and tell me the whole story!"

Pete was many things including a liar, or rather he lived in a world of fantasy but theft was definitely not one of his failings. I had a long conversation with Pete and then phoned the landlady who ap-peared to be, if not completely bonkers, then at the least trying to extort money. In conversation with a solicitor later that week, my first impressions were confirmed as being right: It turns out that she had made a complaint about the theft and was claiming for compen-sation against Pete, by way of damages but she also had two other similar complaints pending aswell. Once again, this was proof that Pete couldn't survive on his own and that I would have to be there for him, to help him through it… I just don't have it in me to turn my back on anyone in need. So Pete came back again and it was agreed that the arrangements would be as before, only this time I told Pete that I'd help him to find somewhere more suitable to live and that, in the meantime I'd deal with the landlady too. I think that she realised she'd finally met her match in me and when she found out that it was my intention to put in a counter claim against her, she dropped the case. With that sorted I was still left with the problem of Pete and after a few weeks he'd started to slip back into his old habits, at which point I'd insisted that he went to his parents for the weekend.

While he was away I'd invited Paul out for a meal with my children; I wanted to gauge their impressions of him, although I'd decided that it wasn't a good idea to take Michael at that point. The kids seemed to like Paul and got on with him well enough, although Lorna said there was something that she felt wasn't quite right. I'd been thinking that he was too good to be true myself; I was suspicious of his travelling every other weekend, all the way to Norwich to see his 'stepchildren.' I understood that he had been with them since they were very young but at the end of the day, they weren't his natural children. There were other things though that I felt outweighed my suspicions; his birthday was on the same day as mine, he had twin grandchildren, one of which had been named Lorna and was born on Lee's birthday, it all looked as if it was meant to be, even so, I still couldn't escape the feeling there was something wrong and I'd decided to cool off on our contact a little. Something that had been made a little easier by the fact that I didn't feel I would be able to spend as much time at the club; even though Pete had said he wouldn't lay a hand on Matthew again, I wasn't about to take the risk. I told Pete about Paul, saying that we were very good friends and he said that it didn't bother him. With everything that was happening the panic attacks and depression began again.

It was April 2001 and just after Mum's birthday, I'd been to see her and was quite shocked by her appearance, although, at the time I'd put it down to her having a really bad cold. Verity had been keeping me informed and I'd told her that if she wanted me to do anything, all she had to do was let me know but she hadn't. Mum, in turn was also concerned about me and my appearance, so I explained everything to her, the problems with Paul, Pete and the kids and even though it justified my lack of visits, I felt guilty about not seeing her more often.

"You need to go out and enjoy yourself!" She'd told me. "Forget everything for a while, do something for you, stop worrying about me and everyone else Jan!"

She was right; I knew that I couldn't stay home, and being there all the time, so Penny and I went out again. I was still on the committee at the club, though most of my duties had to be taken by other members and they'd been very understanding once they had realised the extent of my personal problems but I couldn't escape the feeling that I was letting them down too which was adding to my guilt, although outwardly it wasn't obvious, adept as I was at hiding my inner turmoil.

Penny and I arrived at the club earlier than usual and I called to the bar staff;

"My usual please!"

Then I made my usual first stop at the ladies; something that had become quite a joke with everyone so I would go in regardless. On the way back to the bar I saw another very familiar face from my dart days; I had felt his eyes on me as I'd walked through the club but I'd decided not to look, now though I was face to face with Ken and there it was; that familiar spark from all those years ago.

"I'll speak to you later." I told him,

"I'll look forward to it!" He said with a wink and a smile.

He still had those memorable blue eyes and his dimples and as I stood there looking at him the years seemed to melt away. He had less hair but the large moustache was still there, although the blonde had been replaced by white, he was also very tall at 6'4" and I must admit that I found it very appealing. As I wandered around the club I remembered how we used to chalk up the ladies darts and the conversation we'd had all those years before and that all important wink that he was still doing and it still had the same effect, just as before. I also remembered that he was quite a lot older than me and that he'd been married back then, although I'd wondered whether he still was and with everything that had happened between Dan and I, the divorce, Gary and Pete; it had been over twenty years since the last time that I'd seen him. I'd decided there was nothing else for it; I'd have to get talking to him. At that moment Penny appeared by my side;

"Who was that?" She asked,

"Oh, just someone I used to know." I'd replied,

"Well he obviously fancies you!" she said, "and by the way you've reacted, I'd say you feel the same!"

"You think? And there was me thinking I had covered it well"

"Um, yes," she smiled, "why not meet him again here, tomorrow lunchtime?"

We ran a Thursday club for older members with bingo, lunch and an entertainer, playing old time music on an organ. Everybody seemed to enjoy it, although Penny and I called it 'Gods waiting room!' Penny, not wanting to miss an opportunity to play Cupid said;

"I'll ask him then shall I?"

"He might be married!"

"So! You won't find out if you don't ask will you? And so what if he is? You're only going to talk to him!"

She was heading over before I'd had time to stop her and was back a moment later;

"He's very keen!" She was smiling again. "No hesitation!"

"Really?" I questioned.

"I told him we'd be here at one o clock tomorrow."

"Do you really think I need anymore complications in my life?" I asked

"That's up to you!"

Ken left soon afterwards.

Paul came in the club at about ten o clock, as was his normal routine, so Penny and I went and sat with him but when I'd turned around I noticed that Ken was back again, only this time he was with a couple and a woman in a wheelchair. I was about to go over and speak to him when I'd realised that he was avoiding my look, so I'd thought better of it, instead opting for just saying goodnight as we left the club; it was the normal thing to do to everyone, Penny and I would even kiss several of the older men goodnight and they would get quite upset if we didn't... All in the name of good humour, of course. Paul said he was having an early night because he was going away early on Thursday evening and wouldn't be back until the following Tuesday. I was suspicious once again but had decided that it was probably for the best, especially given my problems at home. I kissed Paul goodnight and Penny and I took our usual taxi home, I'd had so many questions running through my mind: 'What was Paul up to? What was Ken doing with that woman in the wheelchair? What, what, what?' I had to find out.

352

Chapter 41

Thursday lunchtime arrived and I felt strangely nervous as Penny and I walked into the club, I turned to her and said;

"He probably won't turn up!"

"Want a bet?" She responded.

No sooner had we said the words, Ken walked up behind us. I turned to see the smile and the wink;

"Would you like a drink?" He offered,

"No thanks, I already have one." I answered.

For the next two hours Penny kept making herself scarce and Ken and I didn't stop talking, I'd noticed that he was drinking a great deal and that his hands were shaking, I'd also noticed it the night before and found it a little disconcerting, I didn't want to go down that road again but during the conversation that followed I discovered that it wasn't alcohol that caused his shakes, it was nerves and quite understandable once I'd listened to his story: He was indeed married to the woman in the wheelchair, her name was Ruth and she had multiple sclerosis, he had been her carer for ten years, although she went to the day centre two days a week. He told me that they were only really married in name, that they didn't speak and that Ruth treated him very badly. I'd thought he could be saying it to justify his interest in me, that it was just a line; 'My wife doesn't understand me,' but as the weeks passed by, it became very clear that what he'd said was true. I also noticed that while he was talking about her and his experience as her carer, his shaking became almost uncontrollable so I'd change the subject. I told him about life with Pete and we had relived our days of pubs and darts teams, I explained how I'd felt a little uncomfortable at the time with his wife, Doris being in the team and he corrected me;

"We were divorced at the time!"

"Nobody told me!" I said, a little disgruntled, "in fact Doris led me to believe you were very much together, if I'd have known I probably wouldn't have kept my distance. My marriage was just about over then anyway."

"Your sister knew I was divorced," he responded, "so did most of them. I fancied you then but was told that you wouldn't be interested, basically hands off, she's married, so I didn't pursue it." I wished he hadn't taken their word for it; maybe then neither of us would have had twenty years of misery and I was rather annoyed that Verity had told him, what was essentially a pack of lies but perhaps it was fate. I remembered the words of the medium I'd seen when Pete was in hospital;

"You will be involved with someone you already know, a man who drives H.G.V.'s or is involved in transport."
At the time I'd thought that she meant Nick but Ken had been an H.G.V. driver and I already knew him then too... Could this be the person she had spoken about? 'It was too late now!' I'd thought, he was married and to add to my confusion his wife was disabled. Ken told me that he'd been away for two weeks in the March, paid for by Social Services; they had considered that he was in desperate need of a break and couldn't look after Ruth much longer; it was obvious that caring for her had taken its toll on his health. On his return he had decided he was going to leave her and still intended to do so, he mentioned that she was about to go into respite for a couple of weeks and he was looking forward to it; it would give him time to make arrangements, find somewhere else to live and ensure that his wife's care package was in place. Even so, I'd decided that whilst I was still very keen on him, we could only be friends until he'd decided on his future, I didn't want to be responsible for him leaving his wife, even if he didn't love her. He'd said that it was just nice to have someone to talk to outside of his usual social circle... Little did he know it but he would also be my saving grace.

Over the course of the following week, whenever I was in the club, I watched Ruth and took note of her attitude towards Ken. I also spoke to other members, who were also members of another club where Ken was a regular and none had a good word to say about the woman and all, without exception, felt sorry for him. As I watched the two of them together, I tried to assess their relationship, looking for just one sign that he was something other than her carer but there was nothing. She didn't really speak to him at all; if she wanted a drink, she'd lift her empty glass and hold it out to him, while continuing whatever conversation she happened to be having with her friends, Ken would take the glass and go to the bar without so much as a word spoken, even when he put her drink in front of her, no thank you, nothing. She gave the same gestures when she'd needed the toilet too; she would point at him, her wheelchair and then the toilet door and dutifully he'd get up, take her to the toilet, then come back and sit down. I couldn't believe what I was seeing. I happened to be passing by them both, one evening as I'd headed to the bar;

"Hello!" I said,

"Hello, how are you?" He responded nervously, one eye on Ruth.

"Yes, ok I s'pose," I said, "would you like a drink? Ruth would you like a drink?"

"Yes thanks." She said,

"Yes please! Ruth this is Jan, I've known her for over twenty years she was a friend of Doris's." Ken said, with a smile

"Oh right!" She responded without as much as a glimmer of a smile.

'Poor Ken,' I thought, 'he will really be in trouble for this one.' I gave them their drinks and Ken thanked me adding, albeit quietly that he would speak to me later. I already had his telephone number and he had mine but we could only speak whilst Ruth was at the day centre. I rang him the following Tuesday and arranged to pick him up, saying that we could go for breakfast and talk some more. He'd told me that Ruth had been angry, accusing him of having an affair with either me or Penny, although he said that I should take no notice and pleaded with me not to stop calling him, saying that he didn't care what she or anyone else thought, besides it was obvious to pretty much everyone that I was seeing Paul anyway and Ken had told Ruth as much. I then told him of my decision; that we could be no more than friends for the time being and he said that he understood but still wanted to see me as a friend if that was all we could be. I needed him too but I was uncomfortable with the idea of his wife and the attitudes of other people; 'poor woman in a wheelchair' and the thought that people would think of me as an evil woman for stealing her husband... My own growing attractions and feelings needed to be kept in check.

Pete was becoming increasingly controlling again, so I'd told him that I thought he wasn't looking hard enough for a flat, his response was; that he'd hoped I'd changed my mind but obviously I hadn't. He then informed me that he wasn't going to leave until he'd found somewhere suitable to live, which left me either sleeping in Penny room with her or on the settee, in my own home.

Then there was Paul: In the week that Ruth had gone into respite care, I'd met Paul for a drink in another local club. It was a Monday and he'd been away again for the weekend. Penny and I were sat with some friends of his, when one of his mates, Whally asked him;

"Had a good weekend, been up to see Janet, how is she?"

355

"Yes she's ok," Paul answered, obviously very nervous, continually shifting his position in the chair.

"And how's the kids?" Whally continued

"Yes, ok."

Well that confirmed that something odd was going on; by then I already knew the names of his ex wife and her children, although none of them was Janet. Paul looked at me but I'd pretended that I hadn't noticed anything and talked to Penny. I had really fallen for Paul but until that very moment I wasn't aware of just how deeply, my stomach was churning and I'd been relieved when he suggested an early night because he was tired. As we walked back to his flat I knew I was being very quiet but I was afraid to speak; I knew that if I asked the question, he would almost certainly answer and I wasn't sure I really wanted to know but I needed to find out the truth.

"You're quiet, is everything all right?" He asked when we got back to his,

"We'll talk in a minute!" I replied.

I turned the television on whilst he made the coffees, as had become the normal routine and Penny disappeared off to the toilet.

"Come on, tell me." He said,

"No, you tell me!" I said looking straight at him.

"What?"

"Who's Janet?"

"I didn't think you heard. I'm sorry, she's my partner!"

"A recent partner?"

"No, we've been together three years, she lives in Norwich, that's where I go but I do see my kids and grandchildren aswell."

"How could you, knowing how I feel, what I've been through? You should have told me!" I was beginning to lose it.

"I wanted to and I tried so many times but I love you too!"

"Yeah right!"

At that point everything came like a volcano to the surface and exploded from my eyes, all the anger, all the hurt, I couldn't speak and Penny came rushing in;

"God, what's going on?" She asked as I was putting my coat on in a terrible state. "What have you done to her? I only went to the fucking toilet!"

"Ask him, he's been seeing someone else!" I sobbed and it was all I could do to blub those words.

"Is that true?" Penny demanded.

356

"Yes," he answered, "but I never meant to hurt her. Jan, don't go!"

It was too late for that, I was leaving.

"Wait for me!" Penny shouted.

She was chasing after me at the same as she was calling Paul all the bastards under the sun, I was walking towards Ken's, I had to see him, he'd understand and make me feel better. Penny was pleading with me not to do anything stupid, asking me to come back and talk to Paul, while protesting that Ken would probably be in bed anyway;

"Besides, Ruth might be there. Let's go home!" She tried in vain.

"You go home if you want; I'm going to talk to Ken. At least he won't lie to me!"

And there, in that moment the decision was made, I knew as soon as I'd instinctively started towards Ken's, any turmoil or doubt as to who I should choose had vanished. I rang Ken as I walked;

"Can I come round?"

"Are you all right?" The concern clear in his voice. "Yes come round, I'll put the kettle on!"

"I'll be there in a minute!" I said and hung up.

He was waiting at the door and didn't even question me, he just put his arms around me and said;

"Coffee's waiting."

It was as if he knew what had happened between Paul and me and when I eventually calmed down I told him, with the help of Penny what I'd found out. It was difficult to understand why this man would tolerate me talking about another man and my feelings towards him without judgment or resentment. Ken told me that he didn't mind at all, that it was nice I'd thought of going to him, that I could talk to him about anything and that he was there for me. 'If only we'd got together all those years ago.' I thought but there was still the Ruth and Pete situation to contend with; I never wanted to be the other woman but I decided there and then that maybe, just for the week, I could give it a go, spend some time with Ken and take it one day at a time. I dozed off with my head on his lap and him stroking my hair, he was talking to Penny and the deep tones in his voice were so sexy and appealing, it was like music; I obviously had a thing for voices, Paul's soft Irish accent and Ken's deep manly tones. As the weeks past that voice was like a drug, I had to hear it and I'd phoned Ken at every opportunity, just so I could.

It was about six o clock in the morning when Penny and I got home and by the time we'd made some coffee, Pete was up.

"Where have you been, have you just come in?" He demanded,

"Yes!" I answered,

"That's it, I want a divorce!" He shouted

"Ok, you can have one," it was the first time I'd ever answered that threat and it felt good, "I'll find a solicitor first thing in the morning."

"You leave me no choice," he said, looking rather surprised,

"Yes, I know and as I said you can have a divorce, I'll see a solicitor as soon as I can."

Even Penny looked at me in disbelief but I felt calm and very calculated

"Are you really going to do that?" She asked,

"Yep!"

And I did, finally I had made the decision, after all the years of trying to revive another failed marriage, like flogging a dead horse, I finally admitted defeat and gave him what he'd wanted; why else had his things been packed for at least the previous ten years. I should have done it right from the start, instead of wasting my life and letting my children suffer all that he'd put them through. One thing I was sure of was that Michael would definitely be easier to handle, he'd been having tests around that time to find out what, if anything was wrong with his genes, a reason for why he was so backward, then I'd seen a story on G.M.T.V about a child who had very similar problems to Michael, so I took him to the doctor and even though the doctor had told me that he didn't think there was anything wrong, I'd persisted and he finally agreed to a referral. By that time Michael had been to the Assessment Centre three times for various tests and the results had come back with a problem but further tests were needed to be absolutely certain.

I rang and told Ken that I'd made the decision to divorce Pete and that I was going to see a solicitor.

"Come round if you want to," he said, "she's not here!"

So I did and everyday for the rest of the week. On the Thursday of that week, at six in the morning, almost as soon as Pete had gone to work I phoned Ken;

"I'll be round in a minute." I told him,

"I'll be waiting!" He replied.

It was wrong but for us it couldn't have felt more right, although the years of forced abstinence had taken its toll on the both of us and our first time was a complete failure. I felt so sorry for Ken, he kept apologising and even though I'd tried to convince him that it really didn't matter; that just being with him and laying together with his arms around me was enough; I'm sure he didn't believe me.

"I thought that's what you wanted?" he said.

It was but I'd also thought that it was what he'd expected... It's what all men wanted wasn't it? I made the mistake of telling him as much and he got upset that I'd felt that way, he didn't like the comparison and he really wasn't like all men. He then said that maybe he'd never be able to do it; perhaps it was because it had been over ten years but I reassured him that with all we'd both been through, it was hardly surprising.

I kept my appointment with the solicitor and the wheels were set in motion. The Solicitor said that if Pete didn't contest the divorce, it would take about three Months; citing irrevocable differences and an irreconcilable breakdown. It felt different somehow, more poignant when it was written in black and white and seeing the life I'd led with Pete, although it wasn't in great detail, it still hurt deeply. As I walked back to the car my eyes filled with tears; the memories of so many wasted years, of Dan, of Gary, of Pete, then there was Paul's behaviour and Ken's wife to consider. After that came memories of Mum, Dad and my baby Carl and in those few minutes walking to the car, my whole sorry, wasted life went whizzing through my head. 'What if I've got it wrong again?' I'd thought, 'What if Ken stayed with his wife? What right did I have to expect him to leave her anyway? Could I really live with the guilt of taking away her carer and what was the point?' Then my purpose, my logical side returned; my wonderful children were my reason, I had to hang in there for them, whatever the future held I'd always be there for them.

The first night that Ruth came back I had found it difficult to watch Ken back in his position as her carer, with her treating him as badly as before. Penny and I had been in the club for a while when Paul came in and wandered over to our table,

"Sit here if you want to" Penny said, offering him a chair away from me and he sat down.

"Hi, are you all right?" He asked.

I said nothing and Penny answered for me;

"I don't think she wants to talk to you!"

"I know you don't believe me, but I really am sorry." He'd persisted

I replied, forcing myself to answer;

"I'm used to it, I should have expected it!"

"Don't say that, I really meant what I said, I think the world of you."

"Well you can't have both of us; it's your choice pal!"

'Why did I say that?' I wondered, so far as I was concerned; the choice wasn't his to make anymore, then I'd thought that maybe I could use him like he'd used me; from the looks that both Penny and I had been getting from Ruth, it was obvious that she'd suspected something; 'I could use Paul to get her off the scent.' Besides, I knew that it would only be for a few weeks; Ken had said that his mind was made up already and he'd intended on leaving her anyway.

Pete was presented with the divorce petition and almost overnight became even more difficult to live with; he was still just as volatile as before but his depression became much more obvious which made it very difficult to continue with my stand, I even contemplated giving up, cancelling everything and going back to my sad existence with the thought that if I was to do as everyone else wanted, maybe I could retreat and gather my mental strength again. I was exhausted physically and mentally and had decided to resign from the club's committee but when they received my letter of resignation, although they accepted it, it was obvious that all, without exception were reluctant and that went someway to improving my self-esteem; I'd been under the impression that everyone had disliked me, especially as my association with Ken had come to the notice of several members, though no one was completely sure given my obvious association with Paul and it was very hard to keep up the pretence, even Paul had thought that everything was all right until I'd told him about Ken; more to hurt him than anything else. He couldn't understand why I'd picked Ken over him and said as much; mainly because of Ken's age.

"Age," I'd told him, "isn't an issue. Besides, he's only eight years older than me!"

I thought back to the Ken I'd known all those years before, when he'd just come out of the R.A.F. after twelve years service and he was always very smart but to look at him twenty years on, he was a shell of the man I remembered: His blazer was too short in the body and the sleeves, I had wanted so much to buy him a new one but I knew that he'd never have been able to explain it to Ruth. Then there was his hair; too long and swept across the top of his head to cover his bald spot. Paul was also ex R.A.F. having served twenty years and was very well turned out, the training, if nothing else had taught them both how to make the most of their appearance (although the care of Ruth had taken it's toll on Ken.) and both were without doubt gentlemen; evidently this was something that I found very appealing. I had with Nick, he hadn't been in the forces but still opened doors for me where ever we went and whilst these traits are a very big plus to me, the down side is the proud exterior that seems to come with it; the stiff upper lip and all emotions kept in check. Neither Paul or Ken were able to talk about their experiences, which for both of them had been extremely traumatic: Ken had been a medic and had a pilots licence, he'd told me that he'd seen things no one should see, as had Paul but neither of them would ever elaborate further; they didn't need to, the fear and sadness that was written on their faces was enough. I had even wondered, albeit briefly, whether part of Ken's shaking could've been attributed to those experiences, although I didn't push the point; one day perhaps he'd open up but I figured that I'd had enough to deal with at the time and that taking on that sort of information would've been too much for me to deal with anyway. It crossed my mind that I was doing my usual trick of looking for excuses to justify their behaviour and the treatment I was receiving. I knew one thing for sure; I couldn't keep up the facade for too long and Penny was also telling me that I should finish with Ken;

"It's obvious he isn't going to leave Ruth!" She said "He wants the best of both worlds. You would be better off staying with Paul and being his partner down here and Janet (Paul's partner in Norwich,) need never know!"

I considered the idea but I knew deep down that I'd never be able to accept such an arrangement; I was sick of playing second fiddle, always second best, trying to be all things to all people and never being important enough to anyone… I need to be the one and only in a mans life, no matter who it is.

By the middle of June I'd decided that enough was enough, I had to put a stop to it all. I'd backed away from Paul by not going to the club as much, which was fairly easy to do as I was no longer on the committee but equally that meant I didn't have to watch Ken and Ruth together. I arranged to meet Ken in a car park one Tuesday lunchtime;

"I've decided that it's maybe for the best if we called it a day. I don't think you're going to leave Ruth, you just want me to fill in the gaps, the duties she doesn't fulfil."
The hurt was almost unbearable, I had fallen deeply in love with him and it was so obvious that he felt the same and just as I'd expected him to he'd told me that he appreciated my decision and would respect it,

"I'm so sorry!" I said.
I couldn't control my tears as I watched such a big man brought to tears by me but I didn't know what else I could do, I had to try and move on.

"Are you going back to Paul?" Ken asked,

"No, I've done this to make things as easy as possible for you and Ruth and so that she doesn't know about us."

"Well she still thinks it's going on but she thinks its Penny!"

"This will put an end to that idea aswell then!"
As he walked away I fell apart, I was so sick of crying... It seems like I've spent most of my life in that state.

By the Thursday I so wanted to ring and make sure he was all right but avoided it, as was the case for most of the following week but by the Friday evening Penny wanted to go out and I had to admit that I was ready to face the world again. We went to the club thinking Paul would be away and that there wouldn't be a great deal on, we could have a quiet drink, just the two of us. We were wrong, Paul hadn't gone away and we ended up sat with him but as if that weren't enough, Ken was also there with his daughter Maria; I had met her at Ken's home one lunchtime, when Ruth had been at the M.S. Centre, I'll never forget her words to me;

"Pleased to meet you. You must be the one I have to thank for making my Dad so happy!"
I hadn't known quite what to say to that at the time but he certainly wasn't happy anymore. I managed to avoid talking to them and evaded their looks, though I couldn't help but notice how ill Ken was looking; I was sure he was going to collapse, or worse. 'Was I really responsible for that?' The thought must have been written on my face and Penny noticed my look,

"Don't look at them!" She said. "He'll get over it and if she says anything I'll put her straight!"

"No, you won't!" I put her straight. "You and I will definitely fall out if you say anything and I mean it Pen!"

Penny then spent long periods of the evening ignoring me but at the end of the evening, as I went to the toilet, she did her usual thing and followed. Maria walked in behind us;

"Why did you do it?" She questioned, "Do you know how hurt my Dad is?"

She went on to tell me how very worried she was about him and I really wanted to say that I was too, that I wanted him back and wanted to be with him forever but instead I said nothing.

"She's with Paul!" Penny stepped in.

"Is that true?" Maria asked.

I couldn't answer her, Penny did, again;

"Yes, that's what I said, so tell your Dad sorry but that's the way it is!"

It was all I could do to look at Maria

"I'm really worried about my Dad!" She pleaded.

So was I and about Maria and about all the hurt I'd caused.

"Come on Jan, we're going, Paul's waiting!" Penny said, pulling me towards the door. As we were walking out of the club, Ken had gone to the door to leave in front of me but had stopped and held the door open to let me go first;

"I'm sorry," he said, "I told Maria not to say anything."

"Its ok," I smiled at him, "I'll speak to you soon."

"Promise?"

"Yes, I promise I'll call you."

I watched him walk away again and Paul appeared;

"Are you up for a coffee?" He asked,

"No, I'm going home!" I told him,

"Oh come on," said Penny, "I am!"

"No! I'm going home!"

I'd made up my mind; I was going to do what I wanted for a change and all the way home Penny was digging at me saying things like:

"Your going back to him isn't you?" and "If you do, I don't want to know!"

That ended with me telling her to shut it, that I would do what I wanted to and that she really needed to mind her own business, which created even more stress but made me even more determined to keep my promise to Ken. I phoned him and his voice was like instant calm, almost hypnotic and even though the conversation

363

was quite tense and very emotional, I was even more certain that I should be with him, he seemed to sense my feelings and questioned;

"So, I'm not completely out of the running yet then?"

"I can't do this!" I said, "I just don't think that you'll ever leave her."

"I told you I will and I will"

"But I also don't want to be responsible for you leaving your wife!"

"You're not; I'm leaving her no matter what happens. I'd made the decision before I'd met you again and I told you this before!"

I resolved at that moment that only time would tell, in the meantime, I still needed to sort out my divorce and find suitable accommodation for Pete but by the first week of July, I could take no more: Verity had informed me that Mum was ill again, she had Jaundice, so I had phoned Mum and she made light of it, saying that she was on the mend. I explained that I'd tried to get over and see her but with everything else that was going on, I hadn't had the time and she said that she understood but also that she would like to see me, even just for an hour, so I agreed to go over on Saturday the 7th of July. Unfortunately, on that Morning I'd had arguments with both Pete and Penny, Michael was playing up, as was Matthew; although they were obviously responding to the atmosphere at home, I'd avoided seeing Ken that week aswell, even though Ruth was in respite again for the week and Paul was away too. I couldn't take anymore, I had to get away alone, I packed some things into a bag, I wasn't leaving for good, just the weekend, to where I didn't know, I just wanted to get in my car and drive.

"Don't go," said Penny, "you won't come back will you?"

"Yes I will!" I replied, "I won't leave my kids, its just all been too much!"

'I'll have to ring Mum and tell her I won't be able to get there again,' I thought but figured that she'd just have to deal with it; all the old resentments were there in the forefront of my mind and confronted with her at that moment, I was unsure whether I'd be able to contain it. I got in my car and drove, stopping a little way from Ken's home, I needed to phone him and tell him I was going:

"Stay where you are," he said, "I'll be there in a minute. If you're going, fair enough but I want to see you first."

I was reluctant but he persisted and I eventually gave in; I wanted to hear his opinion anyway, he was after all very wise, even with his own problems. He opened the door and got into the passenger seat;

"Ok," he said, "drive!"

"Where?" I asked,

"Wherever!"

We went to a café and chatted then we drove some more and ended up on the beach at Hengistbury Head, it was warm and relaxed, I laid over his lap and he sat stroking my head, Ruth was due back at about four o clock but he said;

"If I'm not there then I'm not there, you're more important!" I felt that he was more important too, more than all of the hurt I'd been feeling. At that moment we were just two people on a summer's day, sitting on the beach, completely in love and the whole world could've melted away. I knew I couldn't give him up and admitted that I loved him;

"I love you too!" He returned.

I dropped Ken off down the road from his home at about 3:45pm and then went home myself, knowing that if it hadn't been for him I would have left and gone somewhere, anywhere but he'd persuaded me that all would be all right.

"That was a short weekend then" Penny said, as I walked through the door

"You have Ken to thank for that!" I told her.

"Oh right, you've seen him then have you?"

"Yep and I'm going to continue to see him!"

She mumbled something about it being wrong, that I'd get even more hurt and then what about Ruth, all the same old things but sensing that it was falling upon deaf ears, she gave up.

Chapter 42

I arranged to call Ken on his mobile the following afternoon at half past two, just to let him know I was all right; it was nearer quarter to three by the time I managed to get around to it. We were chatting away about everything when at about three o'clock my phone started bleeping, someone was trying to get through, whoever it was persisted, so I told Ken I'd have to take it and ring him back. It was Verity;

"Mums gone!" She said.

"What?"

"She's dead!"

"Where are you?"

"At her flat, I've just found her."

"I'm on my way now!"

I hung up the phone and babbled to Penny;

"Mums dead and Verity needs me! Phone Ken, let him know and tell him that I'll talk to him later!"

And with that, I was out of the door and on my way in a state of shock and disbelief, I felt numb. Driving at speed I was at Mums within five minutes and Verity met me at the door;

"Where is she?" I asked,

"On the floor in the kitchen!"

Verity then explained that the paramedics had just left and that they'd told her Mum wasn't to be moved, that we had to wait for the doctor to come and certify her first and then the Coroner's Undertakers would come and collect her. I followed Verity into the flat to where Mum was laying; she was on her back with her body in the kitchen and her head in the hallway, her eyes were partially open and we almost had to step over her to get into the lounge. I hugged Verity and let her talk as I stared at my Mum just laid there on the floor: Verity said that she had rung Mum to tell her that she was going to be late. She explained how she thought that Mum must have been making herself a milk coffee at the time of death as the milk had been boiling over when Verity arrived, although Mum must have only just died because the milk didn't look to have been boiling long. Verity then told me that she had tried to give Mum the kiss of life, that she had been given instructions on how to resuscitate over the phone whilst the paramedics were en route; she said that she'd really tried but she couldn't revive her, that she was sorry and also that Mums mouth had bled; Verity thought that she must have banged her mouth as she fell.

"Have I got blood on my mouth?" She asked,

"No, you're ok!" I told her.

Mum, my Mum, was gone and I'd let her down; I hadn't been there when she'd wanted to see me, I had known that something was wrong, I'd had that feeling. I would never be able to put things right now; she'd never know how I truly felt, how much I really loved her. Poor Verity, with all that she'd had to deal with already, now this. I told her that I was meant to have seen Mum the day before;

"Mum knew you had problems," she said, "its ok, she understood."

… But it wasn't ok!

It was over an hour before the doctor arrived, but his arrival did break the intense emotional state we were in; neither of us had been able to bring ourselves to make a cup of tea, what with having to step over Mum to do it and everything. When we opened the door, it was to an Asian doctor and he was difficult to understand, although we both caught his first words to us: Looking down at Mum he said,

"Oh, I'm so sorry; it must be terrible to finding Mummy like that. Leave
Mummy where she is, please don't move her, you mustn't move Mummy!"

Verity and I looked at each other and had to walk away for fear that the doctor would notice us smiling.

"Who the hell is Mummy?" I whispered and Verity laughed.

"Can you imagine what Mum would say being called Mummy?" She asked.

We were trying desperately to contain ourselves as the doctor continued, saying that although the duty Coroner had been called, it was a Sunday and he couldn't say how long it would be before he'd arrive.

"Even so, please don't move Mummy, ok thank you" He finished and left.

Verity saw him out and we both laughed again, looking at Mum I said;

"She really would have loved that one!"

Then the phone rang and it was Dorset police, the controller asked;

"Would you like someone to come and sit with you until the coroner arrives?"

I was puzzled, 'what had it to do with them?' The controller explained that as it was a sudden death, they had to call and take details; I quizzed Verity, who looked just as puzzled as I was and shook her head.

"No, we're ok!" I said.

I was then told that someone would be along shortly to take details anyway. I put the phone down and turned to Verity;

"Apparently it's a formality? You wait, that'll be the next thing they'll think we, or at least one or the other of us has murdered her!"

'That would be the ultimate joke,' I thought, 'Mum may finally get her own back on me yet!' When the police arrived, Verity told them what had happened and we both breathed a sigh of relief when they left and we weren't handcuffed.

It was half past seven in the evening, more than four hours after Mum had died when the coroner finally arrived. It had been difficult to sit there with my poor Mum, lying on the floor and once or twice, when I'd looked at her I could have sworn that she was breathing. Suddenly, with the coroner there, it was so much worse; they were taking her away forever. Verity and I stood together, looking out of the lounge window, unable to watch whilst they put our Mum into a body bag, I kept thinking; 'Please don't zip it up, she won't be able to see!' But of course they have to. They also took Mums jewellery off too; her wedding ring and her cross and chain, something else they have to do I suppose and handed it all to Verity, Mum had always worn those things and it suddenly made me angry; it felt to me like they were stripping the corpse, though I knew it was a silly thought.

"Mum always said she'd leave this flat, feet first!" I said to Verity,

"Yes and she got her wish."

We watched out of the window as they loaded the black body bag into the back of the black van and the tears were rolling down my face… I'd dreamt that scene so many times and I'd known it was coming but somehow, in my mind, I'd dismissed it; I felt that I was too young to lose my Mum, 'Not my Mum, that won't happen for years!' But it did happen, it had happened and why did I feel like this? I'd never really had a relationship with her but I wanted her, right then, so we could make amends, I wanted to tell her I was so sorry I'd been such a disappointment, all I'd needed was five minutes and then I heard her voice in my head;

"Pull yourself together and don't be so daft!"
She then told me that she was back with Jim now and that it was where she'd wanted to be after all; she'd always said that she had one bad husband and one good one and I had always resented the way she'd spoken about my Dad but I was so glad when she had found happiness with Jim, he was a good man and I know that I'd got on better with him than Verity had.

It seemed very strange in that flat, so empty without Mum there. Verity and I only stayed for a few minutes and even that was almost more than we could stand, we decided to lock up and come back the following day to face it together, that we would handle all the arrangements side by side and that we would go and tell Aaron together too. I knew he'd take it badly because through everything that had happened, he'd always been closer to Mum than Dad, I worried about the effect this would have on him. We weren't close and hadn't spoken for years but he was still my brother and I thought; 'if I feel like this, then he'll probably feel the same,' I wouldn't have wished that feeling on anyone. Then there was Dad, all right he and Mum weren't together but I knew he'd be devastated just the same, I remembered something he'd always said;

"Me and your Mother may not have got on but she was a proper lady!"
That was very true, Mum always was exactly that but Verity had had nothing to do with Dad so I knew I'd have to tell him alone. I hugged Verity;

"I'll meet you here tomorrow morning. Are you going to be all right?"

"Yes, you?"

"Yes I'm ok. Ring if you need me!"
Poor Verity looked so lost; her life had revolved around Mum for all those years, looking after her everyday as she had, I sat and watched her drive away, before I drove in the opposite direction.

Pete had already been told and had phoned me whilst I was still at Mum's flat;

"Is there anything I can do?" He'd asked.

"No, just see to your own dinner and the kids!" I'd told him. While thinking; 'what can he do? He's less than useless in a crisis anyway!' Then he asked if I wanted dinner and I thought; 'what a bloody ridiculous thing to say with my Mum's body lying here and feeling as sick as I am. Yes, why not let's have some steak and chips maybe a bottle of champagne!' I thought it but I didn't say it;

"No thanks!" I said, "I couldn't think of eating right now!"

"What time will you be back?" He Asked,

"How the hell should I know?" I snapped. "Depends when they collect her, they didn't give us a time!"

"I only asked!"

"Yes, ok, see you whenever!" I finished and hung up.

Penny came out to meet me when I'd pulled up outside home, I told her that I was expecting Pete to have a pop at me and I found myself quite surprised when he didn't;

"Are you ok?" He asked

"Yes, I'm fine!" I snapped again, "I've got calls to make!" He walked away and I felt a little guilty, thinking that I shouldn't really have treated him like that, after all; he was feelings Mum's loss too. Penny told me that she'd phoned Ken and that he'd said to phone him as soon as I could, never mind that Ruth was there, his only concern was me and hearing that made me feel a little better; I knew that it wasn't just something he'd said to make me feel better or win some brownie points, he really did mean it and I wanted so much to speak to him, to hear his voice but I had to call my Dad first: The phone rang a few times before he answered and after the initial hello's and how are you's, I said;

"I've got some bad news."

"Oh, what's that then?" He asked,

"Mum's died!"

"Oh my god!" Then silence,

"Dad?" I said,

"Yes, I'm still here."

"Are you all right?"

"Yes, it's just a shock. What did she die of?" He questioned,

"Heart attack we think, we won't know for certain until after the post mortem."

As I told him of the circumstances, he was relaying the information to Diane and by her reaction and tone of voice; she actually seemed concerned.

"Is Verity all right?" Dad asked,

"Yes, she will be, we are sorting things out together."

"Good and what about Aaron, does he know?"

"I'm going with Verity to see him tomorrow."

"Let me know if you need anything and keep me informed."

370

"I will, as soon as I know anymore."

"Thanks for letting me know Janie."

As I put the phone down, I knew by his voice that Dad was deeply shocked; at just sixty-seven, Mum was rather young. I picked up the phone and started dialling again;

"Who are you calling now?" Pete asked,

"Ken!" I replied,

"Who's Ken?" He quizzed,

"A friend!"

I dialled the number and the soothing voice was there, sounding really concerned for me;

"Just say the word and I'll be there!" He'd told me.

I'd have loved to have been able to say; 'I need you now,' but I couldn't without making more problems for myself so instead I said;

"I'll be in touch as soon as I can!"

Although I'd, once again had to explain the circumstances; something I found myself having to do numerous times over the following days, all the while I felt I had to keep control. Verity had informed Mums brother, sister and our cousin, who all lived in Cornwall; after all, I'd had nothing much to do with any of them over the years anyway. Pete had told the kids and in one way I was grateful but in another I resented him; it was my job to tell them, not his and I was supposed to be there to gauge they're responses: They were understandably upset but unlike Verity's kids they had never been that close to Mum. Surprisingly, it was Matthew who took it the worst, especially given the way that Mum and Verity had treated him over the years: They had always said things like; "he was odd" and "he was too up himself" but his reaction proved something that I'd always said; far from being totally insensitive to anyone else, he was quite the opposite; so sensitive to everyone that he'd had to remain aloof, giving the impression of disinterest to protect his own vulnerability.

As agreed, I met Verity at Mum's flat early the next morning, preferring not to go in alone, she had waited outside for me to arrive; I don't think that going in there alone was something that I could have done either. The image of Mum, just lying there on that floor was so vivid in my mind that I was sure she'd still be there and as we walked through the front door, a shiver went through my body and it felt like some part of Mum's spirit was still there: I was sure I could feel her watching and I dreaded going through her things; the cup with her half made coffee, the milk pan, everything just as she'd left it. Verity and I decided to leave again and go to Aaron's first, thinking; 'maybe this will all be easier to deal with later!'

My brother lives in a large bungalow on about two acres of land, at the very bottom of the land there are stables converted into offices where he runs his car business and his cars that are for sale are on the grounds, in front of the stables. There have always been odd shifty characters working for Aaron, for as long as I can remember and they've always had the knack of making you feel uncomfortable and as we drove down the driveway one of these characters was watching us, obviously nervous at an 'unannounced visitor.' As we pulled up by the offices, he tried to ignore us;

"Excuse me, is Aaron about?" I asked,

"No, he's out," he replied, "don't know when he'll be back!"

"We need to speak to him, we're his sisters!"

"Oh," his whole attitude changed, "um, he should be back in a minute, I'll ring him now!" He then disappeared into the office, reappearing a few minutes later; "Aaron said can you hang on, he's on his way and should be here in about ten minutes."

"Thanks!"

Verity and I had a look at some of the cars because Verity had said that she'd needed a new one and as I was looking around at the property, estimating it's worth, I couldn't help thinking how it's said that crime doesn't pay; 'well,' I thought, 'he certainly didn't get all this from hard work!' Then a large, black Mercedes came down the driveway and the man we'd spoken to said;

"Here's Aaron now!"

The car stopped and Aaron got out;

"All right then?" He asked, "how you doing?" He looked puzzled,

"We've got some bad news." I said, "Mum's died!"

"Oh shit!" His expression showed immediately how he felt but just as quickly, the barrier went up; his protective mechanism.

"Just a minute," he said, "I've got to speak to him." Pointing at the man that we'd spoken to, who was back working on a car, Aaron went over, gave him some instructions and walked back towards us, his barrier now well in place; "How did it happen?" He asked and Verity explained the details. "Well, if there's anything I can do, let me know." He said.

"We've got to make the funeral arrangements but we won't know anything until later." I told him

"Did she have any money saved to pay for it?" He questioned,

"Don't know yet, she never made a will. We'll have to go through her papers and then we will know more." Said Verity,

"It doesn't matter anyway," he said, "I'll sort it, just tell me how much and keep in touch ok!" He gave Verity his phone number, "Ring me later!"

We agreed and he walked away, he was so unable to let us see his pain but as he walked away it was so obvious.

Verity and I went back to Mums flat again and systematically cleaned and sorted through each room; organising this, cancelling that and we briefly discussed which undertaker we would use, although nothing was decided and when we'd phoned the Coroner, he had asked who we were considering and to who Mum's body was to be released. He'd also told us that Mum had died from a massive heart attack, that she hadn't known anything about it and that it had been instantaneous, no pain and it had been a relief to know that she hadn't suffered; not then anyway, although she really had suffered in those last few months. During the ten days that lead up to the funeral, Verity and I shed a lot of tears and talked more than we ever had before. There were a lot of funny, almost farcical moments too, where we were unable to stop ourselves from laughing. One such issue was the loss of Mums body:

The Coroner had had to keep Mum's body, to do further tests, so three days after her death we'd phoned the Coroner to find out if Mums body was to be released, only to be told that she had already been released. When we asked where Mum had gone, the poor woman on the phone said;

"The undertakers!"

"Which undertaker?" Asked Verity,

"Oh, I don't know! I'm so sorry; could you ring us back in a few minutes? I'll have to find out!"

Verity put the phone down, turned to me and said;

"They've lost her!"

"What?" I questioned,

"They've lost Mum's body!" She answered,

"They can't have!" I was stunned

"They have! Either that or she's got up and walked out!"

"I wouldn't be surprised"

I could imagine Mum, looking down and laughing; 'this would really appeal to her sense of humour.' I thought and then the phone rang;

"We've found her!" Said the girl on the phone,

"Oh good!" I responded, "Where is she?"

"She's gone to the agreed undertaker." The girl said,

"We didn't agree to anyone, which one?" I asked.

She gave me the name followed by;

"They picked her up at about nine this morning."

"Really? Ok, thanks!"

I hung up the phone and turned to Verity;

"They must be desperate for work body snatching."

Verity contacted the undertaker;

"I believe you have my mother?" She questioned,

"Hand over the receiver," I said, "Should we pay the ransom...? Depending on how much it is of course!"

We couldn't control our laughter and I dread to think what the undertakers must have thought: 'Those poor grieving daughters, who are laughing hysterically down the phone?' We made an appointment for the undertaker to call at mums flat two days later, then phoned and told Aaron; we'd felt that he should be there and have a say in the arrangements and he agreed to be at the meeting. Two days later and Aaron turned up at Mum's flat with a briefcase and when he sat down, he put it beside him on the floor. Shortly after, the undertaker turned up with a similar briefcase and after shaking our hands, placed his on the floor next to Aaron's. Verity and I couldn't take our eyes off the cases; dreading they would get mixed up at the same time as finding the situation very amusing; we had no idea what was in Aaron's case but knowing him, as we did, the contents would most likely disturb the undertaker for life and he was a very solemn man, he had to be I suppose. The undertaker bent down and picked up his briefcase; 'Phew, that was lucky!' I thought and Aaron, now realising why Verity and I were smiling, smiled too, much to the undertaker's confusion but he carried on with the arrangements, picking the coffin, the lining and then the cost. At that point Aaron picked up his briefcase and I thought; 'My God, he's going to shoot him!' But he opened the case and said;

"Well I think the quote is reasonable."

Verity obviously knew what I was thinking but smiling she agreed;

"Yes, that's not bad."

Aaron opened the briefcase fully and it was full of money; bundles held together with elastic bands.

"I'll pay you now!" He said as he took out a bundle of fifty pound notes.

"No, no, we will invoice you afterwards!" Said the undertaker, quite startled.

"Oh ok," said Aaron, "well send the bill here then and I'll pay it."

"Not to my address!" Verity interrupted,

"Certainly." Finished the undertaker.

The poor man couldn't get out quick enough and Aaron left almost immediately too.

It was decided that the wake would be held at Mums flat and that we would hold onto the keys for another week to clear it before giving them back to the council. I spoke to Ken, keeping him up to speed and as he had a van, or rather mini bus with a lift on the back for a wheelchair, I'd asked him if he would be available to help us clear the larger items of furniture and he said he would. Verity wasn't keen on my association with ken and voiced her disapproval but as usual, could give no reason for it except to say that I could do better; I didn't think so and to my mind he was everything that I wanted and all that I needed, although I didn't invite him to the funeral because Pete had wanted to come; he said it was to pay his respects and support me but I know whose support I'd have preferred. Penny came too, she'd liked my Mum and Mum her, although she'd always felt that Penny was a bad influence on me and a constant reminder of my days in care. Aaron turned up, as did all of Mums family and whilst they acknowledged my presence, they were so obviously over the moon to see Aaron… There it was again; confirmation of my position in the family. There were also a number of people, friends of Mum's, who I'd never met but who Verity seemed to know well, they were telling her how sorry they were at her losing her Mum;

"You must be devastated!"

Yes, she was and so was I but I had my children; they were all there, all of them very smart and well turned out in their suits and ties and whenever I looked at them I felt so proud. Matthew had chosen to sing part of a hymn, solo but he'd struggled so hard to sing it and when everyone joined in he fell apart, unable to hold back the tears any longer, which in turn set the tears flowing from all my children and me. I knew mum would have been proud of him and told him

so, although Verity had said that she'd known it was a bad idea, I
on the other hand felt it wasn't, not to Matthew and I told her so.

The wake went quite well; lots of small talk and whilst it
was nice for so many people to have turned up, it was a relief when
they left. Aaron's girlfriend and both of his children came and just
like mine; they were a credit to him. His daughter, a lovely child,
was about eight at the time and his son was four and Aaron was so
obviously proud of them, a doting father. I'd never really seen this
side of Aaron and I was quite surprised by it; I shouldn't have been,
our upbringing had somehow made the importance of our children
so much more precious. Once the older friends and relatives had
left, Aaron disappeared to the Off Licence and came back with bottles of every sort of alcohol and beer imaginable;

"I didn't know what everyone drinks, so I bought one of
each!" He said

"A man after my own heart!" Said Penny, a little nervously.
She was nervous of Aaron, mainly given his reputation and he
knew it, making the most of it and Penny in her amusing way,
played the game, which had amused me no end; especially when
Aaron dropped his mobile phone, making no attempt to pick it up
Penny looked at him and then at the phone, Aaron looked at her;

"You've dropped your phone!" She said,

"Yes!" He grinned at her,

"Aren't you going to pick it up?" She asked,

"No, you can pick it up!" He told her.

It was right by his foot, she cautiously bent down, keeping an eye
on his expression; still the mischievous grin that I remembered so
well, that usually came right before he'd give me a friendly whack.
She picked up the phone and handed it to him;

"Thanks," he said, "about time! I wondered how long it
would take you."

"Cheeky bastard!"

And so the banter continued. Two of Aaron's male friends turned
up, they worked for him and they'd had a job in London but had
got lost on the way back; Aaron was giving them directions over
the phone and calling them all the 'tossers' and 'idiots' under the
sun, much to everyone's amusement but that was his way; he paid
them and they did as he said, like a Mafia Godfather. It was obvious, just by looking at them that they were dubious characters and
when listening to the stories of drugs, guns and prisons, it left no
doubt in anyone's mind, it also left no doubt as to the respect that

my brother commanded and as if that weren't enough; my boy's were impressed by him and the last thing I wanted was for my sons to get involved in his dealings. Lorna seemed to get away with telling him, albeit jokingly what she thought:

"Chauvinist pig! You can buy me a car, it wouldn't hurt you, and you are after all my uncle!"

'That's my girl,' I thought, 'tell it as it is!' And by his amusement and attitude towards her; he definitely appreciated her stand, he even offered to make sure that she passed her driving test;

"No thanks, I'm quite capable of doing it myself!" She told him,

"Don't say I didn't offer!" He laughed.

When he left he kissed me goodbye; something that he'd never, ever done before and I certainly hadn't expected… Maybe he's gone soft in his old age!

We emptied the flat and divided Mums belongings; "Do you want this?" And "Do you want that?" Ken moved everything to either Verity's or my home and took all the rubbish to the tip. We gave him a couple of mum's disability aids thinking that perhaps Ruth would be able to make use of them and Ken said that when he'd given them to her she'd said thank you but I found that hard to imagine.

Verity and I went to the undertakers the following week to collect Mums ashes. Mum had often joked about her ashes and about where they should be placed:

"Pack them in a rocket and send them up in the sky. They'll explode all over the town!"

We had discussed it with Aaron and we agreed that the firework thing was a little impractical, then he told us we could take his boat out and sprinkle the ashes in the sea off of Bournemouth beach, all that he asked was that we let him know when we wanted to do it. On the way to pick up the ashes, Verity had bought two Danish pastries for us to have with a coffee. She had the cakes and Mums ashes on her lap and she decided to take a look at the ashes; which were contained in a dark green plastic container, just like a quality street jar. Unfortunately the window was open slightly and as she unscrewed the lid, a gust of wind blew a small amount of ashes all over her and the cakes. I knew there was no way that I'd be able to eat mine after that but it didn't stop Verity; she ate hers and as she picked off the worst of it she said;

"It's a bit crunchy!" Followed by, "Well, that's one way to get rid of them, eat them!"
We both laughed and it seemed that each time we had to deal with something traumatic, Mum somehow had a hand in it and brought the humour in, leaving Verity and I convinced that she was still there somewhere.

In the years since her death I've had many times of tears and dreams of her, each time she seems to get through in particular a song that was played so often during our week away at the holiday camp: 'Reach for the Stars' by S Club 7. Mum had sat in her wheelchair and each time the line; 'reach for the stars' was sung, she'd raised her arms in the air and laughed... I can visualise that now and gradually that memory is replacing the image of her lying on that floor, I still hear her voice and see her face as I do with Lou and it may seem to the average person that I'm completely mad but I'm sure they are still with me, with the added bonus that even though in her life I felt that Mum was never there; I only have to think of her now and she is.

Chapter 43

The bill for the funeral arrived and Verity spoke to Aaron, he also agreed to sell her a car too. So we arranged to go out and pick up the car and collect the money for the funeral at the same time but we got there to find the place surrounded by police and no one would tell us anything, other than they were searching the house and the out buildings and that Aaron had been arrested; we were given no idea as to why, or where he was being held and wouldn't find out for some weeks. The property was closed and surrounded for two days and that was that; the funeral costs had to be settled from the small amount of money that Mum had left in her bank account and her ashes; they would have to wait and to this day they still sit on Verity's fire place, in that same green container, although, after a little deliberation the police did allow Verity to take the car, believing that she'd paid for it. We were very worried about Aaron's children and the effect that all this would have on them but we needn't have been; they were safe with Aaron's girlfriend and their Grandmother, in Spain and they'd had been out of the way when it had all happened. We then heard that the whole thing had been drug related; something we found very hard to believe, Aaron may have been a lot of things but a drug dealer was never one of them.

As promised I'd kept my Dad informed of everything, including Aaron's arrest; he didn't come to Mum's funeral, saying that he felt it was for the best and I respected his decision. I decided that I should make more of an effort to speak to him regularly, after all he was the only parent that I had left and I knew that I couldn't bare to lose him aswell, I even told him about my plans to divorce Pete and why.

Pete seemed to try and settle in again after Mum's death and I'd had to tell him that her death had changed nothing and that he still had to go. It didn't appear to make any difference;

"There's no hurry," he said, "I think I should stay and support you!"

I had even introduced him to Ken: Ken had been delivering some of Mum's things for me and was a little apprehensive at the thought of meeting him but, just as I'd thought would be the case; Pete took no notice.

Things between Ken and Ruth deteriorated and I knew that he was reaching the end of his tether; mentally he could take no more but I'd decided to maintain my distance, still unconvinced that he would leave her. I'd had a lot of trouble deciding if it were his insecurities or my own; so much had happened that my emotions had been shaken to the core but I felt like I was adding to his problems. He'd been an absolute rock for me but meeting Pete seemed to have changed him a little too and I'd thought that maybe he was feeling the same way, we still spoke regularly on the phone but I knew that he needed space to make a decision for himself, regardless of the future; if any future existed for us. Penny and I were shopping when the phone rang, it was Ken;

"I've left her, I'm at Maria's and she has said that I can live with her for a while. Will you come and see me?"

"I'll be there in a few minutes!" I told him.

Penny was annoyed and started protesting, saying that I shouldn't go and that he would be back with Ruth the next day but I just ignored her; Ken had sounded very shaky and I knew that I had to get there, to be with him as soon as I could. We arrived at Maria's and the meeting was a little strained but then Penny wasn't about to make it easy, especially given her last conversation with Maria and her disapproval of the relationship. Maria's three girls had been thrilled to see me though and seemed to have accepted me like I was already part of the family: Ken had three children, all grown up and ten grandchildren and although they were beautiful children, I was aware that they'd be part of the Package. Just a few months earlier I'd joked with my own children, telling them that I was now prepared to be a Nanny and how nice it would be 'but this,' I thought, 'is a lot to take on board' and I jokingly said;

"I should be more careful what I wish for!"

In the weeks that followed I spent every possible moment with Ken; going out in his mini bus, walking along the beach or going to Maria's and at weekends he'd meet Penny and I at the club and share a taxi home. Invariably, Ruth was sat on the corner of the road, opposite the club, shouting abuse as we'd climbed into the taxi at the end of the evening, I'd always sit in the front, Penny and Ken in the back. Ruth really did believe that it was Penny who was seeing him; which was all the more funny because Ken had said;

"If Penny was the last woman on earth, I still wouldn't be interested!"

Penny in turn had said pretty much the same.

At the end of August I found somewhere for Pete to live: I'd spoken to an American friend called Scott, who had been my neighbour until he'd split up with his wife the year before; she'd thrown him out and I had put him up for a while, helped him to get back on his feet and even helped him to arrange a mortgage, he was now returning the favour by offering Pete a room. Pete wasn't particularly keen on the idea but the offer had been made and I was determined that he should go. Penny too had said that she felt it was time she left again and I didn't argue: There had been a great deal of tension between us around that time; what with her disapproval of my relationship with Ken, my newly found ability to say 'no' to her and in turn, her inability to change my mind, so when a second room became available at Scott's, Penny accepted it. Besides, Lee and Carrie were keen to come and live with me: Lee had told me that it was because he'd had enough of sleeping in a single bed with Carrie but there wasn't enough room for a double bed in her room, although I think the real reason was that he felt I needed looking after and if that belief would bring my son home, so be it and on the 7th of September, 2001, Pete and Penny moved out and Lee and Carrie came home: It was another one of those hectic days, moving people around, although as had become usual; Ken offered to move the furniture and everyone's belongings in his mini bus and without him it would probably have taken two or three days. Even with his help, it was well into the early hours of my birthday before we'd finished and we were sure that Maria would most certainly be asleep and Ken didn't have a key, so I'd told him that he should stay with me. He was so exhausted that he was asleep in no time; I got into bed beside him and was also asleep, almost before my head had touched the pillow. Maybe not the best idea I've ever had, especially as Michael came in at about 9am with a birthday card from Pete, who was also in the house. I went downstairs and Pete was apparently angry, so I'd tried explaining why Ken had been there but he wasn't about to listen, I then got annoyed with myself for even attempting to justify myself to him.

"I don't have to answer to you!" I said, "We don't have and haven't had a marriage for months, years even, remember? Besides, you only lived here because there was nowhere else to go, now leave your key and get out!"

At that moment I felt quite sorry for Pete and found it very hard to stick to my guns; especially as three weeks prior, (a week before his Dads and Michaels birthday,) his Dad had died, which had been another reason for waiting before making Pete leave and another excuse for him to try and stay, although he'd openly admitted that he wasn't really that upset. It was also another funeral to go to and I'd told Pete that I didn't want to go, given the circumstances but he'd pleaded with me, saying that he hadn't told his Mum we were getting a divorce and that she'd had enough on her plate at the time, I liked his Mum and for once had to agree with him; it would have been far too much for her. Even so, it had been difficult to keep up with the pretence, especially with his sister treating me like a leper: I really wanted to tell her that she'd never have to see me again and how her treatment of me at the hospital had confirmed in my mind that my decision to divorce her brother was exactly the right thing to do, 'I would be well out of that family!' A thought I conveyed to Pete on the way home and by the time he left the house, he was shouting the odds, which was something that Michael didn't need to witness but he was surprisingly understanding; he too had grown up and unbeknown to me until then, had agreed with my decision to get Pete out, although he did say;

"He's still my Dad and I want to see him regularly."
And of course I agreed, re-iterating what I'd said to the others all those years ago when Dan and I had parted;

"We, your Dad and I, may not love each other, or be able to live with each other but we both love you very much." Then added something that I didn't say to the others but then it only really applied to Michael anyway; "You are my baby and the only good thing that came out of my marriage to your Dad!"
I decided there and then that if Ken were agreeable, he'd just as well move in with me, especially now that the accusation had been made. We had agreed that we still needed to be a just as reserved as before in the social club and allow people to believe that he was still living with his daughter and even though he kept some of his belongings at my home, he didn't completely move in until the November, at about the same time as Penny moved out of Scott's and back to Blandford, so she could look after her parents. Then Carrie announced that she was pregnant; I was indeed going to be a grandmother… Where did all the years go?

I knew my home would be chaotic with all of us living there but it was suddenly a happy place to be. Mum's death was still raw and I'd cried nearly every day but for the most part, I was quietly happy; the arguments and bickering had stopped and there was no Pete or Penny, trying to tell me how I should live my life, even Matthew and Michael seemed to get on better together. Ken was such a support to me too and he was looking much better and healthier than he did before, his shaking had all but stopped and his children had accepted me too; I'd been a little concerned that if they didn't like me then Ken would change his mind and when I'd told him how I was feeling he'd said that he too felt the same insecurities, I then told him that I didn't want to come between him and his children but he said that it wouldn't happen, that he was with me, where he would always be, where he should have been for the past twenty odd years and that he was madly in love with me; That was a little hard for me to accept at first, even though I knew I loved him: Strong, intelligent, funny, romantic and loved children just as I did, a family man.

Ken's eldest daughter had invited us to stay for a weekend; she lived in Army accommodation near Ipswich and it was the perfect chance for me to get to know her, so we accepted the invitation and for the first time I felt able to leave Matthew and Michael without any worry for their safety. I knew that they'd be safe with Lee and Carrie.

Lovemaking had never really been a priority but that too was just about perfect, even after that first disastrous encounter. Money was the only issue we had; we didn't have any. Ken had been on benefits as a carer for years but somehow it didn't seem that important... Not yet anyway. He had signed on as unemployed and had to take a refresher course for his H.G.V. Licence but in the mean time, he'd spent his days mending and re-doing my D.I.Y and decorating; I'd done my best over the years but it wasn't perfect, mostly nails holding everything together and Ken being a perfectionist set about changing nails for screws. It was difficult for me to accept his help and I felt pretty redundant, although I did help with the decorating and most of the painting was down to me.

That Christmas had been the best in so many years, the only down side was that Pete had seen a solicitor and I'd had to prove, by way of bank statements that he hadn't paid a penny into the house, he'd also attempted to claim back thirteen years worth of rent but that stopped when I'd pointed out that had he lived anywhere else during that time, he would have had to pay rent anyway, which was obviously non-returnable. He was also trying to manipulate me through Michael, who for the first few months had gone to stay at Pete's every other weekend, unfortunately Michael would become very difficult to handle for a few days after each visit but at least he still had the contact. It was around that time that Michael was confirmed as having an Autistic Spectrum Disorder: 'Aspects of Aspergers' and it was a relief to finally find out what the problem was, although my health had taken another dive with the panic attacks becoming far more frequent, coupled with a deep depression and I'd found it very hard to understand why. It was true that Mum's death must have taken its toll, as had the break up with Pete and Ruby was also still causing us problems because Ken had started divorce proceedings and she was refusing to let him have any of his belongings but then; Ken's kids, his Mum and both his sisters had accepted me and my children, which meant that Ken and I had a lot to look forward to and the icing on the cake was that my first Grandchild was due in the June, so to me, my being ill was totally illogical. Once again I went to see the doctor and he told me that he was sure it was the menopause, in addition to the stresses of forty-four years worth of heartache that was like a weight which had been suddenly lifted from my shoulders; my life had been like a drug, a habit suddenly taken away and the after effects were like that of going cold turkey, whatever the reason, it felt no less debilitating. Ken as ever was my support, he sat the refresher course for his H.G.V. Licence and passed it with flying colours and found work almost as soon as he had, Lee too was working and everything in the garden was rosy but I was still looking for a flaw in my life, thinking; 'this is all too good to be true,' forever waiting, as it seemed for the bottom to fall out of my world, again... For the last four years, the struggle has continued.

There was still much fighting over a settlement with Pete: After promising that he'd never want anything from our home, he decided to change his mind and demanded over twenty thousand pounds but finally settled at £7000, that was on the 1st of June, 2002. I couldn't afford to pay him off without re-mortgaging and I certainly couldn't have raised the capitol from my income alone, so Ken offered to put his name on the mortgage aswell and again I was apprehensive; 'What if he decided to walk away and take his share too? Not only that, he would have to give up his rights to re-housing!' It all felt a little bit too final but I really didn't feel that I had any other choice; either lose my home or take the risk? Then

Ken told me that once we were both free, he wanted us to get married and promised that he wasn't going anywhere ever. So there it was, papers signed and Pete gone, on paper anyway.

By then Pete had all but stopped seeing Michael, not since his new girlfriend had threatened Michael anyway: Michael had come home from one of his weekends with Pete, looking absolutely ly terrified and at first he'd been afraid to tell me why but I'd persisted, as I always have and finally he told me everything; she had told Michael that if he was to say anything about her or her life, to me, then his life wouldn't be worth living, that she would hunt me down and hurt me and then she'd get him. He then told me that he was frightened for me and I promised him that there was nothing she could do, to him or to me and that he should never be afraid to tell me anything. Up until that threat, he and all of my children had never been afraid to tell me anything and that I believe is the reason for our being so close. I was seething and confronted Pete;

"I will hunt her down! Nobody threatens my children!" Something that he should have been well aware of; I'm like a lioness with her cubs. The next thing I knew a solicitor's letter had arrived: Pete wanted to fight me for the custody of Michael on the grounds that I was an unfit mother; he'd claimed that Michael was left to walk the streets alone, until all hours and the whole thing would have been almost laughable had it not been so serious. The accusation was soon dispelled after my solicitor had spoken to Michael, proved Pete's story to be a fabrication and then written to Pete's solicitors telling them as much; the letter included a statement from Michael's school and a record of all the visits Pete had made to the school, his threatening behaviour and his abuse of the staff. Pete dropped the case almost immediately and I knew that he was afraid of me and of Ken but he still needed to try and control my life, whether through Michael, or the solicitor's, although I'm also pretty sure that he was becoming aware that it wasn't working and that he was losing at every turn.

On June the 11th, 2002, quite late in the evening, Carrie's contractions started; my first Grandchild was on the way and I was so excited, as was Ken. Lee and Carrie headed off to the hospital at about eleven o' clock, with instructions for Lee to phone me as soon as the baby was born. Ken and I waited and dozed, then in the early hours of Wednesday the twelfth of June, 2002, at about four thirty, the phone rang;

"Well?" I questioned,

"Yes, she's had a girl! Eight pounds ten ounces, born at ten past four."

He went on to tell me that mother and baby were well and I could hear that he was tired but his pride was so obvious in his voice, that I was reduced to tears, Ken laughed at me. 'My little boy a daddy,' I thought, 'me a Grandmother!' Or 'Nanny' as I've become known as, Carrie's mum is 'Grandma.' Carrie's mum, Rose is lovely; I've liked her and gotten on with her since the day we met. Lee had told me that he thought she was like me; completely mad,

"And funny with it!" I added.

Rose was divorced from Carrie's Dad, so at Christmas and every other celebration I invited her to join us. By the time the baby was born she was pretty much part of the family and we phoned to congratulate each other on the birth;

"Hello Grandma!" I said,

"Hello Nanny!" She replied.

Did we feel old? Yes we did. It was agreed that Ken and I would pick Carrie and the baby up from Poole hospital and transfer them to Bournemouth hospital later in the day, something that's quite commonplace; Poole has a special baby care unit so Carrie had opted for that, just in case, whereas Bournemouth only has a maternity unit. I was on cloud nine; the only sadness I felt was that neither my Mum, nor Lou had lived to see this day. The baby's name was to be Lelani Lilly-Anne her middle name after Lou whose full name was Lillian… She would be so proud! Lelani was an angel, all pink with a shock of dark hair, looking so much like my baby's had, especially her Daddy. Carrie looked well and was so evidently thrilled; she's such a lovely girl and even though I've joked with her a lot over the years, telling her that she's a pain and too young for my son, that she's not good enough; at the end of the day it is only a joke and really, I couldn't have wished for better for my son. I quite often say as much too, although I always end it with;

"But I'm not going to tell you that!"

She'd made my son happy and I could not have asked for more. They'd decided that they would stay with us until the council accommodated them, something I knew would take time.

I'd had fears that Ken wouldn't treat Lelani as one his own, the same fears as I'd had with Pete and my own children when Michael was born and in that case my fears were confirmed but as Ken held that little girl in his arms, I could see instant love and I instinctively knew that I'd have nothing to fear… We still had a long way to go but looking at that scene, I knew we could make it work.

Chapter 44

Because of all the problems that Pete had caused and the many obstacles which he'd in turn created, our divorce wasn't finalised until the middle of September, 2002 and what should have taken three months had taken eighteen. Ken's divorce was finalised first and that hadn't been plain sailing either; when Ken had applied for a court order to get his belongings back, Ruby had told the courts that he'd been throwing stones at her windows in the night and then she'd accused him of breaking in and trying to strangle her. I didn't go with Ken when he made his court appearance, I'd thought better of it; I knew that the moment Ruby laid eyes on me, she'd take what was already a bad situation and make it much worse. As it was Ken was very upset by the accusations that she'd made and his shaking had started again, a few days before he was due to appear and on the morning of the court appearance his shakes were just as bad as they'd been when I'd first met him and I had been quite concerned as I'd waited for him to come home but when he did it was good news: The court had seen through her lies and had ordered Ruby to return all of Ken's personal belongings; it wasn't as if he was stripping the bungalow of furniture, fittings or anything that was useful to her, all he'd wanted was his clothes, his tools and the photographs of his children, they were the most precious to him, along with his Elvis mirror but she'd already smashed that, ripped up all of his various certificates of achievement and many of his photographs the year before and then delivered them to the club, torn and broken in a cardboard box. Ruby had handed the box to Penny while she was outside the club, on one of the family days that were held every year. I don't think that Ruby had recognised Penny in the light of day and had said to her;

"Do you know Ken Rogers? Could you give this to him please Dear?"
Penny just said that she did and that she certainly would, although she told me that she wouldn't have if she'd known the contents, or the affect it would have on Ken; she didn't know what was in the box because it was taped shut, so she'd handed it to him in front of Maria and the children, he'd opened it and immediately broke down. Maria rushed outside to find Ruby and give her a piece of her mind but she'd gone and when Maria came back in Ken, her and the children decided to leave and as if that weren't enough for one day, as Ken drove away from the club, he was pulled over by

the police: They'd had a report that he had been drinking, so more embarrassment again in front of his grandchildren; he was questioned and then breathalysed but then anyone who knows Ken also knows that he'd never drink whilst driving. I wondered how she could do such a thing to him, being the gentle man that he was; it was beyond me, I could never do that to any of my ex's, regardless of any ill treatment I may have suffered at their hands, in fact in Pete's case I was quite the opposite; I gave him food and money on the weekends that he looked after Michael and occasionally when he didn't aswell. I had written to Ruby around that time, telling her what I'd thought, at the same time as making her aware that Ken and I were friends and at the time that was all we were and she had written back to me saying that she knew I was married to a taxi driver called Dan, (still thinking that she was talking to Penny,) she'd also claimed that she'd spoken to him. The only thing she managed to get right was the surname and I'd found the letter very amusing, as had Penny but I had felt slightly sorry for Ruby too, although had she been able bodied I would, without doubt have confronted her long before. Still, a year later and it was all over and both of our divorces had been finalised, though Ken still hadn't got his things back, even with the court order and even though we'd managed to replace most of it, he was still understandably determined to get his personal things and wouldn't give up until he did; the precious memories could never be replaced.

To try and rid us of some bad memories, I'd decided that Ken needed a new car, to replace the mini bus with its wheelchair lift; where each rattle was a reminder of his life with Ruby. The mini bus did hold some good memories of our first days together; we had renamed it the love bus, for obvious reasons and I was a little sad to see it go but I'd also felt that Ken deserved a decent vehicle and even though he liked my sports car, being such a big man with his long legs, it wasn't the most comfortable of drives for him, besides, he'd never really owned anything other than cheap run a round's before then either and as we were both working at the time, I thought; 'why not?' We managed to get a good price part exchanging the bus and bought a big four-wheel drive, land cruiser type vehicle that was visibly better for Ken and I could see by the look in his eyes, as soon as he saw it, that it was the car for him and when he first drove it away from the garage he looked like the cat that had swallowed the cream. He was a completely different person from the sad broken man he'd been, just eighteen months earlier, with his new look, his new fitted clothes, his new hair style and now his new car, he was more like the man I'd met all those years before; strong and confident, he'd even seemed taller somehow, as if he were standing straighter, like a weight had been lifted from his shoulders but best of all, he was happy and that made me happy.

We set the date for our wedding; the fifteenth of February, 2003. Ken's birthday is the thirteenth but with the anniversary of Lou's death on the fourteenth and Carl's birthday on the twenty second, I'd thought that maybe the chosen date would take away a little of the sadness of the month and if the marriage didn't work out, at least I'd have the option of condensing all the misery into that one month and as an added bonus I was able to change my awful surname to a far better one: 'Rogers.' The name Rogers had become a bit of a joke, especially as Penny and I had seen Kenny Rogers a couple of years previously and I'd said;

"One day, I'm going to marry that man."

And here I was, marrying Ken Rogers, not the same one, although very similar and with identical hair colour too… I've thought back to that concert several times over the last few years because it was the strangest evening: Penny and I had arrived at the Bournemouth International Centre and had headed to the bar first for a drink but as we'd walked through, all eyes seemed to turn and look at us, I commented to Penny about it and she too had noticed something odd;

"Have we got cabbages on our heads or something?" She asked.

People we didn't know were saying hello aswell, which I found to be really strange. We'd decided to walk away from the bar and Penny had spotted some people that she did know, from Blandford, so we went over and were stood chatting to them, trying to ignore the attention, when Tom O'Connor walked through;

"Hello, how are you?" He asked,

"Fine thanks!" I replied, slightly stunned,

"Just need to use the loo." He said,

"Oh, ok!"

I thought to myself; 'why's he telling us?' Then he came back through and said;

"Behave yourselves tonight girls!"

Penny and I looked at each other and were very puzzled;

"Well, I know we have a reputation," said Penny, "but we must be famous or something!"

Kenny Rogers it seemed also had problems taking his eyes off of us; we were sitting in the third row and he kept sort of squinting to see us, one of his guitarists kept waving and smiling too, it really was the most peculiar experience and we still talk about it to this day... I missed Penny, I knew it was best for our friendship that she didn't live with me anymore and those last few weeks were really difficult and had put a strain on our friendship but we did have so many good times and hilarious nights out aswell.

Ken and I decided on a Registry Office wedding; neither of us wanted to marry anywhere that we'd been before, so we'd decided to go to Ferndown; at least the grounds were quite pretty, with well kept gardens and lots of trees, the only down side being that it was next to a playing field. Lorna decided that I had to have a hen night; it was something I'd never had before. By then Lorna and Barry had moved into their own home, with a mortgage and were working hard to pay it. They were the perfect match for each other, like Lee and Carrie and, as with Carrie's mum, I got on with Barry's parents too: I'd known his mum, Dee when I was a lot younger, although she didn't know me that well, just my reputation and I knew she hadn't thought that much of me back then but having met me again, I was sure that she'd changed her mind. Barry's dad, Mike was really funny too and when he and Dee met Ken it turned out that they'd known him for years and we all became like one, big, extended family.

Lorna made the arrangements for my hen party but I'd been concerned about her at the time because she was ill;

"It's just the flu!" She'd said but was feeling sick all the time. We found out why and I needn't have been too worried: She announced that was pregnant and I couldn't quite believe it; she'd always said that she didn't want children, although that had been when she was much younger. I really couldn't imagine my baby girl as a mother and the thought of her going through the pain of childbirth terrified me but then she'd informed me right from the start that she wanted me to be there with her while she gave birth: I'd been there with Claire and my neighbour when they'd given birth and I'd been extremely worried about Carrie when she'd done the same but this was my own daughter, my flesh and blood and she's never been able to handle pain or illness at the best of times; at this point she'd been living with Barry for about four years and whenever she'd been ill, she had phoned me and said;

"I need my Mum!"

I'd tell her to come home, which she'd do; she'd lay, with her head on my lap, her finger in her mouth, rubbing her bit of silky material, her 'sleep,' on her face and drift off to sleep, with me stroking her head... To me she'd always be my little girl but this time I'd be helpless, I could be there but I wouldn't be able to do anything to take the pain away; she'd have to go through it. On the one hand she was strong, independent and funny but still, at times like this, she was frightened and as her Mum I needed to protect her, at all cost but how was I going to protect her from this one? I'd be helpless, although I really didn't want her to see how panicked I was either.

We had so much fun at the hen night; including Ken's daughter Maria, his daughter in law Emma and Penny, there were ten of us. Lorna had bought several novelties for me including a wedding veil and had made a list of forfeits that were to be completed by the end of the night. We spent most of the night in a pub and the landlord and the men in there made it work, checking my list of forfeits and fulfilling as many as they could; including getting six men to lift me above their heads, which is no mean feat with me being no light weight, another had stripped off completely and the landlord gave me a pair of his underpants and they were all such good sports. We went to a club for the last hour of the evening and everyone, without exception wished me luck; although several men, upon checking my forfeits were a little disappointed that they'd nearly all been completed: I was a little uncomfortable with some of the things I'd had to do in front of my daughter and did wonder, a few times whether it was perhaps overstepping the barrier of what is acceptable in the presence of my children but looking at her; twenty-two years old and pregnant, I knew that I'd have to accept that she was no longer a little girl but a woman. Another thing that was also apparent was that we were friends, with an unbreakable bond; something I'd never had with my Mother but something I knew I would never lose with Lorna. All the thoughts that she had grown up and gone and the irrational feeling that I'd lost her transformed that night, our relationship changed and a natural progression took place: From parent and child, to great friends with a deep respect for each other. This in turn changed the way I looked at all of my children, seeing them all in a different light, I missed my babies but I loved the young adults that they'd all become and if I needed babies; I had the grandchildren and I already had the first, my own little Lelani, living with us. I felt like I was blessed to have been there for her first smile, when she'd first rolled over and when she'd sat up for the first time… I'd be there each step of the way!

Ruby found out that Ken and I were getting married a couple of days before the wedding and threatened to show up at the reception, which was to be held at a local pub. She'd also told Ken that she wanted all of his belongings removed from her bungalow and that it was to be done on the morning of the wedding, insisting that it was the only time he'd be allowed to collect them. Ken refused and told her to keep it all, so she agreed that he could collect it all the day before the wedding and even though the timing was designed to cause as much disruption and upset as possible, her plan was foiled: Lee and Matthew helped Ken and they managed to clear it all in a couple of hours, although she still tried to make it as difficult as possible saying that whilst Ken could go in, his friends couldn't, so Ken passed everything out to the boys who packed it into the four-wheel drive and best of all; nothing she said or did could bring Ken down anymore.

The wedding preparations were complete and I'd made all the bouquets and buttonhole's myself; I was quite pleased with the result, especially considering that the burgundy and ivory lilies and roses I wanted were not easy to find at that time of year. I'd bought an 'off the peg' ivory suit to wear; a little flimsy for the time of year but it covered a multitude of sins and even I felt that it looked quite good and to top it all off; Ken had asked my Dad for my hand months before and Dad, in his usual way had said;

"Take her on!"

Another really good thing for me was that from the moment they'd met, Dad and Ken had got on so well, even though Dad had accepted Pete, it was obvious that he didn't really get on with him, Ken was totally different; the first time that they met, he and Dad chatted about the R.A.F. and where they had both been stationed (Dad had done national service in the R.A.F.) and when we left after that first meeting, Dad whispered;

"You've got a good one there Janie, don't blow it!"

That meant a lot to me: My Dad's approval and had Mum still been alive I'm sure that she too would have approved; I wished she was and I know Dad had wished it as well, her death hit him harder than he would ever admit.

It was a frosty, sunny morning, to my way of thinking; a perfect day. Ken and my children, all looked so smart, as did Ken's Mum, his sisters, my Dad and Diane, my sister and her family and all the Grandchildren, including my Lelani, who was by now getting around in a baby walker, all of them so beautiful standing there together and everyone getting along so well; I loved them all, it was the happiest day for me in more years than I could remember.

The venue for the reception could have been better but with so many friends there, from the clubs and well-wishers, it was a good day, perfect and with Lou's sister, Susan there too, I felt like part of Lou was there with me. I had never seen my Dad drunk either, I'd seen him put away a lot of beer over the years but that day he was drunk, smiling and happier than I'd ever remembered him. He put his arm around me and said;

"He's a good man Jan, I know this time you'll be happy and you deserve to be happy now."

"Thanks Dad!"

I kissed his cheek and he hugged me, He couldn't take his eyes off his Great Granddaughter either and kept saying;

"She's a smasher isn't she? Cor, isn't she a smasher Diane?"

I'd succeeded in something else that day; making my Dad happy and proud and that meant the world to me. The only down side of the day was that Aaron didn't come and I think it would have made Dad's day complete if Aaron had been there; I had invited him and hoped that he'd come but he didn't. Even so, when we put Dad and Diane in a taxi and said goodbye to them; Dad looked content.

It was almost one o' clock in the morning when we finally fell into bed; it had been a very long but happy day that finished with Ken saying he was the happiest man in the world and a kiss;

"Goodnight Mrs Rogers!"

"Goodnight Mr Rogers!"

With that said and done, we both went straight to sleep.

We'd decided that we wouldn't be having a honeymoon as such, we couldn't afford it but we had booked a Monday to Friday break, from the Sun newspaper, £9.50, per person. We planned on going to Hale in Cornwall on Mum's birthday; the seventh of April but again tragedy hit us and on the tenth of March, 2003, Ken's brother in law, Pete died suddenly, he had been just sixty years old. I'd only really known him a few months and he had been at our wedding, happy and laughing; although I had been a little concerned because whenever he'd coughed, he'd gone a very strange colour, when I'd asked him if he was all right he'd replied he was fine. Ken had known him some thirty-five years and was very close to him and Pete had been Ken's sister's first love; they had been inseparable. Poor Ken had been informed by his other sister Shell, over the phone whilst he was driving his lorry and he'd had to pull over. As soon as he had hung up the phone, he'd radioed through to head office and told them that he'd be taking the rest of the day off, then he'd phoned me to tell me what had happened and that he was on his way home; it was obvious from the sound of his voice that he'd been in tears but in his usual, stiff upper lip way, he was in control by the time he arrived at home. The week that followed was a complete roller coaster of emotion and poor Jacky was complete-ly inconsolable. I made the wreaths for the family as their requests were very unusual and would've cost them a fortune: Pete had liked his Bells whiskey, so Jacky had wanted a wreath that looked like a Bells whiskey bottle, she'd also asked for a glass of whiskey from Pete's four boys and a white heart from his grandchildren. Ken and I arranged to take the flowers to the undertakers the night before the funeral, he'd wanted to see Pete but I didn't; emotionally I was unable to face it, the last body I'd seen was Carl, I'd also found Jacky's descriptions of Pete's body in the chapel of rest hard to take: Jacky had told us that Pete looked lovely in his suit with his Bells whiskey in one hand and roll up in the other, I felt it was a little macabre but she'd said that it was what he would have wanted and she was probably right. I think I'd found it so hard to digest because I hadn't been able to see my Mum, on the advice of the undertakers, who had said that it was better to remember her as she was, so the image of her lying on the floor was indelibly etched in my mind.

I followed Ken through the undertakers, carrying the flowers, thinking that they were leading us to the flower room but instead; we were led to the room where Pete's body was laid. He did look just as Jacky had described; like he was asleep with his glass and cigarette, although the sides of his coffin were strewn with pictures and letters from his grandchildren and it was heartbreaking to read the messages and once again my emotions got the better of me, I was distraught: Partly because of Pete but also Mum's loss sudden-ly hit me, very hard; there hadn't been a day since she'd died that I hadn't thought of her and shed a million tears but there, in that one moment, each and every loss I'd ever had, flooded into my mind, I thought I was going to pass out with grief and I was completely certain that it was my turn next. 'Please God!' I thought, 'no more, you win, I've had enough!' But then, as I was sat in the car, in a garage waiting for Ken to fill up with petrol and pay, Mum was there in my head;

"For goodness sake, pull yourself together!" Her voice said, "I'm still here aren't I. All right not in body but I'm here in thought, I'm always with you!"

I was sure I was completely mad but whatever the truth of life after death, whether it be imagination or just wishful thinking; whatever the reality is, over the years these encounters have given me the strength to go on and it was this strength that kept me going through the funeral.

We still had our 'honeymoon of sorts' to look forward to and that kept me going too. I had arranged holiday leave from my job, where I had worked as a chambermaid in a hotel in Christchurch since the August of 2002: It was a job that I could fit in around Michael's schooling and all the other problems I had and it was the best job I'd had since leaving Pontins; there was no weekend work and all the girls were easy to get on with, they'd even come to our wedding reception, armed with a bottle of champagne and, as it turned out, I was taking time off out of season, so I didn't feel as though I was letting anybody down either. Ken and I packed the night before; I really didn't relish the thought of such a long journey, although I was looking forward to us finally being alone together, just the two of us. I knew that Michael would be well looked after as Lee and Carrie were there, although he was ill at the time; he had a chest infection, which in turn had made his asthma worse and I was worried about leaving him but Lee was well versed in dealing with asthma (being as he's also a quite severe asthmatic) and assured me they'd cope;

"So bugger off mother!"

Even so, I insisted on taking Michael to the doctors before we left and it was the usual routine; anti-biotics, steroids and increase inhaler usage for a few days. My plan had been to replace another sad date, (this time mums birthday,) with a happy occasion, I'd managed to do it with February; even though there were still sad anniversaries and memories, there was at least one new, happy memory; 'what a way to start our honeymoon!' I thought… The day had started badly enough with Michael being ill, little did I know how bad it was going to get.

After we had taken Michael to the doctor and collected his prescriptions from the Chemist, we headed home; Ken was driving, I was in the passenger seat and Michael was sat in the back behind me. As Ken turned right to pull into our driveway, a car came from behind us and went to overtake; it smashed into the side of our car at speed and the impact pushed us back out into the road, the other car then collided with a tree that's outside our home. Ken smashed his knee against the central console, Michael and I had whiplash and the other driver, who turned out to be the ex husband of a friend was unhurt. My immediate concern was obviously Michael and because of the shock I didn't notice my own injuries until later, Ken too was in shock but also very angry. The damage to our car was extensive; the footplate and the wheel arch were virtually destroyed. The driver of the other car, Tom was apologising;

"I didn't see you Jan. Make me a cup of tea and I'll ring the insurance company, it was all my fault!"

"I've got a headache!" Said Michael.

I could hardly speak and Ken said nothing, he was livid, I agreed to make Tom his tea but as I did so a taxi drew up and the driver shouted;

"I saw what happened, phone the police!"

"We don't need to involve them," interrupted Tom, "just let me ring my insurance company."

I thought nothing of it and agreed but as we walked inside with him, he was still talking and I caught a whiff of his breath;

"Have you been drinking?" I questioned,

"Just a couple of cans."

"Ken, phone the police!"

He immediately did as I'd asked.

"It will be negative!" Tom was protesting, "I haven't drunk much, we don't much, we don't need to do this, I thought we were friends?!"

The more Tom protested and the more that Michael was complaining about his head and neck, the angrier I became. Luckily I didn't give Tom the tea before the police arrived; somewhere in my mind I'd realised that it could have an effect on the breathalyser reading, just some other random piece of information I'd registered over the years and not realised and something that was confirmed by the police when they arrived. They took both Tom and Ken outside to be breathalysed and as expected, Ken tested negative, Tom tested positive and was arrested. The officer asked if anyone was hurt and I told him what I'd thought was the case, that Ken and I were ok but Michael seemed to have had a problem with his head and neck, the officer called for an ambulance and said that Michael should go to the hospital for a check up,

"Are you sure you're both all right?" The officer asked, one last time.

"Yes."

I was too worried about everything else to have noticed anything wrong with myself; I was worried about the state of Ken's car and Ken, about Michael; 'and what about our honeymoon,' I thought and then there was the car, 'we'd have to sort the car out!'

The ambulance arrived and Michael was examined, the medic told us that he was going to be fine but they wanted to take him to the hospital for x-rays, just to be sure and asked if we could meet them at the hospital as soon as possible but before we could go anywhere, we had to move Ken's car from the middle of the road; which the police helped us to do, they then took a few more details and left. We drove my car to the hospital and three hours later, in the early afternoon we arrived home again, by which time Tom's car had been collected. Michael's arm had been put in a sling, thankfully nothing was broken, just whiplash and a shoulder injury but where I'd had a chance to calm down a little, I could feel that I too had neck and lower back injuries and I was beginning to stiffen up, I also noticed that Ken was limping too, although as always he said that he was fine;

"I've just bumped my knee!"

We followed the breakdown truck, Ken's pride and joy on the back of it, to the Repair Centre, where they told us that it was going to be some weeks before we could have the car back, if at all; it would take time to repair, especially as it was an import. The Repair Centre gave us a courtesy car, bright yellow and so small that Ken had to almost fold himself in half to get in it; it was like Postman Pat's van.

"Well, that's the end of our honeymoon!" Said Ken.

He looked so sad but I knew my car would never have made the distance; it needed a bit of work and whilst it was fine for short journeys, I couldn't trust it on a long journey. Ken said that he had his doubts as to whether the courtesy car would be any better but I wasn't about to give up that easily;

"Michael's all right and we're both ok, let's go!" I said, "if the little yellow car breaks down on the way then we'll get a replacement!"

I didn't want to right off our honeymoon completely and reluctantly Ken rang the holiday park to tell them what had happened and to say that we'd be there sometime the following day. I chose not to tell Ken that I was in considerable pain; I didn't want to let him down, not now and then the illogical thoughts started flooding my thinking; 'Why us?' 'Was this Mum yet again, getting her own back?' 'Well if it is,' I resolved, 'she won't succeed!' We were going to have this break, one way or another, that is as long as I knew Michael was going to be all right;

"No worries Mum, if we're in the least bit worried we'll take him straight to casualty!" Lee assured.

We left for Cornwall the next morning and I was having trouble hiding the pain that I was in, almost immediately my anxiety became evident too, to me anyway; I'd been all right when I was driving my car but then I was in control. Now, in the courtesy car with Ken driving; every break light I saw made me jump, accompanied by thoughts like; 'Are we going stop in time?' Every bump hurt too and we had to make several stops during the two hundred mile journey, which meant that by the time we arrived it was late afternoon. I was in so much pain and my nerves were frayed but it was obvious that Ken was annoyed aswell; mainly with my continual criticism of his driving but it was pretty clear that he was in pain too. I insisted on looking at his leg and found that it was swollen from above his knee, all the way down to his foot, he claimed that it would be all right and I vaguely believed him, until he took some painkillers; that was something I'd never seen him do and it was then that I knew it was far worse than he'd let on. Our accommodation and the camp were very comfortable but because of the pain that we were in, we stayed inside most of the time, although we did manage to see a few sights and went out for one meal but in the end we decided that being as intimacy was pretty much out of the question as neither of us could move, let alone perform we'd just as well go home. We left at about five o' clock on the Friday morning and arrived home at about lunchtime and by the time we got home; I was virtually unable to walk... 'Would this be the end for Ken and I?' I wondered, 'and before we'd even really got started too!' At that moment it seemed to me that there was some kind of a master plan to make my life as miserable as possible.

I tried to return to work on the Monday but by morning break I had to go home again, I went to the doctor the following week and physiotherapy was arranged and to make matters worse; it seemed that I'd lost my nerve where my own driving was concerned, which was totally illogical. Ken too was having difficulty driving his lorry but with my inability to work, he had to keep going. Then, to add insult to injury, we heard that the other driver, Tom had been banned from driving for a year and had been given a fine of just two hundred pounds, he'd even kept his job as a security officer and because he had admitted his problems, (he had apparently been under the influence of alcohol and drugs when he'd hit us,) he'd have been able to get his licence back in six months. 'Where's the justice in that?' I wondered as Ken and I both lost our jobs after a few weeks; we were both unable to work because of our injuries, which meant that we were also at risk of losing our home due to the lack of income and the fact that the benefit system is such that they pay nothing towards the cost of your home, if you are a home-owner, for the first thirty-nine weeks of a claim. We tried every-where for help but to no avail and it was at this point that I decided to try a 'no win, no fee' claim; initially just for my injuries but it was discussed with the company and they advised that we should claim for Ken and Michael too, although had I known of the trouble that this would cause us over the next two and a half years that it took to settle, I'd never have bothered. We had to beg for interim payments just to pay our mortgage and the other household bills, a lot of which resulted in bad debt, which meant we were then unable to secure any credit for the next six years. We were the victims here, weren't we? The settlements for me and Ken were lower to start with because of my previous back injury, 'wear and tear' and Ken's history of 'wear and tear' with mild arthritis but then we had to take away the interim payments and we were left with virtually nothing in the end. Michael faired better though and at least he has something when he reaches eighteen, it may help a little; especially given his problems… I constantly worry for him and what the future holds for him.

Chapter 45

By the June of 2003 we were both unemployed and Ken was on crutches; he'd been put on the waiting list for an operation to repair the damage in his knee. My back was better than it had been and I could, at least look after him, although I was grateful for Carrie and Lee's help too, in fact they all played their part. We also had something else to look forward to aswell; Lorna's baby was due in October 2003 and Ken's eldest daughter, Tina had announced that she too was pregnant with her fourth child, due in the November. By now Ken had decided that Lorna was his 'baby girl' and it had become quite a joke;

"Please daddy Ken," she'd say, "can I have..?"
She'd give that pleading smile of hers, just as she had with Sam all those years before, kiss him on the cheek and that's it; Ken would melt. She only had to ask and she could have had the world and when on the evening of the 1st of October, Lorna's contractions started, Ken was as concerned as I was and more so than I'd seen him be for his own children, although he wouldn't go into the delivery room and I don't think that Lorna would ever have gone that far either but he was close by, just outside the delivery room in the waiting room. Barry and I were with Lorna all the way through and it was difficult leaving her to keep Ken informed but between us, Barry and I managed.

Lorna's waters wouldn't break and she was in so much pain, she kept looking at me;

"Please make it stop!"
I felt completely helpless and thought; 'surely someone's going to break her waters?' No, apparently there was change in policy and they don't do it anymore; well that's what I was told anyway but I knew if they had, the baby would have been here in no time. The male midwife who'd been attending to Lorna had thought that she'd have delivered before he'd gone off shift at about 9pm but it didn't happen, although when it became obvious that the baby was becoming distressed and that the membrane was bulging and discoloured, they decided to break the waters. Within minutes of doing so, precisely what I'd suspected would happen, happened; at one thirty in the morning, on the 2nd of October 2003, Aiden Lee was born. There was concern at first that he could've had an infection and some complications due to the bowel movements he'd had dur-

ing his distress but he was soon given the all clear. A healthy little boy, weighing 6 pounds and 14 ounces and with his shock of black hair, he was the absolute double of his mother, both Barry and I were instantly reduced to tears of joy. Lorna had to have a few stitches, so while that was being done I'd gone out to get Ken, he too had almost been reduced to tears but as usual, he quickly regained control of his emotions and armed with his video camera, he videoed those first few moments of Aiden's life and just as any proud Grandfather would; he held that baby as if it were his own. Ken and I left the hospital and walked home (with Ken on his crutches) and we were so happy again and as we walked along, I sent a text message to Dan informing him of Aiden's birth just as I had when Lelani was born; a year later and he'd never actually seen her so, although I still felt like he had a right to know, I had no reason to believe that he'd make any effort to see this new baby either. Lou would never have allowed him to ignore his grandchildren and as Ken and I walked along, I could see her and hear her voice, telling me how beautiful the babe was, how proud she was of my daughter and how it would all be all right in the end. So there I was, forty six years old, Nanny to two beautiful grandchildren of my own and Step-Nanny to 10 more, twelve grandchildren in total. Then Tina's fourth baby was born on Lorna's birthday, the 1st of November 2003; between them all, Kens and mine, we were having Grandchildren at the rate of two a year and I'd wanted to give every one of them the best of everything but that just wasn't possible.

Christmas 2003 had been a lean one, although an interim payment just in the nick of time had made things a little easier; nobody went without and somehow we just about kept our heads above water. I'd had no luck in finding another job and I was still suffering with the anxiety attacks and a fear of being alone while driving my car, even to the shops and I knew there was absolutely no way that I was going to be able to hold down a job if I did get one.

Lorna needed to return to work as soon as possible; she and Barry had moved into a new home just before the Christmas because the home they'd had would've been too small for them and a baby but the mortgage on the new place was huge and would take both of them working to be able to afford it. Lorna was torn, she really didn't want to leave Aiden and certainly not with strangers, so I agreed to look after him and there it was, from that moment on, two days a week I was responsible for my Grandsons care and I must admit that I was more than happy to do so; it gave me something to think about especially as Lee, Carrie and Lelani had been given a council flat and had moved out the previous October, just after Aiden was born. I knew that they'd had to go but I missed them terribly, especially Lelani: I'd watched her everyday and been there for every new thing that she'd learnt and whilst I was happy for them to finally get their own home, my house had become so empty; Lelani had toddled into my bedroom every morning, with her big smile and given me a reason to get up each day. Ken too had felt the emptiness that their leaving had left, even though the house was tidy without baby things scattered around and none of Lee's instruments or his bits and pieces laying about; my son has never been the tidiest of people and Ken, who is quite the opposite, couldn't understand why their leaving, at least that side of it, had effected me so much but what he hadn't thought of was that the mess and the housework everyday had also kept me busy, when they had gone I'd felt lost. Looking after Aiden had meant that for at least two days a week my house was busy again with the noise of a baby; although Aiden was a very good baby, only really crying when he'd wanted his feed but I could once again watch as another of my grandchildren reached each little achievement, every new development. It was strange for a while and sole care of this helpless little person had made me very nervous to start with; 'What if I did something wrong?' 'What if something happened to him whilst he was in my care?' 'Lorna would never forgive me!' It's different when it's someone else's child, when it's your own you just do it, you get on with it and you take the consequences, when Lelani had been with us for that first year, so too had Carrie and it was Carrie who had taken the responsibility for her, other than taking her out for the occasional walk to the shops, I hadn't had to deal with that side of things at all really. I discussed my feelings with Lorna and she put my mind at rest;

"Don't be stupid Mother!" She said, "I'm all right aren't I? You did all right with us! Do you really think that I'd leave him with you if I thought you couldn't look after him properly? Anyway, I'd rather you than some stranger!"

And so began my very close relationship with my Grandson... The circle of life continues.

My relationship with Ken had been tested every which way since the day we'd met again, with divorces, deaths and car accidents, all of which seemed to have taken their toll on him too; somewhere he'd lost his smile, his sense of humour and he was becoming quite serious and distant. I let it go for a while but as is my way, I finally had to confront him and my fears; I'd started to believe that yet another marriage was on the rocks, thinking that Ken had decided that I wasn't what he wanted and was planning to leave. We ended up having a huge argument, it was the first real one we'd had and it cleared the air, it transpired that like me, Ken too had been feeling insecure, that maybe I wanted him to leave and throughout the argument he'd continually told me that he loved me, I reassured him that I loved him aswell and realised that we hadn't really lost anything, we'd just had so much to deal with that we'd become side tracked. From that day on I knew that even though we may have our ups and downs in the years to come, the one thing I can count on is the love and sincerity of that man. My Dad was right; I had finally found a good one and I knew that I could have an argument with Ken without any fear of violence, that he'd never lay a hand on me, although up until that moment I'd flinched away whenever he'd raised his hand suddenly towards me, even when playing. He assured me that he would never hit me and said that he was hurt that I could even think he would and whilst I'd told him I knew that he wouldn't, until then I hadn't quite believed it. He also said that he'd never intentionally hurt me verbally either but at the same time understood why I'd found it so difficult to trust anyone; I'd gone into great detail and told him everything, about all of my relationships and my past, which was something I hadn't been able to do with anyone before, I'd always skirted around the edges but for the first time in my life I felt like I could open up and be myself. We still had some major obstacles to overcome with both of us unemployed, our finances in a complete mess and all the waiting for the operation to repair his knee had had an effect on Ken; he was old school and believed it to be his job to be the breadwinner, to bring home the bacon and the idea that he'd failed in that respect had been another reason for his unhappiness but once he'd voiced his fears and feelings we managed to iron out a good many of the creases in our relationship… Once again it seemed to me that my whole life had been one major drama after another and I really did feel that it was surely time for us to be able

404

to move on and find a place, even for a short time, to regain some strength to face the next obstacle, the next unforeseen misfortune.

In the May of 2004 Ken finally had the surgery on his knee, thirteen months after the accident and ten of those on crutches. When I'd dropped him off at the hospital I'd been afraid that something terrible would happen; 'the fates are bound to throw something else at me sooner or later, could this be it?' I'd thought. It wasn't, the operation went smoothly and without a hitch, although he had to endure three more weeks on crutches and then a further three weeks healing after that but once he'd had his final check-up, he was given the all clear to return to work. He'd started applying for jobs but had gotten a little down, briefly, when all the places he was applying to were turning him down, he'd begun to doubt whether he'd ever work again, convinced that at fifty-six he was too old but he then signed on with an employment agency and was soon working again. He was a different man and it looked as though we'd got through it all and managed to keep our home too, just, for three months we were on the up but the moment we began to relax, another disaster hit, it was as if the fates were saying;

"No, you're too comfortable!"

Ken had been working for the agency, delivering to a well-known supermarket when he was hit on the back of the ankle, on his good leg, by a large cage full of bottles. He'd reported the injury at the time but had continued to work anyway but by the time he came home he was in extreme pain and his foot had swollen so badly that he could hardly get his boot off and once he had, it was obvious that he'd definitely not be getting it back on again. After a sleepless night and much protesting, I finally persuaded him that he'd needed some kind of hospital treatment and the x-rays showed that although nothing was broken, he had damaged his Achilles tendon; I had visualized a broken ankle and a leg in plaster for months but it wasn't, just very badly bruised, although because of the Achilles tendon damage he was put back on his crutches and unable to work. Back to square one, well almost but the hand of fate threw us a little lifeline and Ken had to do Jury Service; we'd known it was coming up and that he would need to be available for three months and having done it myself, just before I'd met Ken, I knew what it would entail and that at least he'd be able to fulfil the commitment and rest his leg at the same time. The case he was given was to last ten weeks and Ken would be re-reimbursed his loss of earnings, on the days that the court was sitting anyway but then some money was better than no money. There we were, another Christmas looming and another grandchild to add to the list; Maria had had another little girl, which made a total of four girls for her and fourteen grandchildren for us and then Ken's daughter in law was due in the March of 2005.

"Ok, this is now beyond a joke." I said, "Four years ago I didn't have any, just hoping for one or two. This has to be a record, fifteen grandchildren in four years; it has to be a record."
I wanted to treat each and everyone the same but unfortunately that's just about impossible to achieve, so Ken and I decided that Aiden and Lelani, being the lone children in each family should get a little more; Ken had considered them both to be his own grandchildren anyway and had treated them as if they were.

We had hoped that Ken's jury service would've lasted up until Christmas Eve and that Ken would be able to return to work after Christmas but it finished four weeks earlier and there wasn't any work available through the agency either, so more struggle and another four weeks without money... Now I'd already proved that I could 'do it on a shoestring' but I had vowed never again, I realised that I shouldn't have challenged the fates but they also say that you are never asked to deal with anything in this life, that God in his infinite wisdom feels you cannot handle, well all I can say to that is, God must have a really warped sense of humour.

2004 seemed to have been quite a bad year for most but Lorna and Barry looked to have been hit the worst: Barry had been ill and was taken to hospital (he had to stay in hospital twice over the year); he had developed an inherited bowel problem and was diagnosed with Chrones Disease. He was very poorly for most of the year but being self employed meant no money and he and Lorna had come close to losing their home and worse still, he'd missed Aiden's first birthday because he was in hospital at the time. Watching my daughter struggle had been hard to do, Ken and I had done what we could but we didn't have any money either. I wanted to wrap her up in cotton wool, Barry too and shelter them from the reality of life. The same applied to all of my children, I couldn't understand why it was that God had decided they should have to suffer aswell; Lee with his drugs, Matthew with the mental scars from all the abuse over so many years, poor Michael suffering the same fate coupled with Aspergers adding to his problems and now Lorna, although by New Years Eve I really had thought that we were over the worst of it: Barry with the help of drugs was pretty much back to normal and back at work, Ken had work lined up for the first week of the new year, Michael had been learning how to break dance during 2004 and was quite good at it too; this had made me think that maybe he could incorporate it into his future, that perhaps dancing was a possible career, I found out that there was a college course available to him when he left school and surprisingly he'd already chosen Dance as one of his G.C.S.E. options. Matthew had had counselling for his emotional problems but had taken up tai chi and meditation instead and both were having a positive effect on him, he seemed much more able to deal with his experiences and move on. There had been a few jokes though, within the family and with my neighbours too; at any given time of the day, I could look out of my window at the green opposite and there, in front of my elderly neighbours bungalows, you would see Matthew meditating or doing tai chi, then a little further along the green you'd find Michael, with his piece of vinyl flooring, spinning around on his head and even though passers by usually thought they were a bit strange, several had stopped and watched and my elderly neighbours enjoyed the spectacle more than anyone, some of them even attempting to copy the moves, not Michael's but Matthew's; they'd told me how relaxing they found it, how it seemed to have some kind of therapeutic value for them too and I must admit, imagining all those old, less than agile ladies behind their net curtains, attempting those exercises was rather amusing to me, although I did warn them all to be careful, just in case one of them fell over. Whenever anyone has asked about Matthew and Michael I've always jokingly said;

"It's nothing to do with me, I just drawer my curtains!"

So there I was saying that 2005 had to be our year and something good would finally happen for us; I couldn't have been more wrong, I'd obviously not tempted fate enough, I never listen, I'd thought that maybe God would see that I couldn't actually deal with anymore but no, he'd decided that I was more than up for the challenge.

It did seem that at the start of 2005 life had finally turned a corner for the better, my only concern had been Dad; he'd had a severe bout of flu and hadn't been able to go out with his dog, he was trapped in the house with Diane and her wild accusations that their neighbours were trying to get at her and delusions that strange people were following her, she'd even claimed that she was unable to walk up the road alone. These ramblings would've tested even the most sane and logically minded person and they had certainly taken their toll on Dad and even though I was still having difficulties driving on my own, I felt I had to make the effort once a week to take Diane out shopping, if only to give my Dad a break for a couple of hours. I'd been very worried about him; he was very depressed and appeared completely unable to snap out of it, he'd also started having quite severe panic attacks too. The first of which had happened a few weeks prior to the flu; he'd been out with the dog one day and it had got into a fight with another, he'd managed to separate the two dogs and had headed home, it was just as he was almost back at his house that the panic attack had happened. He hadn't been outside of his front door since; his excuse was that he didn't feel up to it and I must admit, he did look quite run down and the slightest thing seemed to upset him. It didn't help when the 'Asian Tsunami' hit on Boxing Day, 2004 and we were aware that my brother had gone on holiday to the area for Christmas; I had told Dad a couple of weeks before when as usual he'd asked if I had heard anything from Aaron,

"So he must be doing all right for himself to be able to afford a holiday like that!" I finished.

When I'd heard the news on Boxing day morning my thoughts were; firstly praying that my brother hadn't been caught up in it, especially as he'd taken his partner and children with him and although I knew that he was on an Island a few hundred miles away, the reports had said that they did have casualties; secondly I was hoping that Dad hadn't seen the news. He had, so I tried to convince him that Aaron was many miles away and that he may have even been on his way home by then, not that I was sure myself but I told Dad that I'd let him know as soon as I knew anything. Then followed a very anxious week, trying to contact anybody who was an associate of my brother. Verity finally managed to contact someone at Aaron's home; he had been caught up in the Tsunami and he'd been injured but everyone else was safe and well. Aaron had stayed a little while after to help some of the local people but he was on his way back home. I rang Dad and told him, he wanted to know all the details but I was unable to tell him at that point, although once again I assured him that I would be in touch as soon as I knew anything. I spoke to Verity the following day, she'd spoken to Aaron and filled in the details; just seconds before the wave had hit, my brother, his wife and the two kids had been waiting to get on board a light aircraft for a site seeing tour, Aaron had seen the wave coming and had shouted;

"Run!"

His partner and his daughter had run towards the higher ground but his son had gone in the opposite direction. Aaron had gone after him, caught him and had managed to keep hold of him as the wave hit, his son was fine but Aaron had been knocked around by some oil drums and debris and had suffered cuts and bruises but as he said;

"I was one of the lucky ones!"

Even so, he was quite shaken and this I felt was yet another reason to see the back of 2004 and welcome 2005. I'd even thought that being as Aaron had had this brush with death, he may have realised how fragile life really is and changed his ways, perhaps even make his peace with Dad but he didn't, although the news that Aaron was all right seemed to lift Dads spirits a little. Then, two weeks after Aaron had returned from Thailand he was arrested but for once he wasn't actually guilty of anything and even though this was eventually proven and the case had been thrown out of court, Aaron had still spent six months in prison on remand before being released. While he was inside he'd complained about pains in his legs and was given painkillers by the prison doctor but the pain had persisted and eventually the authorities decided to allow further investigation. His x-rays revealed that he'd had a broken knee cap, it was obviously damage done by the Tsunami and it proved his ability to with stand abnormal amounts of pain; one of the main reasons that has made me feel he is such a formidable character.

News of Aaron's troubles took its toll on Dad's health, the panic attacks increased in severity and frequency and Dad became agoraphobic; unable to go outside the gate but then came yet another flu type virus and he wouldn't even venture to his gate. I did feel though that it was more the fear of the panic attacks than the attack itself that were the problem having suffered so badly with them myself, although mine, with Ken's support, had eased in the months leading up to this; I still had them, especially when I was alone or when I was looking after Aiden, those same illogical fears that I was aware had been brought about by Mum's death but I was also aware of how Dad was feeling and that he didn't have the support I had. All that Dad had was Diane and as much as he loved her, she was of no help to him at all, constantly nagging; Dad had said that she was always telling him he wasn't a man, that if he was he'd stick up for her and sort the neighbours and that if he were a real man he'd pull himself together. She also moaned that he'd never go anywhere with her and that he was only interested in his garden but to be honest, that was his only way to relax and get away from her, especially as he'd given up fishing five years earlier; he'd told me that he had to give it up because Diane was so nervous about being left alone. Unfortunately, once he'd had the flu and started getting the panic attacks, he'd found it difficult to even go out into his garden and to make matters worse, he had refused to go to the doctor, he just kept saying that he would when he was ready. I contacted him by phone everyday, just to see how he was and called in at least once a week, unannounced, to take Diane shopping and each time, when we'd got back to the house, Dad would laugh at me and ask;

"How'd it go?"

"Yes, all right," I'd answer, "but she's a complete nightmare!"

And she was, in and out of every shop, never looking where she was going, always tripping over curbs or I'd glance at something, taking my eyes off her for a second, turn back and she'd be gone.

"Rather you than me," Dad said one day with a laugh, "I know what she's like!"

It was encouraging to know that he'd managed to retain his dry sense of humour and as much as I found Diane difficult to deal with I, like Dad had learned to ignore most of what she said, she really couldn't help the way that she was. I resolved to appeal to her better side, to try and keep the peace, not for her sake but for Dads.

At the start of February both Ken and I had caught really bad colds, that lasted right through our 2nd anniversary and Ken's birthday and I'd had to stop calling in to see Dad for a couple of weeks but then he caught it anyway and so did Diane; Dad hadn't really gotten over the second bout of flu and was complaining of a sore throat, although he still refused to go and see the doctor. Then Ken's cold turned into asthma, as did Michael's and even though I was very busy with them, I still rang Dad everyday. Michael was also being bullied again, not only at school but at the youth club where he'd been dancing and I wouldn't let him go unless he was with his dance teacher, Darren. Darren had taken Michael under his wing; he was twenty-two, very reliable and an extremely good break-dancer and above all I knew that Michael would be safe with him. Darren had also become Michael's confidant aswell as his teacher, which was something that he needed; Pete hadn't really bothered with Michael for over a year at this point and Michael missed him, he was always asking me why his dad wasn't bothering with him anymore but I really didn't know what to tell him, what could I say? I did however send regular text messages to Pete, keeping him up to date with Michael's achievements, although there was never any kind of response. Michael, Darren and two other boys had entered the 'Inter Youth Club Talent Show.' The fact that they had won it two years in a row had given a real boost to Michael's self confidence and his determination to stick to it, perfect the moves and he really was a perfectionist, something that is also, in part due to his Aspergers; he had to get things exactly right, just as he had with his martial arts. On the down side, he would get very frustrated if it wasn't perfect and then he'd start convincing himself that he was no good at anything and it was a constant battle of words to try and convince him otherwise. Darren and Michael taught other kids within the youth club too, this had been part of the reason that Michael had fallen out with a particular boy; it seemed that the lad was jealous of Michael because he'd been teaching his ex-girlfriend how to dance and he'd threatened Michael several times. I hadn't been too concerned at the time because Darren was always there besides, Michael was fifteen years old and everyone had been telling me that I would have to let him grow up sooner or later. Michael had also assured me that the boy was nothing to be afraid of and that he didn't even go to his school, although the boy had sent messages via other pupils at Michael's school, threatening to get Michael. So on February 28th, when Michael came home and said that he'd had a message from someone, saying that the boy had intended to get him later that evening, rather than having to spend the evening worrying about Michael, I asked him to stay at home.

"If I stay home now he'll think I'm a coward!" He argued, "Besides, I've promised to teach her tonight and Darren will be there anyway, so you don't need to worry."

"Any problems at all and you phone me!" I told him. Something felt somehow different that evening, call it intuition or premonition but I nearly drove Ken mad, repeatedly asking;

"Do you think he'll be all right?"

"Of course he will!" He'd reply.

Then, at about seven thirty the phone rang and it was a youth worker, he was attached to the youth club but was calling me from the main leisure centre, he told me that he was a first aider and that Michael was with him, that he'd been badly beaten up and although first aid had been administered, Michael needed hospital treatment;

"I'll be there in two minutes, phone the police!" I exclaimed and hung up.

Ken and I were on our way within seconds, with my saying;

"I told you, I knew this would happen, I should have made him stay at home!"

The first aider warned me that I may be shocked by my son's appearance and he was right, he'd also told me that he had taken photographs of the injuries that he would give to the police. Michael's face was a mess; he had a broken nose, a black eye, very large lumps all over his head, a chipped tooth and a very deep cut into his bottom lip and we spent four hours at the hospital while he had x-rays and examinations of his head injuries. This did however give him the time to tell me exactly what had happened: Three boys had in fact beaten him up, one of them had been the lad that had threatened him and the other two were twin brothers.

"Where was Darren?" I'd asked,

"The club was shut when we got there, just a notice on the door, so Darren said that he was going home." He replied,

"Why did you stay?" I questioned,

"Ashley (Darren's younger brother) and I were going to come home after I'd been to the leisure centre, I was going to see about starting Tae-Kwondo again but they came from nowhere mum!"

I then received a phone call from Pete, via the casualty department; I wasn't sure how he knew we were there, I just figured that maybe Michael had given his number to the first aider. Pete was ranting and raving; demanding to know who the attackers were and saying that he was going to kill them all, He was spouting the usual hot air, with nothing constructive or encouraging to say, until I finally said;

"Unless you can say something helpful, you should say nothing. If there is anything that you should know, I'll text you!"

"Well you'd better, or else!" He threatened,

"And you will do what exactly?" I questioned

"You'll see!" He said and continued with his ranting.

Apparently it was all my fault and I had never looked after Michael properly but by then I'd heard enough and put the phone down on

412

him. Next started a round of police statements, photographs and a warning from the police that repercussions were likely if we pressed charges against these lads, in particular the twins, they told us that even though they were only sixteen, they were already very well known and had several previous accusations of similar offences and all but one offence had been dropped; the victims had been too afraid to pursue them through the courts. I sat down with my kids, Ken and Michael, discussed the situation and with a promise to protect Michael, especially from Lee, we decided to stand up to them.

Michael had to stay off school for three weeks but when I'd explained to them what had happened they were very understanding. Michael's bruises healed pretty quickly, as did his nose, although I'm not so sure that the emotional scars will ever really heal; the whole experience had resulted in him not wanting to go out and to this day he hasn't fully regained the confidence that he'd struggled so hard to gain. He didn't return to the club until three months after the incident; even though the boys were all given four month Supervision Orders, lifetime bans from the youth club and grounds and were each ordered to pay Michael fifty pounds in compensation; poor compensation as far as I'm concerned, especially considering the injuries and the long-term effects that their malice has had on my son. The only physical scar that remains, which is also the one that still needs treatment and will most likely effect his appearance for the rest of his life is his top front tooth; it has already turned black because the root is dead and eventually he will lose it. I was left wondering: 'Why my son? As if it wasn't hard enough for him before!' And obviously I wanted to give them a taste of their own medicine but the law frowns upon such behaviour; although I have no doubt that I could've made them pay had there been the freedom to do so, especially given my past and at the very least I feel that their parents pay should've been made to pay. Why shouldn't they? To my mind that is where the responsibility ultimately lies and had it been one of mine who had inflicted such injuries on anyone, I would have been the first in line to make them pay but then given the life that they've shared with me, and everything that we've all been through together, I know in my heart that my children have a deep respect for everyone and I feel that they should expect no less in return.

My thoughts were echoed by Dad when I told him what had happened to Michael when I went to see him, two days after the assault, it was his birthday. I hadn't seen him for about three weeks and his appearance had shaken me a little; he had lost a lot of weight but was insisting that it had been the plan, that he'd wanted to lose weight. He then tried assuring me that apart from his sore throat and cough he was fine and working to overcome the anxiety attacks; he'd told me that he knew they were completely illogical, to which I replied;

"You don't need to tell me Dad."
I tried to tell him that he still needed to see the doctor anyway but he refused, insisting that he'd beat it his way and he was as stubborn as they come, there was no way I could convince him. It wasn't until two weeks later that I finally got him there; he'd phoned to ask if I would take him and I didn't need asking twice. I had Aiden that day but as luck would have it Ken was at home too and he'd driven us; which was just as well as Aiden was teething at the time and it was one of the few times that he'd ever made any fuss, so I didn't feel that I could've left him with Ken and taken Dad by myself but then I didn't want to leave it to Ken to take Dad by himself either; I knew that Dad must've been bad to have phoned me and when we got him into the car he was in the grip of a full-blown panic attack and was struggling to breathe. I sat and talked to him for the whole of the journey and by the time we arrived at the doctors he was beginning to come out of it. So much so that he said he'd be all right to go in to see the doctor alone and by the time he came back out he was himself again. He said that the doctor had told him he had 'Global Hysteria,' which had meant that his throat tightened with the anxiety, he then gave Dad some tranquillisers but also asked him to go for a further examination on his throat and a chest x-ray, so I'd suggested we went and did that before we took him home but he refused;

"No, I know what it is now." He said, "I'll think about it, maybe another day.
Besides, Diane will wonder where I am and you know how upset she gets when she's on her own?"
He told us to just drop him outside his gate, said that we didn't need to go in with him and that he'd phone me later in the day and with a kiss goodbye he walked into the garden and shut the gate behind him.

Chapter 46

I knew that Dad would never go for the tests and x-rays but I did think that maybe he was as he said, all right now that he knew what it was and for a few weeks I believed that just maybe he could do it alone; he had seemed to be a lot less dependent on me and when I did speak to him he seemed happy enough; although he had said that even though the panic attacks were less frequent, he found that he was having difficulty eating certain things, this he'd told me was because he had choked on a biscuit. It was then that I realised the anxiety had affected his eating habits and I argued with him, telling him that he couldn't live on soup alone and that I would find him other alternatives when I went shopping for them later that week. Diane had taken to staying at home rather than go with me and Dad would read me the shopping list over the phone, I'd go and get everything and deliver it to them, usually on a Thursday evening; I'd found that easier, I was still very nervous when driving alone, so Ken would come with me, besides Dad enjoyed his chats with Ken and they had become really close over the previous couple of years and with Ken's help Dad had even achieved getting to the end of the road and back a few times. This had been good for Ken too; he hadn't had a Father since his own Dad had died of lung cancer in about 1964, when Ken was fifteen, so in a way it was helping them both.

Then, quite suddenly, Dad took a turn for the worst again and this time he was so bad that he wouldn't even leave his bedroom, it didn't help that Diane was also a complete bag of nerves and that she couldn't cope with Dad; he was convinced that she wanted him out of the way, so her family had tried to take her out as often as possible. Dads throat problem worsened again too, his voice became very croaky and he had all but given up eating anything whatsoever. Diane had had a severe cold aswell and had told me that her ears were very bad; she claimed that she couldn't hear what Dad was saying but I began to think that he'd had a mild stroke because on bad days I couldn't understand him either and as I'd feared, he wasn't about to go back to the doctor but finally, in the June I'd decided that enough was enough; if he wouldn't go to the doctor then I'd bring the doctor to him. Diane had needed an appointment to see her doctor too and hers was at a different practise to Dads, even so I knew that I had to get them both sorted out. I phoned and spoke to Dad's doctor and he was reluctant to come, even when I'd explained that I couldn't get Dad out of the house and that he had a problem with his chest, the doctor just argued with me, saying that Dad had managed to go and see him in the March, so I pointed out that he was far worse now and the doctor finally agreed to make a house call. I arranged to meet him at Dad's, that way I could be there for Dad, explain things to Diane and get the dog out of the way too (I had visions of the dog attacking the doctor) but I'd had to drive there alone because Ken was working at the time. There's something to be said for facing your fears head on and each time I was forced to drive alone, I found it was a little less stressful than the last. When I arrived, Dad was in his usual place, lying on his bed, wearing a vest and without a jumper his weight loss was far more obvious, the stocky man he'd always been was now just skin and bone. It must have shown in my face because Dad asked; "What's wrong?"

"Why are you still not eating?" I questioned,

"I needed to lose weight." He answered,

"Yes but its gone too far Dad!" I said,

"Yes but I'm eating more again now."

"Solid food?"

"No, soups but I have four raw eggs in a pint of milk in the morning too. It's not easy though, it's the damn panic attacks!"

The doctor arrived and examined Dad, gave him a prescription for more tranquillisers and reiterated that Dad had to go for the tests, although he still didn't think that there was anything to worry about. I stopped the doctor as he was leaving and asked if he could give Dad something for his chest; to my mind Dad needed an antibiotic, or an inhaler, anything but the doctor refused;

"Not until he has the tests, he hasn't got an infection, it's his nerves."

"But he's so thin," I said, "he won't eat and I can't get him out of the house, he has panic attacks!"

But nothing I said made a blind bit of difference, the doctor had made up his mind;

"Well maybe if he takes the tranquillisers he will feel a bit better." He said, "Hopefully he'll be able to leave the house and go for the tests!"

And with that he left, leaving me feeling totally helpless. I went back to speak with Dad;

"You see," he said, "I told you it was a total waste of time!"

416

I started remembering back to Gary's brother, Ben and how I'd tried then to make people listen but nobody did and with tragic consequences.

"Dad, please go for the tests," I pleaded, "I don't want to lose you too!"

"What are you talking about?" He asked, "You won't lose me, I'm fine!"

I went to collect his medication and decided to buy him some muscle building milkshake, thinking that if I could get him to drink it, maybe he'd be able to build his body weight back up, which would hopefully give him the strength to fight whatever this was. He promised to try it for me and from then on he drank it three times a day and his weight increased a little. He didn't get on as well with the tablets from the doctor however; he'd tried them for two days and they had made him far worse, he became terrified of the effects that they were having on his ability to think logically and like me he couldn't handle anything that interfered with his normal senses; if it took away the control then we'd end up fighting, trying to keep it and we always seemed to ask the same question too: 'Why do I feel like this?' Constantly analysing everything. I suggested that he reduce the dose and he tried but still couldn't cope. I then found a herbal alternative, so Dad phoned the doctor and explained that he couldn't take the tranquilizers because of the side effects but the doctor re-stated what he'd said before; that Dad would have to take them. He didn't, instead he started using the alternative that I'd found, which he'd tried for a while and had claimed that they helped. So there he was living on milk shakes and herbal remedies, each day phoning me, to tell me how he was and it was very wearing, especially on his really down days, he'd say things like;

"I think I've had it, all my friends have gone!" Or; "Diane's bad, she wants me out!"

I would sit on the other end of the telephone, trying to persuade him otherwise.

Ken then booked us a holiday for the end of June, he said that we needed a break, Michael too; Michael still hadn't recovered from the assault and we decided to take Michael's friend Ashley with us aswell. I'd hoped that it would be good for us all but at the same time I was worried about leaving Dad, although he told me he'd be fine;

"It's only for a few days after all." He'd said.

We'd had quite a good week, unfortunately Michael and Ashley didn't get on as well as I'd hoped but it wasn't too bad considering. They both entered the free style dance competition, break dancing and Michael won it, something that Ashley wasn't very happy about but it was good for Michael, helping to building up his confidence again and he won a free weekend, to go back for the 'Grand Final' in the December, which gave us all something else to look forward to. When I told Dad he was thrilled and the news seemed to help him a little aswell; he didn't appear to have gotten any worse and looked to be holding his own, he'd even started doing a bit of gardening again, although he still wouldn't leave the grounds of the house and every time I spoke to him he'd say;

"I'm going to beat this and I'm winning!"

And for the next couple of months it looked like that he was winning and that he was going to be all right, although I still continued with my weekly shopping trips and occasionally Diane agreed to come with me, especially when I offered to take her shopping for clothes, or out to a market, just to give Dad an extra break. Diane's daughters did the same and with Ken and one of Diane's sons in law doing the odd jobs and the gardening in their spare time, the good days seemed to out weigh the bad, for Dad, not for me, I was crying at some point every day, missing Mum, missing Lou and missing Ken; we hadn't had the time to be just us and any time we did have together was taken up with conversations about Dad, Diane and Michael and what to do about their lives. I was still looking after Aiden two days a week and those were usually the good days and Dad would phone in the evenings but they were always quick calls. I suggested to Ken that we should take a mid week holiday, just the two of us and he jumped at the chance. So in August we went to Somerset and we had a good time just relaxing and getting back to us. It was then that I realised how far we'd drifted apart and how tired Ken was, I just hadn't noticed and as I watched him browsing in the gift shops and looking out over the bay deep in thought, I regained that feeling of how much I loved and appreciated him, quietly supporting me through everything and never mentioning his needs. I realised that I had to put everything else on the back burner if I didn't want to lose this man, although when I'd admitted to Ken that I felt I was going to lose him, if I hadn't already, he said that the idea hadn't even entered his head, he re-affirmed his love for me and then told me that it was as it had always been and so on for eternity. Even so, I decided that I needed to work a little harder to keep the love going strong, we'd been through so much in the four years we'd been together, not to mention our previous lives and time was passing by so quickly that I was left questioning; 'where had all those years gone?' I told Ken of my thinking, of how I thought we should try to spend a little quality time together and he said that he too had felt the same and by the time we were due to go home, I felt we had regained the togetherness that we'd lost and Ken looked so much happier too... Whatever the future held, I knew that we would always be together and I also knew that I was somehow better able to deal with the problems that life kept throwing at me.

The first thing I did when Ken and I arrived home was phone Dad to see how he was, Diane answered and said that he'd been awful, that he'd been crying, that he'd missed me so much and that she'd never seen him like it before but then she asked me not to tell him that she'd told me. When Dad came on the phone it was pretty obvious that he'd been listening in;

"Take no notice of her," he said, "I'm all right!"

"I've brought you something back Dad," I told him, "and your Christmas present too!"

The conversation that followed chilled me to the bone;

"Do you really think I'll be here then?" He asked,

"Yes, of course you will!" I answered.

"I don't think so. I think that's wishful thinking on your part." He sounded quite serious and logical as he continued; "I'm not scared of dying, I've got nothing to live for!"

"Don't talk like that!" I told him, "I'm not going to lose you, Mum was enough!"

"I know she was and I'll do my best not to let you down but I am seventy five and out of the forty people I called friends, I've got just one left, the rest are all gone."

"But you have me" I said, trying so hard to find a reason to persuade him to fight on, then a thought popped into my head; 'Is he talking suicide?' I wondered and asked; "You're not thinking of doing anything stupid are you?"

"No, course not!" He replied, almost laughing at the suggestion.

Then his mood changed again and he was talking about the garden, the dog and Diane. 'What is he thinking?' I asked myself and I knew that I had to get to see him, see for myself exactly what was going on but I didn't want to turn up unannounced because Dad would've figured out that I was checking up on him and I was also a little afraid of what I was going to find when I arrived, I really didn't feel that I could face it alone so Ken agreed come with me the following day. My imagination was running wild that night and I didn't sleep well at all, mainly dosing, slipping in and out of consciousness and then, for the first time since they'd died my Dad's parents, my Grandparents were there in my head, I could see them and hear them;

"Our boy's going to be all right. Tell him that we're watching over him. You have taken the best care of him that you can and remember that we are all here for you too."

That was it, my brain was buzzing: 'Did they mean he'd be all right in life, or in death? If they meant death, did that include me? Was I going to die?' I convinced myself it must've meant that Dad would live and that my mind was playing tricks on me. I told Ken of my visit;

"Well it has to be your imagination," he said, "because you're certainly not going to die!"

When we arrived at Dad's the following day, he was sat in his chair, smiling and happy. I told him of my dream and he wasn't surprised;

"I know that they're here," he said, "I've had similar dreams."

We sat and chatted about it all like it was normal and then he admitted that like me, he and his Mother before him had had many dreams, or visitations over the years and that it had been 'a way of life,' although he didn't really discuss it with anyone because he felt that people thought he was mad enough anyway.

"Just accept that it happens," he told me, "it's something that you've inherited and by the way; you're not mad either, it's a gift!"

"Must be the gypsy in us then eh?" I questioned,

"Yes, that's probably right." He answered.

From that day on we were able to speak about anything and everything and I wanted to know everything; we'd talked for hours face to face and on the phone and I learnt more about my Dad in those few weeks than I'd ever known in all the previous 48 years. Mum had always told me that I was like my Father and her meaning, I'm sure was that I always looked on the black side but for once she was wrong and I was glad to be like him. I love my gardening and I've kept fish for a number of years, just as he did but those were the obvious things and what was less apparent were the similarities between our views of the after life, wildlife, conservation, conversation, even our political views and for once I was proud of our likenesses, I also wondered whether I'd finally found the answers that I'd been looking for. I loved my Dad and most important of all, (to me,) my Dad loved me and I finally believed it. I kissed him good-bye that day and almost every time I saw him after that but I also knew then that he was going to die soon too.

I rang Verity and informed her that Dad was very ill and incredibly frail but she said that she didn't know him and that she really wasn't particularly interested; I could understand how she felt to a certain degree, but at the end of the day he was still her Dad, I'd even tried to tell her that; just as she needed my help and support when mum was ill and dying, so I too needed her help with this and whilst she said that she would've helped had it been just Dad, she admitted that she couldn't face Diane and nothing would make her have contact with Diane;

"She's a hateful woman," she said, "and completely barking!"

Even though I agreed with her opinion to a certain extent, I'd also learnt a lot about Diane: She was without doubt mentally ill, even her own children had thought so but she was also vulnerable and unable to cope alone, living in constant fear of everyone and everything and totally reliant on and devoted to Dad; the thirty odd years that they had spent together were proof of that devotion and for the most part (apart from the last year or so) they had been happy and in between those paranoid outbursts of hers, she was a caring person and I felt she deserved respect for that.

Matthew's twenty-first birthday had been on the 10th of October, 2005 and Ken and I decided that he should at least have a party. It was arranged for the 7th, at yet another social club we had joined in the earlier part of the year; we'd joined mainly because Ken's Mum and his sisters were regulars and it gave us the chance to socialise with them, but it was also a place that we could take Michael and somewhere that he was able to practice his break dancing, which meant I didn't have to worry about him going out alone to the youth club. I was really looking forward to the party, my friends and family all together, under one roof, where I could show my appreciation and love for them all; particularly Matthew, he'd really been through the mill over the years. It was also a chance for

Lee, Matthew and the other members of their band to play a live gig and have a laugh. I did invite Dad but he'd declined, saying that he didn't think he was well enough, instead sending a birthday card and some money to Matthew, although as always I'd had to remind him of the date, he'd never remembered birth dates, all that was except mine, he'd managed to remember my birthday for the three years prior and that year he'd bought me some hyacinth bulbs, they're actually Ken's favourite but it was the thought that counted and he'd made up for it with a lovely card: To my daughter.

Friday the 7th of Oct and the party, although three days before Matthew's birthday, went so well and it was a real lift to my spirits seeing everyone so happy and my children, I felt so proud of the adults that they'd become and of my beautiful Grandchildren too and to make the evening complete the boys and their friends had insisted that I sing; although initially I'd protested, it had been years since I'd done anything like that but in the end I finally agreed. So with Matthew on the drums and Lorna behind me on the stage, dancing along I sang 'Summertime' and when I was done there was a standing ovation and shouts for more, so I finished with 'Crazy' and a;

"That's your lot!"

Someone had suggested that the 'X Factor' might be a good idea but I think I'd replied with;

"I think I'm I little too old for that now."

Even so, it was the one dream, or ambition that I'd always had and I was a little sad to think that it is the one thing I may never get to do, not in this life time anyway, the main thing was that Ken was happy and I'd proven to everyone that I could sing, it wasn't just a rumour anymore. As a complete family, we'd had an almost perfect evening and it showed me that even though life has thrown us some pretty hard times, at the end of the day we are a family and I was glad of that; especially during the next two weeks, I didn't know it then but they would be some of the hardest I'd ever had to face.

Matthew in his usual way had been very appreciative of the efforts that we'd made for him, insisting that if we'd needed any help to pay for anything, he was more than happy to pay for something. He'd also made a lasting impression on several regulars in the club who had said what a pleasant, polite young man he was;

"A credit to you!"

But then that's something I've always been told about them all and it's a phrase I've always been so proud of.

Matthew had phoned Dad and thanked him for the card and they'd talked for a long while, another thing that I'd be glad had happened over the next two weeks.

Tuesday the 11th of October, 2005, I hadn't heard from Dad that day, so I'd thought; 'No news is good news!' I'd been looking after Aiden during the day anyway and was quite tired and Ken had to be up at half past four the next morning, so we'd gone to bed early, just after nine. The phone rang at about eleven o' clock and Ken answered, after jumping out of his skin, then he handed the phone to me thinking it was one of my elderly neighbours but it wasn't, it was Diane;

"Your Dad's collapsed and I can't get him up off the floor!" She then told me that her son had also tried and he couldn't either.

"Have you phoned for an ambulance?" I asked,

"No, I can't do all that."

"Phone them!" I was losing my temper.

"I can't!" She whimpered.

"Then get your son to do it!" I barked, "I'll be there in a minute!"

Realising that something serious had happened, Ken was already up and getting dressed and we were out of the door and in the car in a matter of minutes. In a strange way I'd hoped that something like this would happen, at least then he'd have had no choice but to go to the hospital and have the tests done, only trouble was that by this time it was too late and I knew it was, especially when I'd considered what Diane had said: Apparently Dad had told her not to phone me, even though he was having trouble breathing, he'd said that he wanted more time, Diane had said that they were in bed at the time, that he'd got up to go to the bathroom and that that was where he'd collapsed, she'd said that even then he'd told her not to phone anyone, yet he wasn't breathing. The conversation had been so confused that I'd really had to think about it and I'd talked it through with Ken (who was also very angry that they hadn't phoned 999 immediately); we figured that Dad must have collapsed and become unconscious before Diane had gone round to get her son up, he'd then gone back with her and had tried to pick Dad up, all of which must have taken a good twenty minutes and only then did she phone me, it had taken us around twenty minutes to get over there and the paramedic had arrived at exactly the same time as us, so Dad would've been unconscious for about forty minutes by this point. The paramedics had worked on Dad for an hour but he couldn't be revived and all the while my pulse and my mind were racing; 'Had Dad been right all along? Had she not phoned for help on purpose? Had her son done the same, wanting him out of the way? What would I do without him?' I was so angry and my dad was gone and he'd been right about one thing; he didn't make it to Christmas.

Diane was sat there, crying;

"What am I going to do without him?" "How am I going to cope?" "How could he leave me?"

I couldn't look at her, I had to go outside and as I stood, looking into the garden I could hear Dad's voice, his words;

"I'll always be with you, I won't leave you!"

He'd said it just days before and now he was gone and as the tears started rolling down my face, my thoughts turned again to Diane and of how she could think of nothing but her self and then it happened; I felt a hand on my shoulder, although there was no one there. 'Who could it be?' I wondered with only two possible answers; it had to be either Dad, or my imagination. I went back inside and Diane's son made us all coffee and kept saying how sorry he felt for us and there I was, just as I'd been four years earlier; waiting for a policeman and an undertaker.

The police arrived and took statements; who was I? Who was she? Death was confirmed at twenty five past twelve on the 12th of October 2005. I phoned Verity;

"What's wrong?" She asked.

"Bad news!" I said.

"What?"

"Dad's just died!"

"Can I do anything? Do you want me to come down?"

'A little late now!' I thought but said;

"No just thought I should let you know."

I then told her the circumstance and she said that she too was suspicious at the delay in calling for help

"I'll ring you later" I told her and hung up, I was numb.

The undertaker arrived and Diane asked if she could say goodbye;

"Of course you can," replied the undertaker, "take whatever time you need."

I couldn't go in with her, I couldn't face seeing my Dad on the floor, choosing instead to go outside with Ken and wait for Dad's body to be taken away.

A few minutes later they brought him out, or rather another body bag on a stretcher and they loaded him into the back of a van, then they were gone and I was an orphan.

"I can't deal with the arrangements," said Diane, "how could he leave me with all of this!"

I knew that she couldn't read or write very well but it also seemed to me that she was wiping her hands of it. I looked at Ken to find that he was getting just as annoyed as I was.

"It's ok Diane, I'll do it all." I said, "Ken and I will deal with the arrangements!"

In reality it was probably the better idea for me to do it anyway, I already knew the routine; Verity and I had dealt with Mum's arrangements. Diane agreed with the decision, saying that it was me who had known him best and pointing out that he'd taken to calling me his angel. 'That maybe but where was I when he was dying?' I thought, 'I should have phoned when he didn't phone me!' I didn't want to look at her anymore; I needed to go home;

"I'll be back in the morning, there's nothing more I can do now."

With that said Ken and I left. From then on the coroner and the undertaker had dealt with me and I'd relayed the details to her.

Ken phoned work the following day, telling them what had happened and that he wouldn't be in for a couple of days. He needed to support me, promising to be there and he was. Lee took it the hardest, or at least that's how it seemed, he showed his feelings openly, crying his heart out. Dad and he had been close but as he admitted the loss of Lou came back and hit him hard too and each time he cried, I cried and everyone else followed suit. All that is but Ken, he was keeping his emotions in check, although his pain was apparent in just one line;

"I really liked your Dad but I thought I'd have him for more than four years."

"Dad thought the world of you too Ken" I said, reassuring him.

He had and that was so obvious. I also knew that I had nothing to reproach myself for either, this time I had done all that I could.

The coroner rang the following day and told me that he'd found a large growth in Dad's throat, he would be carrying out a detailed post-mortem and would notify me of the results later in the week. I rang Diane;

"I'll be over shortly to explain but it looks like cancer."

"It can't be," she said, "he told me there was no cancer in your family. I knew it!.." I thought that was it but she continued:

"...They're all here throwing his things out!"

"What?! Who is?"

"My family!"

"My God, Dad hasn't even been dead twelve hours! Tell them to leave it alone, we're coming over to get it now!" I hung up the phone.

I was livid, this was confirmation that they really had wanted to get rid of Dad, he had been right. Ken and I were in the car and on our way over there again and when we arrived I was ready and prepared to smack them all out.

"How dare you, my Dads not even cold!" I shouted at Diane's, suddenly confused looking son and it was then that I realised I should have considered that, as usual Diane had got it wrong and on this occasion I really do think that it was intentional. Diane's son explained that yes, they were cleaning things out and taking up the carpet in the bathroom where Dad had collapsed but Diane had asked them to, she'd told them that she couldn't do it on her own, she'd also told them that I'd be over to collect my Dad's belongings, although omitted what she'd said to me; that they were throwing his things away. As it was he didn't really have anything of value anyway, he hadn't made a Will and all he had to show for his seventy five years on this planet, was a little bit of money that he'd put into a joint account, (he'd said that it was to pay for his funeral but then Diane said that she needed it to live on,) his stamp collection and his fishing tackle, but neither of those were really worth any monetary value and nothing like the amount that we'd needed for a funeral. I had asked Dad to sort everything out, make a Will and get things in order to save this happening, I'd even reminded him of the problems that Verity and I had faced when sorting mums estate but he hadn't done it, he probably thought that he had more time.

Ken and I, with the help of Diane's daughters put most of Dad's things in black bags and loaded the bags into the car; everything, including my Dad had been loaded into black bags, removed and disposed of in just twelve hours. I decided then and there regardless of the cost, my Dad would get a good send off. I did think

426

that maybe, if I appealed to my brother he may help. Verity phoned him and we went over to see him together, just as we had four years earlier, he wasn't home but he was on his way. When he arrived I told him what had happened and how Dad had died but unlike before, he didn't seem anywhere near as upset;

"Thanks for letting me know."

Was I imagining his disinterest?

"Dad asked after you all the time," I told him, "he really wanted to see you!"

Nothing, no emotion. Verity and I left and as we drove home I questioned her;

"Why wasn't he bothered? He was left with Dad, just like me. Mum left us both and yet he was more upset when she'd died!"

"He was closer to Mum and so was I..." Verity replied,

"...Aaron had no time for Dad!"

I couldn't believe it, somewhere they must have felt something, and he was our Dad.

"I'm not doing this for Dad either," Verity continued, "I'm here to support you!"

What could I say? I didn't know, so I resolved to say nothing and thought a lot instead. Dad had been right; my family and I were the only ones who actually cared about him. I didn't need Verity's support, I would do this, and Ken was the only support I needed. If I'd had any doubts about that support they were soon dispelled, Ken was my rock, beside me every step of the way.

The Coroner phoned to tell me the cause of death; it was cancer, complicated by a chest complaint and respiratory failure. I listened but couldn't take it in; by then everything had become so matter of fact, listed in order of things to do: Arrange the undertaker, register the death, cancel his pension and fill in papers for Diane, applying for a death grant towards the cost of the funeral; if she didn't want to part with Dad's money then the least she could do was sign some papers, she didn't want to pay a lot of money for flowers either so I'd had to do those too. I'd had to make an appointment to register the death, it was for the following Tuesday; Verity came with me for that because Ken was working. We stood in a queue, in between Council Tax payers and housing enquiries and when we finally got to the desk the girl said that the Registrar had asked if we could make another appointment as she was running late;

"No we most certainly cannot!"

"Oh, I'll see if she'll see you then." She replied, obviously a little taken back with my sharp response and surprised by my refusal. She disappeared and came back a few moments later; "She will let you in and see you." She said.

"Well that's big of her," I answered, "I should think so!" Verity and I couldn't believe the attitude and Verity told the registrar as much;

"We're ok because we're here together but what if we'd been a poor elderly person, who'd just lost a life long partner, can you imagine the distress that you would have caused?"
The registrar agreed and suggested that we make a complaint in writing. We registered Dad's death and I was recorded as Dad's next of kin and when we were done I thanked Verity for sparing me her time;

"That's ok," she said, "if you need any more help let me know!"

The undertakers were a wonderful, well established company in Bournemouth, run by brothers, a family business that had really moved with the times. Many of our family and friends had been taken care of there and I couldn't help wondering why we hadn't used them for Mum; I did think that maybe it was because the name of the company was the same as Dads surname and that's why Verity didn't choose them, but then there were so many over the top, ridiculous thoughts running through my mind that I didn't really know what I was thinking, all I knew was that this would be handled right for my Dad. I explained to the undertaker that I may have wanted to see Dad and that we hadn't been able to see Mum, he looked at me with a puzzled expression and said;

"I don't quite understand that, but rest assured you *will* be able to view him at any time."
I didn't but at least I knew that the choice was mine this time and that his body would be treated with the care and respect that he deserved. I did ask for a lock of Dad's hair though; he'd always had such an amazing head of hair, even in his later years it kept its dark colour, although in the last few months he had gone a bit grey. I asked Diane if she'd like one too;

"Oh no!" She said, "I couldn't do that, I couldn't have that here!"
I'd known that that would be her reaction and I think that deep down it was my intention to make her feel uncomfortable... A little revenge.

Chapter 47

The date for the funeral was set for Friday the 21st of October and, with the help of the undertaker, I chose the coffin and what I felt was the perfect charity for any donations, perfectly in keeping with Dads beliefs:

'The preservations of our waterways and wild fowl.'

I could picture Dad sitting by the river, fishing; his green hat always perched on the top of his head, always too small. Whenever I remembered his hats, it made me smile; every one that he'd ever owned was always the same, too high up, which meant that the top always looked about four inches higher than it should've been; from the woolly ones that he wore in his garden during the winter, to the wider rimmed ones that he balanced on his head during the summer and then there was the one that I'd bought for him, with a slogan that read: 'I'd rather be in my garden!' Those were always the happiest times for him and they're the images that I will forever cherish.

I had to decide what to write in the obituary column and it was hard trying to include everyone but I felt that it read well when I'd finished and I took it to the undertakers. I also needed to find and contact Dad's brother and sister. I managed to trace his sister, who was actually his cousin; she was Dad's Auntie's (Nan's sister) baby and Nan had adopted her for some reason. Dad's own sister, Madeline had died from meningitis when she was eight years old and Dad's life had then become a round of contradiction and confusion, with an awful lot of skeletons in the cupboards. I did ask Dad to write it all down for me and he had started to aswell, albeit a little reluctantly, saying that he was slightly embarrassed but promising that he would try but he'd only managed to write a few names down before he died. Nevertheless, I'd decided to find out a little more for myself, only I realised during that week, all too late, just how little I really knew about Dad's family. I couldn't even get in contact with Dad's brother before the funeral, there hadn't been any sort of contact with him for years; Dad's sister had told me as much when I'd spoken to her on the phone, she'd also said that she probably wouldn't come to the funeral either but would send flowers.

I had chosen Hymns that I'd thought Dad would like, I knew that he'd had his religious beliefs, I just didn't know what they were, however I did know that he had watched songs of praise every Sunday, for as long as I could remember, that and the cricket, especially 'The Ashes.' I was aware that we'd won them in 2005 because they were one of the highlights of Dad's final few months; I've never understood the sport but I'd listened to him talk about it every day and that was the only reason that I'd known we had won. After much deliberation I chose the song that I wanted playing as we entered the chapel; 'Forever Autumn' by Justin Haywood, not because it was one that Dad knew but because the lyrics were so apt. I also wrote everything that I could remember about him, trying to consider everyone in those memories: His thirty-one years with Diane and her children, my brother and sister, Dad's fishing and gardening, his friends and neighbours, I was so afraid I may've missed someone out and I was worried about my wording too but I needn't have been, the Minister had asked if he could read the eulogy and the poem that I'd written, just as they were.

I'd arranged for Dad to be brought to my home and from there we'd followed him on his final journey; Ken, myself and my children, Diane didn't want him to go from her home, so she had agreed to meet us at the chapel along with everyone else. As we arrived I noticed, standing with Verity and her husband, Dad's brother and his wife and when I spoke to him he told me that he'd seen Dad's obituary column, I apologised for his having to find out that way and he assured me that it was all right and completely understandable. Unfortunately my brother wasn't there but the important thing, as far as I was concerned, was that I was there and I knew that Dad would've been so proud of his send off. Gemma came to the funeral and was sat with Ken and my children; she'd attended not only as my friend but because of the deep respect that she had for my Father too. Penny couldn't get to the funeral but she did come with us the following week when we went to the river, to scatter Dad's ashes in his favourite fishing spot; though this was far more low key than the funeral; just myself, Ken and Penny, my Children, their partners and my Grandchildren, although I'm sure that my Dad's spirit was there too... Somewhere in the afterlife, or in my imagination, they're all there and when I think of them, somehow I'm not so alone.

The life I've led has had its share of struggles and I suppose if I were to dwell on it for too long, I may consider it unfair and let myself be filled with self pity; on bad days maybe I am but if I hadn't experienced all of these things then I wouldn't be the person I am today and in actuality, I quite like that person now and

430

I only have to look at my Children and my beautiful Grandchildren to know that it's all been worth it. My fear of death is still here and I wonder whether at forty-eight I am middle aged or nearing the end, although the important thing is: I've been here, done what I felt was right and survived and to lift my spirits and make 2005 that little bit easier to bear; Michael won the Grand Final Free Style Dance Championship at Pontin's in December, just as Dad said he would and for 2006: My third (or sixteenth) Grandchild is due in the August; Lee and Carrie's second child, conceived about six weeks after Dad's death, just as Lelani was conceived about six weeks after Mum's...

Meant to be? Coincidence? Or reincarnation? Whatever it may be, whatever the reason in the grand scheme of things, I can finally accept and cope with it all and nothing is more than I can handle.

My Dad   2/3/1930 – 12/10/2005

He wasn't a hero, who died in the war,
To me, my Dad, he was so much more,
His occupation? Fitting carpets and things to the floor,
To me, my Dad, he was so much more.

He talked of the World as a troubled place,
How pollution and politicians are destroying our race,
To preservation of wildlife, birds, fish in the sea,
To me, my Dad meant much more to me.

He was loyal, trustworthy and collected stamps too,
He loved gardening and fishing, grew vegetables for you,
He was funny and sarcy and vulnerable, it's true,
But did he do wrong to any of you?

He talked of his ancestors, of the travelling life,
Of the Romany people, the trouble and strife,
He told of the ways things ought to be,
To me, my Dad, meant much more to me.

Although my Dad's gone in my mind I will see,
His face and his smile as he's talking to me,
If God has a garden, that's where he will be,
My Dad, you should know,
You meant much more to me.

Made in the USA
Columbia, SC
30 April 2017